The Reconstruction Era

Recent Titles in
Debating Historical Issues in the Media of the Time

The Antebellum Era: Primary Documents on Events from 1820 to 1860
David A. Copeland

The Revolutionary Era: Primary Documents on Events from 1776 to 1800
Carol Sue Humphrey

The Reconstruction Era

*Primary Documents on Events
from 1865 to 1877*

Donna L. Dickerson

Debating Historical Issues in the Media of the Time
David A. Copeland, Series Editor

GREENWOOD PRESS
Westport, Connecticut • London

Library of Congress Cataloging-in-Publication Data

Dickerson, Donna Lee, 1948–
    The Reconstruction era : primary documents on events from 1865 to 1877 / Donna L.
Dickerson.
        p. cm.–(Debating historical issues in the media of the time, ISSN 1542–8079)
    Includes bibliographical references and index.
    ISBN 0–313–32094–2 (alk. paper)
    1. Reconstruction–Sources. 2. Reconstruction–Press coverage. 3. American
newspapers–History–19th century. 4. Reconstruction–Public opinion. 5. Public
opinion–United States–History–19th century. I. Title. II. Series.
    E668.D545   2003
    973.8–dc21   2003048827

British Library Cataloguing in Publication Data is available.

Library of Congress Catalog Card Number: 2003048827
ISBN: 0–313–32094–2
ISSN: 1542–8079

First published in 2003

Greenwood Press, 88 Post Road West, Westport, CT 06881
An imprint of Greenwood Publishing Group, Inc.
www.greenwood.com

Printed in the United States of America

The paper used in this book complies with the
Permanent Paper Standard issued by the National
Information Standards Organization (Z39.48–1984).

10 9 8 7 6 5 4 3 2 1

Contents

Series Foreword   vii

Introduction: Newspapers during Reconstruction   ix

Chronology of Events   xvii

Chapter 1: The First Year: Expressions of Hope and Concern, 1865   1

Chapter 2: Johnson's Presidential Reconstruction Plan, 1865–66   15

Chapter 3: The Freedmen's Bureau, 1865–72   29

Chapter 4: Black Codes, 1865   43

Chapter 5: Seating the South's Congressional Delegation, 1865   55

Chapter 6: President Johnson versus Radical Congress, 1866   69

Chapter 7: Freedmen's Bureau Act, 1866   85

Chapter 8: Civil Rights Act of 1866   97

Chapter 9: Black Suffrage: Before the Vote, 1865–66   109

Chapter 10: The Fourteenth Amendment, 1866   123

Chapter 11: New Orleans Riot, 1866   137

Chapter 12: Congressional Reconstruction, 1867   151

Chapter 13: Black Suffrage: The First Vote, 1867   169

Chapter 14: The Alaska Purchase, 1867   183

Chapter 15: Impeachment of President Johnson, 1868   193

Chapter 16: Creating the Carpetbagger Myth, 1867–69   207

Chapter 17: The Battle for Woman Suffrage, 1867–70   221

Chapter 18: Indian Policy in the West, 1867–76   235

Chapter 19: Violence and the Ku Klux Klan, 1867–72   251

Chapter 20: Sunday Liquor Laws, 1866–73   267

Contents

Chapter 21: Mormons and Polygamy, 1870–77   279
Chapter 22: Black Suffrage: The Fifteenth Amendment and
            Beyond, 1869–77   291
Chapter 23: Chinese Immigration, 1867–72   305
Chapter 24: Boss Tweed and His New York Ring, 1870–73   317
Chapter 25: The Crédit Mobilier Scandal, 1872–73   331
Chapter 26: The Trial of Susan B. Anthony, 1873   345
Chapter 27: The Civil Rights Act of 1875   357
Chapter 28: The Hamburg Massacre, 1876   371
Chapter 29: The Compromised Election of 1876   381
Chapter 30: The End of Reconstruction, 1874–77   393

     Selected Bibliography   407
     Index   411

Series Foreword

As the eighteenth century was giving way to the nineteenth, the *Columbian Centinel* of Boston in its January 1, 1799, issue printed correspondence from a wise judge who said, "Give to any set men the command of the press, and you give them the command of the country, for you give them the command of public opinion, which commands everything." One month later, Thomas Jefferson wrote to James Madison with a similar insight. "We are sensible," Jefferson said of the efforts it would take to put their party—the Republicans—in power, "The engine is the press."

Both writers were correct in their assessment of the role the press would play in U.S. life in the years ahead. The press was already helping to shape the opinions and direction of the United States. It had been doing so for decades, but its influence would explode following the Revolutionary War and continue into the 1920s and later. The number of newspapers erupted in the United States from fewer than forty papers in 1783 to more than 500 newspapers by 1860. In 1898 Joseph Pulitzer's *New York World* had a daily circulation of 1.3 million. By the beginning of World War I, about 16,600 daily and weekly newspapers were published, and circulation figures passed 22.5 million copies per day with no slowdown in sight. The number of magazines grew even more impressively. Journalism historian Frank Luther Mott counted 600 magazines in 1860 and a phenomenal 3,300 in 1885, up from around 5 at the end of the Revolutionary War. Some circulations surpassed 1 million, and the number of magazines continued to grow into the twentieth century.

The amazing growth of the press happened because the printed page of periodicals assumed a critical role in the United States. Newspapers and magazines became the place where Americans discussed and debated the issues that affected them. Writers, editors, and citizens took sides, and they used the press as the conduit for discussion. The *Debating Historical Issues in the Media of the Time* series offers a glimpse into how the press was used by Americans to shape and influence the major events and issues facing the nation during different periods of its development. Each volume is based on the documents—that is, the writings—that appeared in the press of the time. Each volume presents articles, essays, and editorials that support opposing interests on the events and issues, and each provides readers with background and explanation of the events, issues, and, if possible, the people who wrote the articles that have been selected. Each volume also includes a chronology of events and a selected bibliography. Books in the *Debating Historical Issues in the Media of the Time* series cover the following periods: the Revolution and the young republic, the Federalist era, the antebellum period, the Civil War, Reconstruction, the progressive era, and World War I.

This volume on the Reconstruction period focuses on the issues that affected the nation from 1865 to 1877, from the end of the Civil War until President Rutherford B. Hayes ordered the last federal troops from the South. The papers of this period were highly political in their content and, consequently, served the needs of politics. The Civil War, as one might suspect, shaped much of the press' content in the first years of the period. But as time progressed, economic, religious, and social issues that affected the maturing nation captured increasing amounts of attention from the press. As the United States moved forward from the war, its citizens continued to use the press as the catalyst to debate the issues that concerned them and to shape the United States's direction.

Introduction: Newspapers during Reconstruction

As the Civil War neared its end, President Abraham Lincoln faced two major tasks: how to reconstruct the once rebellious Southern states so that they could once again be part of the Union and how to incorporate nearly five million ex-slaves into a democratic society. However, Lincoln was assassinated before he had an opportunity to develop a comprehensive plan for the South. That job would fall to his vice president, Andrew Johnson. Within six weeks of assuming office, Johnson developed what he would later call "My Policy," a set of criteria each rebel state must meet to be restored to full membership in the Union. However, "My Policy" was much too lenient for Republicans in Congress, who insisted that rebels and former slaveholders not be returned to power and that blacks be protected from their former owners. During the next four years, Johnson and Congress battled it out in Washington as well as in the newspapers. The winner would be Congress.

When Ulysses S. Grant was elected president in 1868, the political wars were reduced to mere skirmishes. Not only was Grant more amenable to Republican wishes but Republicans themselves had moderated their own views on Reconstruction. By 1877, with President Rutherford B. Hayes in office, Republicans abandoned Reconstruction all together. The South returned to the control of whites, and blacks were relegated to third-class citizenship.

As the sole purveyors of news and opinion, the U.S. newspapers bent and spindled U.S. public opinion with little regard for independent journalism and with great regard for party politics. In other words, the newspapers of the Reconstruction era did not serve society's needs but instead served the needs of politics.

In the North, newspapers and reporting had matured significantly during the war. New systems of information transmission were developed, a more professional cadre of journalists came out of battlefield reporting, and more newspapers were becoming profitable business enterprises. But not everything had changed in U.S. journalism. Newspapers remained political entities, as they had been for the past one hundred years, and played the role of pied piper for their favorite political party. The personal editor—the man everyone knew by name and face in the community—was still a hallmark of U.S. newspapers, politics was still the sum and substance of the newspaper, and the editorial page remained the most important page in the paper. Editors were not expected to be independent or objective; instead, they were expected to be leaders of their party on and off the editorial page. In fact, it was not uncommon for reporters, editors, and publishers to serve in Congress or in state legislatures, hold federal jobs, or be employed by state and local governments.

Although newspapers covered a wide variety of stories about murdered prostitutes, railroad accidents, and city improvements, for example, their specialty was politics, just as it had been before and during the Civil War. The front page of the newspaper contained all of the latest telegraphic news from Washington, New York, and around the world. Headlines ranged in size from a single label to several tiers, depending on the significance of the news. In the big city dailies, editorials appeared on either the second or the fourth page and generally took up the entire page. The editorial page was the only page in the newspaper that was written locally. Consequently, it was not uncommon for the large metropolitan newspapers to employ two or three editorial writers who wrote anywhere from four to eight editorials a day. The editorials were lengthy, and the style could best be described as pedantic, flowery, and verbose. After all, it took a lot of words to fill six columns of small type every day. Reconstruction politics occupied much of the editorial space from 1865 to 1870, then other topics such as the monetary system, foreign relations, and economic issues slowly pushed Reconstruction off the editorial page.

Between 1865 and 1877, the Northern press identified itself either with the Republican Party (moderate or radical) or with the Democracy. Sometimes readers needed a scorecard to determine which paper was affiliated with which party and which branch of the party. Initially, the most influential radical Republican newspapers were Horace Greeley's *New York Tribune,* Horace White's *Chicago Tribune,* William H. Harrison's *Philadelphia Inquirer,* and E.L. Godkin's *The Nation.* These newspapers did daily battle with President Andrew Johnson, supported the radical movement in Congress for a more stringent Reconstruction policy, and favored legislation that improved the political well-being of blacks.

The moderate Republican newspapers supported President Johnson for a longer period of time, until they reluctantly determined that his leadership was leading the nation nowhere. Moderates were critical of radical legislation but were more critical of the South's seeming recalcitrance and continued abuse of blacks. The moderates were led by Henry Raymond's *New York Times,* William Cullen Bryant's *New York Evening Post,* Samuel Bowles's *Springfield (Mass.) Republican,* and Murat Halstead's *Cincinnati Commercial.* Then there were Republican newspapers that never seemed to know where they fit—like reeds in the wind, they shifted their editorial stance to accommodate the moment. Prominent among these newspapers was James Gordon Bennett's *New York Herald,* which would verbally flail Republicans as easily as it would criticize Democratic leaders.

The Democratic press was composed of those newspapers, often called "Copperheads," that had refused to support "Mr. Lincoln's war." After the war, these conservative Democratic editors supported Johnson's Southern policy when all of the Republican papers had abandoned him. The Democracy, as it was often referred to, was highly critical of the workings of Congress and believed that most of what the radical Republicans did was illegal or unconstitutional, or both. Northern Democratic newspapers worked hard to heal the divide between the North and South, supporting general amnesty, criticizing the work of the Freedmen's Bureau, and calling for the South to be allowed to determine its own future. They took a very conservative view of the place of blacks in the South, refusing to support the franchise for blacks and arguing that the fate of Southern blacks was best left in the hands of Southern whites. The Northern Democratic press was led by the Manton Marble's *New York World,* Wilbur F. Storey's *Chicago Times,* and John McLean's *Cincinnati Enquirer.*

By the early 1870s, both parties and their press engines slowly began to change into what we think of today as the Democratic and Republican parties. First, the Democrats needed a new source of voters, whom they found among the laborers and immigrants in the northeast. The party became the "working man's party," supporting economic policies that served the middle-class and lower class Americans. Democrats strongly criticized the growing federal bureaucracy and all of its corruption and graft and called for reform in government.

Republicans also were looking for a new direction for the party, moving away from the egalitarian and republican values of Lincoln and toward reforms that would support business and industry. The first attempt to realign the traditional party landscape occurred in 1872, when reform-minded

Republicans, led by a cadre of strong Republican editors, joined with like-minded Democrats to create the Liberal Republican party. These new Democrats and Republicans wanted "the natural order of things" restored in the South through local control, not federal, interference. They blamed corruption in the South on carpetbaggers and illiterate blacks, and while they supported the Fourteenth and Fifteenth Amendments, they did not support the various laws passed by Congress to enforce their provisions and to protect blacks. Among the newspapers that lent support to the new party were the *New York Tribune, Chicago Tribune, Springfield (Mass.) Republican, Cincinnati Commercial, The Nation,* and the moderate Democratic *Louisville Courier-Journal,* edited by Henry Watterson. But this affiliation with a new untried party was short lived. When the Liberal Republicans nominated *New York Tribune* editor Horace Greeley for president, many Republicans returned, albeit sheepishly, to their old ranks. There, despite Grant's lackluster second term, they managed eventually to re-create the Republican Party into one that more closely resembled the Republican Party of the twentieth century.

In the South, politics were more black and white—literally. You were either a black Republican (meaning radical) or a white Democrat. Despite having hard times reestablishing newspapers after the war, Democratic and Republican newspapers throughout the South participated in a raucous, excessive, and biased form of journalism seldom seen before or since in the United States. Robert Ridgway, the editor of the *Richmond (Va.) Whig,* described the role of the "loyal" Southern press: "Our soldiers having overthrown the insurgents, it will now be the duty of our loyal journalists to rekindle the smouldering fires of patriotism, infuse new ideas into the South and win back our deluded countrymen to their first love." The *Richmond (Va.) Times* described the role of the Southern Democratic press:

> There never was a time when the Southern press was performing its duty
> to the South more vigilantly, fearlessly and usefully than now. The evidence ... can be found in the curses, imprecations, groans and yells of all
> the detected, flagellated and exposed military tyrants, unworthy judges,
> thievish cotton agents and mousing agents of the Freedman's Bureau. ... But for the press, these harpies would have stripped our people as
> bare as a pack of coyotes devour the carcass of a buffalo.[1]

Frank Luther Mott in *American Journalism* referred to the Reconstruction years as a time of suffering for the Southern press that did not end until the "reign of terror" brought by carpetbaggers was over. Mott's reference was to political patronage doled out by corruptionists who forced papers to " 'sing low' or suspend." Mott's interpretation followed that of William Dunning, an early historian who viewed Reconstruction as "an era of corruption presided over by unscrupulous carpetbaggers from the North, unprincipled

Southern white scalawags, and ignorant freedmen."[2] In fact, without a broad base of patronage support from both Democrats and Republicans, the Southern newspaper would have barely existed after the war. Also, the purse strings of Republican patronage were not held by the radical rascals of Dunning's Reconstruction but by moderates who, if anything, too easily acquiesced to the compromises that led to Reconstruction's failure. The South's party press was a natural fallout not only from the politics of Reconstruction but also from the South's weak economy. During this critical period, the party press—whether the rural Democratic sheets or the urban Republican papers—promoted political identity, educated citizens in their political responsibilities, and pressed the party line.

The Democratic newspapers were the organs of the "white man" and had very little interest in promoting the cause of Republicans or blacks. Their editorials were vindictive, racist, and filled with Southern demagoguery. They did not hesitate to blast anything that smacked of radical Republicanism—from the presence of soldiers in the towns to the work of teachers in the freedmen's schools. Needless to say, Democratic newspapers and federal occupation forces did not always see eye to eye. While the Northern press fully enjoyed the privilege to criticize Congress, Reconstruction policies, the army, and the president, some of their Southern brethren were arrested and their newspapers suspended for expressing the same opinions. Although such arrests were not widespread, there were enough incidents during the early years of Reconstruction to create an atmosphere of self-censorship among editors critical of Reconstruction policies.

Examples of military interference include the following:

The editor of the *St. Martinsville (La.) Courier de Teche* was arrested for his continuous criticism of military occupation.[3] The editor of the *Franklin (La.) Planter's Banner* was arrested after publishing an editorial about a feud between the local provost marshal and the mayor.[4]

The editor of the *Petersburg (Va.) Daily News* was arrested and jailed in Richmond after ridiculing President Johnson's charges that Jefferson Davis was involved in Lincoln's assassination. He was released three months later.[5]

Both the *Americus (Ga.) Summer Republican* and the *Albany (Ga.) News* were suspended after being charged with disloyalty and failure to promote peace and national unity.[6]

Whatever the reason for suspension or arrest, the newspapers were generally reflecting their communities' impatience with the overt military presence and with what they considered "monstrous and ungenerous outrages" by radicals who "are trampling on the Constitution to effect our degradation and ruin." For the military, which was a legal occupation force, censorship was justified as an expedient means of controlling a rebellious and disloyal population and limiting anti-Reconstruction rhetoric.

Only a few dozen Republican newspapers existed in the South at any one time. As long as there was a federal presence in the South, most Republican newspapers could survive on the money they received printing military orders and legal advertising or by acting as the stationer for the local military commander. In March 1867, Republicans in Congress decided to bolster the Republican press in the South by passing an appropriations act that allowed federal printing contracts to be let to two newspapers in each Southern state. The decision as to which newspapers would receive these contracts was placed directly in the hands of Edward McPherson, a moderate Republican and the clerk of the House of Representatives. In states where there were few Republican newspapers, competition for the contracts was slight. But in Florida, Georgia, and Virginia, competition was keen and boisterous. In the spring and summer of 1867, McPherson was deluged with correspondence promoting various loyal newspapers. But the patronage dollar was very fickle. A Republican newspaper had to toe the correct moderate Republican line or it could lose its contract to another Republican paper. For example, McPherson withdrew the printing contract from the *Jacksonville Florida Times* when its editor began supporting a group of radical Republicans campaigning across the state in a mule-drawn wagon.[7]

In most districts, the granting and denying of printing contracts was a political free-for-all from which district commanders distanced themselves. However, when General John Pope, the commander of the Third District, found it increasingly difficult to carry out Congress's new Reconstruction plan, he issued an order prohibiting officials from giving advertising to any newspaper that had opposed or obstructed Reconstruction. His target was the district's Democratic papers. The reaction of newspaper editors was immediate and rancorous. The editor of the *Jacksonville (Ala.) Republican*, a conservative paper, complained that the "oppressive nature of Gen. Pope's despotic order" had deprived the paper of its "legitimate patronage." He considered selling the paper "to retire altogether from the disgusting arena of modern politics, mixed up as it is with radicalism, leaguism and niggerism" but was unable to get a fair price. The *Mobile (Ala.) Advertiser and Register* was confident that while conservative papers may suffer monetary loss for a time, "they will triumph in the end" because the people would not allow the press to be starved out of existence.[8]

It is more difficult to identify the leading Republican and Democratic newspapers in the South because of the short life span of most newspapers. But the Democratic newspapers that were most frequently quoted by others included the *Atlanta Constitution, Memphis Daily Appeal, Richmond (Va.) Times, Mobile (Ala.) Advertiser and Register,* and *Milledgeville (Ga.) Federal Union.*

Republican newspapers that exerted influence across the South included the *Savannah (Ga.) Republican,* Samuel Bard's *Atlanta New Era, Richmond (Va.) New Nation, Montgomery (Ala.) State Journal,* and Governor William Holden's *Raleigh (N.C.) Standard.* Newspapers edited by or for blacks were most likely to stay true to the Republican cause. Black newspapers were edited by agents of the Freedmen's Bureau and included the *Augusta Loyal Georgian* and *Macon (Ga.) American Union.* The *San Antonio Express* was supported by the Union League, and the *New Orleans Tribune* and the *Mobile (Ala.) Nationalist* were sponsored by local equal rights associations.

A Note about Language

Some of the language in the editorials included is racially offensive. However, because words and images are the primary conveyors of culture and ideas, it is important that readers understand that such language was commonly used and accepted by Americans—even the mostly highly educated—in the nineteenth century. Racial slurs, epithets, and insults were not just part of the everyday language of the period but a central part of this nation's political language and consequently are important in understanding the history and politics of race relations in this country. Therefore, to present an accurate historical picture of the issues, the language has not been edited out, and readers should keep the language and images in the context of the nineteenth century.

Notes

1. Quoted in *Tampa Florida Peninsular,* 14 September 1866, 2.

2. Frank Luther Mott, *American Journalism* (New York: Macmillan, 1950), 368; William A. Dunning, *Reconstruction, Political and Economic 1865–1877* (New York: Harper Bros., 1907). For a more modern version of the Dunning school interpretation, see E. Merton Coulter, *The South during Reconstruction, 1865–1877* (Baton Rouge: Louisiana State University Press, 1947); Eric Foner, *Reconstruction: America's Unfinished Revolution, 1863–1877* (New York: Harper & Row, 1988), xix–xx.

3. Joe Gray Taylor, *Louisiana Reconstructed, 1863–1877* (Baton Rouge: Louisiana State University Press, 1974), 66.

4. James E. Sefton, *The United States Army and Reconstruction, 1865–1877* (Baton Rouge: Louisiana State University Press, 1867), 55.

5. *Petersburg Daily News,* 22 June 1865, 1.

6. *Albany Patriot,* 16 August 1865, 1; Louis Turner Griffith and John E. Talmadge, *Georgia Journalism, 1763–1950* (Athens: University of Georgia Press, 1951), 91–93.

7. Richard Abbott, *The Republican Party in the South, 1855–1877* (Chapel Hill: University of North Carolina Press, 1980), 135.

8. *Mobile Advertiser and Register,* 12 and 27 September 1867.

Chronology of Events

1863	President Abraham Lincoln announces Amnesty Proclamation
1864	President Lincoln pocket vetoes Wade-Davis Bill
	President Lincoln is reelected
1865	Freedman's Bureau is established
	General Robert E. Lee surrenders to General Ulysses S. Grant
	President Lincoln is assassinated
	Andrew Johnson is inaugurated
	President Johnson announces amnesty plan
	Thirteenth Amendment is ratified
	Thirty-ninth Congress refuses to seat Southern delegation
	President Johnson announces former Confederate states restored
1866	Civil Rights Act is passed over President Johnson's veto
	Second Freedmen's Bureau Act is passed over President Johnson's veto
	Fourteenth Amendment is proposed
	Tennessee is admitted to Union
	New Orleans and Memphis riots
	National Union convention meets
1867	Black franchise is approved in Washington, D.C.
	U.S. Supreme Court decides loyalty oath cases *ex parte Garland* and *Cummings v. Missouri*
	Alaska is purchased
	Reconstruction Acts are passed
	Ku Klux Klan violence escalates

1868   President Johnson is impeached; Senate acquits
          Fourth Reconstruction Act is passed.
          Fourteenth Amendment is ratified
          Ulysses S. Grant is elected

1869   President Grant is inaugurated
          Fifteenth Amendment is proposed
          Union Pacific and Central Pacific railroads meet at
             Promontory Point, Utah
          Arkansas, Alabama, Florida, Georgia, Louisiana, North
             Carolina, and South Carolina are readmitted to Union
          Georgia is expelled from Union
          Redemption begins with Democratic victory in Tennessee

1870   South Carolina holds Ku Klux Klan trials
          Hiram Revels is elected to U.S. Senate as first black senator
          Fifteenth Amendment is ratified
          Virginia, Mississippi, Texas, and Georgia are readmitted to
             Union
          First Enforcement Act is passed
          Joseph H. Rainey, first black U.S. Representative, is sworn in

1871   Ku Klux Klan Acts are passed
          Tweed Ring is exposed

1872   Freedmen's Bureau is abolished
          Crédit Mobilier scandal is exposed
          Liberal Republican Party is created; supports Horace Greeley
          President Grant is reelected

1873   Boss Tweed is found guilty
          Congressional hearings on Crédit Mobilier scandal
          U.S. Supreme Court weakens Fourteenth Amendment in
             Slaughterhouse Cases
          Panic of 1873
          Susan B. Anthony is found guilty of voting illegally

1875   Civil Rights Act is passed
          Democrats win majority of seats in House of Representatives

1876   U.S. Supreme Court weakens Fifteenth Amendment in *United*
             States v. Reese and *United States v. Cruikshank* decisions
          Battle of the Little Bighorn
          Hamburg massacre
          Presidential election results in deadlock over disputed ballots

1877   Election commission is created to break election deadlock
          Rutherford B. Hayes is inaugurated
          Redemption is complete
          President Hayes withdraws troops from South

CHAPTER I

The First Year: Expressions of Hope and Concern, 1865

A s the Civil War came to an end in the spring of 1865, the South had every reason to believe that the North would deal with it harshly. After all, more than 600,000 men had been killed on both sides—a terrible social and economic loss to the country.

When General Robert E. Lee of the Confederacy handed his sword to General Ulysses S. Grant at Appomattox, he warned, "Should arbitrary or vindictive policies be adopted, the end is not yet. There remains a great deal of vitality and strength in the South."[1] And Confederate president Jefferson Davis echoed General Lee's warning: "The Confederate Cause is not lost, it is only sleeping."

President Abraham Lincoln had no desire for retribution but instead wished for a swift restoration of the South to the Union. In his inaugural address on March 4, 1865, Lincoln called for "malice toward none; with charity for all; with firmness in the right, as God gives us to see the right, let us strive on to finish the work we are in; to bind up the nation's wounds. . . .to do all which may achieve and cherish a just and a lasting peace. . . ." Even General Grant's terms of peace—to allow Confederate soldiers to keep their arms and return home without fear from prosecution—matched the desire by many for a peace that would be void of revenge or bitterness.

The *Cincinnati Gazette* sent Whitelaw Reid to the South to report on postwar conditions. In one report he noted, "The National Government could have prescribed no condition for the return of the Rebel States which they would not have promptly accepted. They expected nothing; were prepared for the worst; would have been thankful for anything."[2] Part of the South's fear that its citizens would be treated as defeated enemies came in part from radicals like Representative Thaddeus Stevens and Senator Charles Sumner, both of Massachusetts, who called for harsh measures against the defeated rebels. Stevens advocated a broad policy of disenfranchising former

President Andrew Johnson, 1808–75. *Served as president, 1865–68.*
Library of Congress.

Confederates, confiscating their land and giving it to blacks, reverting the
Confederate states to territorial status, and punishing many Confederates
for treason. There also was speculation after Lincoln's assassination that
President Andrew Johnson would adopt a harsh policy toward the South.
As provisional governor of Tennessee, Johnson had been uncompromising
toward rebels, vowing to punish and impoverish traitors. At one point he
stated that treason was "the highest crime that can be committed, and
those engaged in it should suffer all its penalties" and "their social power
must be destroyed."[3]

In the North, there was less certainty about the fate of the South. Many Northerners simply wanted to get back to normalcy. That meant dealing leniently with the South and letting the Southern states decide their own future as long as it did not include slavery. Others preferred, as did Stevens and Sumner, to deal harshly with the rebels and to create a political system in the South that would prevent any future acts of rebellion. But few wanted to see war criminal trials, hangings, or wholesale confiscation or to make the Southern states territories to be ruled by military force for an indefinite period. Southerners, after all, were still Americans.

In the spring of 1865, there was much speculation about "What's next?" What would the postemancipation South look like? How would former rebels resume their place as members of a united nation? What role would newly freed slaves play in the "new" South? Some in the North were upbeat, forecasting that peace would bring prosperity and a new feeling of enthusiasm about the future. Politicians were eloquent not only in their praise for the brave Northern and Southern soldiers but also in their forecasts for the future. They called for a Reconstruction policy that would forgive the rebels and that would be "equitable," "generous," "amicable," "wise," and "speedy."

This chapter's section of writings that endorse a speedy and generous policy toward the South begins with an editorial praising President Johnson as the best possible person to lead the country because he is a Southerner who understands the mind of the South. The second writing is by Horace Greeley, who called for a magnanimous peace unhampered by retribution of any kind. Mixing his metaphors, Greeley compares the war to a path strewn with obstacles, then he compares peace to a great ship sailing on uncertain waters. The next selection, by John W. Forney, places its faith in the nascent Union spirit that has been kept under the Confederate heel for so many years. The last selection, by William Cullen Bryant, is a prayer of rejoicing and praise for the strength of the American people during the war and a plea that the nation will now rest on a strong foundation of democratic principles.

Others were more skeptical and urged caution against placing too much trust in the South's ability to restore itself. In this section of writings, Horace White cautions in the first entry that the South is a bitter loser and will strike back when given an opportunity. The second reading from the *London Times* predicts that the war is only half over and that Reconstruction will be a hard fight. The third entry, by Samuel Bowles, warns against putting the South's future back into the hands of former rebels. The final editorial, by George W. Curtis, predicts that the spirit of rebellion will never die out and that the only way to deal with a South that continued to be unsubdued and unchastened was a strong Reconstruction policy.

A CALL FOR A SPEEDY AND GENEROUS POLICY

Anonymous Writer: "The New Era"

After President Lincoln's assassination, many people placed great hope in Andrew Johnson to carry out a just Reconstruction policy that would punish the rebel leaders but leave most Southerners to restore their states without broad acts of retribution.

Chambersburg (Pa.) Valley Spirit, April 26, 1865

The administration of President Johnson in its work of restoration, will necessarily have many subjects of difficulty to meet. Subjects fraught with important consequences to the country. He has as yet made no declaration of the policy which will govern him in the duties of his position, but promises to deal with questions as they arise and make his policy known by his acts. That he will [be] disposed to punish with severity the instigators and leaders of the rebellion, is most certain, but that he will be lenient and conciliatory to their deluded followers, the masses of the Southern people, is equally beyond doubt. His course, however, in this respect, is only of importance to us in its bearing on the difficult and delicate work of reconstructing, re-organizing and restoring the seceded States to their position in the Union. The policy which will govern in this great work is a matter of great interest to the people of the country at this time, as on it will depend the permanency of peace and the future prosperity of our country and people. For our part we are hopeful, and are disposed to believe that his course will meet general approval and be conducive to the best interests of all.

Mr. Johnson is emphatically a man of the people. Born and raised in the South, there is, perhaps, no public man who so well understands the temper and views of *the people* of that section, or can make better use of those influences on which reliance must be placed, to convince the larger portion of the Southern population that their true interests are adverse to those of the men who excited the rebellion. To secure the cooperation of the Southern people in the work of re-construction, would seem to us less difficult under a southern man of Mr. Johnson's stamp, than under any other, and hence we deem it fortunate that such a man was in a position to succeed our murdered President in the administration of the government at such a critical conjuncture in the affairs of the country. The intellectual ability and force of character possessed by him, and displayed in every position which he has occupied, leave no room to doubt his capacity to fill the high position devolved upon him with credit to himself and his democratic training. He was born and raised a Democrat, and we much doubt if those principles of democracy, imbibed in youth and strengthened in manhood, have lost their hold upon him and given place to their opposites. . . .

Horace Greeley: "The Dawn of Peace"

Horace Greeley was one of the war's strongest supporters and was a foe of slavery. Throughout the Reconstruction years, his editorials endorsed civil and political rights for the freedmen, universal suffrage, and broad educational policies. After the war, he advocated a reasonable peace that was somewhere between severity and weakness.

New York Tribune, April 14, 1865

The path of Peace opens pleasantly before us—There may be thorns in the way as we advance, obstacles to be removed, pitfalls and snares to be avoided, but we look back to the dread road we have traveled for four long and weary and painful years, and the road before us smiles only with Summer sunshine. It is natural for man to indulge in hope, and hope is not always illusive. That the war is over is a mighty fact. The courage, the endurance, the patriotism, the self-sacrifice that have stood the test of this gigantic struggle have born the heaviest burden that can be laid upon the heart and character of a nation, and whatever else may be before us we accept the future with a cheerfulness that needs no abatement, with a joy that should be dimmed with no gloomy anticipations.

There are ships that will encounter the toughest storms and rot to pieces in the calms that succeed them. But ours is not one of these. The storm caught us with our rigging unbraced, our sails flapping, our decks in disorder, our yards unmanned, our rudder unshipped. A ship put in order to encounter peril amid such multiplied danger, and that then rode out the tempest is too staunch and too well conditioned to fear any wind that blows or any swell it can upheave. With flag and pennant streaming gaily out upon the breeze, she takes a new departure upon a smiling sea.

It is a moment only for rejoicing. The hours of despondency—how many we have passed through!—the fears that courage, or strength or resources might fail us, have passed away. The good fight has been fought, the Right has triumphed. We are a nation no longer divided against itself, but one, indivisible, united Free. . . .

John W. Forney: "Will the Union Find True Friends in the South?"

While serving as editor and publisher of the Philadelphia Press *and the* Washington Chronicle, *John W. Forney served as secretary of the Senate.*

As a Washington insider, he probably knew more about the workings of Congress than did anyone else. In this editorial, Forney predicts that Unionism and loyalty will once again find their place in the South.

Philadelphia Press, April 15, 1865

It should be remembered by all who have wondered at the comparative dearth of Union sentiment in the South, that until within a very recent period our armies have been partially held at bay by powerful antagonist forces, and that while a hope of success has buoyed up those who cordially supported the rebellion, an ever-present dread of condign punishment has overawed and restrained those who secretly sympathized with the national cause. Thus, the most powerful leevers that influence the action of mankind has exerted their full force against us.

Sherman's triumphant march, the capture of Richmond, and the surrender of Lee's army, have changed all this. Unionism is no longer a magnet to attract persecution and ignominy, but a badge of honor, wisdom and security. Those who have suffered for their fidelity to the old flag, and those who display an eager promptitude now to seek its protection, must become the influential men of their section, because they alone can advance the interests of the people among whom they reside. Those who are disposed to cling with passionate blindness to the idol of an exploded Confederacy will soon sink into obscurity, and either be compelled by the force of public opinion to abandon the worship of their fetish, or practice it with the secrecy of Pagans seeking to perpetuate heathen rites in a Christian land.

If ever an issue was bravely, persistently, energetically and thoroughly "fought out" the indivisibility of our country has been thus decided.—The rebellious States have not cried "enough" before every available resource was exhausted, every imaginable device tried in vain, nor before men, money, arms and ammunition failing, "unconditional surrender" was the only alternative left. The period has therefore arrived when the rational men of all sections should and will earnestly endeavor, on the broad basis of Union and Liberty, to "enrich the time to come with smooth-faced peace, with smiling plenty, and fair, prosperous days."

If moderation is displayed in the North it is only fair to presume that, when the full purport of our late victories is comprehended and digested throughout the South, that section will not be slow to contribute its share of the labor necessary to consumate the great work of pacification. Experience has shown that, wherever the triumph of our arms was assured, encouragement and assistance have never been entirely wanting. . . . We see that the germ of reconstruction was found everywhere. And now that the pressure of the vigilant and despotic Confederate Government has been almost entirely destroyed, we may fairly expect these evidences of returning loyalty to redouble in number, importance, and influence, until in every deed "the whole, the boundless continent is ours" by the tacit consent of all its inhabitants. . . .

William Cullen Bryant: "Glory to the Lord of Hosts"

One of America's best-known poets, William Cullen Bryant was a religious man who wrote more than 20 hymns. The language in this editorial will remind the reader of language and tempo typically found in hymns.

New York Evening Post, April 10, 1865

The great day, so long and anxiously awaited, for which we have struggled through four years of bloody war, which as so often seemed to "stand tip toe on the misty mountain tops" but which dawned only to go down in clouds and gloom; the day of the virtual overthrow of the rebellion, of the triumph of constitutional order and of universal liberty—of the success of the nation against its part, and of humane and beneficient [*sic*] civilization over a relic of barbarism that had been blindly allowed to remain as a blot on the escutcheon, in short, the day of PEACE, has finally come. It has come, as every wise lover of his country wished it to come, not as a weak compromise between the government of the people and its enemies, not as a concession to an exhausted yet vital power of revolt, not as a truce between two equal forces which lay down their arms for the time, to resume them as soon as they should repair damages and recover strength—but as the result of a stern, deliberate, unyielding determination to vindicate the supremacy of the organic law over the entire territory and people of the nation.

The issue raised by the insurgents was a distinct one; it arraigned the right of the Union to exercise its authority over states which chose to assert a right of secession; the appeal was made to the arbitrament [*sic*] of arms; for four weary years "the weary hours toiled heavy with the unresting curse they bore"; and all the strength, the valor, the endurance, the pride, the energy, the sentiment, the passion and earnest conviction of duty of either side, was put forth in the terrible conflict of principles in an awful and gigantic wrestle for the mastery. Now, when the trial has been made, when the victory abides with us, when the vital question has been decided, when the insane leaders of the slave states and their ignorant followers have been shown what the sovereign people demands as to integrity of the nation and its government, the peace that must follow will be a peace founded upon establishing and enduring principles.

Glory, then, to the Lord of Hosts, who hath given us this final victory! Thanks, heartfelt and eternal, to the brave and noble men by land and sea, officers and soldiers, who by their labors, their courage, their sufferings, their blood and their lives, have won it for us! And a gratitude no less deep and earnest to that majestic, devoted and glorious American People, who through all these years of trial have maintained themselves steady and self-respectful amid all the excitements of an unexampled civil war, who have never given way to despair or terror on one hand, or dashed out wildly on the other in a spirit of vengeance and fury, but through every vicissitude of the times have stood calm, self-reliant, determined, indomitable, conscious of strength, and in the deep prophetic instinct which that strength lent, assured of success.

We need not admonish such a people as to the manner in which they should rejoice in the signal successes of the day. They who are capable of grand achievements in the field are no less capable of magnanimous feeling toward the fallen foe. They will exult in no petty or insolent feeling of triumph over a prostrate enemy, but in a cheerful and generous sentiment of the great general ends accomplished; in a sense of the calamities escaped, of the burdens removed, of the feuds closed, of the blood staunched, of the animosities laid aside, and of the kindly feelings restored; in the prospect of a speedy recovery of our wasted energies, of the return of industry to its wonted channels, of the establishment of our institutions on a basis more indestructible than ever before.

A Call for Caution and a Firm Policy

Horace White: "Reconstruction"

The Chicago Tribune *supported President Lincoln's lenient policy toward the South, but after his assassination the newspaper established a very different direction: "Henceforce, let us treat this hellborn outbreak of slaveholding fiends as a rebellion . . . now let them feel the force of righteousness, retributive justice."*[4] *In this editorial, the editor calls for nothing less than unconditional support of the Union.*

Chicago Tribune, April 26, 1865

The problem of reconstruction must obviously be solved to a great extent by events as they arise. In other words, we must be governed in a considerable measure by circumstances in dealing with those States whose return to the Union has been coerced by superior physical force. The most important feature attending the regeneration of these States is the temper and disposition of the Southern people. We all know that the great majority of them entered into the rebellion with their whole hearts, and that they would be in rebellion to-day but for the overthrow and dispersion of their armies. We know that they feel keenly and bitterly the dismemberment of their treasonable government and we have no doubt they would raise the standard of revolt to-morrow, if they believed it possible to make headway against our armies. Many of them are undoubtedly tired of the war, but even these we apprehend, entertain no good feeling toward the Union. It is to be hoped that these people may take a common sense view, if they cannot take a patriotic view, of their situation, and yield obedience to the law. By so doing they can smooth the way to reconstruction and permanent peace, as no other agency can possibly effect those objects. . . . They can, in a word, have as many of the blessings of peace as they shall honestly strive to obtain. Slavery is not one of the blessings of peace, and slavery they can never again have.

The great question therefore is, how will the masses of the Southern people co-operate in the task of reconstructing the Union? Thus far the indications are not promising. . . . Will they ever make any progress in loyalty, or even in the passive virtue of obedience to laws which they hate? It is unnecessary to inquire whether they have any valid reason for hating the laws which have now resumed their supremacy in the revolted districts. We are dealing with facts, and one of those facts is, that the Government, which they sought to overthrow, has overthrown them, and reasserted its power and majesty. Another of these facts is that a reconstruction must be effected, and that if it cannot be effected with the aid of the Southern people, it must be effected in spite of them. The rebellion was put down in spite of them, and surely the lesser task can be achieved even if they should meet it with active or sullen resistance. There are four millions of colored American citizens, of undoubted loyalty, in the Southern States, who will gladly take the places of an equal or greater number of disloyal whites in the duty of administering a government of liberty regulated by law. Ignorant though they be, they can be educated speedily, under the instruction of competent officers, in the profession of arms and in the duty of putting down brigandage, and preserving social order. The rest will take care of itself. We have an element of power in the very heart of the rebellion sufficient to meet all the requirements of the problem of reconstruction. That that element will play an important part in any future adjustment of the governmental machinery of the South is certain. How important it shall be the white people of the South can determine in some measure for them-selves.

Anonymous Writer: No Title

John Delane was the editor of the London Times, *whose reporters had thoroughly covered the Civil War. Delane, like many British journalists of the era, was never convinced that the war was a "just war" nor that the North was united in what it was trying to accomplish. This editorial, whether written by Delane or not, contains the kind of insightful predictions about Reconstruction that one rarely saw in U.S. newspapers.*

London Times, June 17, 1865

We are an outspoken people, and make no secret of our conclusions, but there is nothing in those conclusions to which any citizen of the Union need object. We have been surprised at the abrupt extinction of the war, but not more so than the Americans themselves. Whatever may have been our speculations or sympathies, we rejoice that the work of carnage is at an end. We cordially reciprocate the expressions of amity which reach us from America, and shall not be disbelieved in our professions of desire for permanent peace. For the rest, we can only wait. We can see nothing of the future, nor will we pretend to believe that the revolution is over. On the contrary, we see that it is but half finished, and that America will certainly never again be the America of the past. But it may well be something better. The blot of slavery at any rate, is effaced from its soil, and one subject of contention is removed. The position, too, of each State of the Union in relation to the whole is now defined and established, if not improved. Then the people have learned truths and unlearned fallacies, besides undergoing that instructive experience which war seldom fails to yield. We expect, indeed, that the Americans of the future will be more like other people and less like their former selves.

We will not attempt to flatter them. They know well enough what we thought of their civil war, and they will be prompt to comprehend that our judgment remains in suspense still. In a few words they have won—won against the expectation of the whole world—but what they have won remains yet to be seen. The result is probably within their own control. Upon their policy it will depend whether the South becomes again amalgamated with the North, or survives only as a blemish and a burden to the republic. The work of reconstruction may be more trying than the work of subjugation. . . .

Samuel Bowles: "Restoration of the Union"

Samuel Bowles was one of the most respected editors in the country, and his newspaper had one of the largest circulations outside of New York City. A moderate Republican, Bowles took the high road on issues in a simple direct style. This editorial calls for placing control of the South into the hands of loyal men but cautions that the South must be watched lest it revert back to its old ways—a call heard in most Republican newspapers.

Springfield (Mass.) Republican, April 20, 1865

We talk of reconstruction, restoration and the readmission of seceded States to the Union, and this loose habit of speech does no harm so long as we do not allow our ideas and acts to be hampered thereby. These phrases are inaccurate substitutes for a thought that cannot be expressed in a single word.

What we want is to put the government machinery of the Southern States into loyal hands and, whatever we may hold as to State rights, the general government must make sure of this, otherwise have the sacrifices of the war been in vain. Nominally, the large majority of all the Southern people have been disloyal. There are not enough men in the seceded States who have stood firm against the general defection to fill the State and local offices.

It follows that we must accept as citizens those who renew their loyalty to the Union or we must govern the entire South by satraps and armies for an entire generation. Which will we do? All questions of reconstruction resolve themselves at last into this single one.

Under the wise foresight of the President, the revival of the loyal State Governments has kept pace with the progress of our armies and with the fall of the military power of the rebellion, all the States now controlled by disloyal Governors and Legislatures are put in a situation to undertake the same reconstructive work. Congress has provided no other mode, and the President's plan will be followed in all States with modifications adopted to the condition of things in each, perhaps with some general changes of his order.

All the theories of reconstruction invented for the purpose of transforming a third of the States into territories or colonies fall with the rebellion as all sagacious men foresaw that they must. They have served only to distract loyal men and embarrass the Government.—They have fulfilled their mission, and their inventors will be glad to have them forgotten.

We stand again on solid ground; the rebel is a citizen of the United States, to be forgiven and restored if he repents—to be excluded from all the rights of citizenship if he continues obdurate—to be punished as a traitor if the public safety requires it. The rebel State is a state of the Union to be recovered from disloyal and placed in loyal hands. This is the work we have been doing for four years, now almost accomplished. . . .

We have not fought our way out upon the firm highway to be cheated of our object at last. The restoration of the Union is a simple and straight forward process, and it will be speedy and permanent. The heresy of secession perishes with the rebellion and slavery ends with the war it provoked.

George W. Curtis: "The Present Peril"

George W. Curtis, whose Harper's Weekly *had covered the Civil War in word and picture, had little faith in the South's ability to reconstruct itself into a loyal state. He repeatedly called for a strong federal Reconstruction policy, enfranchisement of blacks, and a refusal to seat Southern represen- tatives in Congress unless there was complete political freedom for the freedmen. Although lengthy, this editorial describes the fear that many in the North had that the Union lives lost in the war were for naught.*

Harper's Weekly, June 24, 1865

It took seventy-five years to teach this country that fire will burn. Against the instincts of the human heart, against the dictates of common-sense, against reason and all experience we insisted upon yielding every thing to Slavery in a free Government, until Slavery took the Government by the throat, and only by the most prolonged and desperate struggle was thrown off. In like manner, against all reason and experience which assured us that sovereignty is one and can not be divided, that a nation can be injured in no part without suffering every where, that the law of life in communities is like that in individuals, we allowed the mischievous Kentucky and Virginia res- olutions to remain as a vague apology for treason, instead of seeing that where such resolutions could be adopted and defended there was the ut- most necessity of a solemn national renunciation of them by a constitutional amendment forever settling the question. Sufferance made treason insolent; servility made it strong; until the authority of the State struck at the national supremacy, and only by blooding every hearthstone with blood, and load- ing our children with debt, was the national authority restored. . . .

It would be ludicrous, if it were not too sad, to see those who are still stunned by the war doubting whether the men who excited and conducted it can possibly be capable of any naughty action. There are the horrible pens of Millen and Andersonville; the unimaginable suffering inflicted upon in- nocent men; there are the cold-blooded slaughters of Fort Pillow and Lawrence; the hangings and tortures of Union men in East Tennessee, in Texas, in all the South and Southwest; there are the plots to burn great cities, the firing of hotels and museums and theatres full of innocent women and children; there are the plans of infecting whole districts with fatal dis- ease by the yellow-fever rags; there are the massacres of helpless negroes in the streets; there is the murder of the President in a theatre; the murderous attempt upon the Secretary of State lying ill in his bed—and some good soul asks, "Do you really think they would be guilty of murder? They may be politically mistaken, but do you seriously think they would do any thing unfair?"

Could we seriously think otherwise? How is it natural to suppose that those who breed children for sale, whose laws and social and industrial habits are designed to imbrute human beings, would wage war? Is it not by every foul and dishonorable means? Is it not by poison, by assassination, by massacre? Why should not savages be savage? Jefferson Davis was called "a high-toned Southern gentleman." . . .But what his gentlemanhood and high tone were you discover when you read his speeches, in which Yankees are hyenas, and Grant and Sherman are spaniels to be whipped. There were lovely and accomplished women in the Slave States; but when they spoke of slavery their bald barbarity dehumanized them. The blood chilled in the heart to hear their flippant or fiery talk. They were like the smooth-skinned wives and daughters of ogres in fairy tales. . . .

The men who control Southern sentiment are baffled, they are not changed. They are beaten in the war—that is all. Are they less hostile? Do they confess that they had no right to make war? Do they believe that States are not sovereign? Do they acknowledge the equality of human rights? Do they hate Yankees any less because the Yankees have whipped them? The ladies of the rebel States, who are reduced from the luxury based upon the unpaid toil and untold wrongs of human beings to gain a livelihood by mechanical labor or to receive Government rations—are they less bitter and mad than before? The beggared men, who live on charity and sneer with irrepressible hate at the "Federal" Government—are they changed at heart? . . .

Have we learned that fire will burn? Do we yet understand that the chief duty of the loyal people of the United States is to suffer the late slave States to be reorganized only upon such terms as those people prescribe? Do we fully comprehend that the important point is not speedy reorganization, but sure reorganization? Do we see, as we should, that it is better Virginia should be governed as a territory for half a century rather than that she should be recognized as a State by the spirit of State Sovereignty and caste which produced the rebellion? Congress must decide the Question. Let Congress, then, distinctly understand public opinion. Let every body speak out. We are in no danger of treating any body too severely. This country was never yet too severe upon any citizens but those who warned it of the danger of intrusting a free government to the hands of those who had no faith in its principles. We are not in danger of a blood-thirsty policy but of our old obsequious pusillanimity, and a sentimental sophistication in which the true character and relation of men and things at this juncture will be forgotten and the country plunged into new perils. Wise men will insist at every hazard that the lessons of experience shall be heeded, and that the peace and welfare of the country shall be secured by placing the political power of the reorganized States in the hands of those only, and all of those, who utterly repudiate State Sovereignty, and all civil distinction based upon color; for such, and such only, are truly trust-worthy citizens of the United States.

Questions

1. What new role would Southern Unionists play in the reconstruction of the South?
2. What did the *London Times* mean when it wrote that the war was only "half finished"? Was it right?
3. What role could the newly freed slaves play in the political reconstruction of the South?
4. What is the difference, according to George W. Curtis of *Harper's Weekly,* between a "speedy Reconstruction" and a "sure Reconstruction"?
5. The *Harper's Weekly* editorial is an example of "waving the bloody shirt." What is the meaning of that metaphor?

Notes

1. *New York Herald,* 24 April 1865, 4.

2. Whitelaw Reid, *After the War: A Southern Tour* (Cincinnati: n.p., 1866), 24.

3. Brooks D. Simpson, *The Reconstruction Presidents* (Lawrence: University Press of Kansas, 1998), 69.

4. *Chicago Tribune,* 17 April 1865, 4.

CHAPTER 2

Johnson's Presidential Reconstruction Plan, 1865–66

Six weeks after assuming office, President Andrew Johnson put forward in two proclamations his plan for restoring the South. His Amnesty Proclamation restored all property rights (except for slaves) to most Confederates who would take a loyalty oath. However, he excluded wealthy slaveholders and those who held high offices in the Confederate government or army. Those excluded classes were required to apply for pardons directly from the president. His second proclamation established a Reconstruction plan for North Carolina, which would be the template for Reconstruction of all other Southern states. He appointed provisional governors in each state and required states to call constitutional conventions, rewrite prewar constitutions, and nullify secession.

Johnson's announcements ended several months of uncertainty about how the South would be treated after the war. Initially, Johnson's presidential Reconstruction plan was greeted favorably in both the North and South as a continuation of Lincoln's desires. It was sufficiently harsh on the leaders of the rebellion as well as on the old slavocracy, but it also allowed states great leeway in reorganizing their governments to suit themselves. Many citizens believed that this generous policy would lead to swift restoration of the South and a quick return to normalcy. Johnson declared on several occasions that there was no such thing as Reconstruction, believing that the term implied the rebuilding of something that had been torn down. Instead, he preferred to use such terms as "restoration" or "rehabilitation," sending a message that the South would be allowed to return to its former condition—except without slavery—as soon as possible.

Southern states were quick to pledge their loyalty to Johnson and to abide by his policy, believing that the work of the Civil War had ended with abolition of slavery. Republicans, on the other hand, believed that the abolition of slavery was only the beginning and not the end. Radicals expressed great disappointment at the president's failure to provide more protections for blacks, and they warned that the South would quickly return to its old ways. "The Negro Question" would dominate the Reconstruction debate for the next 12 years.

In the summer and fall of 1865, Southern states elected delegates to constitutional conventions and rewrote their constitutions according to the model Johnson prescribed. One of Johnson's requirements, the ratification of the Thirteenth Amendment declaring an end to slavery, disturbed many former slaveholders. Despite the fact that it had been three years since the Emancipation Proclamation, some Southern legislatures believed that former slave owners should be compensated for the loss of their "property." Others resisted ratifying the amendment because, as the *Augusta Loyal Georgian,* a Republican newspaper, explained, "Most of the white citizens believe that the institution of slavery was right and the best condition for colored men and women."[1] Others feared—and correctly so—that to abolish slavery as a condition for readmission opened the door for further federal dictates concerning the freedmen.

Southern legislatures also showed reluctance to meet another of Johnson's requirements—a renunciation of the secession acts as illegal. To do so meant denouncing states' rights—the theory that served as the foundation for many acts of Southern defiance going back to the Kentucky and Virginia resolutions in 1798 when those states attempted to justify their right to disobey a federal law. Rather than declare the secession acts illegal, some legislators argued that it would be better to simply repeal them just as they would any law they had no further need of. But in the end, most states did declare secession null and void.

By the fall of 1865, all of the rebel states had new constitutions and were ready to elect new political leadership. Disregarding the Ironclad Test Oath, which required congressmen to swear they had not voluntarily participated in the rebellion, Southern states elected many former Confederate officers and generals. Johnson seemed to overlook this small indiscretion, but to Republicans it appeared that the president was reneging on a promise to punish the South and aligning himself with the Southern elites. Johnson even ignored the oath requirements himself when he appointed various Confederates to federal posts such as postmaster and tax assessor.

The results of the fall election demonstrated that the South had no interest in creating a new political leadership to replace the old slavocracy. Congressional Republicans not only wanted to see a contrite South reenter the Union, they also wanted to see loyal union men in charge of restoring the South and to grant blacks equal rights. Republicans believed that the only way to answer the "Negro Question" was to give blacks the franchise and allow them to exercise the power of the vote. Once Congress realized that it was moving in the opposite direction from the president, it began laying the groundwork for its own Reconstruction plan. In December 1865, Congress not only refused to seat the South's newly elected congressional delegation but also appointed a joint committee of 15 members to investigate conditions in the South and to bolster their arguments against Johnson's lenient policy.

The editorials that follow represent the views of newspapers during 1865 as Johnson reveals his Reconstruction plan. In the first section are editorials critical of Johnson's policy. The first selection by William Lloyd Garrison was written after Johnson issued his plan for the readmission of North Carolina. Garrison believed that the readmission of any Southern state so soon after the end of the war was too early, as not enough was known of how the South would treat blacks and conform to necessary standards of a Democratic nation. The second entry is a letter from a Union man in Louisiana describing the violence and rebel spirit of ex-Confederate soldiers returning home. The third selection is from the *New York Tribune*, describing what has happened in the South during the six months since Johnson issued his policy for readmitting Southern states. Garrison, still trying to support Johnson, believes the president has been duped by the Southern states. The final reading, by George W. Curtis, criticizes states like South Carolina that have passed laws and constitutions without a majority of the people participating.

Throughout 1865, Democratic and conservative Republican newspapers supported Johnson's policies, if not the man himself. The section supporting Johnson's Reconstruction policy begins with an editorial, by Ben Wood, from the *New York News*, which assures the South that the president will stand against any efforts by radicals to prevent states from being readmitted to the Union. The second entry, by James Gordon Bennett, notes that by disenfranchising former rebels and blacks, Johnson has made enemies of both radicals and the white Southern aristocracy. In the end, it will be the poor whites of the South who will reconstruct the South and bring support to Johnson's policies. The third selection, by Seth Boughton, asks the North to readmit the Southern states quickly so that the South can get back to normalcy. The fourth editorial, by W. W. Screws, uses the adoption of Mississippi's new state constitution as occasion to praise Johnson and his steadfastness against radical elements in Washington. The last entry, by Manton Marble, in this section places great confidence in Johnson and the ability of the Democratic Party to stand up to anything that the radicals in Congress might do to thwart the president's policy toward the South.

CRITICIZING JOHNSON'S POLICY OF MODERATION

William Lloyd Garrison: "The Fatal Step"

William Lloyd Garrison, the most prominent leader of the prewar aboli-
tionist movement, continued his work for the freedmen after emancipation.
In this early salvo against President Johnson, Garrison pleads for a public
outcry against the administration's soft Reconstruction policy and a halt to
admitting any more Southern states until Congress could meet.

National Anti-Slavery Standard, June 3, 1865

If the President has really made up his mind to leave the fate of the negro
in the hands of the whites of each State, there is no hope either for the negro
or the Union. But we refuse to believe that such a scheme is matured, and in
order that it may not be we summon the North to its duty. Everywhere let
protest and denunciation be heard. Let the Administration be compelled at
least to hesitate—and to gain time may be to save a nation. Reconstruction
on this theory is only in the gristle; never let it harden into bone. Keep out
the States this summer and fall. Keep them in military possession til Congress can meet, armed with the indignation of the anti-slavery North, to
check and control the suicidal madness of the Administration. Keep the
bars down, lest when once up it need another revolution to overstep them,
and to give again to the Federal Government the power which it not pos-
sesses to disregard and overrule State rights for the sake of the nation.

"A. R.": Letter to the Editor

This letter, sent from a "Union man" in Houma, Louisiana, describes the
violence against Union sympathizers by ex-Confederate soldiers returning
home. There was a very real fear that such violence would escalate if fed-
eral troops left the state. The New Orleans Tribune *was one of the South's*
few stable Republican newspapers.

New Orleans Tribune, August 3, 1865

Messrs. Editors Tribune—Decidedly the infernal rebellion has come back
among us, and before long another hideous war will again desolate our
beloved country. Secessionists everywhere are appointed, and soon again,
from one end of the land to the other, they will be the supreme rulers. From
every quarter, we hear "this or that (always some Union) person has been
murdered." Contempts, threats, assassination, are the only prospects of the

day. The Union men, chased as wild beasts, and outnumbered by thousands and thousands rebels coming daily from Dixie, will be obliged to quit their homes, to leave the country that they loved so much, for which they have sacrificed everything, fortune, time and lives. Within three months, in the Parish of Terrebonne, the United States flag, the glorious Star-Spangled Banner has been insulted and torn down; once in a public ball given by some loyal citizen, and lately, during the night, in a cowardly and unknown manner. What is going to be? What shall be your fate, men of the Union, if some change does not come soon to dissipate the dark clouds of the political horizon and bring consolation to the painful hearts of the discouraged loyal people?

Will the actual order of things last long again? If so, the country is going to another struggle, but a million times more terrible than the first!! . . . But God is great and just. In Him, we have put our confidence and trust. Let us hope that He will soon confound the wicked and the Light and Truth shall be triumphant everywhere. A.R.

Horace Greeley: "First Fruits of Reconstruction"

By mid-November, five states had met in convention, ratified the Thirteenth Amendment, nullified (or repealed) secession, and created new governments. But what they created and how they went about it did not sit well with Republicans. In this editorial, Horace Greeley recounts what has occurred in the "reconstructed" states to prove that the Southern states were still acting like rebels.

New York Tribune, November 15, 1865

We can best understand the success of the experiment of Reconstruction by looking at the results in many of the Southern States. It is six months since the President threw open the doors of the Union to the defeated Rebels, and invited all who were willing to become good citizens and obedient to the laws to enter and resume their seats at the old family board. History does not present an example of similar magnanimity. . . .

Those who have criticised that policy certainly admit that the President's motives were kind and charitable. Perhaps we can no better illustrate that kindness than by remembering that to gratify the South he was willing to postpone justice to the negro. Those who know how deeply and earnestly the honest Northern heart felt on this subject will appreciate the sacrifice that the President was willing to make to propitiate the South. If any statesman commanded their gratitude, their support, their undeviating kindness, it was the President. They made protestations. They were the President's most sincere friends. They would show him the true devotion of a Southern heart. He was their bulwark against Radicalism. He would stand between them and "abolition ghouls." They on their part, would be his most devoted supporters. They would take up arms for him as they took up arms against him, and under the fostering care of Andrew Johnson, poor white, but now President of all these States, they would assist in building up a Republic that would rival in imperial grandeur the proudest days of the Commonwealth of Rome.

Well, we have tried them and what? Let us go down to Louisiana. Here is a State rich in resources—her great metropolis overflowing with the good things that commerce can bring. . . . We find the negro downtrodden. Men are imprisoned for speaking their opinions about Negro Suffrage. The worst features of the slave laws are revived. . . . If we go to Mississippi, we find not only a refusal to allow the negroes the rights of jurors, but even the rights of witnesses. In South Carolina, the Rebels almost force Wade Hampton into the Gubernatorial chair, merely because such action would be a defiance to the President. . . . As for the Constitutional Amendment it comes by compulsion. South Carolina will vote for it now, that she may kick open the doors of Congress and stand before the Speaker's chair with six electoral votes in her hand—six votes, to our shame be it spoken, that represent a power as great as Connecticut with eighty thousand white men less. Then we come to North Carolina. . . . Not one word about the Constitutional Amendment. As with these States it is everywhere throughout the South. What one State has come back frankly, and accepted all the issues of the war, even the issues of the President? . . .What Southern State has accepted all the Presidential propositions? Not one; and for this reason only that the Rebels will not concede one jot or tittle toward reconstructing a Union that does not eternize Slavery and strengthen the power of the slaveholders. They know full well that if we leave the negro in their hands a freed man, and allow them to group around him laws as degrading as those of South Carolina, they will have little trouble in perpetuating a system more degrading than Slavery. . . .

Let us emphasize these two points. The Rebels play for a winning game. "Let us," they say, "kick open the doors of Congress, and what then? We have our apportionment increased; for the negro being free, he must be counted man for man. At home, we have negro labor at slave prices, and no responsibility. We may turn the negro out to the commons when he is seventy, just as we turn out horses. Our laws compel him to work for us—we may do as we please with him. The Government has released us from our obligation to the negro, and placed an obligation upon him. Altogether we have made a jolly exchange and trumped the Yankees nicely in their own game." These gentlemen of the South mean to win. They meant it in 1861 when they opened fire on Sumter. They meant it in 1865 when they sent a bullet through the brain of Abraham Lincoln. They mean it now. The moment we remove the iron hand from the Rebels' throats they will rise and attempt mastery. . . . Therefore, we not only break faith with the negro, but with the true Union men—with those who went into the caves with Andrew Johnson, and with him suffered for their principles. The first fruits of reconstruction promise a more deplorable harvest, and the sooner we gather the tares, plow the ground again and sow new seed, the better.

George W. Curtis: "South Carolina"

This editorial was written immediately after the South Carolina convention met under President Johnson's Reconstruction plan. The state's decision to repeal, rather than nullify, secession sent a message that it still held fast to the principles of states' rights.

Harper's Weekly, October 14, 1865

South Carolina Convention has also agreed upon its offer and adjourned. As we showed last week, the key-note for its deliberations, struck by the Provisional Governor Perry, was the Dred Scott decision.

The Convention repealed the ordinance of secession by a vote of 105 to 3. It declared by 98 to 8 that as slavery had been abolished by the action of the United States authorities it should never be re-established in the State, and directed a commission to submit a code to the Legislature for the protection of the colored population. . . .

The South Carolina Convention, by merely repealing the act of secession neither denies the right of secession nor the authority of the Convention of 1860. It simply declares that it is now expedient to reconsider and reverse a legitimate action. It repeals the ordinance as a legislature repeals a law which it was perfectly competent to pass. . . . Like the Alabama Convention, that of South Carolina declared all political power to be inherent in the people, and then based the Government upon a minority of the population. The spirit of the Convention may be inferred from the speeches and Message of Governor Perry and the remarks made by the leading members, as well as by its authentic acts. Even that part of the population which is declared to be vested with political power is not allowed to pronounce upon the proposed Constitution.

Is this an "acceptance of the results of the war"? Is there any evidence here that South Carolina, formally or informally, verbally or inferentially, renounces the theory which has distracted this country for more than a generation and finally culminated in terrible civil war? Does she take the least pledge not to renew that attempt; and however futile the supposition of a renewal may now seem, is it not for that reason all the more important that at this time all shadow of legal pretense for secession shall be utterly removed? Shall not the people of the United States—and not a certain class in South Carolina—who are now to decide this question, decide plainly and indisputably and forever, that while the right of revolution for hopeless op-pression can never be renounced, the right of secession and State sover-eignty are fictions too monstrous and perilous to be openly or covertly tolerated for an instant?

It is not an unkind humiliation . . . to require that they shall at least solemnly renounce that [states' rights] plea before they are admitted to an equal share in the Government. It is not an unwise nor unconstitutional ex-ercise of power to refuse to recognize as republican a political system which puts every political and personal right of a majority of the population at the mercy of a contemptuous minority. It is not ungenerous to insist that the condition of the return of the bitterest enemies of the Union to a voice in its government shall not be the proscription and oppression of its most faithful friends. . . .

Supporting Johnson's Moderate Policy

Ben Wood: "The Policy of the President"

The New York News *was a popular newspaper in the South because it supported a strong Democratic line. In this editorial, Ben Wood assures the South that President Johnson will stand fast with his policy of leniency against the threats of radicals in Congress.*

New York News, June 12, 1865

Every day brings to light additional proofs of the conservative policy which has been determined on by President Johnson. It is now well under-stood that in the course of a very few months the great bulk of the citizens of the Southern States will be restored to the enjoyment of all the rights, po-litical and social, which were theirs before the war, with the single exception of the right to hold slaves.

The President is convinced that on no other basis than this can there be any real Union between the States. The Southern people are our fellow-citizens; but they could have no real love for a government which should place them and keep them in an inferior condition, as respects political rights, to their fellow-citizens of New York or Massachusetts. The problem for Mr. Johnson to decide was, how to make good citizens out of the people of the South: how to make them zealously affected toward the Government, and he has very wisely decided that the way to accomplish this is to make them realize that they have an interest in the Government, and more than that, that they are to have a voice in shaping and directing the future policy of the Government; and equal voice with their fellow-citizens of the North. This decision of Mr. Johnson is well known; and while it fills the hearts of all true patriots with joy, it has carried dismay and consternation into the camps of the Radical Republicans.

Some of the far-seeing leaders of the Republican party are already greatly alarmed at the prospect. The only way that they see to avert it is to persuade the President to admit the Southern negroes to the polls, and thus kill the votes of the white people of the South, and to disfranchise a large portion of the citizens of the Southern States upon various pretexts.

But the President utterly refuses to be led by them. He has not been in haste to decide upon his policy; but, having decided, he will maintain his ground.

James Gordon Bennett: "President Johnson's Plan of Reconstruction—Call for a Constitutional Convention"

James Gordon Bennett, owner of the New York Herald, *was a personal friend of President Johnson's and supported the president even after most Republican papers abandoned him. In this editorial, Bennett supports giving control of the South to loyal Unionists. However, within weeks of this editorial, Johnson began pardoning former slaveholders and returning control of the South to the old Southern aristocracy.*

New York Herald, June 2, 1865

The plan of reconstruction adopted by President Johnson, as foreshadowed in the Herald and announced in the recent Presidential proclamations is so simple, clear, strong, practical and constitutional as to command the respect and support of every reasonable man. Its main feature is to throw the political power of the Southern States into the hands of the poor whites of that section, who never had any political control before. The negroes and the former negro owners are excluded for the present from the privileges of suffrage. We estimate the voting population of the seceded States, at say, eight hundred thousand. Of these, two hundred thousand belong to the exslaveholding aristocracy, who used to domineer over the remaining six hundred thousand voters, ruling them for many years and finally nearly ruining them by this rebellion. Now this condition of things is to be completely changed. The six hundred thousand poor whites are to exercise the legitimate supremacy of a majority. Through State conventions, the adoption of new State constitutions, the election of State officers and then of members of Congress, they are to bring the seceded States back into the Union quietly, quickly, and gracefully. President Johnson's admirable plan settles the reconstruction question most satisfactorily.

But as the plan which we have briefly sketched excludes for the present the ex-slaves and the ex-slaveholders, it naturally encounters the opposition of the negro worshippers of the North and the negro aristocracy of the South. . . . At any rate, now that both North and South concede that slavery is dead, we find the extremists of both sections uniting in abuse of President Johnson. He need care nothing for that, so long as the people are with him. He is not the kind of man to be bullied by vituperative orators or fanatical papers. He has determined upon his policy and he will pursue it to the end. We believe it to be the right policy, and we anticipate its complete success. . . .

Any attentive observer of political events can easily see that the effects of President Johnson's plan will not cease with the reconstruction of the Union. That will be its first and immediate result; but the ultimate results will be quite as important. It is a philosophical as well as practical plan, and it will reorganize Southern society and revolutionize our national politics. Reconstruction is but the beginning of the scheme. The poor whites of the South, placed by the president in the supreme political control of the section, will form a union with the war democrats of the North. These two parties will at once rally around Andy Johnson who represents them both; for he began life as a poor Southerner, and he was elected to the Vice Presidency as a war democrat. The President will consequently have the same close hold upon the masses of the people that Mr. Lincoln had, and he will become as invincible. . . .

On the whole, it is very probable that the negro suffrage question, which President Johnson has left to the several States, according to the constitution, will have to be finally taken up and settled by a constitutional convention of all the States. Even the radicals must admit that it would be impossible to give the emancipated slaves of the South the privilege of voting, like white men, while the free negroes of New York cannot vote unless they possess two hundred and fifty dollars worth of real estate. This would be a most transparent absurdity, since the newly freed slaves are totally ignorant, and our Northern negroes are comparatively educated. . . .

Seth Boughton: "Are We to Be Represented in Congress?"

This editorial pledges cooperation in return for a moderate policy controlled by President Johnson rather than a harsh one led by the radicals. Seth Boughton was a strong Southern Democrat but less bombastic in his editorial language than many of his Southern brethren in the press.

Milledgeville (Ga.) Federal Union, **August 1, 1865**

We are told by many of the conservative papers at the North, that it is the intention of the extreme Radicals to prevent the Southern States from being represented in the National Congress. We do not think it of so much importance as to get up a fuss over it, particularly as the party in power at the North having us completely subjugated can do as they please with us; but as a harmonizing and healing policy, we think it best for all parties, North and South, that the States lately in rebellion be allowed a representation in Congress, at the earliest practicable moment after their restoration to the Union. This we know to be President Johnson's view of this particular question. The President rightly thinks that the States are entitled to representation in Congress if they have republican forms of government, and are loyal. What the South needs now, more than any mere political privilege, is quiet and a restoration of business in all the departments of industry. She needs capital, and labor that can be relied on. Politicians just now are played out, and, therefore, Congress is of but little importance to us of the South. Yet as an evidence of good feeling toward us, and as a means of restoring the amity theretofore existing between the sections, we should be pleased to see the party in power in Congress, manifest a spirit of magnanimity, to say nothing of justice, towards the Southern States. We cannot expect the country to prosper as it once did, until all animosities are buried, and all grievances forgiven and forgotten. The people of the South are honest. They have determined to do all in their power to repair the injuries which have befallen the country on account of the War, and they will prove by their acts that they are as earnest as they are honest. It may be a gratification of a mere spirit of spite or hate to the majority of the North, to punish us of the South still farther, but we are certain no good can come of it to them or us. So far as the Army or the men that composed it are concerned, we are willing to trust them, and take the terms they offer us. But there is a party at the North, respectable in numbers and controlled by men of influence, who are not satisfied with the abolition of slavery, but who are determined that the subject shall not be put to rest. They find the platform on which they rose to power suddenly kicked from under them and the party left without a foundation to build upon. We hope that there are wisdom, and prudence and discretion enough amongst the people of the North, to enable them to be just to themselves even though they be not generous to their brethren of the South. We want peace—a true peace—not a patched up thing that has no heart in it, and no meaning in it. We intend to be true to all our obligations, and we sincerely hope that the President will attach no credit whatever to the stories put afloat by designing politicians, that the Southern people are discontented and disloyal. This is a trick to help the Radicals. Our people are not such fools as to do the very thing that the

Radicals desire them to do, viz; throw disturbances in the way of the restoration of the country to law and order.

W. W. Screws: "The President's Policy of Reconstruction"

Mississippi was one of the first states to reorganize under President John-son's Reconstruction policy. Editors looked at Mississippi's success as an indication that Johnson would stand by his plan of Reconstruction and that the rest of the Southern states should follow quickly behind.

Montgomery (Ala.) Daily Advertiser, August 31, 1865

The proceedings of the Convention in Mississippi were concluded with the reading of a congratulatory address from President Johnson, which is a sure indication that no difficulty now exists in the way of a speedy resumption of civil rule in that State.

A general election has been ordered for October, and members of Congress will be elected who can take their seats at the meeting in December next, and thus she will stand as she did in 1860. The interest manifested by President Johnson in the proceedings of the Convention and his expressed gratification at the result of its labors, show that he is anxious for the States to be fully represented, and it makes the war between him and the radicals more fierce than ever.

He has stood out against all opposition in favor of the plan he first announced. . . . No matter what differences may exist in the South upon other matters, he is sustained in his policy by a large majority of our people, and now more than ever since his address to the Mississippi Convention, assuring them that military rule would soon be withdrawn and the habeas corpus restored.

President Johnson has a most difficult part to play in the history of the day; and thus far he has shown that firmness which promises that he will hold out to the end in the course he has adopted in reference to the Southern States and their reconstruction: and while it may not be as lenient as could be desired, yet he will receive the thanks of the entire South for standing out so manfully against those who wish to degrade us by forcing negro suffrage upon us, and will be sustained by those everywhere who have the good of the country at heart.

Manton Marble: "The Political Situation"

Manton Marble was one of the strongest Democratic editors in New York, and he fully supported President Johnson's Reconstruction policy. In the election of 1865, Democrats did not fare well, but they did give resounding support to Johnson. In this editorial, Marble accurately forecasts that radicals will find Johnson a stubborn opponent if they go their own way regarding Reconstruction.

New York World, November 10, 1865

In the late election, the Democratic party did not accomplish all they hoped; but they did enough to blast the designs of the Radicals, and insure the rehabilitation of the Union. . . . The celerity of the consummation depends very much on President Johnson, whose path we have smoothed, and on whose policy we have set the seal of success, if he acts with the fidelity and sagacity to be expected from his character. Had the Democratic party, in this canvass, inscribed on their banners opposition instead of support, we should have lost the election as now; but the consequences would not have been the same. Our prompt and intrepid confidence in the President disconcerted and ham-strung the Radicals in their state conventions. . . . The consequence was, that the reconstruction policy of the President was ostensibly countenanced by the Republicans as it had been unequivocally indorsed by the Democrats. . . .

The pivot of this inquiry is the future action of President Johnson. All our reasoning goes on the presumption that he will not truckle to the Radicals. Supposing him to defy them, what are the advantages placed in his hand for this purpose by the late election? These: that he can count with confidence on the indubitable support of all that numerous body of citizens returned as having voted the Democratic ticket. Though not quite a majority they can be reinforced into one. . . . There can be no doubt whatever that the moment the Republican party, as a party, dares take open issue with the President on his reconstruction policy, men of moderate tendencies will at once desert it sufficient in numbers to convert the great army of Democratic voters into a majority.

The Republican Congress can undoubtedly arrest the President's attempted reconstruction at the coming session. They have the numbers, and a majority of them do not lack inclination. But under existing circumstances, will they dare exert the will? It is indeed, possible that the strategic lines drawn around them by the Democratic party may "give them pause." If the President is firm on his side, all they can do on theirs is to delay, not defeat, the success of his plan. If they arrest his experiment, he has only to appeal to the people in the congressional election, less than a year distant. His supporters would sweep the country, as the Democratic party would have swept it in this election just closed had that issue been madly presented. The Democratic party have engineered the politics of the country into such a shape as to make President Johnson master of the situation. If the Republicans elect to oppose him, he knows where he can find a triumphant majority, even with the Southern States excluded. But if the hopelessness of effectual opposition dragoons the Republicans into his support, our purpose is equally accomplished. The reconstruction policy triumphs; the Southern States come back; political parties will be reorganized with reference to the vote of the whole country. The reconstruction question, having then become obsolete, will be consigned to history. It will be no longer an issue in national politics, and the dividing line between parties will be drawn with reference to other questions.

It is for [Republicans] to say whether they will fight it out on the negro suffrage line, or frankly accept the policy of the President. If they are cunning enough to choose the latter branch of the alternative they may keep their party together till the reorganization consequent to the renewed participation of the South in federal politics.

QUESTIONS

1. What kind of evidence does the North use to demonstrate that the South is not to be trusted?
2. What effect did repealing the acts of secession, rather than nullifying them, have on the theory of states' rights?
3. What major issue stood between Johnson's policy and that of the radicals?
4. Why did James Gordon Bennett believe a convention was the best way to settle the issue of black suffrage?

NOTE

1. *Augusta Loyal Georgian,* 4 January 1868, 2.

CHAPTER 3

The Freedmen's Bureau, 1865–72

During the months before General Robert E. Lee's surrender, slaves and former slaves abandoned plantations and moved toward Union lines. It fell on the government to create a mechanism by which hundreds of thousands of refugees could be clothed, fed, and housed. In some areas, the problem fell directly into the hands of the army. In other areas the ubiquitous "Sanitary Commission"—an agency charged with overseeing the sanitation and health of soldiers—took on the task of dealing with refugees.[1]

In March 1865, less than a month before the Confederate surrender, Congress established the Bureau of Refugees, Freedmen, and Abandoned Lands to deal with what most believed would be a short-term program of moving blacks from slavery to freedom. The bureau's operations, confined principally to the relief of freedmen and to the rental of abandoned lands, was to exist only for the duration of the war plus one year.

The role of the bureau necessarily grew beyond its original charge. In addition to supervising the disposition of abandoned or confiscated lands and property, bureau officers issued food, clothing, and medicine to destitute refugees and freedmen. They established hospitals, schools, and employment offices, as well as camps for the homeless. They registered marriages and eventually assumed the job of helping black veterans file and collect claims for bounties, pensions, and back pay. Most of the bureau agents' efforts were spent overseeing the writing of labor contracts and listening to complaints.

As the first social welfare bureaucracy established by the federal government, the Freedmen's Bureau was an example of the expanding role of the federal government into the affairs of states. Consequently, many saw the agency as nothing short of a usurpation of states' rights, and every attempt was made to undermine and discredit its activities.

The bureau's affairs were directed by General Oliver O. Howard, whose strong commitment to helping freedmen came from his strict religious upbringing. However, the bureau's agents on the front line were a mix of former union officers and Southern whites with varying degrees of commitment and little experience working in a highly politicized environment.

The bureau received its funding from the sale and rent of land. It was authorized by law to rent abandoned and confiscated property to freedmen for three years. After the three-year period, the bureau could sell the land to those who had worked it. More important, it was from the stewardship of their own land that freedmen could begin to distance themselves from their slave heritage. At the end of the war, more than 800,000 acres reverted to the bureau, and during 1865 more than half of that land was rented to freedmen. However, the policy of land redistribution lasted only a few months. In May 1865, President Andrew Johnson ordered General Howard to restore all land to pardoned owners with the exception of that land that had already been sold under court order. By the fall of 1865, almost all of the land that the bureau controlled on behalf of freedmen was returned to prewar owners.

With no land sales or rents, the bureau no longer had a source of funding and no longer actively promoted black ownership of land. Without their own land to work, freedmen were forced back to the plantations, where they entered into contracts that exchanged labor for crops or money. From the perspective of white planters, this was a positive turn of events because they needed a cheap and steady source of labor that could be compelled to stay on the land.

The primary duty of the Freedmen's Bureau quickly turned to the overseeing of contracts between black laborers and white landowners. The result was a system of legalized peonage. Freedmen were required to be under contract, and if they broke the contract they would be punished with imprisonment. These regulations were sanctioned by the bureau, which argued that freedmen needed work and they needed to be protected in the contract negotiation. If that meant exchanging freedom for contracts that provided fair wages, medical care, and clothing, so be it.

Most of the bureau agents' time and energy were occupied enforcing contracts. If freedmen wished to complain to a bureau agent or sue their employers for breach of contract, they had to travel long distances to the nearest town. Going to court was expensive, and courts typically sided with the planters or they delayed decisions. The bureau tried to counter planters' recalcitrance by setting wage guidelines, relocating blacks to areas where wages were better, and prohibiting physical punishment of workers. On the other hand, the bureau too often coerced freedmen to sign contracts, fined or imprisoned workers who struck for higher wages, ordered blacks to leave cities, imprisoned blacks for debts, and forcibly removed freedmen from lands that they were working.

If the bureau can be credited with any singular success it was in the area of education. The freedmen's schools were the first public school systems in the South, and by the time the bureau was disbanded, more than 5,000 schools serving more than 250,000 children had been created in the South. This total did not include night schools.

Initially, the bureau was not allowed to build schools or rent buildings for schools. However, the second Freedmen's Bureau Act of July 13, 1866, authorized funds for the salaries of state superintendents of education and for the repair and rental of school buildings. Freedmen were expected to pay a small fee to keep the schools open, a fee they gladly paid. Freedmen also built schoolhouses or found buildings large enough to seat 40 to 50 students—in a church, in a stable, in someone's house, in abandoned buildings.

Bureau policy also prohibited paying for books and teachers' salaries, so black families were required to furnish board and at least $30 a month for a teacher before opening a school. Most black communities could not afford this expense, therefore the bureau worked closely with philanthropic organizations from the North, particularly the American Missionary Association, freedmen's aid societies, and other church-related organizations that had previous experience establishing schools in the South. These groups sent young women into the South as teachers and subsidized the purchase of books and school materials.

Whites' attitudes toward freedmen's schools ranged from apathy to violent opposition. Opposition came primarily in those areas where teachers used the schools to educate adult freedmen about their political responsibilities—particularly their responsibility toward the Republican Party. The Ku Klux Klan used violence and intimidation to shut down freedmen's schools, from ransacking schools, harassing teachers and students, burning schools, and even murdering teachers.

Eventually, teachers and technical colleges and universities were established by the Freedmen's Bureau to train black teachers, preachers, and doctors. Among those schools were Atlanta University, Fisk University in Nashville, and Howard University in Washington, D.C. (named after General Oliver Otis Howard, the Freedmen's Bureau head).

No matter how much good the bureau did, there were many men in prominent positions, including President Johnson, who did not believe that blacks should have their own bureau or that money should be spent to help blacks move from slavery to freedom. Johnson began his attacks on the bureau a year after it was founded by vetoing the second Freedmen's Bureau Act, which would have extended the bureau's operations for two more years and given it an adequate budget. Congress was unable to muster enough votes to overturn the veto.

To thwart a second attempt by Congress to pass a reauthorization bill, Johnson sent two inspectors—John Steedman and Joseph Fullerton—to the South in April to study the bureau's operations. Although the inspectors heard freedmen in every community praise the bureau and warn against its withdrawal, their report was highly critical, accusing bureau agents of malfeasance, corruption, and swindling.

Despite the damaging report, Congress passed the second Freedmen's Bureau Act in July 1866. The new law extended the agency only until 1868, but it did allow the secretary of state to discontinue the bureau's operations in any states that were reconstructed. Dragged down by high costs, limited budgets, corruption, and excessive patronage and buffeted by white intransigence and presidential disdain, the bureau drew its last breath in 1870.

The first set of readings presenting the Freedmen's Bureau in a favorable light begins with a letter, by Josephine E. Griffing, describing in graphic detail the plight of black refugees in Washington, D.C. The second entry describes the work of the bureau and ends by pleading that should the agents of the bureau be removed, blacks would have no protections. The third reading, by E.L. Godkin, praises the work of the bureau, pointing out that it has done more good than harm for the South's blacks. The fourth entry is a letter describing the difficulties encountered by a white female teacher in a freedmen's school in Virginia. The final piece in this section, by Samuel Bowles, reflects back on the work of the bureau and concludes that it had been a positive force to support blacks and that some of its work should be continued.

The readings against the work of the Freedmen's Bureau begin with a piece by "Bill Arp," one of the South's most popular humorists, who is critical of the bureau's interference. The next entry, by Henry J. Raymond, supports the findings of Johnson's investigators and calls for the bureau to be disbanded. The third selection, by Manton Marble, finds the Republicans' reports of prosperous freedmen an excuse to end the bureau's work.

Favoring the Work of the Freedmen's Bureau

Josephine E. Griffing: "Appeal on Behalf of the Freedmen of Washington, D.C."

Josephine E. Griffing, an Ohio abolitionist, moved to Washington, D.C., in 1864 to help the freedmen who had poured into the city during the war. She was appointed a bureau agent but was fired when General Howard believed that her too-realistic depictions of the freedmen were hurting the bureau's reputation. This letter appeared in one of the last issues of the Boston Liberator, *an abolitionist newspaper originally founded by William Lloyd Garrison in 1831.*

Boston Liberator, November 3, 1865

TO THE FRIENDS OF HUMANITY:

I beg leave to make the following statement and appeal to the Northern States in behalf of the destitute Freed People in and around the National Capital.

The population of Washington, at the last census, was, Whites 60,000, Free Colored, 14,000, and from a recent partial census by the War Department it appears that not less than 25,000 have been added. A large proportion of these are women and children, a few of whose husbands and fathers are still in Government service; but most of them are either disabled, dead, or left with the rebels.

A host of miserable women, with large families of children, besides old, crippled, blind and sick persons, have been driven out of Maryland and sought refuge here. Most of these people have exhibited industry and thrift beyond the expectation of their friends, paying, generally by day's labor—often difficult to obtain—for shanties, garrets, cellars and stables—unfit for human beings to live in—an average rent of $5 to $6 per month.

At the commencement of the winter of 1864, upon personal examination, I found nine hundred families, with an average number of five children, without wood or the means to obtain it; half that number without beds or blankets, and as many without bread or the means of subsistence....

At the same time it was found that thousands of women and children of the latest arrivals were without a change of clothing, and large numbers had no under clothing at all.

A number of infants, of only a few days old, were found without a garment, and in this condition many perished from the cold. Hundreds of old persons and children were without shoes and stockings, and being badly frost bitten, several had their limbs amputated in consequence, and are crippled for life. Very few among the twenty thousand have comfortable beds or household utensils. I find from burying their dead, that the sanitary condition of most of the poorest class conduces much to the fearful mortality among them, as they are compelled to breathe a very impure air within, and a stench without the room, and are often covered with vermin, even after death....

I have lately learned from the Quartermaster's Department, where coffins are issued for those Freedmen too poor to buy, that since the commencement of the extreme hot weather, about 80 coffins per week have been called for, most of which were for children. This mortality is far greater than has before been reported since they came to the city. . . .

In one family of a soldier who lost his life in battle, five out of ten of his children have died since March, 1865, from the above causes. In another, three out of seven children, of a soldier drafted December last, have starved to death within the last three weeks. The mothers, in both cases, were prostrated with sickness, and all their supplies were suddenly and entirely cut off. In the same square, mothers and sons and wives and children, of soldiers still in Government service as Regular U.S. Troops, are suffering for the necessities of life. . . .

The bureau of Freedmen has no appropriation from Congress to meet the wants of these wretched men, women and children. Maj. Gen. Howard, in his circular no. 2, distinctly states this, and also invites the benevolent public, and associations already organized for Freedmen's aid, to cooperate in giving the needed relief to these sufferers until compensating labor can be found for them. . . .

We need large quantities of cloth for these schools, and also yarn for knitting. Bedding of every description is absolutely needed before the coming winter. Household utensils, and a little cheap furniture, should be supplied to those who have none. Sleeping on the shanty and stable floors last winter induced colds and pulmonary disease, that terminated the lives of hundreds, who, with beds and bedsteads to sleep on, might now be living.

Provisions of all kinds are needed for these families, whose rent absorbs much of their scanty earnings.

Correspondent: "The Freedmen's Bureau"

The Mobile (Ala.) Nationalist *was one of the first black newspapers in the South after the war. It was sponsored by the Union League, an organization committed to educating blacks in the politics of the Republican Party, agitating for better labor conditions, and supporting the work of the Freedmen's Bureau. This is a letter to the editor, probably written by a Freedmen's Bureau agent.*

Mobile (Ala.) Nationalist, May 3, 1866

The Freedmen's Bureau is looked upon by most persons in the South as the "old man of the sea," clinging to the back of social and commercial prosperity.

It is almost universally hated and contemned [*sic*]. Its agents are treated with scorn, and those who undertake to conscientiously carry out the principles of right and justice . . . are maligned even by those whom the Bureau is saving from starvation.

The cause of this intense hatred is not necessary to inquire into. It is well understood by every unprejudiced mind.

In order both to enhance the prosperity of the country, and to improve the condition of the freed people of the South, the Freedmen's Bureau devised a system by which planters might depend upon a certainty of labor. . . . To this end, certain rules and regulations were made, whereby contracts made with freedmen might be enforced. The only legal penalty for the violation of a contract is that of damage to the party suffering from such violation. . . . Civil magistrates are authorized under the regulations of the Bureau to enforce such contracts.

What would be the consequences of the withdrawal of the Bureau? Its orders would be suspended. No magistrate could enforce contracts. . . and he could only apply a civil remedy. The contracts now made would not be worth the paper they are written on. Freedmen would be free to come and go, and the planter would have no redress. The results are evident and unquestionable.

The Bureau is now not only protecting the freedmen in his natural rights, but is materially assisting the planter in recovering a portion of his former prosperity. Remove the Bureau and the basis of the prospective prosperity is gone also. . . .

E. L. Godkin: "The Freedmen"

Like most Republicans of the time, E.L. Godkin was not enamored with the Freedmen's Bureau, yet he recognized the good work it had done and understood where the freedmen would be without the bureau and its agents.

The Nation, August 16, 1866

The final report of Gens. Steedman and Fullerton has been made public. Their foregone conclusion is that the Bureau is a nuisance in itself, and is served by unworthy agents; its continuance will be productive of discord and oppression. It is in behalf of the blacks that these commissioners most urgently call for the dissolution of the Bureau. Forgetting the old cry of the slaveholders, that a Negro would not work at all except under compulsion— forgetting the outrageous vagrant acts of the past twelve months, . . . forgetting that the Bureau enforced the making of contracts (whose terms were not prescribed) partly to bridge over the disorganization of labor, partly in deference to the opinion that the freedmen would avoid labor, . . . —these Presidential fault-finders accuse the Bureau of re-enslaving the blacks by contracts which impose wages far below those obtainable in open market by competition. The very success of the Bureau in restoring labor, and in enhancing the value of the laborer, is thus turned against it as a crime; and while to-day it is feeding more whites than blacks, and, with what little military support is still allowed it by the President, is doing its best to promote industry, security, good morals, and substantial justice among all classes of population, it is subjected to these assaults. . . . No one less than the friends of the Bureau will object to the most rigid, so it be impartial and disinterested, scrutiny of its agents and its operations; nor is it to be denied that, from the vary necessities of the case, as well as through errors of judgment, many incapable and not a few corrupt officers have been taken from the army into places under the Bureau. But, on evidence palpably one-sided and inconclusive, with motives undisguisedly hostile, to denounce the very existence of a legally established institution, resembles nothing else than the President's superfluous message concerning the Constitutional Amendment—that is, both are acts calculated and intended to weaken the popular respect for law, simply because certain enactments are not conformable to the "policy" of the Executive.

Anonymous Writer: "How It Looks from a Virginia School-House"

This letter reproduced in the New York Tribune *tells of the hatred held by white Southerners against teachers and missionaries who went South after the war to teach in freedmen's schools.*

New York Tribune, March 27, 1866

A brave young woman, of education and refinement, who has left her home in Brooklyn to devote herself to teaching the freedmen in Virginia, gives, in a private letter to her brother, from which we are permitted to make extracts, some interesting incidents in her daily life. She writes, March 19:

"To-day, as I was quietly returning from school alone, I was saluted with such a volley of oaths that I involuntary turned my head to see the speaker. A man instantly retreated within a gateway, repeating: 'God dam you and send you to hell, you cursed bitch of a Yankee teacher!' Some colored people, who had evidently heard, said: 'Do you know who that is?' I replied, 'No; but I should be glad to know.' They then mentioned his name. When he saw me speaking with them he renewed his curses. I went on, and meeting the Major (of the Freedmen's Bureau), of course told him. He will see what he can do, but not much I expect. He says he was beset on Friday night by a rowdy mob, who woke him up with the cries 'Wake up and come out, you damned Freedman's Bureau;' some shouting, 'Kill him!' others, 'Tear him to pieces!' All this, however, is perfectly natural. I looked for it, and look for much more. It is the first time in my life I have had the honor of an open curse, and I *do* feel it an honor in such a cause.

"*9:45 p.m.*—Just in from school. . . . We went on quietly with our work as usual, when at 9 o'clock a great crash came against the window, and a large rough stone (which is now on the table before me) fell on the floor. It came exactly in a line with the spot where I was standing, and I think we have to thank the calico window-blind, in part, for preventing further damage. Something has been thrown nearly every night lately, but this is the first time a window has been broken. I see they want to frighten our scholars away. Do you think we are reconstructed down here? Ask Mr. Beecher to come down and protect us. Perhaps a little of his smooth eloquence might soften those hard 'loyalists.' The colored people want to celebrate the anniversary of the fall of Richmond, because it is their Independence Day. They are told if they celebrate it at all it shall be with blood. One of the young men says he will celebrate it, if he does it alone. What do you think I should advise him? Of course I hold it to be their right to celebrate their freedom, and I don't like to see them cowed down by the Whites. Yet I don't like to risk bloodshed, though I seriously believe that more blood will have to be spilt before these people will be free."

The writer of this letter little expected it would ever find its way into print. Its simple, unaffected statement, given in an unreserved, sisterly communication, is worth a ten-column speech of ever so able a member of Congress on Reconstruction. . . .

Samuel Bowles: No Title

Even those people most sympathetic to the Freedmen's Bureau believed it was only a temporary bureaucracy and that once blacks received the vote and certain civil and political rights, there would be no further need for the bureau. This article by the Springfield (Mass.) Republican*'s editor was written as the bureau was taking its last dying breath.*

Springfield (Mass.) Republican, November 24, 1868

The expected order for the discontinuance of the Freedmen's Bureau on the 31st of December, according to the act of Congress last July, has been issued by Gen Howard. The operations of the bureau are to be entirely discontinued, except the educational department and the collection and payment of moneys due soldiers and sailors and their heirs from the government on account of military services. . . . That the bureau has been of great service to the freedmen, in their new and changed condition, there can be no doubt; indeed we do not see what they could have done without it. No doubt, too, the blacks will greatly miss, even now, the fatherly protection and counsel of the Bureau officers, and there will be individual cases of fraud and oppression that would not have happened as long as these officials were within reach. But the emancipated negroes must learn to take care of themselves sometime, to appeal to the laws for justice and their rights, and the sooner they understand this the better. It is highly proper, however, that special attention should be given by the general government to providing educational facilities and settling accounts for military services of the freedmen, and this it undertakes to do through the bureau in its modified form and with its diminished resources.

OPPOSING THE WORK OF THE FREEDMEN'S BUREAU

Charles H. Smith (aka "Bill Arp"): No Title

Charles H. Smith, better known by his pen name Bill Arp, was a lawyer and Confederate veteran who began writing for newspapers after the war. This piece probably appeared originally in his hometown newspaper in Rome, Georgia. In 1878, Arp moved to Atlanta and wrote "letters" for the Atlanta Constitution *for 25 years, becoming the South's most popular humorist of the era. His homespun philosophy was written in a down-home style that barely camouflaged strong racial stereotypes.*

Staunton (Va.) Vindicator, November 17, 1865

Then there is another thing I am waiting for. Why don't they rekonstrukt the niggers if they are ever goin to? They've give 'em a powerful site of freedom, and very little else. Nere's the big freedmen's buro, and the little buros all over the country, and the papers are full of grand orders, and special orders, and paragrafs, but I'll bet a possum some 'em steal my wood this winter or freezes to death. Freedman's buro! freedman's humbug. I say. Jest when the corn neede plowin the worst the buro rung the bell and tolled all the niggers to town, and the farmers lost the crops; and now the freedman is gettin cold and hungry, and wants to go back, and there aint nothin for 'em to go to. But freedom is a big thing.

Hurraw for freedom's buro! Sweet land of liberty of thee I don't sing! But it's all right.

I'm for freedom myself. Nobody wants any more slavery. If the abolishunists had let us alone we would have fixed it up right a long time ago, and we can fix it up now. The buro aint fixed it and it aint goin to. It don't know anything about it. Our people have got a heap more feeling for the poor nigger than any abolishunist. We are as poor as Job, but I'll bet a dollar we can raise more money in Rome to build a nigger church than they did in

Bostown. The papers say that after goin round for 3 weeks, The Bostown christians raised thirty-seven dollars to build a nigger church in Savannah. They are powerful in theory, but mighty [weak] in practice. . . .

Henry J. Raymond: "The Freedmen's Bureau—The Results of the Investigation"

The report by Generals John Steedman and Joseph Fullerton was a stinging indictment of the bureau's operation. It convinced many people in the North that the bureau wasted taxpayer money. Congressman Henry Raymond supported President Johnson's veto of the second Freedmen's Bureau Act.

New York Times, August 13, 1866

The hostility which each succeeding report of Gens. Steedman and Fullerton has encountered has certainly not been the product of a regard for the public welfare. The investigation was instituted to ascertain the truth with reference to a Bureau whose working had been the subject of unsatisfactory controversy; and the facts brought to light should have commended themselves to the dispassionate attention of the Press. The systematic attempts that have been made to hide these facts when concealment was possible, and in other cases to pervert and misrepresent them, proves that the faction who have taken the Bureau, with all its mismanagement, under their especial charge, care more for partisanship than for economy and truth.

Briefly, it is shown that the Bureau had outlived its mission and is now a source of mischief. It is shown that in the greater portion of the South the agents of the Bureau have needlessly interfered with local civil authority; and needlessly roused local prejudice. It is shown that vast amounts of public money have been squandered, and that other large amounts, collected by agents under various pretexts have disappeared, none knows how or whither. It is shown that there has been no uniformity in the management of the Bureau—no fixed system in the administration of its varied power, no sufficient restraint upon the action of its officers, no efficient check upon the disposal of the moneys coming into their hands. It is shown that Bureau agents have been concerned in sending northward statements prejudicial to the Southern people, with a full knowledge of their falsity. It is shown that many of the representations which have been employed by the Radicals to commend the Bureau to the Northern sympathy have lacked the quality of truth. . . .

Gens. Steedman and Fullerton have pricked some very pretty bubbles. They have exposed the hollowness of much maudlin sympathy. They have stripped disguise off proceedings that were not intended for the public eye, and have reduced divers humanitarians to the level of peculators, and squanderers of public money.

Perhaps the most provoking of all the exposures are those which show that for some time past the Bureau has operated to the disadvantage of the freedmen, and that the discontinuance of the Bureau is required in the interest of the freedmen themselves. Strange is it not, that these noisy Radicals, overflowing with love for the negro, uphold a Bureau which practically reduces him to bondage? ...

Manton Marble: "The Radical Mission to the South"

The Democratic New York World's editor manages to get every grievance against the Freedmen's Bureau into this editorial—from the bureau's budget, which allowed the building of schools and buying of stationery, to the defunct and unauthorized transportation system that moved laborers from impoverished urban areas to plantations where jobs were available.

New York World, June 5, 1867

We have lately corrected the extravagant and untruthful statements of General Howard respecting the enormous number of negro schools in the Southern states, and the immense amount of money deposited by the freedmen in their own savings banks. But the Southern correspondents of Northern Radical journals continue to send the most flattering accounts of the mental, moral, physical and pecuniary conditions of the emancipated blacks. ... If a tithe of these tales is true, there is every reason for at once getting out an injunction upon the United States Treasurer to prevent him from issuing a single dollar to the Freedmen's Bureau, which is clearly obtaining money under the false pretense of clothing, feeding, protecting and above all, "supplying stationery" to a class of people who are fairly implored to take the highest wages; who build seminaries of learning for their children; who have bank accounts; and who travel from Virginia to the Gulf and back again at government expense. Every tax payer as well as every true philanthropist, will hail with satisfaction all indications that look as if the freedmen were likely speedily to be an entirely self-supporting population. ... The animus which inspires the enthusiastic and extravagant Radical accounts of the progress and general prosperity of the lately emancipated blacks is obviously this: to show that the negroes are entirely qualified to exercise the elective franchise ... and by showing that at every point in the South they can preach Radicalism to large and intelligent colored audiences—citizens, indeed, who have stately school houses of their own building at their backs and bank books with a goodly tow of entries on the right side in their breeches pocket. ...

QUESTIONS

1. What were the major arguments against the Freedmen's Bureau?
2. What was the real motive for sending the investigators to the South to study the Freedmen's Bureau?
3. Why did the South dislike the Freedmen's Bureau?
4. What benefits did landowners receive from the Freedmen's Bureau?

NOTE

1. Information for this introduction comes from Paul A. Cimbala and Randall M. Miller, *The Freedmen's Bureau and Reconstruction: Reconsideration* (New York: Fordham University Press, 1999); Paul Skeels Peirce, *The Freedmen's Bureau* (New York: Haskell House, 1971).

CHAPTER 4

Black Codes, 1865

When the war ended, Southern planters returned to their plantations and began rebuilding the agricultural system that had prospered before the war. That system was built on the concept of large plantations that required hundreds of slaves to plant and pick cotton, harvest rice, or cut sugar cane. To maintain the old ways, plantation owners needed to keep former slaves on the plantation and prevent them from finding other ways of making a living.

The first solution was the creation a new labor system that depended on annual labor contracts that did not pay wages until after a harvest was in. In most Southern states, blacks who were not under a labor contract could be charged with vagrancy and sent to work off their punishment on plantations.

The second solution was to recreate the dual legal system that had existed before the war. Slave codes to regulate the life of slaves had existed in all of the Southern states as far back as the early 1700s, and black codes also had existed to regulate the free blacks. As far as the South was concerned, emancipation meant only that slaves had been raised to the status of "free Negroes," and they were to be treated just as free blacks had in the antebellum days. The black codes, passed to "protect the negro in his rights of person and property," ensured that blacks kept their place in the new social and economic order—a place that had changed little with emancipation.

Mississippi, the first state to pass a black code, required "That every freedman, free Negro, and mulatto shall, on the second Monday of January, one thousand eight hundred and sixty-six, and annually thereafter, have a lawful home or employment...." If blacks did not have a job, they would be arrested for vagrancy, and if a freedman left a job before his contract was up "he shall forfeit his wages for that year, up to the time of quitting" and he could be returned to his employer. The legislative committee that recommended Mississippi's black codes recognized that some of the laws might seem "rigid and stringent to sickly modern humanitarians," but they would "hurt no one."[1]

Other states passed codes to prohibit blacks from owning guns so they could not hunt for a living, from leaving plantations so they could not look for better work, from assembling in groups larger than five to prevent them from instigating insurrection, from living in cities and towns so they could only work as farm laborers, from using public transportation so they could not leave their "home," and from renting or purchasing property so they could not work their own land.

In South Carolina, a former Confederate officer, summing up the need for black codes, said black freedom must be "limited, controlled, and surrounded with such safeguards as will make the change as slight as possible. . . . The general interest of both the white man and the negro requires that he should be kept as . . . near to the condition of slavery as possible, as far from the condition of the white man as practicable." South Carolina's codes prohibited freedmen from following any profession except farmer or servant unless they could pay an annual head tax that could be as high as $100. In Florida, disobedience, impudence, and disrespect of an employer were crimes.

Black codes also made it legal to bind over children to plantation owners when parents were in trouble with the law or were not under contract. Parents were not required to give permission for their children to be apprenticed and often were not informed where their children were sent to work. Minors could be apprenticed at very young ages and kept in apprenticeships well past their majority.

Black codes also kept blacks separated from whites, to prevent the "mixing of races." Segregation laws covered hospitals, insane asylums, schools, hotels, restaurants, theatres, and public transportation. In Texas, separate railroad cars were set aside for paying black passengers and circuses had separate entrances for blacks, and in all Southern states, public cemeteries had separate sections for blacks.[2] If separate accommodations were not available, then it was not uncommon to simply exclude blacks from services. For example, several states had schools for whites only, others did not provide orphanages or asylums for blacks, and most states did not allow blacks to stay in hotels.

Because so many blacks were on the move, traveling from town to town or from one section of a city to another, the issue of public transportation came to a head very early. To see black men sitting next to white women or black women sitting in a streetcar while a white man stood was simply too much for white Southerners' sensibilities. As one scholar notes, underlying the anger against black's disregard for racial etiquette was the fear of "unrestrained black lust and sexuality." Racial amalgamation—or miscegenation as it was popularly called—meant that once blacks were allowed to sit with whites on the streetcars, they would next move into the theatres, then the hotels, then the homes, and finally the bedroom.[3]

In Richmond, Virginia, blacks initially were excluded from streetcars, then they were allowed to ride on the platforms outside (i.e., hanging on). In 1867, after several blacks staged a sit-in on Richmond's privately owned streetcars, the military commander ordered that anyone who could pay the fare could ride on the inside of the cars but that segregated cars would be provided. The blacks-only cars were marked with a black ball on the roof.[4] In New Orleans, the blacks-only carriages were marked with a star—and thus became known as the "black star cars."

The Southern white press rarely if ever mentioned the codes, and when they did they wrote only about the need for more control of blacks. It was the constant editorializing by the black Republican newspapers in the South that brought Northern attention to the black codes. Because the codes were so far reaching, they were seen as the South's attempt to redefine Reconstruction for itself. In the end, the black codes resulted in the Civil Rights Act of 1866, which provided that all citizens would receive full and equal benefit of the laws and be subject to the same penalties. Thus, separate laws for blacks were made illegal. By late 1866, most of the black codes had disappeared on paper—declared void by the courts, the military, or the Freedmen's Bureau. But states found creative ways of maintaining some of the same proscriptions against blacks through economic-based laws. For example, Tennessee passed "An Act to Preserve the Peace and Prevent Homicide," which prohibited the sale of any handgun except those issued by the army or navy. The only persons who owned such guns were whites, either because they served in the military or because they could afford the very expensive weapons. Few blacks could afford them.

The readings opposing black codes begin with an editorial by Horace Greeley, who pleads with the South to do away with their black codes and treat blacks humanely. The second entry, by Julius J. Flemming, hints that black codes have had a negative effect on Northern minds and never should have been passed. The third editorial, by Jean-Charles Houzeau, gives examples of black codes and rhetorically asks why the war had been fought if not to give all men equal rights. The editorial in the *Chicago Tribune* by Horace White points to the black codes of South Carolina and warns against allowing Southern states that act against blacks to rejoin the Union. The last reading, by John Emory Bryant, is from a Southern Republican newspaper, warning Georgia against passing black codes that create separate classes of citizens.

The readings supporting black codes are all from Southern Democratic newspapers. The first entry calls on the military to pass laws regulating blacks who are taking too many liberties with their freedom. The next editorial, by Seth Boughton, calls on the Georgia legislature to devise a system to regulate blacks for their own good. The final two editorials in this section justify black codes with the age-old argument that blacks are inferior beings and must be treated as such.

OPPOSING BLACK CODES

Horace Greeley: "Reconstruction—How Not to Do It"

This editorial details various black codes from Tennessee and concludes with an impassioned plea from the abolitionist Horace Greeley.

New York Tribune, **June 23, 1865**

Here then are the fruits of reconstruction: The Rebel comes back to power and citizenship, his hands red with loyal blood. He has every inducement to come back. He is offered home, property, crops, lands and help from the Government. He can make the negro work for him without wages, and if the negro objects, a convenient provost-marshal awaits his bidding. . . . The negro comes back from Fort Wagner and Port Hudson, covered with the scars of wounds obtained in the defense of the dear old flag. After fighting and bleeding for us—sleeping in the same bivouac and marching in the same column with our sons and brothers—we quietly dismiss him without even bounty, and send him back to Tennessee, where his oath will not be taken nor his children educated—to North Carolina where the provost marshal may put him into the corn field—or to Virginia, where he cannot travel from town to town without a pass. Thus we reward his loyalty!

This is reconstruction: but is it justice? "Well," replies some impatient friend, "you have gained emancipation, whipped the South, and made peace, will *nothing* satisfy you?" None in the world more easily satisfied, good friend. We only ask justice for the negro. Let him alone. Give him opportunity and stand off. If he is lazy, let him starve. He will soon find his level. Give him a fair field, just as you give to the blue-eyed German or the swarthy Pole. He doesn't want protection, nor provost marshals to make him work. God has given him appetites, wants, energies and reason. Stand back and let him use them. Abolish your hateful laws, like those of Tennessee. In reconstructing the South, say to those gentlemen who come to Washington as the disciples of a new faith, "Gentlemen, go back to your people and tell them that, when Slavery died, all things pertaining to Slavery died with it. . . . We have made the negro free: see to it that you do not make him a serf.

He must be as one of you. Pass laws making tests of suffrage if you will, but make those laws apply to White as well as Black. We have made these slaves freedmen, and now must not degrade them." This is the true method of re-construction. We have earned the right and the power to do it by a fearful war. If we let the opportunity slip, then our Peace becomes a mere sheet of ink and parchment. Now is the time; and if our statesmen show wisdom and firmness, they can settle forever the question of Human Slavery, not only in America but throughout the world.

Julius J. Flemming: Correspondent's Letter

Julius J. Flemming was a South Carolina journalist, lawyer, minister, and magistrate. This letter is from a series of "correspondent's letters" detailing life in the South after the war that was published in the Charleston (S.C.) Courier *between 1865–71 under the pen name "Juhl."*

Charleston (S.C.) Courier, **December 31, 1865**

It is apprehended that much of the work of the late legislature will have to be undone or done over. The criminal law as amended is emphatically a bloody code. To make larceny, where a bale of cotton or a horse is stolen, a capital felony without benefit of clergy is to insure the acquittal of everyone arraigned on such an indictment. The juries will not convict where death is a penalty for such offences. . . . Besides, there are features in both the free-man's code and the criminal law as amended calculated to draw upon us fresh and fierce broadsides from the unfriendly majority which now con-trols Congress. Hence, many believe that under the circumstances it would have been better to have made no such ostentatious legal and judicial dis-tinction between the races, but to have slightly modified the common law and left that law to cover and regulate the entire population. This would have been less expensive and onerous to the people and certainly less of-fensive to [Republicans].

Jean-Charles Houzeau: "The Nine O'clock Rule"

The New Orleans Tribune *addresses this editorial as much to Northern readers as to Southern readers, pleading for help in dealing with the injus-tices brought about by black codes. Jean-Charles Houzeau was a Belgian who edited the* Tribune *primarily for New Orleans's black citizens.*

New Orleans Tribune, **July 19, 1865**

There is a general disposition throughout the State to have the old pro-slavery regulations and ordinances revived. We published the other day the remarkable ordinance passed by the Board of Police of Opelousas. In conformity with another resolution from the same Board, that town is now enjoying the blessings of a regular patrol of whites to control and keep down the colored people. We must, however, recognize in justice to the enlightened and progressist Board of Police of Opelousas, that the negroes have been given up to ten o'clock to walk in the street,—one hour later than they had obtained under the old regime. This additional hour is the fruit of our victories in the field; four years of bloody war have been fought to gain that one hour. The world certainly moves in that quarter.

It moves, too, in the Crescent City, although perhaps, not a great deal faster. We hear of masters claiming their slaves, and taking them back to their home, even in the parish of Orleans. We hear of congregations and religious meetings ordered to disperse at the stroke of nine o'clock P.M. In the Third District, the police of the city has been, of late, very particular on that point. Meetings of women and children have been interrupted at nine o'clock when reciting prayers for the soul of President Lincoln, or singing canticles and hymns. Such a course is perfectly lawful in the opinion of our civil authorities. Slavery is abolished; but the ordinances of police enacted to uphold slavery have not been revoked. And according to that reasoning a man may be whipped in the parish prison, at the demand of any other man, provided the victim be not called a slave, but a freedman. It is a truly good thing to well understand each other. . . .

Such is the example of good manners and good morals set to the unfortunate negroes by their masters. This is done in virtue of the principle that men are not equal before the law. We do not know, indeed, if white and colored people are equal, at this time before the laws of the State. But we perfectly know that they are not considered so by the civil authorities and the civil magistrates. If this war has been made to obtain equality of rights for all citizens, it has certainly been, on that point and up to this time, a complete failure—as the object has not been attained. Practically, men are not equal before the law, and not equal before the magistrates as far as Louisiana is concerned.

Will the nation give up the great idea that sustained the masses during this momentous struggle? Will the North accept her virtual defeat, after so many victories in the field—after having crushed her enemies? That is the question that remains yet to be decided—and to be fought again if need be.

Horace White: "Black Codes"

Nothing gave a radical paper like the Chicago Tribune *greater pleasure than pointing to specific acts that demonstrate the South's unwillingness to treat blacks like free persons.*

Chicago Tribune, reprinted in *New Orleans Tribune,* December 24, 1865

At the commencement of the present effort to reconstruct the South on the rebel basis alone, we predicted that the cloven foot would appear when the State Legislatures should come to frame their "Black Codes." It matters not to the late rebels whether their constitution read "slavery is abolished" or "slavery is restored" so long as the masters are at liberty to govern their own "Black Code."

We lay down the fundamental proposition that the whites of a State have no more right to frame a Black Code of any kind than to restore slavery in all its enormity. All laws made for blacks must apply to whites and vice versa. But starting with a white suffrage we must expect a Black Code. We do not gather grapes from thorns, nor figs from thistles, nor equal rights from a partial suffrage.

We rejoice that the Legislature of South Carolina has hatched out the serpent's egg of "Reconstruction" in time for Congress to see its offspring wriggle. We present a few joints of its vertebrae for the inspection of the curious, who think "we must trust it."

South Carolina enacts, in brief, as follows:

White employers shall be called masters, and black persons employed shall be called servants.

The master may whip his servant himself if the latter be under eighteen year, but if he be so old as to make the experiment dangerous to the master, the judge may order him whipped by the Sheriff.

Servants shall rise at dawn, feed and water their stock, then feed their masters, so as to begin work by sunrise.

They shall not leave their premises without a written pass.

If any other person shall hire or harbor them without their master's consent, he shall be punished as for an infamous crime.

Servants must be polite to their masters. . . .

Would we lift the veil from the men who framed these laws? Look at the cases reported and examined by the military authorities at one station, Columbia, for the month of November, as reported to the New York *Tribune.*

Dr. Thorn assaults with intent to kill, and maims for life his former slave.

Dr. L.D. Hobbs, on trial before a military commission, admits he shot Melvin, freedman, but claims to be innocent of murder because the deceased did not die within eight days after Hobbs meant he should. . . .

A few days previously a dead black man was found in the court-house square labelled: "This is a warning to all damn Neggahs in this vicinity." Also, one black boy—whipped to death was found in the streets—one Federal Captain murdered and one more freedman mortally lashed, and two more murdered for information given to the U.S. authorities.

This is given as a sample of a single district. The others correspond. Yet these are the people for whom Southern rebels and Northern Copperheads claim that they have magnanimously accepted all the results of the war, and are entitled to participate in the government.... What avails the passage of a Constitutional Amendment in the face of their Black Code, and their calendar of crimes all committed against the freedom of the emancipated race. To permit the State to come into the Union with such a record uneffaced, would be a mockery to freedom and perfidy to the honor of the Government. We have no words adequate to express our sense of the baseness of such efforts to smuggle slavery back into existence. The North must come up to the position, and the sooner it takes the stand the better that there can be no Black Codes whatever in the Southern States, that all laws applicable to one race shall apply to the other, and that no State shall be admitted into the Union until it shall have adopted a provision depriving the Legislature forever of the power to enact one law for blacks and another for whites.

John Emory Bryant: "The New Georgia Code"

This editorial reports on a legislative committee that was preparing a bill for "laws for the benefit of persons of color." John Emory Bryant was an agent for the Freedmen's Bureau, and his newspaper was edited primarily for blacks in Augusta, Georgia.

Augusta Loyal Georgian, February 3, 1866

This code has been carefully prepared by able lawyers, men who, we believe intended to act wisely and secure justice to the freedmen, but in our opinion, they have labored in vain. What necessity is there for a "negro code"? It is claimed that the freedmen require different laws from white men. This depends upon the intention of the law makers. If they desire to keep the freedmen always in an inferior position and prevent their improvement, it can be most effectually accomplished by a system of laws, like those prepared by the Commission. But, if it is their intention to give the freedmen fair play, and an opportunity to improve their condition, they have, we believe, acted unwisely, for they must be aware, that the effect of such Legislation will be injurious to all persons of color, by denying them rights, which white men enjoy. We object to all such distinction.

It may be claimed with some reason that because the freedmen are and but recently emancipated, the right of suffrage should be denied them, but upon no principle of justice, can men claim that for those reasons, civil rights should be denied them. In the name of 500,000 colored persons in this State we demand that no distinction shall be made before the law. We demand this because it is right, and because being citizens, they are entitled to the rights granted to other citizens.

Laws that are not applicable alike to all citizens are unconstitutional and void, unless the Constitution itself concede the right to make such distinction. But it does nowhere give the right to deprive citizens of their natural rights, except as a punishment for crime, whereof the parties shall have been duly convicted. Therefore no citizen can be deprived of the right to sue and testify, except as a punishment for crime. In a word, all laws, which make such distinction, are null and void.

We notice that a bill is before the Legislature of this State "to exclude freedmen from other States from this State." Such a law would be clearly unconstitutional and void; for, being citizens, they are "entitled to all privileges and immunities of citizens in the several states" or in other words, they shall have the same privilege, exemptions and freedom granted to other citizens and all rules and regulations which apply to one citizen, shall apply to all.

We are surprised that men, as able and as learned in the law as the committee, who have prepared the system of laws, should have fallen into the error of supposing, that one system of laws can be enacted for one class of citizens and different system for another class. We can account for it only upon the hypothesis that they hold that "persons of color" are not citizens. . . .

Let Georgia . . . preserve her dignity by refusing to pass laws that do not apply to all. Governor Jenkins will no doubt veto unconstitutional laws if any should be passed.

SUPPORTING BLACK CODES

"Sioux": "The Negroes of Houston"

The Freeman's Champion *was a short-lived newspaper edited by a former Confederate officer known only as "Sioux," who believed that the military or the city ought to pass restrictions on blacks in Houston, Texas, to keep them "in their place."*

Freeman's Champion, reprinted in Galveston Weekly News, March 29, 1865

Every traveller who has passed through this city, cannot fail to have noticed the demoralized manners of our darkies. We see them in nearly all the groceries, and are disgusted with the airs the scoundrels put on. White ladies are forced to turn to one side of the pavements to allow the "gemmem ob color" to pass, or they would be crowded into the gutters. They are allowed to have their balls and parties weekly, and the public protect them at these licentious gatherings.—Reader, have you ever noticed the manner in which the black population dress! Have you ever noticed the profusion of jewelry and silk dresses the wenches wear? Have you noticed the gold watches and chains the bucks adorn themselves with, then compare their appearance to the worthy white mechanic, or his family? You hear daily of robberies and thefts being perpetrated in this city, some of you lay all this upon our brave soldiery, and many a brave and gallant command has been defamed and charged with rascalities perpetrated by these black scoundrels. Some men allow their darkies to hire their own time, and the scamp is as free as though he were in Boston, and he contaminates and puts devilry into the heads of steady and faithful servants. . . . We see the same free skunks acting as body servants to many of our officials in this department. Why is this? What right have officials to take this privilege? But some will say, "you have no right, sir, to question our military men about these matters," and try to silence us on the ground that we dare not find fault with officials. But here they find themselves mistaken. We claim to be free men. We have stood shoulder to shoulder in the ranks with our brave comrades and assisted in beating back the haughty invader, and now are we to come down and kiss the big toe of officials, and fear to speak the truth? No, never, our aim is for our country's good. Her cause is our cause, her people our people, her soldiers our brothers, and we shall never hesitate to lash without any mercy in spite of the consequences, any and every infringement upon the rights of the people. We demand that some reform be made concerning the darkies of Houston. Every good citizen demands this, and we know our worthy Mayor will take some steps to reform this crying evil.

Seth Boughton: "It Can Do No Harm"

Without using the terms "black code" or "freedmen's laws," the Milledge-ville (Ga.) Federal Union *supports a set of laws for Georgia that will apply to freedmen and not whites—all for the purpose of getting blacks "in the right track."*

Milledgeville (Ga.) Federal Union, **July 25, 1865**

All men see, know, admit that slavery is dead, and now that it is dead, it should be the desire of every good white man to put it away decently, and prepare for the consequences. We, like thousands of others, have seen how indolent and worthless the negro has become, in nine cases out of ten, since his elevation to freedom. The officers of the U.S. Army, in common with us, have deplored the failure of the negroes to settle down steadily to work, and behave themselves as all decent persons should, white or black. . . . Would that the negro understood intelligently what is due to him, and what is ex-

pected of him. But he will not understand. And now we ask which is best—
say nothing about him, do nothing with him, or cast about and see if there
are not some lawful means at hand by the use of which the negro may become, what the honest men among those who made him free intended him
to become, a peaceable and industrious worker in the hive? If we all shut
our eyes to his faults, or the inefficiency of measures adopted for his guidance and control, we are neither his friend nor the friend of the government
that is burdened with his custody. . . . Let us try and get the negroes, who
know so little what freedom is, and how to enjoy it properly, in the right
track. Let no man hesitate to suggest to any officer of the government the
ideas which he may entertain for the good of the freedmen and the welfare
of the country. They *will* hear—they will patiently hear all your suggestions,
because they feel that the great responsibility of the negro's future welfare
and happiness now depends on those who have suddenly discontinued the
relation in which he formerly stood to his master; and they will be glad, yes
rejoice, to find that any improvement, however small it may be, can be suggested. It must be conceded on all hands, that those who have lived with the
Southern negroes all their lives, and know their character and disposition,
are more competent to devise a system for their government, than those
who are but little acquainted with them, and have not until recently been
brought in contact with them. . . .

Anonymous Writer: No Title

*It was believed that the inferiority of blacks was sanctioned by God and sci-
ence, and nothing could dissuade whites to feel otherwise.*

Nashville (Tenn.) Daily Union, **February 11, 1865**

You are told by the enemies of the Government the Federal authorities . . . will make the negro your equal, giving him social and political rights.
Those who make such statements know them to be false, or are so pro-
foundly ignorant that they are unworthy to be freemen. . . .

The negro if freed will fall within the laws governing his race. He is inferior to the white man, and will be controlled and governed by him, subject
to such laws as may be proposed for his government. No one wants to give
him equal rights, and in such a social position equality cannot be attained.
The God of nature has placed His fiat upon it, and no power on earth can
make him the equal of the Anglo-Saxon; but as christian men we can elevate
them in the scale of human beings . . . They are human beings, with immor-
tal souls, and as such, it is our duty as the superior race, to control, govern
and elevate them from the degraded situation in which they are.

Charles H. Wynne: "The Negro Inferior"

Even after black codes disappeared and the Fourteenth Amendment was placed before the country, Southerners still held that blacks were to be treated differently because blacks were inferior.

Richmond (Va.) Enquirer, reprinted in the Mobile (Ala.) Nationalist, July 25, 1867

Platforms may declare that all laws creating distinctions or differences of any sort between persons of different races shall be unconstitutional, null and void, but all such declarations will be as vain as the attempt to combine oil and water by shaking them together. . . . Let there be separate schools, separate colleges, separate churches, separate accommodation in places of entertainment, and in arrangements for sojourn or travel, etc. etc.

Their thick lips and rolling white eyes show every gradation in the ascending and descending scale, from the lower order of animals up through the monkey, the baboon and the ourang-outang [of] the Congo, until the animal finally assumes something like the appearance of a man in the shape of the mulatto and the quadroon. Yes, they must have been monkeys, and now [if] they are left to pursue the bent of their instincts they will return to the monkey again.

QUESTIONS

1. What was the purpose of black codes?
2. What effect did black codes have on radical Reconstruction policy?
3. What were the arguments against black codes?
4. What role did racist language play in convincing people that black codes were needed?
5. How did black codes perpetuate the belief that blacks were still to be treated like slaves?

NOTES

1. James E. Bond, *No Easy Walk to Freedom: Reconstruction and the Ratification of the Fourteenth Amendment* (Westport, Conn.: Praeger, 1997), 36.

2. Howard Rabinowitz, "From Exclusion to Segregation: Southern Race Relations, 1865–1890," *Journal of American History* 63 (1976): 325–50.

3. Leon Litwack, *Been in the Storm So Long* (New York: Vintage Books, 1979), 264.

4. Rabinowitz, 330–31.

CHAPTER 5

Seating the South's Congressional Delegation, 1865

In May 1865, only six weeks after assuming office following Abraham Lincoln's assassination, Andrew Johnson announced his plan for restoring the Southern states. The president's Reconstruction plan appointed provisional governors in each state. It required states to call constitutional conventions, rewrite prewar constitutions, and nullify secession. Johnson also issued a proclamation that restored all property rights (except for slaves) to a large segment of Confederates who took a loyalty oath. However, his amnesty proclamation did not cover wealthy former slaveholders or those who held high offices in the Confederate government or army. Those individuals—about 20,000—would have to apply personally to the president for pardons before they would be allowed to vote.

Johnson's lenient policy was welcomed in the North and the South as a reasonable and generous approach that would result in quick restoration and a rapid return to normalcy. Southern states lost no time restoring their civil governments. During the summer and fall, elections were held for delegates to state conventions. By early fall, most states had new constitutions and were proceeding to elect state officials, legislators, and congressmen.

Although by fall most of the formerly disenfranchised Confederate officials and wealthy landowners had been pardoned and were back on the voter rolls, they were still unable to run for federal office. In 1862, Congress had revised the oath of office taken by all federal civil servants, including congressmen and military officers, by adding a new section known as the Ironclad Test Oath. The new section required federal officials to swear future loyalty to the United States and to affirm that they had never engaged in criminal or disloyal conduct and had "neither directly or indirectly participated in, or in any manner aided" the rebellion. Anyone who could not truthfully take the oath was prohibited from holding public office, holding a military commission, working for the government, or conducting business

No Accommodations. *A Southern congressman-elect asks the clerk of the House of Representatives if he can have his old seat back. The clerk responds, "Sorry, sir. . . . All the old seats were broken up and are now being thoroughly reconstructed."* Harper's Weekly. *Library of Congress.*

with the federal government. For practical purposes, the oath eliminated anyone who had served the Confederacy either in the army or as a civilian. Delaware's third-term Democratic senator James Bayard refused to voluntarily take the oath and warned that after the war, the requirement of congressmen to take the Ironclad Test Oath would block many congressmen-elect from the South, even those who had received a presidential pardon.[1] And he was correct.

The Republican Party was split on the issue of the oath. Some believed that it provided the best excuse not to seat the South's first group of congressmen; others agreed with President Johnson, who argued, "as badly as any of our Southern brethren have acted, they are nevertheless members of our great political family, and must sooner or later be awarded their seats at the family table." Southerners argued that the Ironclad Test Oath prevented their best men from running for office, forcing the election of second- and third-rate men. The only recourse was to ignore the Ironclad Test Oath. Georgia dared to elect former Confederate vice president Alexander H. Stephens to the Senate and 10 of the new Southern senators and congressmen had been Confederate generals. Of seven governors elected in the fall, only the governor of Louisiana could take the Ironclad Test Oath.

The election of so many former rebels into public office, the passage of black codes that controlled the social and economic lives of freedmen, and reports of violence against blacks resulted in an immediate outcry by Northern Republicans that the "spirit of rebellion" was still alive in the South. Even President Johnson expressed dismay that his policy had failed to replace the old slavocracy with a new yeoman leadership. He sent messages south warning that their defiance was impolitic, and he sent direct instructions to some states to stop passing harsh black codes that were viewed negatively in the North.

As the news from the South worsened, even moderate Republicans who had supported Johnson's Reconstruction policy began to shift their stance when they realized that the South had no intention of reforming itself. In November 1865, Speaker of the House Schuyler Colfax delivered a speech in Washington that was a harbinger of things to come. He warned that the South must elect only men who could take the Ironclad Test Oath, that the South must meet new requirements for admission, and that blacks should be recognized as equal before the law.

Colfax's speech was no idle threat. Reacting to what appeared to be Southern recalcitrance, 124 Republicans met in caucus before the opening of the Thirty-ninth Congress and agreed unanimously to create a Joint Committee of Fifteen to investigate the conditions in the South. And, until such time as the Joint Committee made its report, "no member shall be admitted into either House from any of the so-called Confederates States." Although this was an extraordinary move on the part of Congress and considered by Southerners to be an "abuse of Congressional power," it was not illegal. Each house of Congress has the sole authority to establish the requirements of its membership, and neither the president nor the courts can interfere.

On the first day of the Thirty-ninth Congress in December 1865, the clerk of the House of Representatives Edward McPherson called the roll, and under instructions from the Republican caucus omitted the names of the newly elected representatives from the former rebel states. These actions left no doubt that Congress—not the president—would dictate the terms of Reconstruction from now on.

The *New York Herald* called Congress's action "ultra radical and revolutionary." The *Herald* continued, "The opening proceedings foreshadow the practical reduction of the excluded Southern States to the status of Territories conquered from a foreign enemy and still in a state of revolution. Coercion! There is nothing here but coercion."[2]

Southern congressmen who arrived in Washington ready to do the nation's business turned around and headed back home. A few stopped at the White House on the way south to seek Johnson's intervention, but most quietly left the capital, not surprised by the action of the Republican Congress. In his annual address to the Congress, Johnson criticized the Congress for not admitting the South's elected representatives, but he did concede that Congress alone had the authority to review and accept the credentials of its members.

In part to answer criticisms and to strengthen its own resolve on the issue, each house of Congress passed a concurrent resolution in March agreeing that it would not admit representatives from the South without the concurrence of the other. This was also a singularly unusual resolution, as it was traditional for each house to decide its own membership without any consultation from the other side.

Moderate and radical Republican newspapers supported the decision not to seat the Southern delegation, reminding readers that the South had brought these problems on itself by exhibiting an unrepentant rebellious spirit. The first entry in the section against seating the Southern delegation begins with an editorial from a small Michigan weekly that believes President Johnson will go along with Congress in all that it requires for the seating of delegates as well as for the reconstruction of the South. The second entry, by E.L. Godkin, argues that refusing to seat the South's congressmen had made no difference, because Johnson's policies were giving the South what it wanted, including control over blacks. The third reading, by Horace White, demonstrates that until the Southern states give blacks the vote, they cannot reenter the Union on an equal footing with other states. The final selection, by William W. Harding, explains that once Southern states ratify the Fourteenth Amendment they will be readmitted and that no further requirements will be set forth.

The section favoring the immediate seating of the Southern delegates begins with an editorial by W.B. Phillips addressed to the clerk of the House of Representatives, suggesting he should abide by the wishes of the president and not by the prodding of party politics. The next two readings are from Southern Democratic newspapers that chastise Congress for using the Ironclad Test Oath to exclude its best men from public service. The final selection, by S.W. Mason, advises the Southern people to be patient and eventually the tyranny of radical Reconstruction will disappear.

OPPOSING THE SEATING OF THE SOUTHERN DELEGATION

Anonymous Writer: No Title

The Hillsdale (Mich.) Standard, *like so many small-town Republican newspapers in the North, wanted to believe that President Johnson would work with, rather than against, Congress as Reconstruction plans were worked out.*

Hillsdale (Mich.) Standard, December 12, 1865

The Hon. Schuyler Colfax has made a speech at Washington, in which he alluded to the reconstruction policy likely to be pursued by Congress. He took the following positions:

That Congress is the law making power on the subject of restoration.

That Congress will sanction the action of the President in requiring the State conventions to annul the secession ordinances, in requiring their Legislatures to ratify the constitutional amendment abolishing slavery in repudiating the rebel debt.

Congress will also protect the freedmen as entitled to all the rights referred to by the Declaration of Independence when it declares that "all men are created equal."

Congress will require that their amended State Constitutions, embodying this principle, shall be ratified at the polls by a majority of the Southern people.

Congress will exclude all who can not swear they have not voluntarily supported the rebellion.

And finally in all the work of reconstruction Congress will proceed slowly and deliberately.

A special to the New York Herald says that the President is opposed to the policy here laid down, and favors the admission of Southern representatives to Congress without taking the test oath. This may be true, but we do not credit it. We do not believe that the President desires to have rebels admitted to Congress and thereby given a voice in the direction of the government. There are enough men in the South who can take the test oath, and show themselves free from the stain of treason, men quite as talented and able as those who were foremost in the rebellion, who may be sent to Congress, and until a majority of the voters in the South desire these in preference to men whose hands are foul with rebellion and treason they should have no representation. Moreover we believe that President Johnson does not desire to take the whole responsibility of the policy of reconstruction on himself, but to wait for the action of Congress, and instead of opposing that body he will heartily carry out the plans which may be laid down by it.

E.L. Godkin: No Title

Although E.L. Godkin approved the joint resolution against seating the Southern delegation, he was not hopeful that such action would have a great deal of effect on the behavior of the Southern states as long as President Johnson gave them what they wanted.

The Nation, January 4, 1866

In an early number of The Nation we expressed an opinion that the powers of mischief of the Southern malcontents were to be feared in the local legislatures as well as in Congress; that the great question really was, how to keep them out of the former—which called down upon us a good deal of indignation, particularly amongst our Baltimore friends, who were at the time greatly agitated by the alleged probability that the Clerk of the House would admit the whole Southern delegation to their seats before organization. Well, the Clerk of the House has done nothing of the kind. There does not seem to have been at any time the slightest ground for supposing that he would do anything of the kind. There is in Congress, as we then predicted there would be, a "powerful Northern majority," who will not consent to the re-admission of the South until it has given ample security for its good behavior. But what great difference does this make as regards the condition of Southern society? What the South wanted most of all to get back into Congress for, was its deliverance from military rule. That it is now securing without getting back into Congress. President Johnson is handing over the States one by one to the State authorities, and delivering to them the management of their own affairs. This to them is the essential thing. It gives them the control of the negro—within certain limits, it is true, but wide limits. It enables them by stay laws to bid defiance to their Northern creditors; by vagrant laws and labor laws, such as all the States are passing, to "keep the negro down" and "make him feel his inferiority;" and to build up on, in short, the ruins of the old social system a new one, very much better, no doubt, but still marked by features repugnant to the spirit of our institutions, and likely to prove a fertile source of trouble in the future. And what can Congress do to prevent all this? The exclusion of the Southern delegates does not interfere with it in the least. As far as we can judge, the delegates are willing to stay at home as long as the House pleases, provided the President refrains from interference; and the President has given, and is giving, the strongest proofs that his interference is nearly at an end. So that, important as the power of keeping them out of the House and Senate undoubtedly is, it is by no means all-important. The successful exercise of it does not, as we now see, enable us by any means to reach the core of the Southern difficulty. The mere adoption of the Constitutional Amendment does not do it, nor will the Freedmen's Bureau do it, unless it is supported by more force—brute force—than it has now at its disposal. It remains to be seen what can be done by enforcing the Amendment.

Horace White: "The President's Arguments"

On April 2, 1866, President Johnson declared that the war was at an end, that all states but Texas had met his requirements for restoration, that there was no longer need for military forces in the South, and that the Southern delegations should be admitted by Congress. His proclamation fell on deaf ears, because everyone knew that restoration was now in the hands of Congress.

Chicago Tribune, April 24, 1866

It is a singular fact that every principle which the President urges as a reason for admitting the seceded States to seats in Congress immediately furnishes, when fairly applied, the exact reasons why they ought not be so admitted. He says you ought not to tax any portion of the people without giving them representation, therefore you should admit the Southern Representatives to vote in Congress before you try to govern the South. Congress replies, the loyal States have the same right to tax the Southern States without admitting their Representatives that the white citizens of the Southern States have to tax or govern the black without representation. Therefore, in order to maintain the President's principle, we must defeat his policy, reject the present State governments of the seceded states, and require them not to tax the colored citizens of the South without giving them the vote.

Again, the President says our Constitution makes all states equal, therefore Mississippi has as good a right to seats in Congress as Illinois. Congress will reply in due time that the Constitution does make all States equal, and that the seceded States, as presently constituted, would have twice as many Congressmen as the same voting population anywhere in the Northern States, therefore the Johnson policy is a gross violation of the principle of equality of States.

The President says military law is a great evil. Now, until you give the late rebels equal political rights with yourselves you must govern them by military law, which always tends toward despotism and away from liberty. Congress will reply: Agreed, but if to avoid the necessity of governing the South by military law we must give them equal political rights, then the whites of the South can only avoid the necessity of governing the negroes by military law by giving them equal political rights. We perceive that in Mississippi, Georgia, South Carolina and nearly every reconstructing State, militias have been formed to govern the blacks. Where no system of military law prevails, irresponsible military bands of regulators govern them. We know that in South Carolina, where blacks are to the whites as three to one, and in Louisiana and Mississippi, and in portions of other States where the colored people are more numerous than the whites, military force will be necessary to govern them, unless both blacks and whites are made politically equal. By our very desire to banish military force, which always carries with it military law, with all its liability to oppression and injustice, we are compelled to abolish any reconstructing State governments which make distinctions in the right of suffrage on account of color, for we are warned in advance by the formation of your State militias, that you intend to govern the disfranchised portion of your population by military law.

William W. Harding: "The Re-admission of Southern States"

The Philadelphia Inquirer *wanted a quick restoration of the Southern states. Almost a year after Congress initially refused to seat Southern congressmen, editor William W. Harding instructed the South that if it ratified the Fourteenth Amendment, its representatives would be seated. Within a year, Harding changed his opinion of the radicals and became "one of them."*

Philadelphia Inquirer, **November 10, 1866**

Among the reasons given by the Southern opponents of the adoption of the Constitutional Amendment; for their opposition is one which may have some strength in it, they say that no guarantee is given them that the ratification of the amendment will insure that their Representatives in Congress will be admitted. It is true that Congress has given no guarantee to that effect, but the admission of Tennessee upon the ratification of the amendment, shows that there is no intention to insist upon further stipulations, or to urge further humiliation of the South. It is true that certain members of Congress have, in the heat of political debate said, very foolishly, that it is not certain that the ratification of the amendments by the Southern States will admit them to Congress. But if it is inquired who these members are it will be found that they were opposed to the admission of Tennessee, and that they were overruled by the majority. What is called the "radical policy" is not contained in the Constitutional Amendment. The "radicals" in Congress opposed them bitterly, and were defeated. The intention of Congress must be gathered from the acts of the majority, and not from the declarations of a violent minority. We know enough of the feelings of the majority of the Northern people to assert that in the late elections they intended to sustain the moderate policy of the Constitutional Amendments which were passed despite the "radicals." We believe, also, that although there is no guarantee now, that the Southern States shall be admitted upon the ratification of the Constitutional Amendment, that such was the expectation and intention of the vast majority who voted to sustain the policy of Congress. A refusal to admit a Southern State after such ratification would be looked upon as a gross wrong, and any member of Congress who would go contrary to the popular feeling on this subject, would arouse a storm of indignation against him which he could not withstand, and which would soon bring him to a sense of his duty. It would be perfectly proper at the commencement of the next session to pass a resolution, clearly guaranteeing the right of representation to every State that ratifies the amendments, and we hope that such action will be resolved upon without any needless delay.

FAVORING THE SEATING OF THE SOUTHERN DELEGATION

W.B. Phillips: "Are the Southern States to Be Represented in the Next Congress?"

Several months earlier, the New York Herald *predicted that representatives who could not take the Ironclad Test Oath would not be seated. However, the paper did not support Congress's exclusion of all of the South's representatives. Nine months later, the* Herald *changed its tune and turned away from President Johnson and supported much of the radical Republicans' agenda.*

New York Herald, October 30, 1865

At the assembling of the next Congress in December, the first important question that will arise will be upon the admission of representatives from the States lately in rebellion. It will come up before that body will be organized even, and in the process of organization. And, however it may be decided by the Clerk of the old House of Representatives . . . the question of their right to seats, with all the political bearings, will be discussed. . . .

The action of the Clerk, then, is of the highest importance. There is no one to control him. Congress does not exist till organized. Neither the President nor any other officer of any department of the government has authority in the matter. If he should adopt the theory of the administration, that the late rebel States never have been out of the Union, and never have ceased to be members of it; that, in fact, they have not absolved and could not absolve their federal relations with the other States, he ought to place the names of their representatives on the roll, provided the President should declare the rebellion suppressed and the States to be exercising their functions again as heretofore, and provided there be no law hindering him from doing so. It is said by the radicals, who oppose the admission of the Southern members, that there is a law which will prevent the Clerk giving to these members certificates of admission to the floor of Congress till their claims and eligibility to seats be determined by the House. On the other hand, it is said that this act referred to, which was passed during the rebellion, is neither applicable nor constitutional. Without discussing this question, it is evident that a grave responsibility rests upon the Clerk. He must decide what his duty is legally in the case; and if there be a doubt as to the legality or constitutionality of refusing to place the names of these members on the roll he should decide in accordance with the restoration policy and wish of the President, and for the peace, harmony, and best interest of the country. . . . But, looking at the political character of the House, if organized without them, we apprehend the conflict on the subject would be fearful. Indeed, it is doubtful whether they would be admitted at all. The radical element may be so strong and determined that these gentlemen may be sent back to their homes, and the country kept in a state of anarchy. We recommend Mr. McPherson to ponder well over these things, and above all to put himself in *rapport* with President Johnson. Let him learn what the wishes and policy of the President are, and act in accordance with these. He will be right then, and will obtain the commendation of the country. . . .

James Sledge: "The Test Oath"

One of the keys to seating Southern representatives in Congress was finding men who could take the Ironclad Test Oath. Like so many Southerners, editor James Sledge saw the oath as a way to ensure that only idiots and uncaring Southern men were ever elected to Congress.

Athens (Ga.) Southern Banner, November 15, 1865

We think it doubtful whether in all Georgia there are nine men whom the people would elect to any office or whom they would trust in any way, who could take the oath prescribed for Senators and Representatives before they can take their seats in Congress. . . .

It is true we see men now eager to assert their uninterrupted devotion to the Union who, to our knowledge a year ago, waved their hats high in air for Lee or Johnston and who either lacked sincerity then or now, but they cannot take the oath. No repentance, no contrition, no mental reservation of loyalty, no amount of honest abhorrence of the Confederate Government, would suffice to come within the pale of the oath, if the applicant for a seat in Congress ever gave a dollar to a Confederate soldier, be he father, brother, or son, or ever voluntarily did any thing which proved him in sympathy, however remotely, with the mass of his countrymen.

But suppose such men could be found, and the people could be induced to trust them, and suppose them seated in Congress—all seven in a row—having taken this test oath. What would the Northern members think of them? Would they trust them? Could they respect them? Let the bitterest opponents of the South during the war, ask themselves in their hearts and consciences, if they were obliged to choose for their associates Southern men who fought for their honest convictions of duty and right, and who, when resistance became hopeless . . . renewed their allegiance to the United States, and put their shoulders to the wheel of reconstruction, or Southern men born and educated at the South, with their friends and kindred all around them, who, during the four long years of the war, acted so that they can, without perjury or equivocation, take the test oath for a seat in Congress, which would they choose? Which would they trust in their families? Wade Hampton, or the Southern man who can call God to witness that he never gave a meal or a dollar to a Confederate Soldier, and that he saw his relatives, his friends, and his neighbors go to the war and never expressed or felt a hope that they might succeed? To find such an individual, search must be made among the "idiots;" he cannot be found among the children.

As a people we have earnestly, honestly, endeavored to restore our political relations with the North. Frankly and without complaint we have acceded to all the requirements of the Executive authority. We have done all that we could. We shall elect to day, we hope, honest, faithful men to represent us in Congress—men who will zealously aid President Johnson in his conservative policy, and whose claim to general confidence is based on the record of their lives—men, who, though unable to take the Test Oath, are as loyal to the United States Government as any man at the North, be he who he may, and far more loyal than many, who for selfish and factions purposes are vindictively, tearing open the wounds made by the war, embittering old animosities, rekindling sectional agitation, and using all their energies in defeat the benevolent plans of the President of the United States.

S.G. Reid: "Is There Any Peace in the Land?"

As the official Democratic paper in Alabama, the Montgomery Daily Advertiser *reflected the general attitude of many Southerners who saw Congress's rejection of their "best men" as a signal of worse things to come.*

Montgomery (Ala.) Daily Advertiser, December 13, 1865

No concession, it seems, is to come from the other side, and powerless to do otherwise our people must meet the demands made upon them, in order to secure the uncertain good which may come from submission to things which our judgments do not approve.

In nearly every instance the people have elected conservative men to places of honor and trust. The newly elected Governor of Alabama, both Senators and most of the Congressmen belong to the highest type of conservatism known in the politics of this State. None of them can take the oath, and very few in the State can, but they have been elected because men of extreme views before the war, have refused to offer [themselves] for places of position, although we doubt not in many instances, they could have been elected. The "radical dogs of war" are, however, upon the track and intent upon blood. Not content with the utter degradation of the South, they insist upon writing across her fair brow words and deeds of darkest infamy.... All the conditions which it was said were required of the South to entitle her to representation in Congress have been complied with, and yet the doors are violently shut in the faces of our representatives by a set of radicals whose blood thirsty instincts show them to be more fit representatives of the days of Robespeirre [*sic*] when France was deluged with blood, than of this day and generation, when all classes *profess* a desire for peace and harmony.

S. W. Mason: "What Is Wanted of the Southern People"

The issue of seating the Southern delegation brought out the philosophical side of this editor, who seemed resigned to suffer the retribution of Congress's radicals.

Savannah (Ga.) Daily Herald, December 17, 1866

How frequently we hear the question asked, what is to become of the great interests of the South under the vindictive government of the Radicals? Will they deprive the Southern States of all their powers? Will they appoint Provisional Governors over us? ... And then, why should the Southern people concern themselves for readmission into the Union? Will the mere fact of their having a representation in Congress conduce any to their present temporal welfare? Recuperation is now what they require above everything else. Instead of hanging about the halls of Congress for admittance, and becoming discontented because the doors are unjustly and even contemptuously closed against them, they should rather reconcentrate all their energies and labor upon the task of restoring its former prosperity to their ruined section. ...

It is, therefore, most earnestly to be desired that every one should study patient and persevering attention to his own domestic affairs, which he can control, leaving those in power to manage the affairs of government and to solve the question of reconstruction at their leisure. That they are disqualified by prejudice and ignorance for the task, we all admit. . . . They require the Southern people not only to acquiesce in the legitimate results of a war in which they were overcome by superior numbers and resources, but, to "make treason odious," they expect us to exult over the death of Jackson, over the fall of Richmond, over the surrender to Lee. They insist that we rejoice at the capture of Davis, and that we concede that he has merited a traitor's doom! This is *against nature*. It is demanding *an impossibility*! It is requiring the Southern people to sign and seal the bond of *their own infamy;* to acknowledge before the world, not only that they are slaves, but that they are knaves and poltroons. The Southern people cannot put on sackcloth and repent in dust and ashes over political sins, for they are consciously innocent. "They did what they did" not in enmity to the Union, *per se*, not in hatred of the Northern people, but in honor of the principles handed down from Jefferson, Madison and Monroe, and in defence of the rights they had inherited from their fathers—principles which, in their heart of hearts, they believed essential to the maintenance of public liberty and constitutional government. We *cannot* now—and, God helping us, whatever the consequences, we *will not*—dishonor the memories and trample upon the blood of those who fell before Richmond, who conquered at Chancellorsville, who waded so calmly through the fire at Gettysburg, and who wrestled so desperately for victory with overwhelming numbers from the Wilderness to Cold Harbor. The Southern people *cannot do this*. An overpowering sense of self degradation forbids it. . . . The South, in the midst of her desolation and voiceless woe, can now do nothing to avert such a catastrophe; but history, experience, philosophy, the past, all declare in prophetic tones that the duration of such a government must be short, and that it will expire amidst the universal execrations of the people who have been scourged by its intolerable oppressions.

Questions

1. Why did Republicans not want to see former rebels representing the South in Congress?
2. Why did some argue that the Ironclad Test Oath should be abandoned after the war?

3. If Southern rebels could not be elected to Congress, who in the South could? Why was that a problem for Southern whites?
4. Had the South's representatives been seated in December 1865, what could have been the effect on future congressional actions regarding the reconstruction of the South?
5. What were the South's arguments for having their representatives seated?

NOTES

1. In 1868, Congress was forced to create an alternate oath for Southerners unable to take the Ironclad Test Oath. The Ironclad Test Oath was repealed in 1884.

2. *New York Herald,* 5 March 1866, 4.

CHAPTER 6

President Johnson versus Radical Congress, 1866

As provisional governor of Tennessee, Andrew Johnson had been uncompromising toward rebels, vowing to punish and impoverish traitors. At one point he stated that treason was "the highest crime that can be committed, and those engaged in it should suffer all its penalties" and "their social power must be destroyed."[1] These words brought hope to Northern Republicans that Johnson's Reconstruction policy would be tough but fair. But that hope was soon dashed when the president, in the summer of 1865, began issuing pardons wholesale to the Southern leadership, making them eligible to vote in the fall elections. Republicans also began losing hope when Johnson appeared to overlook acts of violence against blacks and when he spoke about allowing the Southern states to rule their newly freed slaves as they wished. To Republicans it appeared that the president was reneging on a promise to punish the South and was instead aligning himself with the Southern elites.

Disappointed in the president's leniency toward the South, congressional Republicans began laying the groundwork for their own Reconstruction plan as early as December 1865, when they refused to seat the Southern congressional delegation. At the same time, they appointed a Joint Committee of Fifteen to investigate conditions in the South. The committee's investigations resulted in the Freedmen's Bureau Act, the Civil Rights Act, and finally the proposal for the Fourteenth Amendment.

Rather than cooperate with Congress, Johnson chose to fight it on every corner. He vetoed the Civil Rights Act because he did not believe the federal government should interfere in states' prerogatives over their own citizens. He vetoed the Freedmen's Bureau Act, arguing that it was too expensive and that blacks did not need special protections and services from the federal government. After the Fourteenth Amendment was approved for ratification in June, Johnson criticized the proposal as an abridgement of states' rights. With the signing of each veto, the rift between the Congress and the president widened.

Johnson adamantly believed that what he called "My Policy" not only appealed to a large segment of the country but also crossed party lines. In some ways Johnson was correct—many Republicans and Democrats saw Johnson's plan as a mirror of their own political beliefs in white supremacy, states rights, and a speedy restoration of the Southern states. But the news from the South cast a cloud over Johnson's policy and made it increasingly difficult for even Johnson's strongest adherents to support. Riots in Memphis and New Orleans during the summer of 1866, a punitive labor system designed to keep blacks in a condition as close to slavery as possible, and a failure of courts in the South to provide justice for blacks all proved that Johnson's Reconstruction policy was a failure.

But Johnson appeared oblivious to the conditions in the South and continued to believe his policy was popular enough to give him a second term in the presidential election of 1868. He was convinced that if he could unite Democrats and conservative Republicans into a new National Union Party he would eventually run the radicals out of Washington. However, like so many third-party movements, the National Union Party simply could not stand on its own. Not only did the party fail to attract any Republican or Democratic leaders but many of his supporters found Johnson's vetoes of legislation to protect blacks arrogant and divisive. He also disappointed conservatives when he made embarrassing and unpresidential speeches that blasted Republicans and called Republican leaders traitors.

By the fall election of 1866, the National Union Party showing was disastrous. Moderate and radical Republicans gained control of more than two-thirds of the seats in the House and the Senate. Bolstered by this unprecedented showing of popular support, Republicans could now take on the president openly and begin building a congressional plan for restoring the South.

The first selection, by George W. Curtis, reflecting the radical viewpoint during 1866 educates the reader about the difference between conservatives and radicals. The second editorial, by Charles Nordhoff, calls on Johnson to moderate his stance and to listen to the voice of the people as spoken during the election. The third entry, by E.L. Godkin, declares the election an unprecedented declaration by the people that the president's policy is dead and that the South must bend to the radical will. The last editorial in the set, by Henry J. Raymond, is the first indication that the *New York Times* is withdrawing its support from Johnson, who has neither the support of Congress nor the trust of the people.

The conservative press, on the other hand, continued to support Johnson's policies, and the Southern newspapers continued to have faith that Johnson would defeat the radicals. The first entry, by Seth Boughton, under the conservative viewpoint wonders what will happen if Congress continues to force its radical policies on the South. The second reading, by Manton Marble, defends Johnson's intemperate speeches, calling them a barometer of Johnson's commitment to defend his policy. The third entry, from the *New York Herald,* calls on Johnson to recognize his foes in the Republican Party and to fight back by uniting conservative Republicans and Democrats into a new Union party. The reading from the *New York Times* criticizes Congress for leaving the nation and the South in limbo during the summer of 1866. The final selection by a Southern editor directs Southerners to be patient yet strong in the face of a Northern enemy.

THE RADICAL VIEWPOINT

George W. Curtis: "Radicalism and Conservatism"

This editorial sums up the major differences between the radicals and President Johnson's conservative followers and describes the issues that would drive the coming fall election.

Harper's Weekly, April 21, 1866

In every political contest in a Constitutional system the names of Conservatism and Radicalism will be applied to the opposing policies, while the history of such governments show that the policy which truly conserves the principle and spirit of a free system is that which is called Radicalism. . . .

In this country at this moment both Radicalism and Conservatism, as the names of a policy of national reorganization, are very easily defined and comprehended. Thus Radicalism holds that the late rebel States should not be suffered to take part in the government of the Union which they have so zealously striven to destroy except after searching inquiry into their condition, and upon terms which shall prevent any advantage having been gained by rebellion. By the result of the war the suffrage of a voter in South Carolina weighs as much as the vote of two voters in New York. Is that a desirable state of things? Would any fair-minded voter in South Carolina claim that he ought to have a preference in the Union because, however honestly, he has rebelled against it? . . .

Radicalism holds that equal civil rights before the law should be guaranteed by the United States to every citizen. It claims that the Government which commands the obedience of every citizen shall afford him protection, and that the freedom which the people of the United States have conferred the people of the United States shall maintain. Is that a perilous claim? Is any other course consistent with national safety or honor?

Once more: Radicalism asserts that, as the national welfare and permanent union can be established only upon justice, there should be no unreasonable political disfranchisement of any part of the people. It denies that complexion, or weight, or height are reasonable political qualifications. . . .

This is Radicalism. Is it unfair? Is it unconstitutional? Is it anarchical or revolutionary? It denies no man's rights. It deprives no man of power or privilege. It claims for the National Government nothing which is not inseparable from the idea of such a Government. Does it demand any thing that every prudent and patriotic man ought not to be willing to concede? . . .

In our present political situation Conservatism is the policy which declares that the late rebel States are already in a condition to resume their full functions in the Union. . . . It denies that the United States ought to protect the equal civil rights of citizens before the law, and would admit the absent States to Congress before requiring their assent to an amendment equalizing representation. Conservatism is the policy which, forgetting that the United States are bound by every moral obligation to secure the freedom which they have conferred, apparently believes that that freedom will be best maintained and the national peace most truly established by leaving those of every color who were heroically faithful to the Government during the rebellion to the exclusive mercy of those who sought to destroy it.

These are the distinctive points of the Conservative policy. Are they agreeable to an honorable and intelligent people? . . . Who are the present Conservatives? . . . The Conservative party, or the supporters of the policy we have described, is composed of the late rebels and of those who justified and palliated rebellion, with a few Republicans. . . .

Radicalism has not a single vindictive feeling toward the late rebel States, but it does not propose to forget that there has been a rebellion. It has the sincerest wish, as it had the most undoubting expectation, of working with the President to secure for the country what the country has fairly won by the war, and that is, the equal right of every citizen before the law and the full resumption by the late insurgent States of their functions in the Union only upon such honorable and reasonable conditions as Congress might require. All reasonable men who support that policy will not lightly denounce those who differ with them. They will strive long for the harmony of those with whom during the war they have sympathized and acted. . . .

Charles Nordhoff: "The Moral of the Election"

The New York Evening Post *hopes that President Johnson will "heed the voice of the people" spoken during the election and begin to work with rather than against Congress.*

New York Evening Post, October 11, 1866

On Tuesday the people of four great states of this Union gave their decision on a question which had been forced upon them. The question was clearly put—Are you for the President or for Congress? . . . As any man who knew the people of the northern states might have foretold, the people in the four states to which we refer have declared for Congress.

Three months ago the Republican party was divided upon several important questions. A large and respectable part—perhaps the most thoughtful part—favored the immediate admission of loyal representatives from the southern states. But when the President rashly took a course which made the election a direct hand-to-hand contest with Congress, it seemed to a vast proportion of the true men of the party which had sustained the cause of the Union during the war, that no alternative was left but to stand by Congress, and to put off to another time all issues of less immediate interest, however important and however far reaching in their consequences to the country.

Let us hope that the President will take a lesson from the voice of the people. He may well do so. His main purpose has been and is, if we understand him rightly, to bring the country back as quickly as possible to constitutional government. The shortest way now to reach that desirable end, is the adoption of the Constitutional Amendment. Those who oppose that now, labor for the perpetuation of disorganization; and are not wise or true friends, either of the southern states, or of the country. Mr. Johnson has gained, we are told, great influence over the southern whites. If he is a wise statesman, he has an opportunity to use that influence now for the pacification of the country. Let him urge the adoption of the amendment upon the southern voters. . . .

On the other hand, when Congress meets again, with the immense popular vote at its back, we have a right to expect that it will be moderate; that it will remember that harmony, and not strife, is what the country needs and anxiously demands. . . .

On their moderation and sound judgment as much depends as upon the President. The country desires nothing so much as to see the two branches of the government working in harmony together. It demands that each shall do its part towards this; and it will not tolerate violence or manifestations of hatred in either. . . .

E.L. Godkin: "The Northern Elections"

The election of 1866 was a major affirming event for Republicans, who swept local and national elections in the North. The vote was considered a resounding vote against President Johnson's Reconstruction policy.

The Nation, **November 5, 1866**

Mr. Johnson has now seen the groundswell of popular indignation of which he has so unweariedly discoursed since February last. It has not, indeed, been quite of the kind which he predicted; in fact, the popular tide on which he counted so much has overwhelmed him and all his schemes. The conductor of the train, as Mr. Seward so felicitously termed him, has found out that the train has run over him, instead of his having run away with it. . . .

This is the most decisive and emphatic victory ever won in American politics. Not only is the majority the largest ever given in the same section of country, but it is given upon the largest vote ever polled. . . . Under all the circumstances, this is an unprecedented occurrence; and it demonstrates that the elections this year have stirred up the nation more thoroughly than any that have ever before taken place. Nothing could add to the weight, the force, the earnestness, the intensity of this determination of the people. . . .

What, then is the meaning of this impressive popular demonstration? It is not surprising that upon this point there should be some difference of opinion, since the battle was fought upon different grounds in various places. But we think that all reasonable men can unite upon a few leading points as at least forming a portion of the verdict.

The first point which has unquestionably been passed upon is, that the people will not trust the South, or its ally, the Democratic party of the North, to rule in our government. The second is, that the South shall not be restored unconditionally to its privileges in the Union. The third is, that Congress, and not the Executive, is to name the conditions of restoration. The fourth, that the conditions already proposed are abundantly liberal to the South. . . .

The splendor of its victory should not, however, blind the [Republican] party to its increased responsibility or to the perils which it must yet pass. . . . The Southern question *must* be dealt with boldly and settled finally within the next two years. It *should* be settled within six months. The people are ready to have an end put to further controversy as to the foundations of our national structure, in order that the work of rebuilding may go on. And more than ever we believe that the truest policy for all interests, and the truest humanity towards the white population of the South, which may otherwise be led on to destruction by its insane advisers, demand the prompt and complete establishment of equal suffrage as the basis of reconstruction, or, if anybody likes the phrase better, the removal of all political distinctions based on the color of the skin.

Henry J. Raymond: "The President and the People"

By the end of the campaign season, the writing on the wall was clear—the president's policy, no matter how "practical," was not being endorsed by the people or by the New York Times.

New York Times, **November 8, 1866**

That the dominant sentiment of the country differs at this time more widely than ever from the position of the President, is proven beyond dispute by the result of the late elections. The President, by his messages to Congress, and by his speeches upon his late tour, has given the people every opportunity to comprehend fully his policy. He has not only stated it repeatedly in definite terms, but he has enforced it by all the arguments which he could command from the Constitution, from the principles of reason, and from the grounds of statesmanship and the public welfare. He has been thoroughly in earnest in the matter and has himself unquestionably been governed by the reasons which he has brought to bear upon others, and through which he has attempted to convince his opponents. But Neither Congress, as was demonstrated by the votes, nor the people, as had been shown by the elections, appear to have been affected by the President's arguments, or, at least, they have not been affected in such a way as to bring them to the conclusions at which he is firmly anchored. On the contrary, the divergence between them has been steadily growing greater, until today the policy of the Administration seems hopeless of popular triumph in any State of the Union, if we except the State of Kentucky.

The forms of our civil polity are such, that, while they give great power to the president in legislation, as well as in his Executive capacity, they establish a very positive limit beyond which he is entirely subordinate to the Legislature. . . . Not only so, but Congress can compel him to be the administrator and Executive agent of a policy which he opposes, both as regards domestic and foreign affairs, and can enforce upon him courses of action against which he has exerted his whole power. . . .

The Executive being thus powerless in law and in fact, when the legislative body is opposed to his policy and action, and the Legislature being possessed of power to enforce upon him a course that shall be in conformity with his own will, there would seem to be but one course for a discreet Executive when he unfortunately finds his policy to be adverse to that determined upon by the Legislature. It is to voluntary conform his policy as nearly as possible to that of the latter—to give way voluntarily as far as he can, and by every means to try and reconcile differences and settle in a pacific and republican manner the conflicting ideas and measures which are for the time being before the country. If this method be not adopted, there will inevitably be a solution reached less agreeable to at least one of the parties, and at the same time, more positively adverse to the policy of the Executive.

THE CONSERVATIVE VIEWPOINT

Seth Boughton: "Our Situation"

Although President Johnson was fighting Congress on every front against its many attempts to legislate the future of the South, some Southerners expressed disappointment that he was not doing enough to stop the radical Republicans.

Milledgeville (Ga.) Federal Union, February 13, 1866

Men nor States should act blindly with regard to their affairs. It matters not how unpalatable the truth may be, it is always best to look it squarely in the face. The President has flattered the States at the South with an early restoration to all their rights in the Union, and an equal participation with all the States in the benefits as well as in the burthens of the Government. For some reason, best known to himself, he has withheld from us the promised relief. In the face of the recommendation of Gen. Grant, he still quarters regiments of negro troops in our midst: Thus increasing every day the irritation of the old wounds which were healing so kindly. . . . The President knows that these negro troops are not needed in Georgia to keep the peace. Why, then, add to our troubles and still further vex and irritate us? Is he afraid of Congress? We have given him credit for moral courage and firmness of the Jacksonian stamp, but we must confess we have seen no manifestation of either, for some time past. All the while Congress is going on with its high-handed legislation, and gradually undermining the Constitution and actually changing the form of Government—yet we see no decided stand on the part of the President to arrest these wild and wicked notions of the Disunionists. . . .

Our State Legislature is moving on it is true, and our Governor does pretty much as he used to do before the War, but who knows how long it will be before the Congress of the U.S. shall step in and set aside all the acts of both touching the laws for the control and government of the Freedmen. In Virginia it has already been done; and it is these acts on the part of Military Commanders, that makes us utter even a feeble remonstrance against the silence and apathy of the President, who promised us protection, and who has the power to send Mr. Stanton home to-morrow, and to dismiss every U.S. Officer who dares to set aside the civil laws of a State. . . . If the President will not help us stem the current of unjust, unequal and unconstitutional legislation by Congress, or use his power to crush the despotism of Military Commanders, what have we to hope for, or live for, in the future of this Country? He may be powerless to check Congress—but he is omnipotent to crush the despotic edicts of his Military Commanders, and the suffering people of the South, ask and expect him to do it.

Manton Marble: "President Johnson's Recent Speeches"

President Johnson's intemperate and unpresidential speeches during the late winter and spring of 1866 against the radical policies drew a great deal of criticism from Republicans. Democrats were willing to forgive the president and assign the incendiary speeches to his heightened indignation, but others believed that the president was drunk on the occasion of some of his extemporaneous speeches.

New York World, April 20, 1866

Many Republicans have entertained a faint hope that, since the triumph by Congress in passing the Civil Rights bill over the President's veto, he would show a disposition to compromise. But the President's speech to the soldiers and sailors on Wednesday, and the short speech to the colored people yesterday, effectually dispel all such delusive hopes. Mr. Johnson shows himself as firm in all his leading positions as if the victory had been on the side of the veto; and the feeling of indomitable hostility with which he regards the Radicals is expressed with more vigor than even in the speech of the 22nd of February. . . .

It has been so industriously pretended, by a certain class of Republicans, that the difference between the President and Congress is not of a character to disturb the harmony of the party, that it is of the highest importance to disabuse the country of that idea. . . . It is important that the country should know that President Johnson repudiates any such milk and water twaddle. There is a wide gulf between him and Congress, and as he does not intend to surrender his policy, but to appeal to the country in the next Congressional elections, it is of the very first consequence that the people should know from some perfectly authentic source, that the President regards the breach as important enough to arouse, and to justify him in expressing, his energetic indignation. When he denounced the opponents of his policy with the unsparing severity he used on Wednesday, no one who reads his speech will fail to see that he does not regard the opposition made to his policy as a slight or trivial matter. How can he appeal from Congress to the people but by emphasizing the difference which, as often as an election occurs, the Republicans so perversely deny? . . . If he is incensed, the people will readily infer that he thinks he has something to be angry about; and so far as they respect his judgment, they will cease to regard the difference between him and Congress as of minor importance. But in what way can a man so effectually convince others that he is angry, as by exhibiting the signs of anger in the old-fashioned genuine way. . . .

It is important for the public interests that the facts should be weighed and in no other way could they reach so many people or secure so much attention, as when uttered by him. At present, as well as when he was facing his rebel neighbors in Tennessee, Mr. Johnson has more important things at heart than a fastidious regard for his personal ease or dignity. He speaks to carry his point, and without thinking, or caring, what small *litterateurs* may say of his style, he uses such language as will make the intended impression on the great body of his countrymen, who are not small *litterateurs*, but plain people who neither in their own practice nor in judging of others, enter into the refinement of expressing indignation in restrained language. . . .

W.B. Phillips: "The Fall Elections—The Coming Political Revolution"

Editors are never embarrassed to give political advice to presidents. In this editorial, the New York Herald *advises the president that unless he can unite conservative Republicans and Democrats into a strong National Union Party, there will be no way to defeat the radical Republicans in the fall elections.*

New York Herald, May 26, 1866

The public mind of the Northern States is ripe for a political revolution in our approaching fall elections. The people are ready. They need only the active organization of a national Johnson Union movement to bring them into line. The enthusiastic Johnson meeting held in Philadelphia on Saturday evening last, and the spirited popular gathering on the same night and the same platform at Westminster, Maryland, of republicans and democrats, show how the tide is drifting. The people are spontaneously falling in with President Johnson's policy and they need only a little active work in the way of organization to put an end to the factious and impracticable doings of the present Congress in the Elections for the next.

Congress has been nearly six months in session, and what has it done in the way of Southern reconstruction and restoration? It has given us the scheme of the Joint Committee of Fifteen which is now before the Senate— a scheme the manifest purpose of which is the exclusion of the lately rebellious States from the coming Presidential election, and their indefinite exclusion from the two houses. This scheme is ingeniously covered up with the leading measures of President Johnson's policy; but the issue remains substantially the same. The President's policy is Southern restoration to a voice in the government; the policy of Congress is Southern exclusion. This is the issue which will be submitted to the people in our approaching September, October and November elections; and upon this issue, we say, the public mind of the North is ripening for a great political revolution.

Between the so-called conservative republicans and the democrats in Congress we ought to have had ere this the downfall of Thaddeus Stevens. These two opposing factions, possessing, if combined, a majority against him, have each, to suit their factious purposes, played into his hands. The democrats in Congress are mostly, if not all, of the copperhead tribe, miserable tricksters or desperate revolutionists, whose tactics would disgrace the rowdies of a New York democratic primary election. The conservatives of the House of Representatives are mere playthings in the hands of Stevens. He is amused when they speak in support of the administration, for he has tried them and knows that at the crack of his whip they will be dumb and submissive. Treacherous or temporizing, copperheads and conservatives have less respect for each other than for Stevens, and thus he uses the one faction or the other as occasion may serve him. The radical faction rule Congress because they are united bold and aggressive. Their purposes may be bad, their measures may be vicious and revolutionary but in their fight they show those qualities of courage, skill, tenacity and energy which invariably command respect and give even to a bad cause more or less of popular strength.

Thus the President has failed in Congress to secure a party capable of accomplishing anything. His professed and noisy adherents have their own axes to grind, their own selfish or paltry party purposes to serve, and they are like Joseph's coat, of many colors. Hence, against the radicals the opposition elements of Congress are as powerless as so many squads of bushwhackers against the advances of a regular army. Hence the necessity of a bold aggressive movement from what Stevens calls the "the other end of the Avenue." . . . President Johnson must advance his standard. . . . This is the way to commence an effective organization of a national Johnson Union Party, and in view of a wholesome revolution in our fall elections. . . .

Henry J. Raymond: "The Radicals in Congress—What Have They Done? What Gained?"

Henry J. Raymond was elected congressman from New York City for one term (1865–67), during which he was a stalwart supporter of President Johnson. It was not until Raymond left Congress that he became more critical of the president. In this editorial, Raymond is criticizing himself and his fellow congressmen for their failure to do anything significant during the year.

New York Times, July 16, 1866

The wise men of Washington grow weary of their labors. Despite the frantic appeals of those who seem to fear a recess as a child fear darkness, the end of the session approaches apace. Hot weather has come providentially, to upset the proposal of the ultra of the ultraists, in regard to a permanent session, and there is a likelihood that in little more than a week hence the legislators of the nation will have departed for their homes. . . .

The excitement on the closing days of a session hardly admits of calm reflection. There are intrigues on the floor, intrigues in the lobby, intrigues in the caucus—intrigue and bustle everywhere. The present has more calls than moments, and the future looms up so largely that the conscience has little chance of squaring accounts with the past.

Away from Washington, the case will be different. Brought face to face with their constituents, members will be unable to escape the reckoning that awaits them. Sins of omission and sins of commission will rise in judgment against them. . . .

And how will that account appear. To answer the inquiry we must see how the account stood when the balance was last struck, just before the opening of the Capitol doors in December. The war had then been ended some months, and the country was congratulating itself upon the early consummation of the work of restoration. Much had been already done and gained. The policy indicated by Mr. Lincoln had been adhered to by his successor with the happiest results. The terms dictated by President Johnson had been acceded to by nearly all the conquered States, if not with alacrity at least with completeness and an apparent sincerity that left little to be desired. It was felt that the States so lately in rebellion, having given the required guarantees of future loyalty, only awaited the friendly action of Congress to resume their old privileges in the Union. . . . It was expected that with the assembling of Congress would come the full and final process of restoration—the recognition of loyal Senators and Representatives from the South and the spectacle of a reunited nation legislating constitutionally for the common interest of every part.

In December then, the balance was largely in favor of the President and against Congress. . . . Is the work of restoration one iota nearer completion than when it passed from the hands of the President more than seven months ago? Has Congress done a single thing to advance or complete it? Instead of furthering the work, has not Congress obstructed it? Has it not evaded the question of Southern representation, and rudely repulsed Southern senators and members of unquestioned fitness? Has it not shirked its constitutional duty by referring the subject to a joint committee, appointed for purposes which each House was bound itself to fulfill. Has not the labor of this Committee been abortive, amounting to no more than the preparation of a Constitutional amendment, which passed only after vital modification, with but a slight probability of ratification by the States whose consent is essential to its validity? Is not the prospect of restoration more gloomy than it was seven months ago?

There is perhaps a ready answer. The questioned may say to his questioners that Congress has a policy of its own, differing radically from the policy of the dead and living President; and that Congress has preferred adhesion to its own policy. . . . Let us see how they will improve the matter.

Has it passed any measure dealing with [the states] as territories? . . . Has it enacted the punishment of the Southern people? Has it provided for the confiscation of Southern property? Has it conferred upon the negro the right of suffrage? These are all Radical ideas—all parts of the great Radical plan, which members of the House will tell their constituents has been deemed preferable to the President's plan. But the difference between them is this: The President's plan, whatever are its defects, is practical; he has applied it practically and with good results; while the Radical plan is impracticable, and has amounted to nothing except as an obstruction. The inquiring citizen will, then, complete his catechism by asking: If the majority in Congress were resolved to hinder and cripple the President's scheme or restoration, were they not in duty bound to commit themselves definitely to some counter-scheme? Having evaded this duty, must not the inference be that the Radical policy has been a failure, and that the session has been an occasion of disappointment, and sorrow, and shame to those who have struggled, and waited, and hoped for the restoration of the Union?

John Forsyth: "The Situation"

Throughout 1866, Southerners had been deluded into believing that President Johnson's policies would triumph and that the radical agenda would go down in defeat in the elections of 1866. When the opposite proved true, Southern newspapers began an "incessant harangue" against the North, rhetorically pushing the myth that everyone in the North hated the South. The enemy was no longer the radicals but the entire North.

Mobile (Ala.) Advertiser and Register, November 15, 1866

Our quondam ex-Confederate readers will remember how often, in times past, while war flamed, and we had need to animate drooping spirits in an unequal contest, we used to indite editorials on "the situation." Well, near two years have gone by since that war closed, yet "the situation" is a topic as pregnant of serious reflection and as gloomy in its surroundings as at any period during that eventful struggle. As defeated belligerents, we stand in the presence of a conqueror (represented by the Northern popular majority at the polls), "unsated by victory and unappeased by complete submission." We are regarded as political outcasts, unfit for fellowship, unworthy of clemency, and so sinful that the virtue of magnanimity would be wasted upon us. . . . On the sixth of the present month, ten states out of twelve proclaimed at the polls that their prostrate enemy, who laid down his arms eighteen months ago, is not sufficiently punished or adequately humiliated to satisfy their magnanimous souls. . . . The declared enemies of this land and people are in the uncontrolled power of the Government of the United States. We are helplessly at their mercy, and unless by miracle, God softens their hearts and breaks the sceptre of their sway, we have little to expect besides grinding taxes and political servitude. This is "the situation," but who is wise enough to forecast the time and the method of exodus from it? We have yet to encounter that prophet. . . . We must be patient under wrong, do our duty in spite of injustice, bear with fortitude and resolutely make up our minds that however our once countrymen, by now enemies, may choose in their power to degrade us, we will never, by word or deed, degrade ourselves. For the rest, our only trust is in the goodness of Heaven, for the mercy of man has failed us.

QUESTIONS

1. Why did the Republican press react so negatively to President Johnson's harangues and accusations against congressmen?
2. Why did the *New York Herald* believe that the time was right for a political revolution?
3. Why was the vote of 1866 so overwhelmingly in support of the Republican Party?
4. What were the major controversies between President Johnson and Congress in 1866?
5. Compare the *New York Times* editorial of July 16 with the editorial of November 8—on what points had the *New York Times* changed its opinion?

NOTE

1. Brooks D. Simpson, *The Reconstruction Presidents* (Lawrence: University Press of Kansas, 1998), 69.

CHAPTER 7

Freedmen's Bureau Act, 1866

When President Andrew Johnson assumed office after President Abraham Lincoln's assassination, it appeared that he would support the notion that the restoration of the South would require a strong hand by the federal government. But as months went by, his Reconstruction policy began to soften. Early removal of troops, wholesale pardoning of rebels, restoration of confiscated lands, blocking the work of the Freedmen's Bureau, and lack of concern for the escalating violence against blacks all reflected a lenient policy that ensured the return of white supremacist governments in the South.

Johnson had little interest in protecting freedmen, believing that the future of blacks should be left in the hands of the Southern states. But reports of violence against blacks, the passage of punitive black codes, and the inability of blacks to receive or even seek redress in the courts in the South were proof that Johnson's states' rights policy had not worked. Congress reacted by constructing its own protections, and in the process, set Reconstruction on a different course.

The first test of President Johnson's willingness to compromise on the issue of black civil rights came with the debates over the extension of the Freedmen's Bureau. The bureau, established at the end of the Civil War, had no appropriation and was expected to last for only one year after the war ended. Yet, the job of the Freedmen's Bureau and its director General Oliver O. Howard had grown tremendously. The bureau was responsible for feeding, clothing, housing, educating, and finding jobs for more than four million ex-slaves in the South. By the winter of 1865, the work of the bureau was just beginning, and there was not a realistic end in sight.

To determine exactly what was happening to freedmen in the South, Congress created the Select Committee on Freedmen's Affairs. Members spent several months reading reports and correspondence of bureau agents, which were replete with tales of violence and intimidation against blacks, of the failure of the civil courts to provide justice, and of the effect of the black codes. In January 1866, Senator Lyman Trumbull of Illinois, a moderate Republican and former Johnson supporter, presented the Freedmen's Bureau Bill, which would extend the bureau's operations for two more years and provide an annual appropriation of $12 million. But it was the provisions protecting the civil rights of blacks that were the most radical. The bill authorized agents or the military to hear cases wherever blacks could not get a fair hearing in the civil courts and allowed the bureau to punish and even remove state officials who denied blacks their civil rights.

That the federal government could operate courts in the Southern states as they did during and immediately after the war came from the theory that because they had not been readmitted to the Union, the former rebel states were still subject to martial law. Therefore, if and when Congress recognized these states, such enforcement power would cease.

Johnson had no intention of supporting any bill that he believed gave blacks more protections than whites. He prepared to do battle. In early February, he met with a small group of black leaders, including black abolitionist Frederick Douglass, and in a 45-minute lecture told them in unambiguous language that he would not support black suffrage, that he would not make blacks equal to whites, that blacks themselves were to blame for poor Southern whites hating them, and that the best recourse for blacks was to remove themselves to Africa. He ended the meeting by telling his visitors that the future of blacks lay in the hands of those who knew them best—their former owners.

A week later, President Johnson vetoed the Freedmen's Bureau Bill. In a lengthy veto message, Johnson criticized the imposition of military jurisdiction over the South when he believed that the existing civil courts provided sufficient protection for blacks. Johnson criticized the bureau for its "immense patronage" and for the tremendous financial burden ($12 million in the first year) it placed on the federal government. Congress had never, charged Johnson, provided relief, established schools, or given land to "millions of the white race, who are honestly toiling from day to day for their subsistence."[1] According to Johnson, the authors of the Constitution never contemplated such a system of welfare.

At the end of his veto message, Johnson called the bill "taxation without representation" and declared that such matters should be decided only when all states are fully represented in Congress. With this statement, Johnson threw down the gauntlet and threatened to veto any bill affecting the South that passed while the Southern states remained unrepresented.

Congress was unable to muster enough votes to override the veto. Bolstered by his success and to thwart a renewed effort later by Congress to pass a reauthorization bill, Johnson sent two inspectors to the South in April to study the bureau's operations. Many agents wrote General Howard complaining that the inspectors' visits were superficial and their reports filled with inaccuracies.

Congress finally passed the second Freedman's Bureau Act, overriding another Johnson veto in July 1866, before the inspectors completed their report. The bill gave the president the power to establish the rules under which the military and bureau agents would assume jurisdiction over cases concerning equal rights. Allowing Johnson to maintain influence over the bureau's judicial policy was a bit like allowing the fox to guard the chicken coop. Johnson was slow in approving rules and regulations, resulting in great confusion among bureau agents as to the extent of their authority. By December, the issue became moot when the U.S. Supreme Court ruled in *ex parte Milligan* that it was unconstitutional to use military tribunals whenever civil courts were open. With that decision, military courts disappeared in the South, leaving enforcement in the hands of untrained bureau agents.

The Freedmen's Bureau was needed not only to help former slaves understand their freedom but also to provide them with protections against their former masters. The first reading in this section, by Horace Greeley, criticizes the South's contempt for blacks and argues that the bureau is the blacks' only friend in the South. The second entry, by George W. Curtis, accuses the president of inconsistency when he stated that the bureau was a wartime measure and was no longer needed when at the same time supporting wartime measures in other areas. The war did not end with the fighting, says Curtis, but will end when the freedmen are secure in their citizenship. The last piece in the section, by E.L. Godkin, declares that the Freedmen's Bureau is absolutely necessary to see the war to its right conclusion and to ensure that former slaves are not again reenslaved by their former masters.

The editorials denouncing the Freedmen's Bureau Act begin with a reading, by W.B. Phillips, that announces that blacks will always be shiftless and lazy and all the bureau will do is increase the dependency of blacks on handouts. The second entry, by John Forsyth, is a broad denunciation of radicals and a rallying cry for President Johnson. The third selection, by Manton Marble, criticizes everything from the amount of money appropriated to the bureau to the use of government funds to build schools.

FAVORING THE FREEDMEN'S BUREAU ACT

Horace Greeley: "The Veto of the Freedmen's Bureau Bill"

The New York Tribune *was growing weary of President Johnson's failure to provide necessary protections for blacks. In this editorial from the* New York Tribune, *one can read a warning between the lines that Johnson's days were numbered.*

New York Tribune, February 20, 1866

We call President Johnson as our first witness—though there are many others—to the fact that the Whites of the South too generally regard the Blacks with contempt and aversion. We think the President goes too far when he asserts that the Whites would rise again in insurrection and exterminate the Blacks if the latter were admitted to equal political rights with the former; but that an antipathy very generally exists, is beyond dispute. Only "make the negro know and keep his place"—under the heel of a master—and the Southrons like him as a man likes his dog or a wolf his mutton; but let the Black seem to say, "I am a man and I claim all the rights of man," and he becomes "impudent," "insolent," presumptuous; and every White of the dueling, deep-drinking, gambling class feels obliged to take him down. If servile and cringing, he is tolerated as a useful implement; but he is allowed none of the rights of Humanity.

The Freedmen's Bureau is the Nation's right arm, gently but firmly outstretched to keep the peace between these warring classes. Its principal objects are three: 1. to save the Blacks from famine, abuse and massacre. 2. To set them at work. 3. To see that they are kindly treated and fairly paid for their labor. It is a gigantic enterprise, and has achieved a marvelous success. Hundreds of thousands are now industrious and comfortable laborers, with roof over their heads and food in their cabins, who would have been prowling, thieving, hunted and famishing vagabonds in the absence of the Bureau. It has patiently and generally disabused the Blacks of the notion that they are to share their masters' lands and goods; it has planted schools, inculcated obedience and diligence, and been foremost in all the good that has lately befallen the South. . . .

Yet the President has vetoed the bill providing the continuance and greater efficiency of the Bureau. We deeply regret this; and we think he will live to regret it even more keenly. . . .

Of course the Freedmen's Bureau is anomalous. There is no dispute as to that. Nay more: it indicates a blind roundabout way of doing partial justice when complete justice was (with the President's consent) easier and safer. Three lines in the Federal Constitution abolishing and inhibiting all laws and ordinances that bestow or withhold privileges because of Color, would be worth several Freedmen's Bureaus. Justice—Equal Rights—the recognition of his manhood—these the ex-slave wants—not coddling and petting. Say, if you will, that he must read before he can vote; but then do not let White villains burn his poor school-house. Say, if you will that he must have property before he can vote; but be very careful that the law secures to him all he earns, and gives him every needed facility for maintaining his right. If you deny him the Right of Suffrage because of his ignorance, look well to it that you do nothing calculated to perpetuate that ignorance, and that you incite him to learn by proffering him enfranchisement as the reward of his diligence and acquirements. In short, make your laws rigidly just, then abolish your soup-houses. But until then—

Mr. Johnson has made a grave mistake. He has relieved those who elected him of a great responsibility by taking it on his own shoulders. Hereafter, whatever wrongs may be inflicted upon or indignities suffered by the Southern Blacks, will be charged to the President, who has left them naked to their enemies. Times will show that he has thereby precluded a true and speedy restoration of the South, and inflicted more lasting misery on her Whites than on her Blacks.

George W. Curtis: "The Veto Message"

George W. Curtis points out one of the major difficulties Republicans had with Johnson—his inconsistency. This editorial insists that blacks in the South can be protected only with the Freedmen's Bureau.

Harper's Weekly, March 3, 1866

The Senate did wisely in adjourning after the Veto Message was read. Legislation under such excitement is not likely to be dignified or sagacious. That the Message was a sore disappointment to the truest friends of the President can not be denied. Their regret may be measured by the rejoicing of those who would fain use him for their own purposes. . . .

Of the President's sincerity there is no doubt. That he honestly wishes, as he says, to secure to the Freedmen the full enjoyment of their liberty we fully believe. But he seems to us not entirely master of his own positions. Thus he acknowledges the usefulness of the Freedmen's Bureau as established by the act of last March. But he regards it as a war measure, and war having ceased, he is of opinion that the matter should be left to the States. Yet, if war has ceased, why does he support General Terry's military order reversing the action of the Virginia Legislature? So the President says that in his judgment the late rebel States "have been fully restored, and are to be deemed to be entitled to enjoy their constitutional rights as members of the Union." Yet if this be so, why in his late proclamation restoring the privilege of the writ of *habeas corpus* did he except the late rebel States? The Constitution defines the conditions under which the right of suspending the privilege may be exercised. It is only when in case of rebellion or invasion the public safety may require it. Yet he expressly exhorts us in the Message not to suppose that the United States are in a condition of civil war.

The Freedmen's Bureau is exceptional, but it is so only because the condition of the country is exceptional. All the President's acts in initiating the reorganization of the late rebel States were exceptional. But the question of the hour is very simple in itself, however difficult it may be to answer. How can the United States most surely and judiciously and temperately secure the fruit of the victory they have won? Having given liberty to millions of slaves, how can the authority that conferred it maintain its perpetuity? . . . The President says that a system for the support of indigent persons was never contemplated by the authors of the Constitution. Certainly not, and this bill is no more such a system than an appropriation for military hospitals would be. It is a simple necessity of the situation. Shall these homeless, landless, forlorn persons be left to the mercies of those who despise and hate them, or shall the United States say, "We cut the bonds that bound you to the ground, and we will protect you while you are struggling to get upon your feet?"

If the President believes that the word of the nation sacredly pledged to the freedmen will be kept by the black codes of South Carolina and Mississippi, his faith would remove mountains. And if he proposes to abandon the freedmen to civil authorities created exclusively by those who think that the colored race should be eternally enslaved, who deny the constitutionality of emancipation, and who have now a peculiarly envenomed hostility to the whole class, we can only pray God that the result may be what we have no doubt he honestly wishes it to be. We believe that he is faithful to what he conceives to be the best interest of the whole country. And while upon this question we wholly differ from him, we differ with no aspersion or suspicion.

E. L. Godkin: "The Fallacy of the Veto"

E.L. Godkin was a strong proponent of giving blacks civil and political rights, and he saw the Freedmen's Bureau as necessary machinery for achieving that end. In this editorial, he argues that the results of the Civil War—the freeing of four million slaves—made it imperative that extraordinary measures be taken to ensure true freedom.

The Nation, March 1, 1866

The President's message, vetoing the Freedmen's bill, is based throughout on the assumption that in the late war we simply suppressed a rebellion. If this were true, there is no doubt that much of what he says of the propriety of at once admitting the revolted States to a full share in the Government would be well founded. The luxury of reigning over a conquered people is one which no republic can enjoy with impunity. No man who has read history to any purpose, or who knows anything of human nature, would deliberately propose to keep eight millions of Southerners in a state of vassalage merely as a punishment for having rebelled. . . .

But the war has not been simply a contest between two sets of men, one maintaining the authority of a government and the other seeking to overthrow it. The fighting of the last four years has not simply, as Mr. Johnson assumes, re-established the jurisdiction of the United States over a certain territorial area, and over a certain number of people. It has wrought a social revolution, which for magnitude, for rapidity, and for the gravity of its consequences has never been equaled in history. . . . In our case, four millions of men have been lifted from a legal condition hardly superior to that of beasts of the field into that of free citizens. It is therefore a fallacy, and a very gross one, to tell us that when the war which did this thing is over, all is over. All is not over.

The great question after all . . . is how to assist the freedmen in passing through the transition state between slavery and freedom and independence without increasing or embittering the hostility between them and the whites. . . . In short, Mr. Johnson believes it more safe and prudent, and therefore a more honorable discharge of responsibility to the liberated slaves of the South, to trust solely to the . . . enlightened self-interest of their late masters for their being treated justly and mercifully. . . . And it is upon this point that the question arises between him and Congress.

Now, let us ask ourselves plainly what it is that the blacks of the South need that they may become intelligent and useful members of society in the shortest possible period. Is it not, first of all, the education of civilized life, the means of becoming familiarized with the use of their new rights and the discharge of their new duties? Must we not rouse in them, or encourage in them, a love of industry, a love of accumulation, and a respect for property? . . . Has any society ever prospered, ever been anything but a dead and decaying carcase [*sic*], in which any considerable portion of the people were deprived of this assurance? . . . We must, in short, if we mean to regenerate Southern society, take care that no portion of it is left outside the law.

Now we do not pretend, nor does anybody, that there ought to be a perpetual Freedmen's Bureau maintained for the purpose of nursing the negroes, although we believe it will take some time for the Southerners to learn to treat them as men of like rights with themselves. . . . But in nearly every [Southern state] measures have been passed since the close of the war for the avowed purpose of keeping the blacks down, and withholding from them those common rights and liberties which white men enjoy. And we say deliberately that there could be no better mode of disheartening the freedmen, trampling out the sparks of social ambition in their hearts, than thus meeting them on the threshold of civilization with a penal code; and it is to this code, and not the ordinary laws of the country, that they are committed whenever the Freedmen's Bureau expires. . . .

OPPOSING THE FREEDMEN'S BUREAU ACT

W.B. Phillips: "The Freedmen's Bureau Bill before the President"

Most Democratic newspapers balked at the idea of having a large bureaucracy to care for the freedmen, believing that it would only promote idleness and dependence.

New York Herald, February 17, 1866

The bill ought to be called an act to support the negroes in idleness by the honest laborers of white people, or an act to establish a gigantic and corrupt political machine for the benefit of the radical faction and a swarm of office holders. Either would be a correct title. There might have been some excuse for the establishment of a freedmen's bureau during the war and before the negroes were placed on an equal footing with white people by the amendment to the constitution. There is not the least excuse for it now. Instead of enlarging its powers as this bill enlarges them, the former set out to be repealed. In whatever point of view we look at the measure it is full of evil. The professed object of the bill, which, in fact, is not the real object—to protect and benefit the negroes—cannot be attained by any such legislation. On the contrary, it will destroy that very independence of character and action which inspires a feeling of manhood, by making them dependent upon government. Never disposed to work more than they could help, and having always been taught to rely upon others to provide for and direct them, they naturally will be shiftless, idle, dependent and useless to themselves or others under the special guardianship and control of government. . . . Then, how can the planters and other employers get along with these people as laborers when the caprices, corruption, passions, arbitrary will of the thousands of agents of the bureau scattered all over the country stand in the way?

And where could the victims of this gigantic and arbitrary machine find redress? Let the negroes and white people of the South—the laborers and employers—make their own arrangements, conduct their own affairs and take care of themselves as people in the North and elsewhere do. They know what is best to be done for their mutual interest. The negroes are free and cannot be enslaved in any manner whatever. Their old masters are willing to employ them, and indeed wish to do so as free laborers. They understand the negroes better than any other people do, and as a class are more kindly disposed toward them. Why then should we not allow the natural laws that govern labor and capitol, employers and employed at the North, to operate there? Why should we be burdened with a great charitable institution to support the negroes in idleness at the cost of many millions—maybe twenty millions or more a year? Why should the white working people of the North pay for this, as well as the necessary army of office holders that would be required to carry out the law? It would really be a monstrous fraud upon the country and a great evil to both negroes and whites in the South.

We hope the President may find it to be his duty, after mature consideration, to veto the bill, notwithstanding the abuse he may receive and the ghosts of negro suffering that may be raised. The issue between him and the radicals has to be made, and it is better that it should be made now and on this measure than hereafter. Let the bill go back to Congress with a full review of its features and his general policy as connected with it, and the country will sustain him. If Congress should pass it over his veto let them do so. He will have done his duty, he will find out who are with him and who against him, and the question will then be fairly laid before the public.

John Forsyth: "The Action of the Senate on the President's Veto"

Southern Democratic newspapers placed great confidence in President Johnson and his willingness to fight every radical measure that came before him. That confidence, Southerners would soon realize, was misplaced, as Johnson lost the confidence of the whole nation.

Mobile (Ala.) Advertiser and Register, February 27, 1866

The telegraph yesterday evening, brought us the gratifying intelligence that the Senate had failed to pass the "Freedmen's Bureau Bill" over the presidential veto. The vote was thirty-two to sixteen to constitute the requisite majority.

This, as we have said, is gratifying. Another favorable feature in the news is the hasty promptness with which the question was disposed of. The

ordinary rules of official courtesy would have required at least the semblance of sufficient respect for the President's opinions to allow a reasonable time for considering them. In this case, it is evident that the Radical
leaders were afraid of delay. They were aware that their actions would not
bear examination or reflection. They dreaded the effect of the President's
arguments, acting upon the popular judgment and reacting upon Congress.
They felt that there would be danger in delay. Hence the unseemly haste
with which the matter was taken up and acted upon. It is a good sign.

The President has gained the first step—the *pas qui conte*. The majority
was large enough against him, however, to prove that the battle is not yet
won. The enemy will yet make a stubborn fight. All other political questions
of the day dwindle into insignificance in comparison with this momentous
contest. The motley and multitudinous hosts of Puritan fanaticism, infidel
Jacobinism and sectional malignity are arrayed on the one side under the
banners of the ambitious chiefs of the Radical majority in Congress. It remains to be seen what force the President can rally to the tattered and
drooping standards of Common Sense and Constitutional Right.

We of the South, can do little, except to look on and cheer.

Manton Marble: "The Negro-Trading Bureau"

The staunchly Democratic New York World *saw the Freedmen's Bureau
as a gigantic patronage scam that would put more money into agents'
pockets than into the hands of the freedmen.*

New York World, May 4, 1866

It is noteworthy that ever since the patronage panic has been epidemic
in Congress the Radicals have had very little to say about the rights, privileges, or even the protection of the three million sable sufferers at the
South, who counted some four millions before they were righted, privileged and protected by the government. The negro has been neglected.
Contrary to the general expectation, the claims of the colored brother to the
suffrage were scarcely considered in building up the new Radical party platform, facetiously called, and literally to be "considered" by Congress as the
report of the Committee on Reconstruction.

The colored brother is suffered to go his way for this time, provided his
way does not tend in the direction of the ballot-box.

But, not to be too hard upon him, he is allowed to linger yet another year
under the grateful shadow of the Treasury Building while the modest sum
of twelve million dollars—a million only for every month—is drawn out for
the benefits of the philanthropic people who have abandoned all other pur-

suits in life, and who propose to devote their entire attention to the protection of the negro.

No bill was every more aptly termed an "appropriation." It was a deliberate appropriation of twelve millions of the people's money, under a pretense of protecting negroes, to profit the pockets of party pets. . . . The sum of two million dollars to build negro school-houses for the current year only is probably a larger sum than the aggregate original endowments of all the colleges in the Northern States; but it is only two thirds of the amount estimated for the new negro luxury, and we must be duly thankful. . . .

QUESTIONS

1. What did Horace Greeley mean when he called the Freedmen's Bureau "anomalous"?
2. How did President Johnson propose to secure freedmen their rights?
3. What did E.L. Godkin of *The Nation* mean when he wrote that the Civil War "has wrought a social revolution"?
4. Why did Republicans and Democrats believe the Freedmen's Bureau should be a temporary agency only?
5. Why did Democrats believe the Freedmen's Bureau would do more harm than good for the freedmen?

NOTE

1. James D. Richardson, ed., *A Compilation of the Messages and Papers of the Presidents, 1789–1897,* 1 (Washington, D.C.: Government Printing Office, 1896–99), 399–405

CHAPTER 8

Civil Rights Act of 1866

When Illinois senator Lyman Trumball introduced the Freedmen's Bureau and the Civil Rights Acts in early 1866, he was reacting to a state of affairs in the South that was beginning to trouble not only the radicals in Congress but also many moderate Republicans. In 1865 and 1866, many Southern states passed laws known as freedmen's laws or black codes. These laws, similar to earlier slave codes, ran the gamut from prohibiting blacks from owning land and limiting them to certain jobs, to establishing curfews and travel pass systems for blacks. In many states, blacks were subject to criminal punishment for infractions that would be handled in civil courts if the defendant were white. Blacks who broke contracts, who could not get out of debt, or who were perpetual "vagrants" could be forced to place their children into apprenticeships—virtual slavery—to whites.

Reports of violence against blacks and daily reports of new black codes being passed in Southern states went against the grain of a party that prided itself in its dedication to humanity and justice. It was no longer enough to say that slavery had been abolished; it was now time to take the next step toward civil equality for blacks.

The Civil Rights Act of 1866 was not, as many detractors claimed at the time, a radical measure. Senator Trumball, himself a moderate Republican and long-time supporter of President Andrew Johnson, made certain that the law was a conservative one. It said nothing about black suffrage, the right of blacks to hold office, or about the broad area of social equality. The law declared that every person born in the United States (except Indians) was a U.S. citizen. It guaranteed to every citizen the basic rights of being able to enforce contracts, to sue, to be sued, to give evidence, and to inherit, purchase, lease, sell, and hold and convey real and personal property. Citizens would receive full and equal benefit of the laws and be subject to

the same penalties. The act also had a penalty clause that made it a misde-
meanor under federal law to deny anyone equal rights. Although the Civil
Rights Act did not mention blacks, it was clearly an attempt to respond to
the violence and the black codes in the South.

After Congress passed the Civil Rights Act, Johnson was flooded with
telegrams and letters from Democrats and Southerners who were "looking
for another veto." He also was visited by moderate Republicans in Congress,
who hoped to persuade him to sign the bill.[1] Trumbull met with Johnson on
several occasions to convince him that the bill not only was the right thing to
do for blacks in the South but also was the politically safe thing to do to retain the support of moderate Republicans. Republicans were confident that
Johnson would sign the bill if for no other reason than political expediency.

Johnson vetoed the bill, to everyone's surprise. In his veto message, he
stated in no uncertain terms that he did not believe that citizenship should be
conferred on blacks as they were unfit for the responsibilities. Without citizenship, the rest of the bill was moot. Johnson also opposed equality of laws,
believing that laws that discriminated between whites and blacks were necessary, particularly in the area of social relations. He raised the specter of miscegenation as a possible consequence of equality. He also was concerned that
once equality in the law was established, it would open the door for other
rights such as voting and office holding. To Johnson, black equality was a radical and dangerous idea that would lead blacks to claim even greater rights
over whites. He also argued that the law violated states' rights and was nothing more than "another step, or rather stride, towards centralization, and the
concentration of all legislative powers in the national government."[2]

Why Johnson vetoed the bill despite pleas from friends was clear to the
few who knew him well. First, Johnson was a racist. In his speeches, meetings with whites and blacks, and actions, he was consistent in his belief that
abolition of slavery was as far as he would go to protect blacks. Second, believing that black equality was a radical idea, Johnson hoped that by his veto
he could split the radical Republicans from the rest of the party. However,
had he simply looked at the vote in Congress, he would have realized that
radicals, moderates, and conservative Republicans supported it. Whatever
his reasons, Johnson's veto united rather than split the Republican Party.
Moderate Republicans like Senator Trumball felt they had been deceived
and could no longer trust the president. Johnson had created the common
enemy—himself.

The House and Senate lost no time overriding the veto. Although Congress believed the Civil Rights Act would improve legal protection for blacks
in the South, its promise was not easy to fulfill. Many states repealed their
black codes or made them race neutral; nevertheless, their effect lingered.
Federal courts in the South were overburdened, and the delays in dispensing
justice were a deterrent to blacks. In addition, most federal judges and U.S.

attorneys were Southerners who had been appointed by Johnson and thus were less than willing to enforce civil rights where blacks were concerned.

With the veto of the Civil Rights Act, most moderate Republican editors ended their support of the president and joined radicals in calling for a stronger stance in the South. The first section presents arguments in favor of the Civil Rights Act. The first entry, comparing the Civil Rights Act to the old Fugitive Slave Law, argues that sometimes it is imperative that Congress pass laws to thwart illegal activities by a large segment of the population. The second selection, by Samuel Bowles, criticizes President Johnson for trying to use the veto of the Civil Rights Act to split the Republican Party. The third entry, by George W. Curtis, points to the black codes as evidence that the Civil Rights Act is necessary to protect the rights of the freedmen in the South. The last entry, by Horace Greeley, declares that if the president will not support civil rights, the only way to protect blacks is with the ballot.

The selections against the Civil Rights Act are a good illustration of the use of bombast and demagoguery, the last resort when there were few if any cogent arguments against the bill. The first entry, by W.B. Phillips, is a selection of "squibs" run by the *New York Herald* as fillers between news articles and editorials throughout the issue. The entries describe the various evils that will come as a result of giving civil rights to blacks. The next two entries, by John Forsyth from the *Mobile (Ala.) Advertiser and Register,* give no arguments against the Civil Rights Act but instead blast the "black republican party" in Washington and all of its evils. The next editorial, by Manton Marble, reasons that the new law will be a failure because no Southern jury will convict a white man under it and no machinery can be put in place to enforce it. The last entry in this section, by James R. Sneed, declares that the law will bring about mistrust, violence, and worst of all, miscegenation.

SUPPORTING THE CIVIL RIGHTS ACT

Anonymous Writer: "What Is the Civil Rights Bill?"

This editorial compares the Civil Rights Bill with the Fugitive Slave Law that was passed before the Civil War when Northern courts refused to return runaway slaves to their owners in the South.

New York Evening Post, March 20, 1866

It is a bill empowering certain judicial officers of the federal government to do justice in cases where the state or local courts refuse or neglect to do it.

It is the office of the state courts, under our system, to administer justice between man and man, to enforce contracts, punish offenders against the state laws, protect the innocent against wrong, &c. Sometimes it happens that, by reason of the bitterness of popular prejudices, state courts and state officers do not or will not perform one or other of these functions. For instance, it was generally held that under the Constitution it was the duty of state officers to return, on the requisition of the governor of another state, fugitives from justice, or from slavery. But in time the feeling that slavery is wrong, to run away from slavery is right, and to return the fugitive to bondage is inhuman and wicked grew so strong in the northern part of our country that some states no longer fulfilled their part—or, at least, not with sufficient vigilance to satisfy the slaveholders.

Thereupon congress was urged to enact a law under which this work, which the state courts and officers neglected, was to be done by agents of the general government. . . .

That which was in those days done and suffered to protect the slaveholder in his legal title to his slave, the Civil Rights bill now seeks to do to protect the freedman in that liberty which the latest constitutional amendment guaranties him. It does not surprise us to find men and journals who were formerly loudest in their demand for the enforcement of the Fugitive Slave law, now opposing the Civil Rights bill. There is a small party in this country who now, as for many years are ready to yield everything to slavery, but who are firm as adamant when liberty asks but the smallest security. . . .

In practical operation the Civil Rights bill will, if it becomes a law, be beneficial to the southern people. It will satisfy that almost universal sentiment in the North, which insists inflexibly that the freedmen shall be secured in their rights of life, liberty and property, and also that men of the northern states shall be equally protected—for the bill is for the security of whites as well as blacks. It will thus do away with the reasons which are now offered for keeping the southern states out of Congress. . . . We regard it as an important step in the work of reconstruction, and hope the President will sign it; and we believe that sensible southern men will concur with us in this hope; for such men cannot fail to see that nothing is so much needed in their states, now; to draw to them capital and labor, and re-establish them in prosperity, as to set impartial justice there on a firm foundation.

Samuel Bowles: No Title

Samuel Bowles was one of the most respected editors of his day. He was conciliatory and eloquent in his support of moderate Reconstruction policies. He was also a consistent supporter of President Johnson until the veto of the Civil Rights Act. In this editorial, he criticizes Johnson's attempts to use the veto to split the Republican Party.

Springfield (Mass.) Republican, **April 4, 1866**

Instead of driving off from him a small minority of the republican party, or even the half of it, [Johnson drives] off substantially the whole of it. There is but one voice among republicans on this point. . . . If Mr. Johnson is to stand by the doctrine of [his veto], he must inevitably part company with all the great body of his old supporters, and rely for his friends upon the northern democrats and the reconstructed rebels of the South. . . . For though [Republicans] might give up everything else; waive universal suffrage, concede the admission of southern Congressmen, abolish the test oath, grant general amnesty, they cannot give up national protection to the weak and minority classes in the South.

George W. Curtis: "The Civil Rights Bill"

This editorial dissects the major points of President Johnson's veto and concludes that the law is not only just but also necessary to protect blacks in the South from black codes as well as from violence and intimidation.

Harper's Weekly, **April 14, 1866**

The Civil Rights Bill was drawn with simplicity and care for a very necessary purpose. It declares who are citizens of the United States, defines their rights, prescribes penalties for violating them, and provides the means of redress. The power to do this springs from the very nature and function of a supreme government. But the power being conceded, it is fair to demand that any measure of legislation shall be shown to be necessary, politic, and constitutional. . . .

The policy of such a measure is plain from the fact that the civil rights of millions of the native population of the United States are destroyed in certain parts of the country on the ground of color; that this invasion springs from the spirit and habit of slavery, and that, if not corrected by the supreme authority, the inevitable result will be a confirmation of that spirit, and a consequent perpetual menace of the public peace. . . .

Having freed a man from chattel slavery, is the Government bound to look on passively and see him reduced again to virtual slavery, by a State vagrant law, for a trivial offense? The President, indeed, asks in his veto whether the present laws are not sufficient to protect the rights of the freedmen. What rights? If they are neither citizens, nor domiciled aliens, nor foreigners, what rights have they? Clearly their status must be determined before their rights can be defined; and then, if existing remedies are adequate, they are not impaired by the bill. If they are not adequate, the bill is plainly necessary. . . .

But the serious objection to the veto lies in the fact, which is evident throughout, that the President thinks enough has been done to redeem the sacred honor of the United States, not of the separate States, pledged to the emancipated class. He says indeed that he will cooperate with Congress to protect them; but Congress has maturely considered and presented two methods of protection, and he rejects both. What is the President's plan? Is it to leave them to the Black Codes? Is it to call them free, thereby exasperating the late masters, and then suffer those masters unchecked to forbid them to own property, to bear arms, to testify, and to enjoy any of the rights of freedom? Is it to trust to time, and to hope that when the present generation, to whom we gave our word, is exterminated, some kind of justice may be done their posterity by those who come after us? The present danger to the Union is not in the direction feared by the President. It is not from the United States doing a simple Constitutional act of justice; it is from the States perpetuating the old injustice from which our troubles sprang. State rights interpreted by slavery brought us bitter alienation and bloody war. State rights interpreted by liberty can alone give us Constitutional unity and enduring peace.

Horace Greeley: "The New Veto"

This editorial shows Horace Greeley at his best. In clear and simple language, he ties President Johnson's vetoes to the argument that the only way to protect blacks against the machinations of the president and the South is with the ballot.

New York Tribune, March 28, 1866

We feel moved to thank Andrew Johnson for his undesigned but most important demonstration of the vital truth that no class or race can be trusted with the rights of another, but that the only security for Liberty and Justice inheres in the securing of All Men's rights under the only safe guaranty of All Men's Votes.

Let us thank Mr. Johnson that his Veto is so sweeping. He might have phrased it more cunningly; but he has chosen to let us know that it is not this particular bill that has provoked his opposition, but that any measure whereby Congress shall attempt to protect the Southern Blacks against White abuse and oppression must encounter his determined, deadly opposition. It is not to a mode of doing the thing, but to the thing that Congress proposes to do, that Mr. Johnson's main objection lies; consequently, it is idle to hope that any bill which provides—no matter how cautiously, timidly—for the protection of the Blacks, will receive his sanction. It is therefore, idle to consider his reasons in detail; since his main objection is not to any detail, but to the purpose and necessary scope of the measure.

Let us rejoice, then, that it is thus made still clearer that the blacks can have no other protection than that of their own votes. The Freedmen's Bureau must go; the Civil Rights of the Blacks must remain such, and only such as their respective States choose to accord them. If, then, they are to remain subjects and Pariahs in the land of their birth, they can have no rights at all; for the bone thrown by contemptuous pity to a beggar's dog is not his by right but by grace and favor. The Blacks must vote, or those who hate them will verify their own predictions that they cannot live free among us, but must perish from off the face of the earth. Happily, there is another issue—that to be attained through a legal recognition of the truth that "all men are created equal, and endowed by their Creator with certain inalienable rights, among which are life, liberty and the pursuit of happiness;" and that "governments derive their just power from the consent of the governed." When these vital truths are recognized and obeyed, as they must be, then will our land have true, enduring peace.

OPPOSING THE CIVIL RIGHTS BILL

W.B. Phillips: Editorial Notes

These fillers were inserted throughout the editorial page of the New York Herald *after the passage of the Civil Rights Act as teasers to those who shared the editor's racist attitudes.*

New York Herald, **March 30, 1866**

Is a negro five times better than a white man that the former should vote immediately, while the latter has to undergo five years' probation, if he brings his skill, labor and money to this country from abroad? The Civil rights bill declares that the negro is five times better.
***

Shall Negroes sit in Congress, in the Cabinet and other high stations side by side with white men? The Civil Rights bill says that he may.
***

Shall the Negro intermarry with our daughters, and take an equal place in our households? The Civil Rights bill says that he shall.
***

Is the White Man's government for white men? The Civil Rights bill says that it is not.

***

Are we to have Negroes representing this government as United States ministers at the Courts of France and England? The Civil Rights bill says that we are.

****

Shall our children see a negro in the Presidential chair? The Civil Rights bill provides for such a contingency.

***

Shall Negroes intermingle with our refined ladies in steaming hot theatres, ballrooms and opera houses? The Civil Rights bill declares that they must.

***

Shall a Negro supercede Grant as General-in-Chief of the United States Army? The Civil Rights bill says that he can do so.

John Forsyth: "The President's Veto"

Few Southern editors practiced the art of demagoguery better than John Forsyth. Rather than deal with the substance of the bill, he pays homage to President Johnson.

Mobile (Ala.) Advertiser and Register, March 20, 1866

Few of our readers we imagine, had any idea of the sweeping character of the attack upon the rights of the States, contained in that bill "of unconstitutional abominations," called the Civil Rights Bill, until it was exposed by the searching analysis of the President's veto message. When we see to what perils the very foundations and framework of the Government are exposed by the enemies of Republican institution in Congress, we begin to form some idea of the magnitude of the service the president is rendering to his country, and the immense value of his life to the cause of free government. Upon the minds of the most skeptical of disbelievers in the doctrine of special providence, the thought must sometimes obtrude itself, that it looks as if the finger of Heaven were in the dispensation that prompted the black radical party to choose this man of the constitution, this democratic statesman, to occupy the second place on the Lincoln-Presidential ticket. Suppose the choice had fallen on one of the school of Stevens, Sumner and Wendell Phillips! How pitiable had been the conditions of the country! How utterly overturned and prostrate had been the fabric of free government under which it had lived for the best part of a century! President Johnson stands like a "stonewall" between the constitution he has sworn to defend, and its would be destroyers. . . .

The second veto will add immeasurably to the respect in which good men all over the civilized world will hold him. In circumstances most difficult, trying and dangerous, he has proved himself "every inch a man," and won a guerdon of gratitude and admiration that American generations unborn will acknowledge and pay. If he does, to the end, carry this "great nation successfully through [this] perilous crisis, by firmness, moderation and wisdom," no statesman will fill with his deeds a brighter page in history. . . .

John Forsyth: "The Civil Rights Bill"

This editorial continues John Forsyth's demagoguery, this time blasting the radical Republicans for their insolence against the South.

Mobile (Ala.) Advertiser and Register, **April 8, 1866**

The telegraph informs us that this odious bill has been passed by the Senate, over the Presidential veto. We see but little reason to hope that it will not be urged through the House also, unless some providential interposition should avert the calamity.

The passage of the measure, so soon after the Peace Proclamation, indicates a reckless determination to push the war upon the Constitution and upon the cause of justice, humanity and fraternity, to the very knife. It reminds us of the exclamation of the Psalmist: "When I speak to them of peace, they make themselves ready for war." It shows a fixed resolve to trample the very life out of the conquered South, if possible.

How long we might ask—how long is this reckless and wicked spirit to rule in the halls of Congress? But we had almost forgotten that we are as yet only spectators of the great struggle between the powers of good and evil. If it is to come to a final issue, perhaps it were best that it come quickly. Let them go on: remonstrance is thrown away upon madness.

Manton Marble: "The Political Situation—Plans of the Republican Party"

Manton Marble insisted on calling Congress the "rump" Congress after Southern representatives were denied their seats in the Thirty-ninth Congress. In characteristically blunt language, the editor predicts the law will be an utter failure and blames the radicals for the defeat of President Johnson's agenda.

New York World, **April 17, 1866**

The Civil Rights bill has not been passed with the expectation that it will have any effect as law, but as a preliminary snare for entrapping the President, and more especially as a means of fomenting alienation between the North and the South. Who believes that it can be enforced? Violations of it are made punishable as crimes. . . . A Southern jury will no more convict under this law, than a Northern Jury would have done under the Fugitive Slave law, from which some of its provisions are copied. There are still other reasons why it will not be enforced. The Judges of the United States Courts are so few, and so distant from each other, that their courts afford no adequate machinery for the administration of such a law. . . . The District Judges are also few and widely separated. . . . The bill authorizes the Circuit and District Court to appoint as many Commissioners as they may deem necessary. The office of Commissioner is worth nobody's acceptance but that of a local resident. Southerners will neither stand up against local opinion and accept these offices, nor can they take the test oath if they did. It is plain, therefore, that the Civil Rights bill will not be executed. There will be no adequate machinery for this purpose, and Southern juries would not convict under it even if there were. This must have been perfectly obvious to the concocters of the bill, and to members of Congress who passed it over the President's veto.

What then was their object? It was to find in its non-enforcement new topics of invective against the South, and new grounds of accusation against the President. The real obstacle to the success of the law is the repugnance of the Southern people to its provisions, and their disbelief in its constitutionality; in consequence of which Commissioners will not serve nor juries convict. But its failure will be attributed to the neglect and opposition of the President. . . .

James R. Sneed: No Title

This editorial is typical of the racist editorials found in Southern newspapers whenever Congress passed a law protecting blacks. However, the editor was correct in his prediction that the Supreme Court would correct the problem.

Macon (Ga.) Daily Telegraph, April 24, 1866

Negro equality will reign in all its transcendent beauties. Negroes and Yankees cheek by jowl in the churches, in the hotels, in the theatres, on the throughfares, everywhere, even in the nuptial bed. We wish them joy of the delightfully odorous sensations that await them. It will be a glorious consummation that the negro-worshippers will at last be in the full embrace of their idol, at least until they shall cry for mercy and the Supreme Court, a year or two hence, shall come to their relief.

QUESTIONS

1. What were the arguments in favor of the Civil Rights Act of 1866?
2. Why was the Civil Rights Act important to the Reconstruction of the South?
3. What aspects of the Civil Rights Act interfered, according to Southerners and President Johnson, with the concept of states' rights?
4. Why did the *New York World* believe the Civil Rights Act would be a failure?
5. What were the arguments against the Civil Rights Act of 1866?

NOTES

1. LaWanda Cox, *Freedom, Racism, and Reconstruction* (Athens: University of Georgia Press, 1997), 103.

2. Ibid., 90.

CHAPTER 9

Black Suffrage: Before the Vote, 1865–66

One central theme in the Reconstruction story is the efforts to expand the rights of Southern blacks in the face of racism. Everyone—those who supported black suffrage and those who did not—knew that nothing was more fundamental to a democracy than the protection of an individual's right to cast a ballot at the polls. Those who supported the right of blacks to vote acknowledged the importance of the franchise not only as a basic democratic principle but also as a measure of political expediency. Those who fought against black suffrage feared that if blacks voted, the white South would die.

Although black suffrage was never part of either President Abraham Lincoln's or President Andrew Johnson's Reconstruction policies, it was certainly part of the radical Republicans' plan, even before the end of the war. The radical leadership in Congress believed that the franchise was the only way to avoid a return to slavery in the South. But conservatives and moderates warned that the enfranchisement of freedmen would be a dangerous move that could once again tear the nation apart. Southerners believed not only that blacks were incapable of appreciating and using the vote but also that the franchise would disrupt the newly instituted contract labor program that had been used to force freedmen back to the plantations.[1]

President Johnson initially noted that states might want to consider enfranchising former slaves who were literate and propertied and had served in the war. But the decision to give even limited rights of suffrage would be left to the states, not to the federal government.[2] Johnson even went so far as to suggest to states like Mississippi that if they would enfranchise those who could read and write and who owned at least $250 worth of property then the South would "completely disarm the adversary" and "the Radicals, who are wild upon Negro franchise, will be completely foiled in their attempts to keep the Southern States from renewing their relations to the

Union. . . . "[3] Mississippi did not heed Johnson's advice, nor did Johnson give similar advice to other Southern states.

But despite the radicals' support of the black vote, a solid backing by a broad spectrum of Republicans did not exist. Moderate and conservative Republicans feared that black enfranchisement would hurt the party, and suffrage would be so divisive as to halt any Reconstruction efforts. Democrats also had several well-rehearsed arguments, including the belief that radicals were using suffrage as a way of punishing the South.

In the South, nothing created a greater fear among whites than giving the vote to blacks. Newspapers warned that Negro suffrage meant Negro supremacy and the ruin of the South because blacks were unfit for the political life. The *Richmond (Va.) Times* wrote that if suffrage were extended to Negroes "we shall next look for a movement . . . to endow baboons and monkeys with electoral privileges, and, perhaps during the present generation, beef cattle, hogs and all other livestock will be admitted to the polls."[4]

Southern newspapers urged blacks not even to think about voting. Instead, freedmen should settle down, go to work, and leave politics and voting to the Southern white men who are the black man's natural guardian.

Many in the North and South argued that it was hypocritical for Republicans to advocate suffrage for Southern blacks when blacks in the North did not have the vote. In 1865, only six Northern states allowed blacks to vote, each with varying degrees of discriminatory qualifications. That year, Wisconsin, Connecticut, and Minnesota failed to pass amendments or referenda extending the franchise to blacks. Between 1865 and 1869, only 2 of 11 referenda to amend state constitutions to allow blacks to vote passed in the North. Those two were in Iowa and Minnesota—and only after two earlier defeats in each state.[5]

Meanwhile, Johnson took every occasion to express his views about blacks voting. In February 1866, he met with a small delegation of black leaders, including black abolitionist Frederick Douglass, and told them that giving the vote to blacks would endanger their freedom as well as incite a race war. He explained that if blacks were not satisfied with their life in a South ruled by white racists then they were free to leave the country. Johnson believed, as did most Southerners, that blacks were intellectually incapable of exercising the franchise.[6]

Although freedmen did not have the right to vote or hold office, they nevertheless organized themselves politically to speak as one loud voice to whites in the North and South. In almost all states, blacks participated in statewide freedmen's conventions, where they discussed problems facing the newly freed slaves. Taking up leadership positions in the conventions were not only former slaves but also free blacks from the North, many of whom were agents with the Freedmen's Bureau. The conventions addressed local problems, drafted petitions to the white governors, and read letters from Northern supporters. But their main work was to bring to the foreground their desires as a newly freed people for civil and political equality, for freedom from black codes and violence, and for the right to vote.

Blacks also participated in mock elections—with registration, polling places, and ballots. Organized by the Union League, Equal Rights Leagues, or the local Republican clubs, these elections served as training ground for the future exercise of the vote. In some cases, the black votes were added to the "legal" white-only election and sent to the state legislature or to Congress with an appeal to have the election legalized.

The message being sent by Southern blacks on the issue of suffrage was very clear—without the vote, blacks would have no hope of ever enjoying their freedom. As one Virginia freedman stated, "The only salvation for us besides the power of the Government is in the possession of the ballot. Give us this, and we will protect ourselves."[7] To the argument by whites that blacks were too ignorant to vote, blacks countered that ignorance knew no racial boundaries. If ignorance were to be the test for voting, then as many whites as blacks would fail.

Throughout 1866, the voices calling for enfranchisement of blacks grew louder. After listening to speeches by Douglass and suffragist Anna Dickinson, members of the Republican convention meeting in Philadelphia voted (albeit only by a slim margin) on a resolution calling for black suffrage. But as Leon Litwack writes, it was not the activities of Southern blacks, Northern abolitionists, or even radical Republicans that brought about the extension of suffrage to black Southerners. Instead, it was "the insistence by white governments in the South that the essentials of the old order be maintained without a modicum of concession and the equally unyielding determination of the president to validate the work and the spirit of those governments."[8]

Initially, few Republican newspapers supported giving the vote to blacks, believing that the decision should be left in the hands of white Southerners. But as the South returned to its old habits by passing black codes, forcing blacks back to plantations, and committing violence against blacks, attitudes in the North changed. The readings favoring black suffrage begin with an editorial by George W. Curtis of *Harper's Weekly*. Curtis, one of the first editors to speak out in favor of the franchise, argues that if ignorance is a reason not to enfranchise blacks, it should be a reason not to enfranchise other classes of Americans. The next reading is by Horace Greeley, who eloquently explains why the vote is important to protect freedom for blacks. The next entry, by John Silsby, is an editorial from a Southern black Republican newspaper expressing disagreement with Johnson's contention that black suffrage should be determined by the majority and that black suffrage would antagonize whites. The final selection, by Henry J. Raymond from the *New York Times,* proposes that suffrage should be based on all voters' ability to read and write.

The first antisuffrage reading, by Moses Beach, declares that the issue of black suffrage should be left to the states to decide. Of course, that meant the issue should be left to white voters. The next reading, by W.B. Phillips, typifies the kind of scare tactics often used by Democratic newspapers. In this case, the argument against the franchise and black equality replaces miscegenation with communalism. The last reading, by Samuel Bard, calls on Southerners to stop fighting black suffrage and instead embrace it and use it just as the Republicans would.

FAVORING BLACK SUFFRAGE

George W. Curtis: "The Blacks and the Ballot"

One of the enduring questions regarding enfranchising blacks was if they would be required to meet a higher standard than whites to vote. If education were a prerequisite, would the South educate freedmen?

Harper's Weekly, May 20, 1865

The question of the hour then is, when the Government is ready to allow an election for any purpose whatever to be held in any such State, who shall be permitted to vote? . . .

That the mass of the population at the South, both white and black is ignorant, is very true. But so are great masses of the Northern voters. Education is a good thing; but it appears that some of the staunchest patriots in the land can not read, and that some of the basest traitors are highly educated. . . .

The question is not whether, abstractly, political privilege should depend upon education. It is, whether . . . we shall require conditions of our black fellow-countrymen whose fidelity has saved the nation which are not required of the whites in the same States, nor in other States of ignorant foreigners who can not speak our language, and who have no especial interest in our institutions. Instruct them, say some, and their political rights will follow. But why is that not equally true of the whites? If ignorance is the difficulty, why intrust [*sic*] the States to ignorant white men? By such a plan a discrimination is made at the outset based upon color. The Government says, in effect, that ignorant loyal men who are black are not fit to vote, but ignorant loyal men who are white are fit. The Government thus flings its whole weight against the ignorant men who have been true to it, and favors those who have been false. The mischief is incalculable. For by that act it recognizes what is called the inferiority of the blacks, which has been always urged as the reason for enslaving them. . . .

The colored race was brought into this country against its will and by our inhumanity and cupidity. It has wonderfully increased until there are now some four millions of them among us. Their blood in every degree is mingled with the blood of the whites. They are men and Americans as much as we. Their ancestors came from Africa, as ours from England, Holland, Germany, or Ireland. They are an essential, integral, inevitable, most valuable and important part of our population. . . .

We have now the power and the opportunity of settling this question of the colored race in this country which has rent us from the beginning, and will heave and harry us until it is put honorably to rest. We have already declared them to be men and citizens. Our Government rests upon the broad principle that governments justly exist by the consent of the governed. For that principle the colored men fought with our fathers in the Revolution; and side by side in the fiercest fields of this war they have defended it side by side with our brothers. Within the enemy's lines they have been the guides, the messengers, the friends upon whom we have uniformly relied. To see a black face was to find a true heart. Do we mean to be as faithful and honorable and friendly as they have been? Do we mean to trust them as they have trusted us? Do we mean to give them the chance of securing their own welfare as we have the chance of securing ours? Do we mean to be just? If we do, we shall give them a vote in the Reconstruction of the insurrectionary States. If we are unwilling to do it, our victory has come too soon, and we shall pay the penalty of premature success.

Horace Greeley: "Suffrage for the Weak"

For Horace Greeley, the franchise is the ultimate sign of freedom and the only weapon against tyranny.

New York Tribune, June 14, 1865

A vote has two values. It is, first, the expression of an opinion, which may or may not affect the material interests of the voter, but which he esteems as the performance of his relative duties to his fellow creatures—as something which he owes to the aggregate interests of society. But, in the second place, a vote is the weapon which, so far as the infirmity of the human device will permit, protects natural equality from the obtrusion of artificial distinctions, diminishes the undue influence of accidental position, and asserts the supremacy of the individual will over dictation, compulsion and the selfishness of the mass. . . . The right to vote implies the duty of acquiescence in the will of the majority; but, when that right is ignored or speciously withheld, the disfranchised citizen . . . owes no obedience to those laws, to the enactment of which he did not consent. . . . But now we ask the reader to consider the perilous condition which the Freedman is placed, not, it must be remembered, by any act of his own, but first, through the besotted ambition of his quondam owner, and in the next place our own act, by the act of this nation, in changing his social position. We have, it must be remembered, called the Black to the performance of new duties; we have, in a word, liberated him from galling and grinding bondage. . . . We have made this slave nominally free. But of what value will this freedom be to him, if it bring no means of preserving and of protecting it. If the old Slaveholders are to retain in the reconstructed States the old supremacy, are to dictate measures, without any check, are to domineer after the old fashion, this gift of freedom to the Black will be only a cruel mockery, leaving him still at the mercy of his oppressors, who may hamper his movements, harass his life, check his progress, keep down his wages, and make his last state worse than his first. . . . On the contrary, as he will be more heartily hated, so will he be more heartily oppressed. Are the Blacks to be left in this hideous limbo, vibrating between freedom and slavery, in an anomalous and hopeless position, free in name and serfs in fact? . . . We have made the Blacks "free." But what is "freedom?" Let the honest voter, who is equally proud of his vote and of his honesty answer the question! . . . Would he consider himself "free" if the right of voting were taken entirely away from him, and bestowed exclusively upon men who were two inches taller or shorter, a little richer, a little poorer, a little blacker or a little whiter than he? There is not a voter in this city who, if he were thus disfranchised, would not loudly and lugubriously howl to the world that he was made a slave.

The Rebel Man-Owners have lost much—houses, lands, beasts of burden, cash and credit; but if we wish to bestow upon them a substantial consolation, and give them an excellent chance of recovering the old power which they have lost, nine times intensified, we have only to leave them in their position so often claimed of "superior race." The Blacks will be down again in twenty years, and we Northern Whites will be down with them.

John Silsby: "The Colored Delegation"

President Johnson met in February with a small delegation of black men, including abolitionist Frederick Douglass. At the meeting, Johnson told the men that he did not favor black suffrage and believed that blacks were better off under the management of their former white owners. Needless to say, the report of this meeting did not sit well with black Republican newspapers such as the Mobile (Ala.) Nationalist.

Mobile (Ala.) Nationalist, **February 22, 1866**

Two special reasons seem to be offered by the President for withholding suffrage from the colored man at this time. First, that it would be unjust if a majority of citizens are opposed to it; and second, that the mutual hostility of the lower classes of whites and the negroes might thus produce a war of races.

If the right is to be withheld so long as the majority of the people of the State are opposed to it, then in South Carolina and Mississippi, where a majority of the people are colored, this objection cannot obtain. In those States, not only should the colored people be enfranchised, but the question should be duly tested, whether a majority of the people will concede the rights of suffrage to the whites. Mark, this is simply an application of the principles to which we have referred. We do not believe that any majority, however great, can rightly disfranchise a minority however small. The right of suffrage pertains to all men, in virtue of their being men. But if the question of suffrage pertains to the States, to be decided by a majority of the citizens thereof, then the disfranchisement of the whites of South Carolina and Mississippi must be acquiesced in, if the colored people, who there are in the majority shall so decide.

The assertion that the enfranchisement of the negro will breed a war of races, is the objection against emancipation revived, and which the history of the last four years so completely disproves.

We confess to a feeling of deep disappointment in regard to our President's recent speech. We had thought that the noble utterances which he had put forth from time to time were the indices of more resources that would prove equal to any actual emergency. We would not suffer ourselves to believe that a man who could utter such noble sentiments could do otherwise than follow up his principles to their logical conclusion. When lo, to our astonishment, we find him enshrining that grim old monster id[ea], negro hate, whose loathsome form we had hoped would never again be permitted to stalk forth from his cave; and under the plea of an impending war of races, insisting that the African shall again be immolated upon the altar of human skulls. Mr. Johnson teaches that, as in the days of Buchanan, black men have no rights which white prejudice may not deny. We fear that much sorrow is yet in store for us, unless we show more willingness to learn the lessons of God's providences.

Henry J. Raymond: "Amnesty and Suffrage"

Some moderates who wanted to see the Southern states return quickly to the Union offered a compromise—if the South would accept universal suffrage for blacks, the North would accept amnesty for all rebels. This moderate compromise, however, had detractors in the North and South and in both parties. The New York Times *favored an "impartial intelligence suf-frage"—qualified privilege based on the ability to read and write.*

New York Times, November 22, 1866

During the last session of Congress, Senator Stewart, from Nevada, pro-posed Universal Suffrage and University Amnesty as the basis of restora-tion;—that is if the Southern States would adopt universal suffrage, they should receive a general amnesty—and be restored, as states and as individ-uals, to all political rights which they enjoyed before the war. The proposi-tion elicited but little discussion at the time, as it seemed to embody what was most obnoxious to both sections, and likely to be acceptable, therefore to neither. The Tribune afterward adopted it, and has urged it with a good deal of zeal. But it is not seconded by a considerable portion of the Press, nor can the proposition be said as yet to have been seriously entertained by the country.

Whenever it is we think it will be condemned. Neither branch of it is cal-culated to meet public approval. There is really but a small portion of the people of the Northern States who desire universal negro suffrage, though nine-tenths of them hold that color alone should not debar any man from voting. Whatever may be the practice, in theory at least, voting is still held to involve responsibility and to require some sort of qualification. Voting makes our laws, chooses our rulers, and carries on the whole machinery of civil society;—and nobody capable of holding any opinion on any subject, can doubt that making laws, choosing rules and administering the affairs of a great nation, require some qualifications of intelligence and character. Everybody knows, too, that a large proportion of the negroes of the South,—those employed as field hands during the reign of Slavery,—are utterly igno-rant,—utterly incapable of exercising the slightest judgment, or acting with the least intelligence, in political matters. If admitted to the suffrage, they will not vote; they will be simply the tools of somebody who will. This is a necessity of their condition. It is not their fault but their misfortune. Not be-cause they are black, therefore, but because they are ignorant,—too ignorant to be wisely and safely intrusted [*sic*] with such a power, it is undesirable that all the negroes should be admitted to vote in the Southern States.

Equally unacceptable would be the proposition for a *universal* amnesty. Such an amnesty would readmit to every right of citizenship, to every civil and political privilege, to every office, State and Federal, in the United States, every man who was engaged in any way in the rebellion. To this we do not believe the people will assent. They may excuse those who were dragged into secession,—or even those who went into it, under a sincere be-lief that their first allegiance was due to their State Governments; and they may be willing to see them again in office. But they will not consent that the original authors of the rebellion . . . shall again resume the official power which they so grossly abused. . . .

Universal suffrage, therefore, instead of being an offset to the objections felt against a universal amnesty, being itself objectionable, would only aggravate the hostility against that measure. A *qualified* suffrage and a *limited* amnesty would be much more likely to command the approval of the people. If the South would extend suffrage to the negroes, in common with all citizens, basing it upon certain conditions, intelligence, payment of taxes, or whatever other qualifications they might prescribe, an amnesty which would remove all disabilities from persons engaged in the rebellion, except that the original authors of the movement should be forever excluded from Federal office, would undoubtedly be conceded by the North.

The question is not likely, however, to come up for practical action. It is the purpose of the extreme leaders of the dominant party in Congress to secure the exclusion of the Southern States from political power until after the Presidential elections. This is their specific aim. Questions of amnesty and suffrage may be brought forward and discussed and possibly acted upon,—but not as substitutes for the Constitutional Amendment. That will be insisted upon as a *sine qua non*—at least until the South seems likely to accept it.

EXPRESSING CONCERNS ABOUT BLACK SUFFRAGE

Moses Beach: "Negro Suffrage in the South"

Most Democratic newspapers in the Northern cities refrained from racist language and instead argued that the issue of black suffrage should be left to the voters, not to Congress or the president.

New York Sun, May 9, 1865

The people have been led to believe that the war which is just closing would forever put the detested "negro question" at rest, as an element of political discussion. But no sooner is the first glimmer of peace discerned, than the politicians begin to dig up this apparently irrepressible question, with a hope of making it once more a subject of contention in the realm of politics. Slavery has been sunk so deep by the war that the most persistent partisan will hardly attempt to make political capital out of the institution; but the negroes remain, and the settlement of their status under the new order of things is already exercising the minds of party leaders. "Negro suffrage" is the successor of "negro slavery" as a subject of political division. The radicals claim that every negro, from saddle color to ebony, shall be entitled to the same rights, with respect to voting, that white citizens enjoy. They insist, also that this right shall be granted them in settling the questions of "Reconstruction," and that it shall be protected by the military power.—

On the other hand the "conservatives" contend that unrestricted negro franchise would be productive of great social evils and that it would be highly pernicious to the interests of the South. Now the truth is, that neither party takes the right view of the question. We hold to the old Democratic doctrine that the States have the right to "regulate their domestic institutions in their own way, subject only to the Constitution of the United States." The constitutions of the several Southern States are valid at the present time, just as they were before the war. They have not been abrogated by the act of secession, nor have they been repealed or changed in a legal way.

According to these instruments, negroes have not the right to vote, the people of each State have the power to amend the Constitution thereof, and if they desire to grant the elective franchise to negroes, no power can lawfully prevent them. . . . A state is supreme, with regard to the regulations of its own government, so long as there is no conflict with the Federal Constitution, and the people have a perfect right to permit or refuse negro suffrage, to make a distinction of shade, allowing for the saddle color to vote, to make property qualification or make any other regulations of that character that they deem advisable. Therefore, it is a waste of time for politicians to trouble themselves about what should or should not be done about the question of "negro suffrage" in the South. The people will settle these matters in their own way, just as the people of the Northern States do, and it is for them to say whether negroes shall or shall not vote.

W.B. Phillips: "The Abolitionists and Their New Crusade"

The most often used scare tactic against black suffrage was that it was but the first step toward "amalgamation and miscegenation." Massachusetts senator Charles Sumner, the strongest proponent of black suffrage, often was called "that old miscegenator" by Democrats. In this article, the New York Herald *adds another weapon, Fourierism, which is a philosophy developed in the 1840s that advocated communal living where everything, including husbands, wives, and children, are shared.*

New York Herald, August 7, 1865

Well may every lover of his country exclaim, what next? Is there no limit to their revolutionary demands? No end to their agitation and disturbance of the peace and prosperity of the country, or are the Abolitionists determined to continue their crusade until the people are forced to either adopt the social and connubial equality, free and universal amalgamation of races and sexes of the Fourierite phalanx order, or to resort to the alternative of a war of races, and the extinction of the blacks on this continent? One or the other of these dreadful results must follow as the logical result of the renewal and continuation of the agitation of these philosophers. The severe lessons of the past, the bitter fruits of a fierce war, and the development of crime in its most horrible phase, which is now following in the wake of war, appears to have no effect upon these agitators; but they are, on the other hand, entering upon a new contest, more dangerous in its character, more disastrous in its results, than any which has agitated the nations of the civilized world, either in ancient or modern times. . . . It is well that the public is forewarned as to their intentions, and it would be still better if it was as clearly understood as to the real concession demanded by the Abolitionists or the alternative of war. . . .

Like the Jacobins of France, their tastes of blood has but sharpened their appetite for more. Unable to obtain full political control of the nation through the abolition of slavery and freedom of the blacks, they are renewing their efforts to accomplish that end in some other way. They now demand that the right of voting shall be universally conferred upon the blacks. Through this they hope to obtain full political supremacy throughout the country, and thus force upon us the Fourierite phalanx millennium which they failed to inaugurate at the early stage of their first crusade. This is evidently the end which they are laboring for which is nothing more than the political reign of the Abolitionists, with universal negro suffrage, universal free love and amalgamation of races. Such, at least, is the inevitable tendency of their new crusade, if their past course is any index to the future. Are the people ready for the inauguration of a millennium of that kind? If not, then let one and all rally to the support of the practical policy of President Johnson, and put a final quietus upon the new crusade of the Abolitionists, of which the exponent of the Fourierite phalanx doctrine, *The Tribune,* had become the special organ.

Samuel Bard: "A Southern View"

The reader might be puzzled to learn, after reading this editorial, that the Atlanta New Era *was a Republican newspaper. However, like most Republican newspapers in the South at the time, it had a decidedly conservative bent. Samuel Bard, a native of Louisiana, saw the black franchise as inevitable even though he did not favor it. The question now was how to manipulate the black vote toward President Johnson's National Union Party.*

Atlanta New Era, June 17, 1866

The negro will ultimately vote if he stays here. Every thoughtful man sees this in the not distant future. We are powerless to prevent it. We are without voice in the government; without political power, without the means of asserting our rights under a written constitution. The scheme of the radicals must succeed temporarily. But that very success will prove their ruin as it did the ruin of their ancestors in the days of Cromwell. It will put a weapon of defense into our hands.

Shall we hesitate to use it? Shall we vote the negro and through him control radicalism? Or shall radicalism vote the negro and through him control our local as well as Federal policy? Shall we use this power in legitimate self-defense, or shall the radicals seize it to complete our destruction? How do we propose meeting this issue? Final decision and action cannot be delayed a great while longer. The crisis is not distant. It is here now. What shall be our decision? Pride, or something else, prevented the skillful use of a defensive weapon during the war, and the instrument of destruction, was naturally enough, turned against us. Shall this pride, or this something else, induce similar indiscretion now? Let us begin to think earnestly and seriously on this matter. We have abandoned all hope of a separate nationality. Shall we likewise abandon all manhood, all hope of civil and religious liberty? Should we not, in common with the conservative Union men of all sections, rather change tactics, come down from our stilts, waive mere formalities where vital interests are at stake and fight the devil with fire?

QUESTIONS

1. What were the political consequences of excluding blacks from voting in the South? Were those consequences as great in the North?
2. Why did so many people believe education should be a test for blacks to vote but not for whites?
3. Why did so few people accept the concept of universal suffrage, or suffrage without qualification?
4. What role did hyperbole play in the verbal sparring about black suffrage?
5. According to white Southerners, who should determine if blacks could vote?

NOTES

1. Eric Foner, *Reconstruction: America's Unfinished Revolution, 1863–1877* (New York: Harper & Row, 1988), 220.

2. Ibid., 180.

3. Brooks D. Simpson, *The Reconstruction Presidents* (Lawrence: University Press of Kansas, 1998), 79.

4. Quoted in Donna L. Dickerson, " 'Got no Souls . . . ': Racism in Southern Reconstruction Newspapers," *Proceedings of the Association for Education in Journalism and Mass Communications, Southeast Colloquium* 1 (March 1992): 18–26.

5. LaWanda Cox, *Freedom, Racism, and Reconstruction* (Athens: University of Georgia Press, 1997), 137.

6. Leon Litwack, *Been in the Storm So Long: The Aftermath of Slavery* (New York: Vintage Books, 1979), 530.

7. Ibid., 531.

8. Ibid., 537.

CHAPTER 10

The Fourteenth Amendment, 1866

One of the most infamous cases ever decided by the U.S. Supreme Court was *Dred Scott v. Sanford* in 1857. In this case, the Court ruled that Congress was prohibited from abolishing slavery and that blacks—free or enslaved—were not citizens of the United States. Without citizenship, said the Court, blacks could not claim rights under state or federal law. Ten years later, the *Dred Scott* decision had been nullified by a war, by statute, and by two constitutional amendments: the Thirteenth Amendment abolished slavery, the Civil Rights Act of 1866 guaranteed citizenship and protected the equal rights of all citizens, and the Fourteenth Amendment made citizenship and civil rights a constitutional guarantee.

But despite the legal end to slavery, Southern states continued to insist they had the sole authority to define the status and determine the rights of their people. Freedmen continued to be kept in a state of bondage through repressive black codes and economic intimidation, and local courts refused to prosecute whites who abridged the personal and property rights of blacks.

While President Johnson sanctioned much of this behavior, Congress had other ideas. In December 1865, Congress established a Joint Committee of Reconstruction (sometimes referred to as the Joint Committee of Fifteen) to investigate conditions in the South. For the next five months, the committee read reports and heard testimony from Southern governors, military officers, Southern blacks, white Unionists, and even such notables as General Robert E. Lee and former Confederate vice president Alexander H. Stephens. The committee concluded that the former Confederate states were not entitled to representation in the Congress until "adequate security for future peace and safety" was guaranteed. The only way to guarantee such safety was to protect the civil and political rights of all the citizens.[1]

Although Republicans had gone to great lengths to embed these guarantees in the Civil Rights Act of 1866, it was important to give them constitutional status since laws are subject to repeal or can be declared unconstitutional by courts. So, Congress placed the principles and policies of equal rights beyond the reach of the president and the Southern states by embedding them in a constitutional amendment.

The Fourteenth Amendment, composed of four separate resolutions, often was referred to in the press as the "amendments" because it had so many sections. Section One states that all persons born or naturalized in the United States are citizens of the United States and of the state in which they reside. The amendment guarantees private rights against state interference, stating "no State shall make or enforce any law which shall abridge the privileges or immunities of citizens of the Untied States; nor shall any State deprive any person of life, liberty or property without due process of law; nor deny to any person within its jurisdiction the equal protection of the laws."

Before the war, a slave was counted as three-fifths of a person for purposes of representation in the House of Representatives. Under Section Two of the new amendment, freedmen would be counted as full persons but only if they were allowed to vote. Should Southern states choose not to enfranchise black men, their representation in the House would decrease significantly. Section Three barred from public office those men who participated in the rebellion after having previously taken an oath to support the Constitution. The purpose was to disenfranchise former rebels who occupied many public offices in Southern states. Congress removed this disability in 1870. Section Four prohibited the payment of wartime debts incurred by the Southern states.

The Fourteenth Amendment was a compromise. It did not call for universal suffrage, confiscation of rebel lands, or economic relief for freedmen. While Republicans saw it as a compromise and supported it, Democrats and Southerners viewed it as a radical document initiating a fundamental change in the relationship between the federal government and the states.

The amendment passed Congress on June 13, 1866. Although proposed amendments cannot be vetoed by the president, President Johnson denounced it. He did not believe that the states would ratify an amendment that threatened to destroy their autonomy. Throughout the summer of 1866, Johnson campaigned against the amendment, particularly warning the Southern states not to ratify it.

The ink had scarcely dried on the document when Tennessee, ignoring Johnson's protests, ratified the new amendment and was granted readmission to the Union. At this point, there had been no directive that ratification was a requirement for readmission, but in drafting the joint resolution readmitting Tennessee, Congress strongly hinted that such would be the case for all states. However, Congress adjourned in July before making such a pledge.

The Fourteenth Amendment became the central issue in the campaign of 1866. Despite Johnson's hope that the amendment would lead to the defeat of Republicans, it actually increased Republican officeholders from Congress on down. The key to the Republican success was the moderates' assurances that the Fourteenth Amendment was, in fact, a compromise between Johnson's policy of immediate restoration and the radical platform of suffrage and confiscation. Throughout the campaign Republicans "waved the bloody shirt," reminding people that if the amendment was not ratified then the lives of thousands of young men lost in the war (as well as the blacks and Unionists who had been killed in recent riots in Memphis and New Orleans) had been wasted.[2]

Although Southerners believed that the section basing representation on qualified male voters would eventually lead to black suffrage, the clause that generated the greatest resentment was the one disenfranchising former white officeholders. These were the South's leaders, and to ratify the amendment meant a repudiation of those men. By February 1867, 10 Southern legislatures had followed Johnson's instructions to reject the amendment.

But rejection gave Congress additional justification for creating a more drastic plan for Reconstruction. Through the winter of 1867, Congress labored to create a policy that would once and for all bind the South to Republican principles. The result was the Reconstruction Act of 1867, which divided the 10 remaining Southern states into 5 military districts, each with a military commander. Existing civil governments were declared provisional and subject to military oversight. Voters—all black and white men—not disqualified by the terms of the Fourteenth Amendment were to elect delegates to constitutional conventions. The states also must ratify the Fourteenth Amendment.

In 1867 and 1868, Southern states were forced to reconsider the Fourteenth Amendment, and this time the votes were in favor of ratification.

The section in favor of the Fourteenth Amendment begins with an editorial, by George W. Curtis from *Harper's Weekly*, that argues that the amendment is indeed a compromise and one that everyone should accept. The second entry, by William W. Harding, explains that a constitutional amendment is necessary to keep the South from reverting to its old ways once rebel states are readmitted. The next selection, by Charles Nordhoff, is directed at Southerners, urging them to accept the amendment or suffer the consequences. The last editorial, by Alexander G. Murray, from the *Griffin (Ga.) American Union* reminds the editor of the *Athens (Ga.) Watchman* that the radicals are in charge and must be obeyed.

The readings in the second section begin with an editorial, by Manton Marble, accusing the Fourteenth Amendment of being a black suffrage amendment that no Southern state will ratify, thus ensuring that the Southern states will forever remain outside the Union. The second and third entries by Samuel Mason and John H. Christy reject the suggestion that the South should acquiesce. The next editorial, by John Forsyth, calls on Southerners to spurn all attempts by the North to control the South. The last two editorials are examples of the demagoguery so often found in Southern newspapers when discussing any radical policy.

SUPPORTING THE RATIFICATION OF THE FOURTEENTH AMENDMENT

George W. Curtis: "The Congressional Plan of Reorganization"

Although George W. Curtis would have preferred a more radical constitutional amendment, he admits that the Fourteenth Amendment is a good compromise between President Johnson and the radicals, and one that answered some of Johnson's concerns about the South.

Harper's Weekly, May 12, 1866

The propositions of the Reconstruction Committee will strike every thoughtful citizen as perfectly reasonable. They seem to us to justify the hope of the most truly intelligent and patriotic persons that Congress would propose no policy upon which the whole Union party of the country, including the President, might not agree. Some concessions of opinion were inevitable upon all sides. Those who held with Mr. Thaddeus Stevens that there should be general confiscation, or with Mr. Sumner that impartial suffrage should be immediately established throughout the country, or with the President that no farther conditions whatever were necessary, must have seen that the opinion of the country did not support them, and that all must meet upon some firm and moderate middle ground such as the Committee now offer.

The objection to what is called the President's policy is plain and conclusive. It is that, by allowing the late rebel States to resume their full relations in the Union immediately, and without further provision, those States would have actually gained political power by the rebellion. This gain arises from the fact that every colored man, as a slave, counted as three-fifths of a man in the basis of representation; but as a freeman he counts as five-fifths. In a State like South Carolina, therefore, where the colored population is half or even more than half of the whole, and where that half is disfranchised, every voter has practically twice the power of a voter in a State like

Connecticut. This is an absurdity and injustice so conspicuous as to demand instant adjustment.

On the other hand, the objection to the imposition of equal suffrage by the National Government as a precedent condition of resumption of full rights in the Union is practical and twofold. In the first place, it is hardly to be presumed that the States which prohibit equal suffrage, or deny it to a colored skin altogether, would insist upon its adoption by the suspended States; and, in the second place, such a proposition would have been very widely regarded as a radical blow at the most sacred of State rights, and a consummation of centralization. . . .

But we see no good reason for supposing that all reasonable and patriotic men should not sincerely unite upon the propositions presented. . . . They declare simply, in the first place, that no State shall abridge the privileges of citizens of the United States. Such a proposition is its own irresistible argument. A citizen of this country should be equally a citizen everywhere in it; this is plain, and therefore all his civil rights as a citizen of the United States should be sacred wherever the national flag floats. . . .

In the second place, whenever the elective franchise shall be denied to any portion of the male citizens of a State who are of age, except for crime or participation in the rebellion, the basis of representation shall be reduced in the proportion which the number of such male citizens shall bear to the whole number of male citizens not less than twenty-one years of age. In other words, if South Carolina shall choose to disfranchise 100,000 of her citizens because of their color, or New York shall choose to do the same thing because of want of property, then each of those States shall suffer in the national representation just in that proportion. . . .

These are the propositions of the Committee, which we trust will be unanimously adopted by the Union vote in Congress, because they are perfectly just and moderate, and because they do not claim to reap more than has been sown. They simply define and secure the legitimate result of the war as recognized by the general conviction of the loyal country, and as it has been often strongly stated by President Johnson. They contain nothing vindictive. . . . Here is the plain proof that Congress seeks only the speediest reorganization of the Union upon the most temperate and reasonable conditions.

William W. Harding: "The Constitutional Amendments"

William W. Harding, a moderate Republican, expresses concern that without requiring Southern states to ratify the Fourteenth Amendment, anything that the South does to get back into the Union will be undone once they are readmitted.

Philadelphia Inquirer, October 1, 1866

As we have hitherto said, the policy of the President is to admit the States lately rebellious to immediate participation in all the rights which they possessed before the war without further guarantees for their good behavior than can be derived from the adoption of the Constitutional Amendment abolishing slavery. All the rest that has been done in the South is founded upon State action, and unless some additional security is taken, may be set aside by the same authority which ordained it, just as a law which is enacted may be afterwards repealed. The President thinks that these agreements are sufficient, and entitle the Southern States to a restoration of the rights which they forfeited by the Rebellion. Congress, however, looks at the matter in all its aspects, and is anxious that whatever may be arranged shall be riveted by measures which have the strongest and most binding effect, and which cannot be set aside without difficulty. In short, Congress wants Constitutional guarantees that the peace of the country is assured as strongly as is possible by human laws. It is well enough for State conventions to annul secession ordinances or repeal them, as was done in some cases, to abolish slavery and repudiate the Rebel debt. But as a State does these things, so may a State undo them, and there could be no interference with such action. The President is satisfied with a knot which can be unloosed by those who tied it. Congress is not. It demands such material fastening as cannot be undone, and in order to secure it propose that the Constitution of the United States shall be amended by important additions relating to this controversy. . . .

Charles Nordhoff: "Congress and the Southern States"

This is one of many editorials printed in the New York Evening Post *that pointed out the problems the South will encounter by its refusal to ratify the Fourteenth Amendment.*

New York Evening Post, December 18, 1866

It is strange the southern men do not see that to reject the amendment is to subject themselves to harder terms. Already several plans of reconstruction are broached in Congress, any one of which is more distasteful to the southern leaders than the amendment. A well-informed correspondent writes us from Washington: "There can be no doubt that the opportunity for the adoption by the excluded states of the terms offered in the constitutional amendment is rapidly passing away." Congress will not wait very long.

As soon as it is satisfied that the southern states will not have the amendment, it will proceed to other measures.

It is useless to argue against such a course; the people in the recent elections have demanded and justified it. It is of no use to show that the whole proceeding is extra-constitutional, for the people reply that defiant and unpunished traitors shall not take advantage of constitutional forms to gain unfair advantages; they will not have such a condition of things as makes a vote in the South represent twice as much as a vote in the North; they will in some way exclude from power the leaders and originators of the rebellion. If it is said that measures necessary to obtain such legislation are extra-constitutional, and to the extent revolutionary, the people reply: We accept the risk. Justice is to be done, safety secured, and treason punished, at all hazards.

Alexander G. Murray: "Sensible"

The Griffin (Ga.) American Union *was a moderate Republican newspaper, and like many Republican newspapers in the South during this period it took a great risk in supporting Republican policies. This editorial is a response to John H. Christy of the* Athens (Ga.) Watchman, *which appears in the following section.*

Griffin (Ga.) American Union, reprinted in the Mobile (Ala.) Nationalist, July 10, 1866

Why, my brother Christy, do you not know that the word "Rump," as you use it, is a direct insult to the ruling power in the government? Do you not know that such an insult to the government, and the general haughty, defiant tone and temper of the Southern press, have defeated the President's policy, and made the constitutional amendment necessary?

Do you not know that the constitutional amendment making certain classes at the South ineligible to office, is one of the restraints of the government, and that it is applied to supplant the leaders of Southern ideas and politics, so as to make room for those who can readily harmonize with Northern feeling and sentiment, and that, if this restraint should be insufficient, others will be added? Do you not know that Northern ideas and sentiments now control the government, and that the rebel States can never be fully restored until they all harmonize with those sentiments? Do you not know that the result of the war has settled the question forever, that the South is to be no longer "the South," as it used to be but that henceforth the South is to become Northernized in feeling, sentiment, ideas and politics?

Do you not know all those things and that the only effect of opposition in the South is to multiply and increase in intensity the woes and miseries with which our people are already overburdened? Do you wish to distress our people more and more (for that is all you can do) in order to gratify a selfish price, and maintain a haughty and defiant tone and temper toward those you call "enemies"? . . .

Come, brother Christy cool down! Take a sensible, reasonable view of things as they are. Cease your opposition to the ruling power in the government. Learn to respect the position men occupy, even if you cannot cherish a friendly regard for the men, and let that harmony be restored which is so essential to the well-being of our people. . . .

Opposing the Ratification of the Fourteenth Amendment

Manton Marble: "The Constitutional Amendment"

Democratic newspapers like the New York World *initially would concede nothing to the Fourteenth Amendment despite the fact that it was a truly moderate proposition. Instead, they saw the amendment as a bag of tricks, each one meant to snare the South into ratification.*

New York World, June 15, 1866

As our readers are apprised the constitutional amendment has passed both Houses of Congress by a two-thirds vote, and awaits the ratification of the States. As the Republicans have succeeded in giving the last touches to the platform, we suppose our readers may be curious to see it "with all the modern improvements." Here it is—nigger suffrage with its toilet made:

[Followed by a copy of the amendment]

[The radicals] have with the dishonesty of thorough-paced demagogues, undertaken to rebut the charge of having deliberately adopted a futile and impracticable plan. They expect to make unthinking people believe that the amendment will be ratified by the requisite three-fourths of the States. Their argument is, that the States not excluded from Congress will adopt it at once, and that only two of the remaining eleven, are needed to make it a part of the Constitution. They are already holding out hopes to Tennessee and Arkansas, designing, by this means, to cajole the North into believing that those States may be induced to ratify. This is only a trap to catch simpletons, as may easily be demonstrated.

It is against all probability that either Kentucky, Maryland, or Delaware, will ratify the amendment. Those states are all strongly opposed to negro suffrage. Being already in Congress, they have no motive for ratification. It is against their interest to have the number of the representatives reduced. Why then should they ratify? The eleven excluded States have reasons for refusing, almost as cogent. To be sure, they wish restoration to Congress, but they have no guarantee, not even a promise, that their acceptance of this amendment would reinstate them. Congress, with a view to allude the vote, postpones till the next session the passage of a bill defining the terms of readmission; and if the Republicans carry the fall elections, they will be more likely to raise their terms than to relax them. If Congress would say to the excluded States, "ratify this amendment and you shall for[th]with be admitted," it would practically counterbalance their repugnance. But as the question is presented to them ratification would be an act of gratuitous servility—a pusillanimous surrender of clear constitutional rights, without even the promise of a compensation.

The proposed amendment accomplishes all that the Radicals ever aimed at. Their chief purpose has all along been, and is, to keep the South unrepresented until they adopt negro suffrage. The proposed amendment has negro suffrage concealed in its belly, like the trickish Greeks in the belly of the Trojan horse. "There is a nigger in the fence"—skulking, instead of standing up in plain sight. If the amendment were to be ratified there can be no doubt that the Southern States would adopt negro suffrage rather than lose a third of their representatives. As they outnumber the negroes, they could, on all purely Southern questions, outvote them—to say nothing of their chances of controlling their political action. If the amendment is ratified, negro suffrage will immediately follow; and negro suffrage is the "paradise of fools" for which all devout Radicals offer up their morning and their evening prayers.

Samuel W. Mason: "Appeals to the South"

This editorial challenges Northern newspapers that were calling for acquiescence and asks if they would give up in the face of the same circumstances.

Savannah (Ga.) Daily News and Herald, October 15, 1866

The New York Times and other professedly conservative journals are making most earnest appeals to the Southern States to accept the Constitutional amendment adopted at the last session of Congress. They say that in view of the Radical ascendancy in the next Congress, it would be not only inexpedient, but exceedingly unwise not to accept it, and that speedily. It is urged by them that the only parts of the amendment open to serious objection are temporary in their operation. That by changing the rates of representation their political power is reduced, but only until we find it wise and safe to apply the same qualifications for suffrage to both blacks and whites. That in the ordinary course of things, this result must be obtained before many years. . . .

Would the editors of the journals referred to—after conforming to all that Congress said was the object of the war, and all that President Lincoln declared was necessary for re-admission, and all that President Johnson said was required, adding even more conditions than was prescribed by President Lincoln—consent to new terms and when the Sumners and Butlers, the Stevenses and the whole host of radicals declare that the amendment is but the beginning of new demands—would they, we ask, in view of all these facts consent to this unjust pressure? We do not believe they would thus vote, and what they would not do themselves let them not exact of others.

If negro suffrage is so good a thing as these editors would have the Southern people to believe, and it is but justice to the negro to permit him to vote, as they contend, why do not the Northern States confer the privilege upon him? We wait for the ratification of the Constitutional amendment. . . .

If it is not good policy to admit the negro to equality at the polls at the North, it is not at the South. So far as any policy injures the South, it is injurious to the whole country, and so long as the Radicals insist upon negro suffrage in the South, they can only vindicate their consistency by adopting it in the North.

We all know that we must submit to what is inevitable, but this does not require us to falsify our own judgment or convictions by testifying approval of that which, in fact, we do not approve. If we go aright we must take principle for our guide. It will not do always to sacrifice conscience and principle to expedience, which is the main element in the argument of the journals referred to. We can accept for ourselves the legitimate results of the war. We can suffer the penalties of failure, but we have no right to trade off the rights of the future—the rights of others as well as ourselves—by establishing precedents of subserviency that will afford excuses for similar submission, and, of course, similar stretches of power and oppression, in coming years.

John H. Christy: "All Hope Gone"

The Athens (Ga.) Watchman *expressed a sentiment that was echoed throughout the South—that it was better to remain forever unrepresented than to accept the degrading terms of the radicals.*

Athens (Ga.) Watchman, July 3, 1866

The passage by both Houses of the Rump Congress, of the amendments to the Constitution published in last week's issue, and their almost certain adoption by a sufficient number of States to give it the force of law, extinguishes the last hope of our people. Nothing but a patient, manly endurance of evils and insults, that we are powerless, for the time, to avenge, remains.

Let no Southern State so far lower its haughty crest, or stain its spotless shield, as to debate, even the acceptance or non-acceptance of these infamous terms. If our enemies can pass them without aid, they will not deign to call on us; if not, and the cup is presented to our lips, let us spurn it as a draught that will, in the end, bite like a serpent, and sting like an adder. Our enemies may degrade us. Let us look well to it that we do not degrade ourselves.

John Forsyth: "No Amendment—Stand Firm"

Through the fall and winter of 1866, Southern states one by one rejected the Fourteenth Amendment. In this editorial, so characteristic of John Forsyth's demagogic style, he pleads with the Alabama legislature not to vote for the amendment.

Mobile (Ala.) Advertiser and Register, January 9, 1867

Desolate in heart, broken in fortunes, isolated in politics and enduring all the trials and mortifications of a people subjugated by arms, the South has yet solemn duties to perform. It has temptations to avoid, the wiles of politicians to resist, and a noble fortitude to foster and cherish, in order to bear affliction with patience and hope and thus safely pass through the present, last and not the least of its many crises. We see danger in this Radical Constitutional Amendment . . . It is a Trojan horse sought to be introduced into our gates, with the difference that its armed enemies are not even concealed in its belly. There never was a clearer proposition . . . that the excluded States owe it to themselves, to their heroic leaders, like Davis and Lee, to their fellow Americans in the other States of the former Union, and to the genius of Constitutional freedom, resolutely to decline to become parties, by consent to this degrading amendment. . . . Granting that we get back into the Union, so called, at the price of this sacrifice of constitutional right, State character and honor, as a people, what do we gain but dead-sea fruit? We go back bound, hand and foot, and as much at the mercy of a Radical majority, whose sway will have been prolonged by our act, as we are now or could be under an act of territorialization. We go back with our heads hanging in shame, and our names blasted for all time to come, as a people who have sold their God-like Lee for thirty dirty pieces of silver. Do it not, men of the South! Let them not do the deed, women of the South! . . . We now implore you to stand firm in spurning self-degradation, to hold fast to the vantage ground of your present position, to be true to yourselves and the friends of liberty throughout this once free land, and show yourselves as faithful to principle and honor in defeat, as your dead and living soldiers were brave in war.

Let us be true to ourselves, stand firm and fear not. Radicalism is travelling a road that must come to a speedy end. They are driving the car of revolution with electric speed and a smash-up is inevitable unless the teachings of human history are all false, and the everlasting laws of cause and effect are to be suspended for Radical benefit.

Carey Styles: "Vote It Down"

Although Southern states initially refused to ratify the Fourteenth Amendment, they were forced to reconsider the issue when congressional Reconstruction established ratification as a condition for readmission. The conservative Atlanta Constitution, *a newcomer to Georgia, represented the Southern response to ratification. At the time, Georgia was under the military command of General George Meade.*

Atlanta Constitution, July 3, 1868

Congress provided Georgia with an act of Reconstruction, said to her, call a Convention, frame a Constitution, ratify it by your popular vote, and we will re-admit you into the Union. Georgia did what her rulers required of her. This done, another test is applied. She must ratify an amendment to the Federal Constitution in return for the gracious privilege, or remain out in the cold. It was not enough that she should adopt measures of injustice, establish impartial negro suffrage, sanction Congressional disfranchisement of her best white citizens—nay, it was not enough that she should thus humiliate herself. Now she is coolly informed that her measure is not yet full. She must still deeper degrade herself; lick again the boot with which she has grown so familiar; eat a little more dirt; get down on her knees; crawl upon her belly in the dust, would she be admitted to fellowship with the loyal sisterhood. We would advise her to stay out until she can go in on better terms. Meade's military are preferable to the "loyal militia" proposed by Congress for the Reconstructed States. See to it, Democratic members of the Legislature! that this last act in the drama of degradation is not played. Vote this amendment down, and by your vote prove to the world that Georgia is yet true to herself, and this whole scheme of Reconstruction is a mockery and a lie.

Anonymous Writer: "Vote It Down"

In much of the South, the way to appeal to poorly educated whites was through the kind of demagoguery and scare tactics used in this editorial.

Bossier (La.) Banner, March 28, 1868

If you don't want negro equality forced upon you, go to the polls and vote against the proposed Constitution, framed by the social banditi, domestic bastards, catamites, scalawags, slubberdegullions, cow thieves and jay-hawkers of Louisiana.

If you don't want your State, District, Parish and Ward offices filled with negroes and white vagabonds, vote down the black vomit spewed up by the scrofulous vermin, late of the Mechanic's Institute.

If you don't want negro jurors, go to the polls and vote against the new constitution.

If you don't want to be ground down by taxes to educate negroes, go [to] the polls and vote against the new constitution.

If you don't want your wives and daughters to be insulted by insolent and depraved negro vagabonds, go to the polls and vote against the new constitution.

If you don't want negroes and Yankee thieves to be your masters and rulers, go to the polls and vote against the new constitution.

If you are opposed to amalgamation and miscegenation, vote against the new constitution.

If you wish the respect of all honest white men, go to the polls and vote against the new constitution.

If you prefer the Southern white man to the Northern thief as an office holder, go to the polls and vote down the infamous libel proposed as a constitution.

If you feel like stealing something, and wish to associate with negroes and white jayhawkers the balance of your life, go to the polls and vote FOR the new constitution.

If you want your children to go to the same school, eat at the same table, and sit in the same church pews with negro children, and wish to turn negro and jayhawker yourself, go to the polls and vote for the cow thieves' constitution.

QUESTIONS

1. Why did Northern newspapers urge the South to ratify the Fourteenth Amendment?
2. Why was the Fourteenth Amendment considered "moderate" and a "compromise"?

3. Why did Congress not include black suffrage in the Fourteenth Amendment?
4. Why did the South believe that ratification of the Fourteenth Amendment was an "unjust" requirement for admission?
5. Compare the editorials written by Carey Styles of the Atlanta (GA.) Constitution and John Forsyth of the Mobile (Ala.) Advertiser and Register. Which do you believe is the most effective?

NOTES

1. House Reports, 39th Cong., 1st sess., no. 30, pt. 1, vii–xxi.

2. Brooks D. Simpson, *The Reconstruction Presidents* (Lawrence: University Press of Kansas, 1998), 109.

CHAPTER 11

New Orleans Riot, 1866

Throughout the Reconstruction years, the South witnessed more than two dozen race riots in which at least one person was killed. Those who precipitated riots, typically whites, justified their murder and mayhem as the necessary means of guarding liberty and states' rights.

The New Orleans riot of 1866 was notable not only because of the 48 who died and more than 146 injured but because it served as a turning point in Reconstruction policy. The riot, one of the first and most bloody after the Civil War, resulted in the first serious calls for the impeachment of President Johnson. The riots also served to further unite radicals in their effort to bring about a more comprehensive Reconstruction policy.

Louisiana was the only state in the Deep South that attempted to return to the Union under President Abraham Lincoln's wartime Reconstruction plan. Lincoln offered that once 10 percent of a state's 1860 electorate swore an oath of allegiance and rewrote constitutions that abolished slavery, they would be readmitted to the Union. In Louisiana, the result was the Constitutional Convention of 1864, dominated by New Orleans moderates and conservatives. The new constitution written by the convention neither disenfranchised rebels nor granted blacks the right to vote. However, the constitution did allow any future legislature to approve a black franchise. In 1865, freeborn blacks and freedmen in Louisiana, with the help of white Republicans, campaigned for full voting rights. But at each turn they were met by a secessionist Democratic regime composed of former rebels who countered the suffrage issue with stringent black codes. Since there was no chance of getting a franchise law through the Louisiana legislature, the only alternative was to rewrite the conservative state constitution so as to disenfranchise former rebels and enfranchise blacks. But, with the Louisiana legislature made up of Democrats and former rebels, it would be impossible to persuade them to call for a new constitutional convention. Also, President

Andrew Johnson had warned that a new constitutional convention might hurt Republican chances in the fall 1866 elections. The solution—supported by Republican governor James Madison Wells—was to reconvene the convention of 1864. This was possible because the 1864 convention adjourned with the proviso that it could be reconvened by the convention president.

Agitated at the thought of a radical-led constitutional convention and the potential damage it could do to white supremacy in the state, conservatives and Democrats declared the assembly illegal and sought ways to prevent it. Leading the effort to stop the convention was Louisiana's Lieutenant Governor Albert Voorhies and New Orleans's newly elected Mayor John T. Moore, a former Confederate.

In June 1866, Republican organizers announced that the convention would reconvene in New Orleans on July 30.[1] Several days before the convention gathered, a mass meeting of Republicans—black and white—was held at the Mechanic's Institute where intemperate speeches were made decrying the state of affairs in Louisiana and denouncing President Johnson. One of the speech makers was Dr. Paul Anthony Dostie, a dentist who moved to New Orleans from Chicago during the war. Dostie warned that if anyone attempted to interfere with the convention, "the Streets of New Orleans would run with blood." Dostie led several hundred men, mostly black, in a loud procession down Canal and St. Charles streets to City Hall, where he admonished the men to return home quietly and ignore the jeers and taunts of white men, "but if they strike you, kill them."[2]

Believing the rally to be a harbinger of trouble to come, Voorhies threatened to arrest the delegates should they meet. He also sent President Johnson a telegram asking if the military should be involved in the arrest. Rather than supporting the delegates' right to assemble and cautioning against overreacting to the situation, Johnson instead denounced the impending meeting as illegal and authorized federal forces to help local police suppress the unlawful assembly.[3]

Meanwhile, General Absalom Baird, federal commander in New Orleans and head of the Freedmen's Bureau in New Orleans, wrote Secretary of War Edwin Stanton asking for instructions, as he did not feel it appropriate to break up the convention and arrest delegates. City authorities had assured Baird that peace would be maintained and that no outbreak was anticipated. Stanton never responded to the telegram, so Baird kept his troops at the ready, but at some distance from the convention hall.

Meanwhile, the mayor told the New Orleans police chief to make certain that his entire force reported to their stations on Monday morning, armed. However, their instructions were to stay at the stations and not interfere unless trouble started. Because the New Orleans police force was composed mostly of former Confederate soldiers, there was little chance that they would act to protect the delegates. In fact, they were prepared to disrupt the convention when the opportunity arose.

On July 30, only 25 of the 150 delegates (all white) along with several hundred black supporters assembled at Mechanic's Union Hall. Lacking a quorum, the delegates adjourned while Sergeant at Arms Dostie rounded up the rest of the delegates. The convention was to reconvene an hour later. No sooner had Dostie stepped out of the building than he was shot and beaten. Meanwhile, a group of black supporters (mostly Union veterans) marched up the street carrying a U.S. flag. A shot was fired at the procession, and more shots were fired outside of the convention hall. Delegates and supporters retreated into the building.

Another melee of gunfire and brick throwing several blocks away escalated, and the alarm was sounded for the police to move in. Police chased blacks down streets, into alleys, and through gardens. Three black men were killed before order was restored. The police then moved on the Mechanic's Institute, surrounding the building and shooting into the windows. Inside, delegates and several hundred black and white supporters (some of whom had guns) waved white flags at which point police entered the building. The police fired indiscriminately as men tried to make their way down the stairs to exit the building. Those men who escaped the shooting inside the building were fired on by police and armed citizens outside the building.[4]

By the time General Baird's troops arrived, the massacre was over. Although there is no exact tally of wounded and dead, the official count is 45 blacks and 3 whites killed, and 119 blacks and 27 whites injured. Dr. Dostie and the convention's chaplain, the Reverend Jotham Horton, died of wounds several days later, and former governor Michael Hahn was severely wounded. Those not killed or wounded were immediately arrested and taken to jail; none of the police or armed citizens was arrested.

Although General Philip Sheridan, military governor of Texas and Louisiana, was aware of the potential for violence, he left New Orleans for Texas before the convention. On his return, he wrote General Ulysses S. Grant that the police had attacked the delegates and black supporters "in a manner so unnecessary and atrocious as to compel me to say it was murder." A day later, as Sheridan learned more about the riot, he wrote Grant again: "It was not a riot. It was an absolute massacre by the police. . . . It was a murder. . . . Furthermore, I believe it was premeditated." He urged that the leaders on both sides—the mayor and the governor—be arrested.[5]

The New Orleans massacre dealt a severe blow to Johnson's Reconstruction policy as well as to his attempts to create his new National Union

Party. Radicals used this incident as well as a riot in Memphis in July to discredit Johnson and his conservative allies and to show that the South was still in rebellion. In a counterattack, Johnson repeatedly blamed the riot on the radicals and their schemes to promote black suffrage. Johnson showed no remorse for the deaths.

Congress reacted to the massacre by appointing a committee to investigate the incident. Its report, presented to Congress in March 1867, showed that the riot was planned well in advance by the mayor. Evidence indicated that before the convention assembled, police and firemen were withdrawn from their posts, supplied with additional arms, and told to wait until given the signal to attack. The report also showed that many of the victims were assassinated by police—sometimes with a bullet to the head or directly to the heart. The committee also presented a bill that provided for the disenfranchisement of former rebels and the establishment of a new civil government in Louisiana that would be elected by loyal citizens and blacks. The Louisiana Bill was eventually combined with the Military Bill, a product of the Joint Committee of Fifteen's investigation of conditions in the South, to become the pivotal Reconstruction Act of 1867.

The first set of readings focuses on the conservative reaction to the riot. The first selection, by Charles Wynne, praises President Johnson for ordering the military to interfere with the convention and criticizes General Baird for not following those orders. The second entry, by Samuel Mason, blames the riot on political agitators such as Dostie and insolent blacks. The next entry, by John Forsyth, declares that Southern whites, not the incendiary radicals who precipitated riots, are the true friends of blacks. The last two selections, by Henry J. Raymond, are from the *New York Times*, which in 1866 was a strong supporter of Johnson. The first reading accuses the radical Republican press of making martyrs of the convention delegates. The second entry counters those who contended that the riot was an infringement of free speech and assembly. Written before the findings of the congressional investigation were released, the editorial blames the riot on an organized mob of convention supporters and delegates.

The section expressing the radical response to the riot begins with an entry by George W. Curtis, declaring that the president knew that New Orleans was kindling waiting for a match but did nothing to stop the bloodshed. The second reading in this section, by Horace Greeley, denounced the president for going around the governor of Louisiana and ordering troops to interfere with the convention. The editorial by William Cullen Bryant from the *New York Evening Post* asserts that had the rebel states been readmitted six months earlier, the president would not have dared to interfere in the political affairs of Louisiana. The fourth selection, by E.L. Godkin, expresses puzzlement at President Johnson's lack of remorse at the loss of life.

The final selection, written by Thomas J. Durant, a Louisiana Republican who fled New Orleans on the day of the riot, frames the riot as an abridgement of freedom of speech.

CONSERVATIVE RESPONSES TO THE RIOT

Charles Wynne: No Title

Many Southerners believed that once their states reorganized under President Johnson's lenient plan, whites would be back in control, Johnson would defeat the radical conspiracies, and the federal army would leave with their tails tucked under. Instead, the New Orleans riot strengthened the resolve of radicals to use it and similar incidents of violence to punish the South.

Richmond (Va.) Times, August 2, 1866

RADICALISM, REVOLUTION, TREASON and INSURRECTION in the Southern States have just received a death-blow at the hands of the President. His order to the military in Louisiana, which we publish elsewhere, crushes in the egg the atrocious Radical conspiracy to bring about an immediate war of races at the South. It arrays, by an imperative order, the army against the [Republicans] and all others in rebellion against the existing State Governments and laws. There is to be no more temporizing with the vile incendiaries who have been instigating the negroes to organize regiments, clamor for equal suffrage, and overthrow, by force, the present State Governments.

It is a fact, as disgraceful and infamous as it is undeniably true, that these demoralized traitors and revolutionists have had the sympathies of not a few military officers holding important commands at the South. One of this class of Radical tools was, beyond question, the Federal General to whose criminal remissness the late riots in New Orleans are justly ascribed.

He permitted an illegal assembly to convene composed of men whose objects were the disfranchisement of nine-tenths of the white inhabitants of Louisiana, and the enfranchisement of the negroes. He also allowed the streets of New Orleans to be thronged by shouting, yelling, malignant negro companies, armed and ripe for deeds of lawless violence. Sympathising with these negroes and their vile white associates, he failed to lend timely assistance to the State authorities. A white citizen of New Orleans was insulted and outraged by a negro procession, and an alarming riot at once commenced, which resulted in the loss of many lives. . . .

This wicked and gigantic conspiracy, Andrew Johnson crushed by the order to which we have referred. The whole power of the Government of the United States is hereafter to be employed to annihilate these traitors. . . .

It is providential that there is no disloyal Congress in session to break the force of this crushing blow at Insurrection, Rebellion and Treason. The President is master of the situation at last, and the Radical satrap who refuses to obey the order of his commander-in-chief will now have his head sent spinning from his shoulders.

A splendid opportunity is offered to all the military tools of Thaddeus Stevens to indulge in *harri karri*. They must obey their master or rip themselves up. The dilemma is painfully embarrassing, but should they elect the "happy dispatch" the sabers of the squelched negro companies are at their disposal. It is the favorite weapon of the disgruntled Japanese officials when they disembowel themselves at the gracious command of the Tycoon.

Samuel Mason: "Who Is to Blame"

This editorial is typical of the response to the riot in the Southern conservative press. Radicals were blamed for agitating blacks to take up arms in support of an illegal convention.

Savannah (Ga.) Daily News and Herald, August 13, 1866

It is gratifying to learn from [reliable sources] that the press and authorities of New Orleans not only advised but importuned the people to abstain from any interference with the Convention, notwithstanding the illegality of the proceeding; and the people generally observed the recommendation. Those who happened to be precipitated into the conflict by the pressure of surrounding circumstances, had been attracted to the locality by curiosity, and the collision which so unhappily occurred, was sought by the blacks, whose insolence, owing to the instigation of Dostie and his confederates, was of the most aggressive character. . . .

The truth is, as light is thrown upon the doings of the convention which met in Louisiana in 1864, and which sought to perpetuate its power by overthrowing the present government of the State, the more infamous it appears. To sustain their jacobinical conduct, and to galvanize into life a convention which had been dead for two years, negroes were furnished arms, and every preparation made to precipitate the conflict. And when the spirit caused by these wanton outrages broke out, the Revolutionists whose leaders in Congress had prophesied the result, . . . now charge upon the Administration, the crime and the deeds of blood which they alone brought upon the country.... That the leaders of this mock convention were political agitators, and that the action of the convention was calculated to produce a breach of the peace, no rational man can doubt. It was so intended, for its getters-up knew that when their programme was seen it would necessarily produce riot and bloodshed, and yet, with the facts before them the Radical press insist upon it that the blood is not upon their hands.

John Forsyth: "Inciting a Riot"

The New Orleans and Memphis riots raised concerns among Southerners that their town would be the next victim of a bloody riot by blacks, instigated by Northern radical agitators.

Mobile (Ala.) Advertiser and Register, August 3, 1866

Are there no means of protecting the South against these incendiary attempts to excite a war of races in our midst? There would be no danger of any such bloody calamity if the negroes were left to their own instincts, but so long as their excitable natures are inflamed by white scoundrels, the danger is imminent. If the relations of the races were left exclusively to the management of the Southern State authorities, untrammelled [*sic*] by Freedmen's Bureaus and official and volunteer emissaries of the Radical party, there would be peace and growing good will and sense of mutual dependence between the whites and the blacks. For after all, the Southern people, of all white people, feel most kindly to the negroes, and it is among them that they find their best and most disinterested friends. The love of the Radicals for them is exactly measured by what they can make out of them in political capital and money. The more intelligent of the blacks are fast finding this out, and it is a common remark among this class, if they want a favor, their old masters and Southern friends are to be asked for it. The perils to which Southern communities are exposed by these agitators constitute a powerful motive for an early and complete restoration of the State governments. Then seditious incendiaries can be looked after and punished by law for their crimes, and then the true friends of the colored man in the North will find their condition greatly improved in the South. Until this happens we are constantly liable to a repetition of the late unhappy scenes in New Orleans. It is not in the nature of any men to sit quietly down while scoundrels are whetting knives and lighting torches to be put into the hands of negroes, infuriated by their arts and machinations.

Henry J. Raymond: "The Falsehood and Exaggeration of the Radical Press"

While most moderate Republican newspapers had moved away from President Johnson by mid-1866, Henry J. Raymond was alone among Republican editors fighting for the president. In this editorial, Raymond argues that the radical newspapers—probably pointing directly at Horace Greeley's New York Tribune—*had exaggerated the New Orleans riot and were using the incident as fuel for their antiadministration schemes.*

New York Times, August 3, 1866

The course of the Radical press in regard to the New Orleans riot would be more tolerable if it conveyed an impression of disinterestedness or sincerity. Considerable allowance might be made for the extravagance of an attack upon the population of a great city, if the aim clearly were to bring the population into some hearty accord with the Republic. The elevation of slaughtered negroes into martyrs might be excusable if there were any tenable ground for believing that it proceeded from a human and unselfish concern for an ignorant and hardly-used race. But for this charitable interpretation of the course pursued by Radical journals there is no room. It is at variance with the indisputable facts, for their course is intelligible only when we start with a distinct understanding that the aim of Radical journalism is to intensify sectional bitterness, not to promote sectional harmony. . . .

Thus considered, the intemperate misrepresentation of affairs in New Orleans, the unscrupulous and unjust abuse of President Johnson for his conduct in relation thereto . . . become clear to the most superficial observer. They are parts of a well-considered scheme to help the Radical Party in keeping the South out of the Union. . . .

Nothing is too great, nothing is too small, for this purpose. The spirit which seizes upon the New Orleans riot as a partisan godsend, and swells with a malignant perseverance upon its every incident, does not disdain the murder of a solitary citizen. All is good fish that comes to the Radical net. All is made to render precious service to the Radical cause. The same process of perversion that represents a riot begun by negroes as a war upon the negroes, is used to convey the idea that an assault upon a loyal citizen, or a robbery from which a loyal citizen suffers, or a squabble in which a colored individual loses an eye, or a fight in which a rebel rowdy kills a Union rowdy—must be regarded as an indication of general lawlessness and disloyalty. The intention is the same in every instance. It is to keep alive ill feeling between North and South, and between races in the South, with the view of justifying the programme proposed by the Radicals. . . .

Henry J. Raymond: "Free Speech and Free Fight"

Henry J. Raymond lays the blame for the riot at the feet of the convention-
ists and New Orleans's black population.

New York Times, August 8, 1866

Despite the incendiary utterances of the speakers, no attempt was made
to silence them. The license accorded them on this occasion is proof that
freedom of speech is as much a verity in New Orleans as in any city in the
North. The difficulty was not about free speech, but free fighting, and we
protest against all attempts to palliate the latter under a pretence of uphold-
ing the former. There was nothing in the assembling of the Convention, or
the intended arrest of its members, that involved a breach of peace. But the
Conventionists organized a mob to resist and overawe the civil authorities;
and hence the conflict. Freedom of speech did not depend for its assertion
upon a negro mob.

RADICAL RESPONSES TO THE RIOT

George W. Curtis: "The Massacre in New Orleans"

The most bitter denunciations were against President Johnson's failure to
stop the riot. As Harper's Weekly *points out, the volatile situation in*
New Orleans called for a calm voice, not one that would further inflame
the situation.

Harper's Weekly, August 18, 1866

The President knew, as every body else knew, the inflamed condition of
the city of New Orleans. He had read, as we had all read, the fiery speeches
of both parties. He knew, unless he had chosen willfully to ignore, the
smothered hatred of the late rebels toward the Union men of every color.
He may have considered the "Conservatives" wise, humane, and peaceful.
He may have thought the Radicals wild and foolish. He knew that the Mayor
was a bitter rebel, whom he had pardoned into office. He knew that the
courts had denounced the Convention, and he was expressly informed that
they meant to indict the members. He could not affect ignorance of the imminent danger of rioting and bloodshed.

And he knew, as he knew his own existence, that a simple word to the
military commander to preserve the peace at all hazards would prevent

disorder and save lives. He did not speak that word. Assuming to plant himself upon the Constitution, which by his very act he violated, he telegraphed to the Attorney-General of the State. He threw his whole weight upon the side of those from whom he knew in the nature of things the disorder would proceed, and from whom it did proceed. He knew the city was tinder, and he threw in a spark.

Horace Greeley: "President Johnson's Responsibility"

Horace Greeley criticizes the president for communicating with the attorney general (and the lieutenant governor) rather than with the governor and for setting a tone in Washington that was interpreted as presidential approval of the violence.

New York Tribune, August 1, 1866

If any doubt existed as to President Johnson's connection with the massacre in New Orleans it will be removed by reading his dispatch to Attorney General Herron of Louisiana. This dispatch, written with the knowledge that loyal citizens of the United States were dying from wounds received by a rebel mob assumes the responsibility of the deed. The policy that prompted Mayor Monroe and his followers finds its inspiration in Washington.

This conclusion fills us with inexpressible sadness, but we cannot resist the facts. It is a dreadful thing to arraign the President of the United States as being in any possible sympathy with the unlawful shedders of blood, but when a plain fact is to be stated, the plainest words are the best. In the first place the President recognizes a usurped power to communicate his wishes. James M. Wells is the Governor of Louisiana, and the official representation of the state. To him the President should have spoken. But Gov. Wells, a duly elected Governor by rebel votes, had called this convention together and the President steps over the theory of State Rights, and sends his commands to an officer of his Cabinet—his Attorney General.—one Andrew S. Herron—a conspicuous Rebel in the days of treason. The President directs him to call upon Gen. Sheridan for "sufficient force to sustain the civil authorities in suppressing an illegal or unlawful assemblies." If the President really believes that States have rights, and Governors of States privileges, then his course in recognizing an officer of Gov. Wells's Cabinet as the proper authority to call out troops is a usurpation. . . .

It is folly to use soft phrases in speaking of this appalling crime. The policy of Andrew Johnson engendered the demon fury which has shed blood in the streets of the Crescent City. His statesmanship has once more raised Rebel Flags in New Orleans. . . . The time has come for the people to speak—

and let it be in tones so distinct and unmistakable that even Andrew Johnson will not dare to disobey the warning.

William Cullen Bryant: "President's Blunder"

The New York Evening Post *was a moderate Republican journal that supported most, but not all, of President Johnson's policies—until the New Orleans riot. Beginning on July 31 and running through August 10, the* Evening Post *ran an editorial daily about the riot. Each day, the tone became harsher toward the president.*

New York Evening Post, August 6, 1866

The President has made a blunder, he has done an act directly contrary to all his written and spoken policy. We shall expose his false step and point out its illegality and its dangers, just as faithfully as we denounced Congress for refusing to admit those Southern representatives who were qualified and could take the oath. If the Tribune and some other Republican journals had with us demanded the admission of loyal and qualified Southern members to Congress, they would now be in a better position to oppose the President's illegal assumption of power.

Mr. Johnson has committed a very grave blunder; and the sooner he retraces his misstep, and confesses his error, the better it will be for him and for the country.

In this present unfortunate condition of things in Louisiana, thoughtful men may see how supremely important it is that the country shall be brought back as quickly as possible to strict constitutional forms and proceedings, to the orderly and harmonious working of all the part of our complex system of Government. Had Congress, by the admission to his seat in either body of every member who was duly qualified and could take the prescribed oaths, thus reestablished constitutional order, and set all parts of the Government, State and Federal, to working, each in its proper orbit, the President of the United States would not have dared to commit such an act as the displacing of a regularly elected Governor and the substitution in his place and authority of an agent of his own. It is the habit of some Republican journals, like the Tribune, to ascribe to Mr. Johnson many mischievous notions, and a desire to favor defiant Rebels at the expense and to the injury of Union men. Similar sentiments and aims were imputed to Mr. Johnson by leading Republicans in Congress. It ought to have occurred to these persons that, if the President were really such a person as they believe, or pretend to believe, it was the more vitally important, for the safety of the country, to limit and lessen his powers, by bringing the Government back at once to the old, strictly defined, well-known and well tried "constitutional forms."

E.L. Godkin: "The Silence That Condemns"

During the entire controversy over the New Orleans riot, President Johnson never expressed sympathy for the dead and injured, nor outrage at the violence. His silence on the issue cost him a great deal with Republicans.

The Nation, August 16, 1866

Fifteen days have elapsed since Mr. Johnson took the government of Louisiana into his own hands, and allowed it to pass into the charge of a ferocious and bloodthirsty mob. Fifteen days have passed since he learned of the wholesale massacre of unarmed and loyal men, by those to whom he had deputed his authority. When appealed to by pardoned rebels to suppress a peaceful convention and to depose the governor of a State, he lost no time. He could not wait from Saturday to Monday, but hastened upon Sunday to tie the hands of Gen. Baird, and to direct the forces of the United States to be used in support of the "thugs" of New Orleans. The thugs have acted according to their nature. We cannot believe that Mr. Johnson *meant* that they should enact the scenes of diabolism which they did. We cannot suppose that he intended arrests to be made without the shadow of legal warrant, the assassination of defenceless [*sic*] and unresisting prisoners, the deliberate massacre of unconvicted and unresisting men. But the deed has been done.... Why cannot the President speak?...

We have not heard a word from Mr. Johnson or his organs. The Saratoga Convention has met and endorsed all the acts of Mr. Johnson. Long speeches were made on the occasion, but we do not notice a single expression of horror over this narrative, which half the members must have read on their way to the place of meeting. They could go out of their way to pledge an affected sympathy for the soldiers of the Union at the North, but could not spare a word for the discharged soldiers who had just been massacred by paroled rebels at the South. The president of the convention declared that he held out his hand to the loyal men of the South, whom he justly called our brothers; but to the blood of these brothers, spilt before his eyes, he was blind; to their cries for help and rescue he was deaf....

Thomas J. Durant: " 'My Policy' in New Orleans"

Thomas J. Durant, former attorney general of Louisiana, was a reformer who had worked many years for universal suffrage in Louisiana. Al-

though he did not participate in the convention, he witnessed much of the violence from his home and fled New Orleans the night of the riot after receiving threats on his life. His comments regarding freedom of expression in Louisiana and in the South were part of a lengthy speech given at a meeting in Philadelphia a month after the riot.

New York Tribune, August 31, 1866

These unfortunate men (Southern unionists), whose circumstances permit them, are now flying from their homes in the South to seek refuge and hospitality in freedom of voting and discussion here in the North. How long is this to continue? How long is it before the loyal people of the Union will give the loyal man in the South a government where opinion is free, where every man shall have the right to express his sentiments in vote and in words, where he shall have the right and the privilege of communicating in every respectful way he thinks and what he has to say? Do you not know that now the liberty of speech and the liberty of the press is dead in New Orleans? Do you not know that American citizens are slaughtered in the streets of New Orleans, under the American flag, without provocation? There is no liberty in discussion unless you discuss the merits of the President's policy, or the glories of Lee and Davis. That is the way in New Orleans.

QUESTIONS

1. According to Southerners, what advantage would radicals gain by instigating the New Orleans riot?
2. What effect did the New Orleans riot have on the election of 1866?
3. Why did some Republicans believe the riot was a free speech issue?
4. Why did Republicans believe Johnson was partly to blame for the riot?
5. Would the New Orleans riot likely have taken place if the Southern states had already been readmitted?

NOTES

1. Eric Foner, *Reconstruction: America's Unfinished Revolution, 1863–1877* (New York: Harper & Row, 1988), 263.

2. House Report no. 16, *Report of the Select Committee on the New Orleans Riot,* 39th Cong., 2d sess. (Washington, D.C.: U.S. Government Printing Office, 1867; reprint, Freeport, N.Y.: Books for Libraries Press, 1971), 38–39.

3. *The New Orleans Riot: Its Official History. The Dispatches of Gens. Sheridan, Grant and Baird—The President Answered* (n.p., 1868?), 3.

4. An excellent account of the riot itself can be found in James G. Hollandsworth Jr., *An Absolute Massacre: The New Orleans Race Riot of July 30, 1866* (Baton Rouge: Louisiana State University Press, 2001).

5. *The New Orleans Riot*, 5–6.

CHAPTER 12

Congressional Reconstruction, 1867

Republicans in Congress, angry at the South's refusal to ratify the Fourteenth Amendment and at President Andrew Johnson's policy of rewarding rebels and thumbing his nose at Congress, began as early as November 1866 to develop new guidelines for the admission of the South. Their planning was informed not only by the findings of the Joint Committee of Fifteen's investigation of conditions in the South but also by reports from journalists who toured the South and reported on Southern attitudes toward the North, radicals, Unionists, and, most of all, blacks. Southern violence against blacks including the riots in New Orleans and Memphis also helped put resolve in the Republican cause.

On March 2, Congress passed "An Act to Provide for the More Efficient Government of the Rebel States." Johnson vetoed the bill on the same day and just as quickly Congress overrode the veto. The law provided that the 10 Southern states would be divided into five military districts, each under the direction of a commanding general selected by the president. It further stipulated that delegates to constitutional conventions shall be elected by male citizens—black and white—21 years or older who have not been previously disenfranchised. Delegates were to meet in convention and rewrite constitutions, which would include a guarantee of black suffrage. Legislatures were required to ratify the Fourteenth Amendment. Once all of those conditions were satisfied, Congress would admit the states' duly elected representatives. Meanwhile, existing civil governments were considered provisional.

The new Reconstruction policy was more moderate than radical. It did not create additional classes of disenfranchised whites, did not guarantee blacks the right to vote after states fulfilled the provisions of the act, saw the military presence only as temporary, did not institute land confiscation, and

**White Man's Vote: "Everything points to a Democratic victory this fall—South-
ern Papers."** *This illustration shows a black man holding a Republican ticket trying to
vote at a poll open only to whites. On the wall is a poster calling for members of the White
League to report for drill. The poll watcher is holding a gun to make sure only Democrats
vote.* Harper's Weekly. *Library of Congress.*

placed the future of the black population totally within the discretion of
local governments. The *Atlanta New Era*, a Republican newspaper, accurately forecast the outcome when it wrote, "If the white men of Georgia are
unified they can secure the control for their new state government, elect
their Congressmen, and as soon as the State is once more in its place . . . they

can amend their Constitutions, disfranchise the negroes and restore suffrage to the disfranchised whites."[1]

Southern Democrats campaigned fiercely against voter registration and the convening of constitutional conventions, believing the end would be a mongrelized government run by incompetent blacks and deceitful carpetbaggers. They warned (or advised) blacks to stay away from politics: "Money in the pocket or corn in the crib and plenty of meat in the smoke house will be found to be better friends to the colored man than all the political speakers in the land. . . . The right to vote will never fill the stomach of black man. . . ."[2]

Moderate Southerners—cooperationists—promoted voter registration and office seeking, arguing that a strong white turnout would dilute the black vote. They believed that if the South's best men did not seek office, the worst men would, and governments would pass into the hands of those who would abuse it the most.

Black leaders, carpetbaggers, and scalawags (Southern Republicans) all worked to unite the black vote in favor of Congress's Reconstruction mandates. The first major Republican victory was in the 1867 fall elections to elect delegates to state constitutional conventions. While more than half of the qualified white voters boycotted the fall elections, black voter turnout ranged from 70 percent in Georgia to 90 percent in Virginia—all voting for the Republican ticket.

In the winter and spring of 1868, convention delegates—both black and white—traveled to their state capitals to begin the job of creating new governments. Conservative newspapers greeted this experiment with an unending barrage of racist rhetoric against what they called "mongrelized," "black and tan," or "bones and banjo" conventions. They ridiculed the delegates in the strongest racist language seen to date. The *Mobile (Ala.) Advertiser and Register* warned that the conventions would be composed of "wooly heads, empty heads, stolid ignorance and base venality," and described the members of the Alabama convention as "long-haired barbarians fastening upon Alabama a mad and impossible experiment of . . . government by wild beasts."[3]

Taken together, the conventions in the South were composed of only about 25 percent blacks. Of the 265 black delegates, 107 had been born slaves, 81 had been born free, 28 were from the North, and 40 had served in the Union army. Most were ministers, artisans, teachers, and farmers.[4] While black delegates from the North were educated, the majority of those from the South had little formal education, although almost all could read.

Voters ratified new constitutions and elected state officials and legislators during the late spring and summer of 1868. Some legislatures met quickly to ratify the Fourteenth Amendment. The first states readmitted in

June 1868 were North Carolina, South Carolina, Florida, Arkansas, and
Louisiana. Alabama followed a month later. Other states spent time squab-
bling over such issues as public education, subsidies for railroads, home-
stead laws, and taxes. States that had not ratified the Fourteenth
Amendment by February 1869 were required to ratify the Fifteenth Amendment. Virginia, Mississippi, Texas, and Georgia were readmitted in January,
February, March, and July 1870, respectively.

Among those elected to public office were Joseph H. Rainey of South
Carolina, the first black U.S. Representative, and Hiram Revels from Mississippi, the first black U.S. Senator. At the state level, a number of blacks held
such state offices as lieutenant governor, state treasurer, secretary of state,
and associate justice of the state supreme court. In the state legislatures, the
black delegations ranged from 5 percent in Arkansas to 70 percent in South
Carolina. Black legislators served primarily in the lower house and rarely
chaired important committees. The *Rome (Ga.) Weekly Courier*, joining other
Democratic newspapers in condemning the "black" legislatures, described
the Georgia statehouse with the following verse:

> Parrott in the Chair, Monkey on the floor,
> Scattered round the hall, five and twenty more,
> Hundred odd of white skunks, mean as they can be
> That's the *tout ensemble* of this Menagerie. . . . [5]

Although a lot of effort was put into creating biracial governments, Republican state governments found that legitimacy was a major problem. Republican state governments did not have the support of the majority of
citizens in their state and thus were considered "sham governments." The
only way that white-dominated Republican governments in the South could
build legitimacy was by courting more white voters. The inevitable result
was not only factionalism within the Republican Party but also a bartering
away of black leadership. To assure whites that the party would not be a
"black man's party," Republicans moved blacks out of party leadership positions and refused to support black candidates for office. Blacks often acquiesced because they did not want to heighten the factionalism nor did they
want their presence to hurt the Republican Party at the state level.

Other factors slowly undercut the power of Republicans—both black
and white. Black demands for equality in the social arena created a division
between blacks and white Republicans, who were willing to give political
equality but not social equality. As spending for public schools, railroads,
and public improvement increased, so did taxes. The tax burden landed on
the shoulders of white landowners who refused to pay. Kickbacks for rail-

road subsidies often ended up lining the pockets of both Democrats and Republicans, while the states went further into debt. All of these factors—and many more—eventually led to the downfall of Reconstruction and the abandonment of blacks.

As early as 1870, conservative white rule had been redeemed in states such as Virginia and North Carolina. By 1877, all Southern States were back under the control of the Democratic Party. The *Tuscaloosa (Ala.) Times* celebrated "the rule of the state by the white leaders and masses of the Democratic and Conservative party in place of a rule by the mongrel leaders and the masses of the radical party."[6]

The section favoring the congressional Reconstruction policy begins with an article by Frederick Douglass that outlines a policy that will give blacks social, civil, and political rights. The second entry, by Henry J. Raymond, accepts that radicals in Congress will now dictate the terms of Reconstruction but asks that any new policy be no harsher than absolutely necessary. The third selection, by Horace Greeley, takes an optimistic view of the South's acceptance of the new Reconstruction policy and believes that with the exception of a few ex-rebels, the process will move along quickly. The next reading, by E.L. Godkin, accurately predicts that while the new Reconstruction policy is worthwhile, there is a real danger that it will create a large patronage problem that will lead to graft and corruption. The final entry, by Thomas Wentworth Higginson, makes it clear that the Republican Congress is now in charge and that the Democrats have done nothing but create an atmosphere of disloyalty.

The section against the new congressional Reconstruction policy begins with an article warning Southern whites that the new Reconstruction policy is a fact and that the best thing to do is to rally all Democrats to vote. The second reading, by R.H. Glass, denounces the fact that blacks will be able to vote and hold office but says that even this evil will be overcome with patience and time. The next two editorials come from Southern editors who see the issue of white participation in constitutional conventions quite differently. One editor, John Forsyth, supports a total white boycott out of principle, and the other editor, W.W. Screws, argues that a boycott will do no good except to ensure that the conventions are totally controlled by blacks. The fifth selection from the *London Times* reviews the past two years of Reconstruction, then accurately predicts that moderate and conservative Republicans under the leadership of a more cooperative president can bring Reconstruction to a speedy end. The final reading, by S.A. Atkinson, is from a Southern Democratic newspaper, which expresses in racist language its sentiments regarding the new constitution of Georgia.

FAVORING CONGRESSIONAL RECONSTRUCTION POLICIES

Frederick Douglass: "Reconstruction"

Frederick Douglass, the great black abolitionist, chastises President Johnson's policy and warns Congress against allowing the South to continue its prewar political system; otherwise slavery in another guise would return. Douglass provides Congress a blueprint for enfranchising blacks, protecting blacks from violence, and creating a new South that protects the civil rights of blacks and whites.

Atlantic Monthly, **December 1866**

The assembling of the Second Session of the Thirty-ninth Congress may very properly be made the occasion of a few earnest words on the already much-worn topic of reconstruction.

Seldom has any legislative body been the subject of a solicitude more intense, or of aspirations more sincere and ardent. There are the best of reasons for this profound interest. Questions of vast moment, left undecided by the last session of Congress, must be manfully grappled with by this. No political skirmishing will avail. The occasion demands statesmanship.

Whether the tremendous war so heroically fought and so victoriously ended shall pass into history a miserable failure, barren of permanent results,—a scandalous and shocking waste of blood and treasure,—a strife for empire, as Earl Russell characterized it, of no value to liberty or civilization,—an attempt to re-establish a Union by force, which must be the merest mockery of a Union,—an effort to bring under Federal authority States into which no loyal man from the North may safely enter, and to bring men into the national councils who deliberate with daggers and vote with revolvers, and who do not even conceal their deadly hate of the country that conquered them; or whether, on the other hand, we shall, as the rightful reward of victory over treason have a solid nation, entirely delivered from all contradictions and social antagonisms, based upon loyalty, liberty, and equality, must be determined one way or the other by the present session of Congress. The last session really did nothing which can be considered final as to these questions. The Civil Rights Bill and the Freedmen's Bureau Bill and the proposed constitutional amendments, with the amendment already adopted and recognized as the law of the land, do not reach the difficulty, and cannot, unless the whole structure of the government is changed from a government by States to something like a despotic central government.... All that is necessary to be done is to make the government consistent with itself, and render the rights of the States compatible with the sacred rights of human nature. . . .

Slavery, like all other great systems of wrong, founded in the depths of human selfishness, and existing for ages, has not neglected its own conservation. . . . Custom, manners, morals, religion, are all on its side everywhere in the South; and when you add the ignorance and servility of the ex-slave to the intelligence and accustomed authority of the master, you have the conditions, not out of which slavery will again grow, but under which it is impossible for the Federal government to wholly destroy it. . . . The true way and the easiest way is to make our government entirely consistent with itself, and give to every loyal citizen the elective franchise,—a right and power which will be ever present, and will form a wall of fire for his protection. . . .

It is not, however, within the scope of this paper to point out the precise steps to be taken, and the means to be employed. The people are less concerned about these than the grand end to be attained. They demand such a reconstruction as shall put an end to the present anarchical state of things in the late rebellious States,—where frightful murders and wholesale massacres are perpetrated in the very presence of Federal soldiers. This horrible business they require shall cease. They want a reconstruction such as will protect loyal men, black and white, in their persons and property; such a one as will cause Northern industry, Northern capital, and Northern civilization to flow into the South, and make a man from New England as much at home in Carolina as elsewhere in the Republic. No Chinese wall can now be tolerated. The South must be opened to the light of law and liberty, and this session of Congress is relied upon to accomplish this important work.

The plain, common-sense way of doing this work, as intimated at the beginning, is simply to establish in the South one law, one government, one administration of justice, one condition to the exercise of the elective franchise, for men of all races and colors alike. This great measure is sought as earnestly by loyal white men as by loyal blacks, and is needed alike by both. Let sound political prescience but take the place of an unreasoning prejudice, and this will be done.

Henry J. Raymond: "The Majority in Congress— How They Should Use Their Power"

By December 1866, Henry J. Raymond realized that Congress would now be in charge of dictating the rules for readmitting the Southern states. In this editorial, he argues for doing nothing more radical than is absolutely necessary.

New York Times, **December 7, 1866**

The firmness of the Union majority in Congress cannot be doubted. There will be no flinching from the responsibilities of the hour—no evading the work to be done or doing it imperfectly. And that moderation will be mingled with firmness, and the exercise of power tempered with prudence seems at least probable. . . .

If there were the slightest hope that the restoration question would be settled on the basis of the Constitutional Amendment, the difficulties of the position would be comparatively inconsiderable. A little patience might then suffice for the occasion. But the hope does not, cannot exist. Other measures, of some sort, will be inevitable, unless we consent to acquiesce in the indefinite exclusion of the South, which would be unwise and unsafe for both sides. The country looks for a settlement, and will probably prefer it on a plan as near as possible to that sanctioned in the recent elections. But more radical measures may be a necessity. Restoration may have to make room for reconstruction. Of one conceivable substitute we have a foretaste in Mr. Sumner's resolutions and a little thought will bring others to view of a character for which the public mind has yet been but imperfectly prepared.

What is preeminently desirable is, that nothing shall be done or attempted of a nature more radical than circumstances render absolutely necessary. The policy required is essentially a policy of gradual, deliberate development. If the Amendment be, after all, ineffectual—if other steps must be taken to realize the results which the Amendment has been intended to produce—let the exigencies of the position be made so apparent that the loyal people of the country shall be reconciled to both the agencies and the consequences. Their minds are fixed upon the cardinal point: they intend that all the States shall be brought into the Union upon terms satisfactory to the judgement of the states that subdued the rebellion. If one measure will not accomplish this, other must be tried. But in conjunction with this positive purpose is an unwillingness to employ more coercion than is manifestly indispensable. . . .

Horace Greeley: "Progress of Reconstruction"

Horace Greeley's picture of the South's acceptance of congressional Reconstruction was far too rosy. But Greeley wanted reconciliation so bad that his opinions on Reconstruction seemed inconsistent, contradictory, and too conciliatory. For example, while Greeley was the strongest advocate of impartial suffrage, he also wanted to provide amnesty and full restoration of the voting rights of rebels.

New York Tribune, March 11, 1867

The Reconstruction act, which passed the late Congress over the President's veto is already virtually accepted by the South. It is (of course) denounced and execrated by certain noisy ex-Rebels (mainly of the bomb-proof variety) but not many, even of these, talk of resisting it, while the policy of "masterly inactivity" has few advocates, and their number is rapidly dwindling. And for this there is excellent reason, in the fact that, if the ex-Rebels refuse to organize their States under the act of Congress the Unconditional Unionists (White and Black) will organize each of and by themselves. If then, the ex-Rebels should insist on testing the constitutionality of the act before the Supreme Court, they will simply compel the court to decide whether a State organization by loyal men in obedience to an act of Congress or a rival organization by ex-Rebels in defiance of Congress shall be recognized and upheld by the authority and power of the Union; and it does not seem probable that a majority even of our present Judges will decide that issue against Congress and the loyal organizations.

The ten Rebel States are to be reorganized under the late act of Congress and are to choose Representatives and Senators to claim seats in the present (XLth) Congress. So much is already assured. And it is morally certain that the great body of their people, irrespective of past differences of politics or condition, will participate in such reorganization and election.

Nor is there any symptom of violent perturbation or deadly collision likely to result from the act which was so lately stigmatized by its enemies as one "to organize hell" in the South. On the contrary, the prospect is decidedly favorable to a nearer approach to peace and order than has been exhibited at the South for years. Outrage and violence are less prevalent there than they have been; and there is reason to hope that the Reconstruction at hand will be marked by no such hideous tragedies as those which in 1866 disgraced the cities of Memphis and New Orleans. . . .

On the whole, the good work of Reconstruction is progressing favorably and rapidly. Those who have for years vociferated that the Radicals were bent on keeping the Southern States unrepresented and in chaos until after the next choice for President, will be singing a very different song in December.

E.L. Godkin: No Title

E.L. Godkin praises the military commanders who will be sent South and expresses great hope for the future. But he warns Congress that federal patronage, graft, and corruption will soon follow—a warning that would come true within a short time.

The Nation, March 21, 1867

We think it is safe to say that in all that concerns Reconstruction, affairs have never yet looked so bright as at this moment. There appears—if we are to judge from the selection of generals to command the military districts at the South, under the new law, and from the course already adopted by General Schofield, the only doubtful one of them all—to be no disposition on the President's part to frustrate or evade the execution of the Congressional scheme of Reconstruction, and there are abundant indications that the new act, and the restoration of military protection under it, are facilitating the formation of a real Union party in every State in the South, of which the negroes will form a strong and valuable portion, as there seems no reason to doubt that they do know their friends, and are as capable of party discipline as any other set of men. We may, therefore, fairly expect to see several of the States pass into new hands under the new constitutions. In fact, there is only one black spot in the political sky, and that is the increasing disposition of Congress to use the present enormous revenue for the perpetration of jobs on a great scale, in the shape of bounties, land grants, pensions, and what not. This tendency, if not promptly repressed by the people, will, before every one, launch us on a sea of trouble, compared with which that on which we have been tossing is only a duck-pond. Combinations are already being formed in all parts of the country for a share of the plunder, and we therefore warn all whom it may concern against all schemes for the grant either of lands, or goods, or money, to men of any race, hue, or creed, as merely—we care not how high the character of the proposers may be—swindles in disguise, of which hordes of knaves stand ready somewhere to reap the fruits. The principle of this Government is "a fair field and no favor" for everybody, black and white, male and female—no restrictions, but no loans or gifts.

Thomas Wentworth Higginson: "Moral Significance of the Republican Triumph"

Thomas Wentworth Higginson was a Unitarian minister, abolitionist, and lifelong radical. After President Grant's election in November 1868, Higginson is optimistic about the future of the Republican Party and believes that the fraud and intimidation conducted by Democrats will be that party's undoing. He is much too optimistic. The election was close, and if anything, warned Republicans that their hold on the White House was tenuous.

Atlantic Monthly, January 1869

The victory which the Republican party gained in the November election, after the most fiercely contested struggle recorded in our political history, is the crowning victory of the War of the Rebellion, and it's real close...

After the armed Rebellion was crushed by arms, and the meaner rebellion of intrigue, bluster, and miscellaneous assassination began, both parties had reason to be surprised at the issue. The Rebels found that their profoundest calculations, their most unscrupulous plottings, their most vigorous action, only led them to a more ruinous defeat. Their opponents had almost equal reason for wonder, for the plan of reconstruction, which they eventually passed and repeatedly sustained by more than two thirds of both Houses of Congress, would not have commanded a majority in either House at the time the problem of reconstruction was first presented. . . .

Though the plan of reconstruction eventually adopted is called the "Congressional Plan," it was really the plan of the government of the country. In our system, a mere majority of the Congress is impotent, provided the President, however, "accidental" he may be, however mean, base, false, and traitorous he may be, nullifies its legislation by his vetoes; but Congress becomes constitutionally the governing power in the nation, when its policy is supported by two thirds of the Representatives of the people in the House, and two thirds of the Representatives of the States in the Senate.

In spite of executive opposition Congress had succeeded in getting new State governments organized at the South, and the representatives of the legal people of those States were in the Senate and the House of Representatives. Mr. Johnson and the Democratic party pronounced these reconstructed State governments to be utterly without validity, though their Representatives formed part of the Congress of the United States, and though Congress has by the Constitution the exclusive right of judging of the qualifications of its own members. . . . The intellect of the Democratic party is concentrated, to a great degree, in its Copperhead members; and these had become so embittered and vindictive by [Reconstruction], that their malignity prevented their ability from having fair play. They assailed the Republicans for not giving peace and prosperity to the nation, and then laid down a programme which proposed to reach peace and prosperity through political and financial anarchy. [In 1868 they] selected unpopular candidates, and then placed them on a platform of which revolution and repudiation were the chief planks. Perhaps even with these drawbacks they might have cajoled a sufficient number of voters to succeed in the election, had it not been for the frank brutality of their Southern allies. To carry the North their reliance was on fraud, but the Southern politicians were determined to carry their section by terror and assassination, and no plausible speech could be made by a Northern Democrat the effect of which was not nullified by some Southern burst of eloquence, breathing nothing but proscription and war. The Democratic party was therefore not only defeated, but disgraced. . . . To the infamy of bad ends it added the additional infamy of bad means; and it comes out of an overwhelming general reserve with the mortifying consciousness that its few special victories have been purchased at the expense of its public character. The only way it can recover its *prestige* is by discarding, not only its leaders, but the passions and ideas its leaders represent. . . .

OPPOSING RADICAL RECONSTRUCTION POLICIES

Anonymous Writer: No Title

The Charlottesville (Va.) Chronicle *advises a "cooperationist" stance, believing that the best course for white Southerners is to participate in the calling of conventions and the writing of constitutions. The sooner Southern states can meet the congressional demands for readmission, the sooner they can regain control of their affairs and disenfranchise blacks.*

Charlottesville (Va.) Chronicle, March 6, 1867

There are three courses for the Legislature to take: the first is to fight. The second is to fold arms and do nothing. The third is to call a State convention.

There would be a unanimous voice in favor of the first, if we had any power to make a decent resistance.

The question is between the second and third. The third leads to an acceptance of the cruel and merciless terms imposed upon us. The second leads to the same thing—and to much more.

The question, now is, Who shall get the control of the State under the new dispensation of universal suffrage—the whites or the blacks?

The provisional government, with universal black and qualified white suffrage, is already upon us. The court-house bells in all the counties will soon summon white and black alike to the polls. In addition to this, while the provisional government lasts, we shall have martial law in Virginia—the liberty of every man in the hands of federal officers.

It has been said that we had better have military law than submit to such degradation as implied in the acceptance of the terms. This is true ten times over.

But military law is not the alternative. It is military law and negro suffrage and the proscription of our leading men. These three things come upon us without our lifting a finger.

This is not all; *there will be a convention* to ratify the terms proposed. . . . [The radicals] will have a convention and they will put the state back in the Union, and they will give us a State constitution. That constitution will be like the constitution of Tennessee; it will perpetuate the power in their hands.

There are 600,000 whites in Virginia. We can control the State; we can guide, if we cannot arrest, the storm. And the more rapid our movements the more complete will be our masterships of the situation. Wait—and wait—and wait, and the Radicals will organize the negroes against us.

A state convention can be framed in literal compliance with the act of Congress, which will take all minor elections from the people—leaving only the Governor, the members of the General Assembly, and members of Congress to be elected by the popular vote. And it may be that a property and educational qualification can be secured as a condition of holding office of any kind.

We are therefore, for a convention—at once. It is not worth while to resist the deluge; the man who trusts in God will build the ark that shall float upon the tempestuous waters.

We are very far from despair, black as the prospect is. The immediate aim of our State should be to get back in the Union as quickly as possible. There we shall be measurably at least shielded from the Radical storm. If we stay our course much longer, we shall have confiscation added to negro suffrage. There we have at least reached a *resting place;* there we can get control of our State affairs; there we can *make another State constitution.*

R.H. Glass: No Title

This editorial was the typical reaction of Southern editors to the new Reconstruction Act. Editor R.H. Glass's "grin and bear it" attitude also reflected the South's belief that radicals would eventually pass away and leave the South alone—even if it took another generation.

Lynchburg (Va.) Republican, **March 10, 1867**

We suppose the new military bill may now be considered as in full operation in the five military districts of the South, and that Virginia is no longer a State, but a subjugated province of the Empire. Those whom the President has appointed to command the several districts, are Generals Schofield, Meade, Sherman, Hancock and McDowell, and we are glad to say that all of them are considered conservative in their views, liberally disposed to a fallen foe, and gentlemen in their character and deportment. With the instructions which they will receive from the President, and their enlightened views of public policy, we have little fear that our people will be very seriously oppressed by the military despotism that has been forced upon a people that could once boast of liberty and independence. Galling as this rule is to free born men, we should welcome and endure it with cheerfulness for indefinite years, if that were the only evil that is put upon us. But it is far from being so. The rule of the military is a small matter—a real blessing—to that rule and that state of things which will ensue from the revolution which is made in the social, and political and industrial systems of the South. To be ruled by white men, even in uniform, is not dishonorable in a subjugated people, but to be ruled by an inferior race of another color and low instincts—to have them admitted to the ancient franchises of which our best and most honored white population has been robbed—to have them in official station, and in our common schools, and in every other offensive position, is the intolerable part of the new dispensation. Let us, however, endure as best we can, for a season, this state of things. It is obliged to have an ending some of these days in the very nature of things, and if we do not live to see it, perhaps our children may. The disgrace which impartial history will attach to the transaction, will not fall on us who are unable to resist the outrage, but upon those who have wantonly and cruelly imposed it upon us at the point of the bayonet. . . .

John Forsyth: "The Argument of Numbers"

The Mobile (Ala.) Advertiser and Register *was the leading conservative Democratic paper in the Alabama. As such it advocated a total boycott of all elections and referenda, believing that to do otherwise was to abandon principle. The "S.S.S. Bill" is the Sherman–Shellabarger Senate Bill—or the Military Reconstruction Act.*

Mobile (Ala.) Advertiser and Register, June 27, 1867

The Montgomery Advertiser publishes a list of the Alabama papers that stand with itself in favor of the Congressional plan of reconstruction, pure and simple. The argument of numbers is the poorest of arguments. In seasons of passion, majorities are almost certain to be wrong. . . .

Those who go for the S.S.S. bills in their totality, simply submit to be radicalized by Radicalism. No amount of pretty talk, warm professions, or plausible excuses, serve to veneer the stubborn fact of abandonment of the Constitution of the Nation, and the hopes of liberty in the future to the pressure of Radical threats and Radical force.

If we know ourselves, we think only of the good of the country. But we do confess to a strong and mastering personal ambition to keep our own record clear and to do no act in these times of trial that will bring the blush of shame to our cheeks or to those who bear our name. We will not, therefore, ratify and endorse and pronounce good a system of legislation expressly framed to degrade the South and dethrone constitutional liberty in our whole country, and thereby give rule and power to the open enemies of free government. Others may bend the knee to expediency and abandon principle, submit to tyranny in the blind hope that humility will purchase liberty in the end, but as for us and our house we will serve only the constitution of our country, in our hearts and in our deeds.

W. W. Screws: "Why Oppose a Convention?"

This is the Montgomery paper's answer to the Mobile (Ala.) Advertiser and Register, *provided above. The editorial urges whites not to boycott the holding of a constitutional convention.*

Montgomery (Ala.) Daily Advertiser, **June 28, 1867**

A few men in this state oppose the holding of a Convention. Why, it is hard to tell. If they believe that negro suffrage can be prevented by it they are very credulous. Let's see. There is to be an election soon as to whether or not the people want a Convention. Every negro that is registered will vote. At the same time there will be an election for delegates to the Convention who will assemble in this city in case the vote is in favor of a Convention. Every registered negro will vote. The constitution adopted by that Convention, will be submitted to all the voters, black and white. Suppose the majority of voters is against a Convention or elect members that will reject the terms offered. What next? The term of the present Congress lasts until December year and if the present offer is rejected it will disfranchise the great body of [unreadable] whites, and reconstruct the State by the vote of the negroes alone. Its temper has been sufficiently shown already to convince any one that it will not take a step backward.

Anonymous Writer: No Title

The London Times, *and the British in general, remained neutral during the Civil War, but words and deeds clearly placed them in sympathy with the South. In this summary of the events of 1867, the negative opinion of radicals is very visible.*

London Times, **November 23, 1867**

The great question of the Reconstruction of the Southern State of America seems destined to remain for some time yet unsolved. . . .

Plan after plan of Reconstruction has been suggested and withdrawn. There have been bursts of vigour followed by intervals of reaction. At this moment the result of the November elections throughout the North appears to show a people quite unable to decide what should be done. It. . . . is well to inquire what have been the principal causes of the failure. . . . Being mistaken enough to treat the former register as still existing, they felt bound, in self-protection, to strike off from it all the prominent persons in the South, and it was the resentment against this special disability which caused the rejection of the Amendment. There has been, however, a second cause equally potent in delaying a permanent solution of the question of Reconstruction. The struggle between the president and the Congress last year was carried to the polls at the autumn elections, and the result apparently showed an overwhelming majority against the President, and in favor of the Congressional plans. All the States, beginning with Maine in September, and ending with New York and Massachusetts in November, returned the Republican candidates, and the majority in Congress re-assembled with increased power and a more determined will to force on their designs. They succeeded in carrying through the Legislature a revised scheme of Reconstruction under which some singular particoloured Conventions are now in Session in the South, but the result is a dangerous success. The Conventions have not yet decided upon anything, but the preliminary discussions have served to alarm their promoters. . . .

The imprudence of President Johnson in the autumn of last year gave [radicals] a power which threatens to prove their ruin. They have set on foot a Reconstruction movement in the South, but before it has produced any effect they are themselves deserted by popular support. It appears to be beyond the sagacity of the wisest in America to conjecture what will come next. The adoption of a more revolutionary programme by the Republican party during the remainder of their tenure of a majority is the expectation of one, while a speedy return of the Democrats to power is the dream of another. The Democratic party, however, obviously owe their recent victories to the mere sentiment of reaction against Republican excesses, and they have themselves no definite policy capable of sustaining pretensions to power. The more probable course appears to be that the moderate Republicans will free themselves from the disastrous leadership under which they have suffered, and, in alliance with the best men now in office and under the presidency of some candidate of practical wisdom, such as General Grant, will offer terms of Reconstruction which may admit all the members of the nation to participation in its political life without risking the results of the great war.

S. A. Atkinson: "The Supreme Hour Has Come"

The new Reconstruction constitution for Georgia was placed before the voters in March 1868, and it included many provisions supportive of black civil and political rights, including suffrage. The Athens (Ga.) Southern Banner *was one of many Democratic newspapers that called for the defeat of the constitution.*

Athens (Ga.) Southern Banner, March 13, 1868

Radicalism has so far advanced in its infamous work as to call for the full exercise of every energy that can be enlisted in its defeat. The purpose of that abandoned and shameless organization to control the political destinies of the state by an alliance with negroes and Northern adventurers is too manifest not to be seen and scorned by every just right-minded citizen. . . .

Every white man should gird on the armor for a good fight with the hydra-headed monster which assails civil liberty. If the Constitution framed by the Radical Convention is adopted we do sincerely believe that the State will be controlled by the negroes as certainly as though every whiteman [*sic*] in the State were disfranchised. One hundred thousand men, voting as a unit cannot fail to attract to their embrace a large element of abandoned wretches, like many of those in the Convention, who could never make a sign among decent white men. We believe also, that the adoption of this hell-born conspiracy against the white race, must result in violence and strife, if not in the extermination of either the white or black race from the State. Two races, so nearly equal in numbers, never have lived in a free government on terms of peaceful equality. We value the well being of the black race too much to willingly see them deluded into a conflict which cannot fail to be fatal to them, as well as, fearful for the whites. We value the peace of society too much to be silent when a heaving earth quake is about to belch forth its horrid fires upon us. We shall therefore enter upon the great canvas with every energy enlisted—every impulse aroused, and we hope to have the active aid of every white man, and every prudent and sensible black man in this portion of the State. We have no object to observe but the good of society.

Already the Radical papers are being circulated in every neighborhood, full of ingenious appeals in support of the monstrous frauds embraced in the new constitution. Let the county committees see to it that Democratic papers are sent to counteract the poison instilled by these Convention organs. Let those who need relief be shown that the method proposed is a cheat and a swindle, and cannot stand. Let it be shown that with 100,000 negroes at the ballot box, the white men of Upper Georgia forever lose the control of the State which their numbers have long commanded; and that this populous section becomes but a province, an appendage, of a negro oligarchy.

We appeal to our readers to wake up to the magnitude of the struggle before us. It is no common issue—or ordinary campaign, involving only a choice of individuals. It is the crisis of liberty. Let us meet it like the sons of the fathers of freedom—like honest men, who value honor, integrity, and justice, beyond the glitterized bribe of political power, or the tempting chances of pecuniary advantage.

QUESTIONS

1. What were the most significant changes brought about by congressional Reconstruction in the South?
2. In what ways was congressional Reconstruction a compromise?
3. Compare and contrast *The Nation*'s editorial of May 1867 with that of *The London Times* of November 1867.
4. What role did congressional Reconstruction play in increasing corruption in the South?
5. Why did Southern cooperationists believe that going along with congressional Reconstruction was the best course?

NOTES

1. *Atlanta New Era,* 4 January 1868, 2.

2. *Staunton (Va.) Western Democrat,* 7 May 1867, 2.

3. Quoted in Donna L. Dickerson, " 'Got No Souls . . . ': Racism in Southern Reconstruction Newspapers," *Proceedings of the Association for Education in Journalism and Mass Communications, Southeast Colloquium* 1 (March 1992): 21–23.

4. Eric Foner, *Reconstruction: America's Unfinished Revolution, 1863–1877* (New York: Harper & Row, 1988), 317–19.

5. *Rome (Ga.) Weekly Courier,* 28 February 1868, 2.

6. *Tuscaloosa (Ala.) Times,* 31 January 1872, 2.

CHAPTER 13

Black Suffrage: The First Vote, 1867

Early resistance by the Southern states against giving freedmen civil and political equality led to the Civil Rights Act of 1866, the Fourteenth Amendment, and the suffrage vote in the District of Columbia. All of these laws moved Republicans closer to a broad commitment to black suffrage from which they could not—and would not—retreat. The next step came with the Reconstruction Acts of 1867, which stipulated that delegates to constitutional conventions shall be elected by male citizens—black and white—21 years or older who had not been previously disenfranchised.

In the minds of white Southerners, Reconstruction had been reduced to a single scheme by the federal government "to reverse the social pyramid and expect it to stand on its apex" by replacing the "virtue and intelligence" of the white man with the "Devil's own race."[1] Yet, most Southerners went along reluctantly, knowing that blacks could be intimidated, manipulated, coerced, and eventually disenfranchised by nefarious means. As one Georgia editor said, "Reconstruction does not make Negro suffrage a permanency. If the white men of Georgia are unified they can secure the control of their state government, elect their Congressmen, and as soon as the State is once more in its place . . . they can amend their Constitutions, disfranchise the Negroes, and restore suffrage to the disfranchised whites."[2]

Blacks were not prepared for this awesome civil responsibility and would need to be educated in how to use their newly won political power. They would need to be instructed on how to register, how to organize politically, and how to vote. More than 90 percent of Southern freedmen were illiterate, and slavery was not the best school for learning about civil and political responsibility. A black politician told the Georgia legislature that considering that freedmen had been enslaved for more than 240 years, "it is not be expected that we are thoroughly qualified to take our position beside those who for all ages have been rocked in the cradle of civilization."[3]

169

Churches and freedmen's schools were often used for political rallies and speeches by ministers and teachers who traveled throughout the South urging blacks to register and vote. Most of these black itinerant organizers were clergymen, teachers, or small tradesmen who worked for the Union League or Freedmen's Bureau or were associated with newspapers. For example, Holland Thompson, a young black Republican who worked as a promotional agent for the *Mobile (Ala.) Nationalist*, a black newspaper, traveled throughout the state calling meetings in churches and schools, reading newspapers to eager listeners, and urging blacks to subscribe to the newspaper as well as to the Republican cause.[4]

For blacks openly supporting the national Republican administration, there was one important political machine—the Union League, an organization whose primary objective was to educate blacks to vote the Republican ticket in major elections. The Union League began in the North during the Civil War as a patriotic organization supporting Lincoln. After the war, the Union League spread into the upper South, appealing to Unionists and small farmers in the mountains of Tennessee. But with the advent of black suffrage in 1867, the Washington-based organization employed organizers to organize leagues in the Deep South and enroll blacks in the Republican Party.

By the time elections rolled around in the fall of 1867, more than a half million blacks in the South had registered to vote. Black turnout in the elections for delegates to constitutional conventions ranged from 70 percent in Georgia to 90 percent in Virginia—all voting the Republican ticket. When it was apparent that the black voters were not going to line up behind the Democratic ballot box, white supremacists launched a counterrevolution.

In Mississippi, the Ku Klux Klan and other groups such as the Knights of the White Camellia succeeded through terrorist tactics in keeping enough blacks away from the polls that the proposed constitution was defeated. The Ku Klux Klan even threatened the life of the carpetbag governor of Louisiana. In South Carolina, a local white rifle club was given orders to kill the leaders of the local Union League. General George Mead sent troops into Alabama to arrest night riders and issued orders that forbade Klansmen to put up posters with death threats.

This early violence did not intimidate most black voters. Turnout at elections to approve new state constitutions was good. Black and white delegates were elected to state legislatures, and Reconstruction began to move forward. But by the national elections of 1868, violence was having a significant impact on black voter turnout. For example, by the November elections, more than 2,000 blacks had been murdered in Louisiana. In South Carolina, the president of a local Union League was killed, and plots to kill the Republican governor were later revealed.

Violence and intimidation moved Congress to make black suffrage a national mandate. In 1869, the Grant administration not only approved the Fifteenth Amendment to grant blacks the right to vote in federal elections but it also began passing a series of enforcement laws to try to contain violence and protect the black vote.

The readings in this chapter examine the black vote under the Reconstruction Acts, before the Fifteenth Amendment mandated black suffrage. The readings against suffrage in the Reconstruction Acts begin with an editorial by Charles Dana that predicts that Republicans will back away from black suffrage when they realize that blacks will vote the Democratic ticket. The next two entries from Southern Democratic newspapers use economic blackmail and fear to intimidate blacks into staying away from politics. The fourth reading in this section, by Manton Marble, warns Republicans that if they support black office holding, they will see important elective offices in the South go to blacks. The selection from the *Atlanta Constitution* is one of more than a dozen editorials written during the summer of 1868 that denounced blacks, Republicans, Reconstruction, and carpetbaggers. Editor Carey Styles uses racist language to assert that blacks are inferior and barbarous, thus unfit to hold the franchise. The final entry predicts that once conservatives replace radicals, the black franchise will be removed.

The readings in support of black suffrage in the Reconstruction Acts begin with Horace Greeley's answer to the *New York Sun*. Greeley argues that blacks will vote according to their needs and desires just like every other voter. Those needs will include social and economic freedom, which only the Republicans can offer. The second editorial, by William W. Harding, denounces the violence by whites against schools for blacks and suggests that education and reading are the best tools for ensure that black voters use their franchise wisely. The writer of the third selection, Louis Jennings, wants to see the Southern states back in the Union but only if black enfranchisement is guaranteed. The final entry, by "Karinus," is critical of Northern Republican governments that refuse to grant black suffrage at home yet at the same time demand it for the South.

OPPOSING SUFFRAGE UNDER THE RECONSTRUCTION ACTS

Charles Dana: "Perplexity of the Radicals"

Although Republican support of voting rights had antagonized many Northern Republicans, the party's commitment to black suffrage had not

*been diluted. Also, there was little doubt that Southern blacks would vote
the Republican ticket. See the* New York Tribune'*s response below.*

New York Sun, March 21, 1867

A new trouble has suddenly presented itself to the Radical leaders. They
have latterly had their eyes so firmly fixed upon the attainment of Negro
Suffrage that they never cast a glance ahead to see what the freedmen
would do if that privilege were granted to them. The unexpected acceptance
by the South of the new Reconstruction plan has made the establishment of
Negro Suffrage a certainty; and the Radicals are just beginning to see that
the anticipation of their favorite idea was far more pleasant than the realiza-
tion is likely to be. They are now in a state of deep anxiety and perplexity
with regard to the course which the negroes will take in politics. Without reflecting upon the subject, the Radicals took it for granted, before Negro Suffrage became a certainty, that the freedmen would vote with the party which
gave them their liberty. Now, however, they are examining the matter more
clearly, and the further they extend the investigation the less hopeful they
feel of securing the negro vote. . . . The negroes will vote as the Whites vote,
if the latter do the right thing. The mistake which the Radicals made consisted in not considering the consequences of Negro Suffrage before they
went so far. Their object was simply to make political capital by pressing the
subject upon the South; but they ought to have taken all the contingencies
into account. From the tenor of the Radical journals, it will not be surprising
if the party yet attempt to back out of the Negro Suffrage business. The great object of the Radicals is to maintain the strength and influence of their party;
and, if they conclude that such interests are endangered by suffrage extension, they will not hesitate to take the backward step.

W. W. Screws: "Attending Political Meetings"

The Montgomery (Ala.) Daily Advertiser *was considered cooperationist,
but it did not believe blacks should be part of the Reconstruction process.
Editor W.W. Screws warns blacks to stay away from politics—and the
polling booth—otherwise lose their jobs. Compare this approach with the
one used by the* Mobile (Ala.) Advertiser and Register, *provided below.*

Montgomery (Ala.) Daily Advertiser, May 22, 1867

If the right to vote ever filled the pocket, or the stomach of a voter, the
privilege was greatly abused. In ninety-nine cases out of a hundred such is
not the fact, and those who, in the effort to make use of this great right are
neglecting their business, do a positive injury to themselves and the community at large. One planter in this county told us yesterday that all his la-

borers left home, twenty-two miles from the city, on Thursday last and remained in town until after the speaking on Saturday. The time they lost will of course be deducted from their wages, and we venture they lost much more by coming off to attend league and political meetings than they will ever gain. This evil is generally complained of and more particularly do we find it spoken of in our North Carolina exchanges where the political agitators have been continually getting up public meetings. The Henderson Index estimates that the county of Granville lost fully $5,000 in labor by the late gathering of freedmen at a meeting in that town. Some 3,000 were in attendance, nearly all of whom lost two days from their work. We do not object to their being fully informed on the subject of their rights, but we do in all sincerity say that the best thing the black man can do is to work and strive to make something for his wife and children. If evil white men tell you the government will provide for you at the expense of your white neighbors and thus toll [*sic*] you off from your labor, you are listening to evil counsellors who only wish to use you for their own political advancement. If you have a good place with some money in your pocket, corn in the crib, and meat in the smoke-house, you will find them better friends to you than all the political speakers from Maine to California. You will not be in this desirable fix if you continually neglect your business, for the more you lose from your work the less money you have at the end of the year. In these hard times no laboring man can afford to lose one day in each week, and it is wrong for any one to induce him to do so. Let political meetings alone, is our advice to the blacks, and we believe the whites, too could get along very well by staying away from them.

John Forsyth: "Antagonism of Races"

As the fall elections neared, the nervousness of Southern whites increased. The political activity of the summer had confirmed that blacks would vote with the Republicans and for measures that would drag down white Southerners. In this editorial, John Forsyth uses threats and fear to intimidate blacks from following the Republican Party.

Mobile (Ala.) Advertiser and Register, August 13, 1867

It is the prevailing opinion among intelligent and thinking men at the North that the inevitable tendency of Radical political teaching at the South is to a war of races. We are persuaded that this is a result that the negroes do not desire, and we know that their white league leaders take the greatest pains to impress upon them that there is no such danger in store for them. But if the negroes were taught by these men to put matches and a bundle of lightwood splinters under a frame dwelling, they might as well be told there was no danger of burning the house. There is not only danger, but the thing is certain to happen, if the black people allow themselves to be arrayed in solid mass against the dearest interests of the white people.

If a colored man joins and votes and acts with a party that proposes to disfranchise me, a white man, and threatens not only to degrade me from my political freedom, but to rob me of my property and means of earning a living, there is not a thousand reasons enough in the Christian religion to make me a friend of that colored man. But there are a thousand instincts of human nature to cause me to hold him as an enemy to be antagonized, opposed, fought and overcome. This is the individual view, and it applies to the whole race. The present course of the negroes of the South tends to make for them enemies in every man of white blood except those reckless and inhuman wretches who for their own selfish purposes are dragging the negroes to this fearful pass of dangerous hostility. We think we have shown, as we know we have felt, a genuine and honest interest in the welfare and happiness of the negro race; and more for their sakes than for the sake of our own race, we have grieved to see them putting their destinies in the keeping of the prowling hypocrites whose only object is to control them for their own personal aggrandizement. If the end comes, as it will, as surely as the laws which govern cause and effect, continue to operate, they will be the greatest sufferers, for the whites not only of the South, but of the whole country will be on one side, and three millions cannot stand against twenty-seven millions. If it comes the negroes may read their fate in that of the Indians. They will be exterminated or driven out of the country.

But there is no necessity for this deplorable result. It would not happen if the Radical serpent of the everlasting meddling and proselytizing Yankee had minded his own business and kept his prying nose out of our domestic affairs. But as the serpent has come into our garden, there is but one safety for the blacks; it is to close their ears to her hissing lies, and to remember that they are of the South, and must have one destiny with the South, and that the happiness and well being of both races in the South can only be found in mutual friendliness, good will, and confidence between the whites and blacks in the South. Whoever teaches them otherwise is an enemy, a hypocrite, and a falsifier of God's truth.

Manton Marble: "Negro Voting and Negro Office-Holding"

In the summer of 1867, the National Anti-Slavery Standard *ran an article stating that some blacks were challenging the Republican Party's sincerity by demanding that a black man be nominated for vice president in*

*the next election and that in all state and local elections blacks be elected to
a proportionate share of offices. This is the* New York World *'s response.*

New York World, July 6, 1867

We admit that the qualifications to vote and to hold office do not in all
points tally and coincide. The same citizen who may vote when he is twenty-
one cannot be a member of Congress until he is twenty-five, not a Senator
until he is thirty, nor President or Vice President until he is thirty-five. . . . But
every argument in favor of the negro's right to vote on the same condition
that the white man votes, is equally an argument for the negro's right to hold
office on the same conditions that the white man holds office. The argument
is, that the rights of men have no relation to the color of their skins. . . . All
distinctions founded on color are proclaimed by the Republican party to be
unjust and absurd; a doctrine which they must either abandon or accept as
necessary consequence that negroes have an equal right with white men to
hold office.

The Republicans in our Constitutional convention must therefore be
consistent and open the door for negro governors, negro mayors of cities,
and negro occupants of every grade of office State and municipal. It is their
great mission to erase the word white from the vocabulary of politics. The
eligibility of negroes to all public offices will be a harmless innovation in
this State, their numbers being so small. . . . But in the South the boot will be
at work upon the other leg. There, the voting negroes, instead of being an
insignificant fraction of the Republican party, will form the great bulk of it.
They will be a majority of ten to one in every caucus, and their delegates will
be proportionally strong in every nominating convention. . . . This is a result
on which the Republican party may not yet have reflected, but it is one
which they cannot prevent. Equality in office-holding follows as legitimately
from their principles as equality in voting. They dare not confer the one and
withhold the other, lest the negroes, indignant at the inconsistency, should
turn against them and vote with the other party. The Republicans are under
a delusion if they suppose the Southern negroes will give all the votes and
take none of the offices. A fat office is as valuable to a negro as to a white
man, and will be coveted by him all the more eagerly as a means of removing the badge of inferiority put upon him by his color. That the negroes will
vote themselves into office wherever they have the power is as certain by the
principles of human nature as it is by the law of gravity that unsupported
bodies will fall to the earth. Black governors and black legislatures in the
Southern States, black Senators and Representatives sent from those States
to Congress, will be the natural and necessary fruit of a policy which confers
the ballot upon the negroes and organizes them into a party of which they
will form a large majority. It is equally certain that the Southern whites will

be restless and recalcitrant under the insolent rule of their former slaves, a certainty that opens a hideous vista of bloody brawls and military domination at which humanity stands aghast and patriotism shudders. These hideous consequences will be the natural fruit of the Radical policy of forcing negro suffrage on the South.

Carey Styles: "Not Our 'Brother' "

Few Southern newspapers were more antagonistic to black suffrage than the Atlanta Constitution. *During the summer of 1868, editor Colonel Carey Styles wrote more than three dozen editorials denigrating blacks as being barbarous savages without the intelligence to share political equality with the white race. This editorial, written only a week after Styles began publishing the* Constitution, *sets the tone for the paper's fight against congressional Reconstruction, radicals, and blacks.*

Atlanta Constitution, June 24, 1868

The advocates of negro suffrage do not base his claim on any natural or acquired right. In a state of nature he is without law or government. As a slave, he has taken no step in civilization. We do not trace to him any of the achievements in the art, science and literature, which mark the progressive developments of mankind. The ancient Egyptian and the modern Congonegro were as widely different as any two species of our race. In this country, unlike the Indian, the negro had no normal right. His slavery was the penance of sin or the cupidity of African slave-dealers. He had no natural right to the soil, he has acquired none. . . . He was ignorant by his own incapacity. Today, as then, he is unfit to rule the State. In contact with the white man he has advanced some—the nearer the approach the higher the development. The Democratic party is opposed to giving him this prerogative. It does not believe him capable of wielding it for the good of the country. It regards him as inferior by nature to the white race—as even below the Indian, and with less claim than the latter to the franchise right. Should he in time prove his capacity for self-government, the Democratic party will concede it to him. The Democratic party accepts the negro as "a man"—not as "a brother." The latter it will never concede. It is his friend. It will protect him in every civil right. It is unwilling, however, to make him Congressman, Governor, and Judge. It will not consent to degrade its own race by elevating an inferior above it. It is unwilling that the foreigner, when he emigrates to this country, shall go through years of privilege before he shall vote, when the negro, but recently from the barbarism of Africa, shall exercise that right without restraint. . . .

We are willing to treat the negro as "a man;" to encourage him in his industrial pursuits and in the elevation of his moral and mental being, but not to accept him as a "brother." As such we have no affinity for him. He is farther from our ideas of brotherhood than the Indian or the Chinaman. . . . We simply claim that the Caucasian race has ever stood and will continue to stand in the foreground on the drama of the world. . . .

Anonymous Writer: No Title

Among those newspapers in the North that favored a speedy return of the South to normalcy were the commercial newspapers. These newspapers wanted to see the old economies of the South (sugar, cotton, and rice) return to their former dominance. That would occur only if the blacks remained the laboring force of the South. The editor's predictions that black suffrage would eventually end would come true within a few years.

New York Journal of Commerce, **July 2, 1868**

No law in creation can fix negro suffrage into permanency. It is but an experiment. If it works well, contrary to the experience of mankind up to this time, it will remain incorporated in the constitutions of Southern States. If it proves a lamentable failure, degrading in its effects upon whites and black alike, the sturdy good sense of the Saxon race will throw it off like any other fetter which binds its progress. No law of Congress, no Constitution of any State, no amendment to the Constitution of the United States, is unrepealable. Congress has shown to mankind with what facility the most sacred charters, the most solemn compacts may be rent to pieces, where party interests require it. At some time not far distant, perhaps the Conservatives may have the supreme power, as the Radicals now have. It will be their duty to revise and correct errors of Radical legislation. One of the first questions that will come before them will be that of the repeal of all negro suffrage enactments and provisos. Unqualified negro suffrage will then have been tried upon its merits on the large scale. If on the whole it is a good thing it will not be molested. But if it is, as clearly apparent, evil and nuisance, nothing can save it from being sponged out of existence.

FAVORING SUFFRAGE UNDER THE RECONSTRUCTION ACTS

Horace Greeley: "Negro Voting"

This editorial is Horace Greeley's response to the New York Sun*'s contention that Republicans were backing away from black enfranchisement out of fear that Southern blacks would vote with their former white—and Democratic—owners.*

New York Tribune, March 23, 1867

Yet, the Blacks will not all vote with the Republicans. Many of them are mean, scampish loafers, who choose to live by thieving, selling rum, or pandering to lewdness, rather than by honest industry; and these will probably vote as Whites of like proclivities usually do. Some Blacks, who were kindly treated while slaves, and have been since, by their old masters, will vote under their influence. Some, being grossly ignorant, will vote under the influence of fear, or, being dependent, will vote so as to curry favor with the powerful. Yet it is a base calumny to say of the Blacks as a body that "they will vote as the Whites want them to do." They are men; and will vote under the impulse of diverse motives, just like other men. And one motive will obviously be that of relieving their brethren from the disabilities still crushing them in Kentucky, Maryland, Delaware, and other States under Democratic rule. If the Democrats want the votes generally of negroes, they will make haste to remove those disabilities.

The Negro Vote will be thrown solid for those whom *The Sun* terms Radicals, we have never taught nor believed. That the bulk of it will for some time be so cast as to compel the general repeal and abandonment of all acts and constitutional provisions which disfranchise or degrade men because of their color, we do joyfully trust.

William W. Harding: "Ignorant Voters"

This editorial gives the reader a peek into editor William W. Harding's real passion—books. Not only was Harding a newspaper publisher, he was also one of the best-known and most prolific printers of Bibles—particularly family Bibles. He was passionate about reading and education.

Philadelphia Inquirer, August 26, 1867

The opponents of reconstruction are complaining most bitterly that under the acts of Congress a flood of ignorant voters will overwhelm society in the South, and at the same time are busily engaged in shutting up all the avenues of instruction. A letter from an intelligent colored soldier, received by General Hawkins, asks for a supply of books by which the freedmen may learn to judge for themselves, and thus be able to obtain political knowledge without having recourse to oral information. There are schools established for the very young, but books distributed among the men and women of middle age could be used to great advantage during the long hours of the winter evening. The former masters in Virginia are ordering the colored men to vote for disunionists, under penalty of being dismissed, and driven out of the country. Of course, the voters must be taught that their tyrants of other days have not the power to control the polls. In Appomattox county the schoolmaster has had his life threatened, and on one occasion nearly became the victim of lynch law. Under these circumstances, knowledge must be obtained under great difficulties, and if teachers cannot be sent to every county in Virginia, the next best means of instruction should be used. General Hawkins' correspondent, who writes under the penalty of being called seriously to account of his boldness, says that every colored man and woman he meets asks for a Speller and Reader. In every quarter of the South the freedmen are earnestly striving for an education, and with this well attested fact before their eyes, the politicians have the assurance to prate about ignorant voters.

Louis Jennings: "Admission of the Southern States into the Union"

The New York Times, *like so many Republican newspapers, is impatient for the South to rejoin the Union but is not willing to take it back if it is a "white man's" South only.*

New York Times, May 26, 1868

It is quite time [the Southern] states were restored to their "practical relations" to the Government of the Union. . . . Their aid is needed at Washington in legislation for the nation. Representatives are wanted in Congress, familiar with the wants and necessities of the South and capable of advising such action as they require. . . . The people of the South are now fully capable of taking charge of their own affairs, and there is every reason why they should be allowed to do it.

The only objection urged against their prompt admission, by any of their own people, is that the blacks ought not to vote. The whites claim for themselves all the powers and political rights of government. They would rather remain under their present military regime than share authority with the negroes and prefer not to come back into the Union, until they can come back without any such partners in political powers. So far as their objection takes this shape, it is not entitled to weight. Their objection to negroes voting because they are too ignorant to vote intelligently is, in our judgment valid; but it has been overruled by Congress, and besides, it is an objection which loses force with every day that passes. The efforts made to educate the Southern blacks and the success that attends them, will very speedily make them quite as capable of voting intelligently as the great body of white voters there are today. But the protest against their voting, which rests on the bare fact that they are black, is utterly invalid and scarcely entitled to respect. This is not a "white man's government" alone; it is a government of the people,—that is, of all who are the subject of it. Whatever we may say or think of the principle as a matter of natural right, the theory and practice of our Government alike teach that all citizens, who are required to obey the laws, are to have a voice in making them. . . .

The union should be at once restored on the basis of equal suffrage, which Congress has prescribed. . . .

"Karinus": Letter to the Editor—"Equal Suffrage in Michigan"

In 1868, several Northern states, including Michigan, voted on the issue of granting the franchise to blacks. None of those referenda passed, because Republicans, who supported black enfranchisement in the South, voted against them.

Hillsdale (Mich.) Standard, March 17, 1868

Occasionally we hear an avowed Republican proclaim his aversion to the clause in our new constitution granting the elective franchise to the colored freedmen of the State. Of these we would simply ask, are they Republicans from principle? Are they, in pursuance of that principle, supporters of the reconstruction policy of the Government? If they are supporters of the policies of the government, which is but the principle of justice, upon what principle do they justify their opposition to Equal Suffrage in Michigan? It is much more difficult for a professed Republican to assign a cogent reason for such a position than for the "Democracy. . . . " But because of the patriotic tendencies of the negro, in late years, the democracy regard him as a "degenerated son of noble ancestry," and refuse him fraternal fellowship. None of these causes, however should control the sentiment of Republicans. The Republican and the negro, when Democracy inaugurates treason and rebellion, fight a common battle for a common cause. . . . Shall Michigan, then who has so nobly stood by the policies of the government, contradict and stultify herself by refusing to do in her own dominion what she has commanded Congress to do for the whole domain? Shall they contravene every vote given by our Senators and Representatives in Congress, who were elected by the same people to represent the same principle in Congress that they are called upon to enforce in their own State next Spring? . . . We are at a loss to account for this sudden retrogration from the magnanimous standard of the fathers of the republic, which is meant to be the rule and guide of modern Republicanism. All the State constitutions adopted after the declaration of Independence up to 1792, except South Carolina, extended the right of franchise to legal voters irrespective of color. None of the alarming consequences grew out of that prerogative in those

days which are predicted as being the result of a like prerogative at this time.
. . . In view of these antecedents it is very difficult to account for the seemingly unhappy instinct which move men of late to curse a nigger. Whatever
may have been the modernly progressive tendency of things in reference to
art and science, it seems to have been terribly retrogressive in regard to
prejudices among races. . . . It is reduced simply to the fact that the negro, as
a general thing, will vote the Republican ticket. Shall it be then, that for this
offence the Democracy shall deprive the freedman of his vote, by the aid of
renegade, unreliable Republicans? We shall see.

QUESTIONS

1. Why did Southerners believe that blacks would (or should) vote the Democratic ticket?
2. Why did Southerners warn blacks to stay away from politics and attend
   to their labor and families?
3. What kinds of threats are implied in John Forsyth's editorial in the *Mobile (Ala.) Advertiser and Register*?
4. What were the arguments against allowing blacks to vote?
5. Why did Republicans support black suffrage in the South but not in the
   North?

NOTES

1. *Florida Peninsular*, 27 July 1867.

2. Quoted in Donna L. Dickerson, " 'Got No Souls . . .': Racism in Southern Reconstruction Newspapers," *Proceedings of the Association for Education in Journalism
and Mass Communications, Southeast Colloquium* 1 (March 1992): 18–26.

3. Edmund L. Drago, *Black Politicians and Reconstruction in Georgia: A Splendid
Failure* (Baton Rouge: Louisiana State University Press, 1982), 29.

4. Howard N. Rabinowitz, "Holland Thompson and Black Political Participation
in Reconstruction," in *Southern Black Leaders of the Reconstruction Era*, ed. Howard N.
Rabinowitz (Urbana: University of Illinois Press, 1982), 251–53.

CHAPTER 14

The Alaska Purchase, 1867

In what was the largest voyage of discovery of its day, the Great Nordic Expedition left Russia in 1741 to find and map the coasts of Siberia and the United States. Headed by Vitus Jonassen Bering and Aleksey Ilich Chirikov, 10,000 men set out for the peninsula of Kamchatka on the far western coast of Russia, below the Arctic Circle. Bering and Chirikov then sailed east to Alaska across what would later be named the Bering Sea. Chirikov's ship became separated in a storm and Bering's ship was wrecked on Bering Island, where Bering died. Survivors of the expedition stayed on the island until spring when they managed to sail back to Kamchatka.[1]

Russian explorers and fur traders immediately began to exploit the natural resources of Alaska, establishing lucrative fur, fishing, sealing, and whaling trade companies. The first permanent colony in Alaska was established in 1784 on Kodiak Island. In 1792, Catherine the Great gave the Russian American Company a complete monopoly over fur trading in Alaska, and in 1799, the company was granted control over all trade, government, and religion in Alaska. No foreigners were allowed to fish or engage in any trade with Alaskan natives. With the elimination of competition from other fur traders, the Russian American Company quickly realized large profits for its shareholders, which included members of the royal family.

However, the Russians were not self-sufficient in Alaska. Harsh winters and a lack of food resulted in periods of starvation. Needing to purchase wheat, cattle, sheep, and other food products, the company expanded southward from Alaska, at one time establishing a colony on the northern coast of Spanish California for the purpose of harvesting sea otter pelts and growing wheat. The company also contracted with U.S. and Spanish companies, exchanging Alaskan salmon and furs for food, seed, and livestock.

Despite the prohibition against foreign trade in Alaska, British and U.S. ships openly traded with Indians, exchanging muskets and gunpowder for furs. This resulted in an escalation of animosity between the Russian American Company and other large trading companies, such as the Hudson's Bay Company and Northwest Company.

By the late 1840s, overharvesting of furs, hostility among the Alaskan Indian tribes, inadequate supplies, declining company profits, and instability at home led Russia to consider selling Alaska. In 1853, Russia was preoccupied with the Crimean War against Turkey. The situation worsened when Britain, with its large navy stationed in almost every corner of the world, threatened to join Turkey. Britain's entry into the war put Russia's far-flung territories, especially Alaska, at great risk. To reduce Alaska's vulnerability, Russia decided to enter into negotiations with a U.S. trading company to temporarily transfer Alaska to private U.S. interests. After the war Russia would reclaim the territory. Russian delegates presented the idea to the U.S. government, which decided that the deception was too obvious. But the first seed of the idea to sell Alaska to the United States had been planted.

The United States had not made a secret of its desire to acquire territory beyond the North American continent, particularly its wish to establish a robust commerce in the Pacific. Consequently, Britain agreed to consider Alaska neutral territory, perhaps fearing that Russia would cede the land to the United States permanently. When the Crimean War ended in 1856, Russia faced a large debt. Selling Alaska not only would help with the debt but it would also allow Russia to focus its trading in China and Japan. Selling Alaska also would give the czar an excuse to get rid of the Russian American Company, which was expending a great deal of the Russian navy's energy as it interdicted illegal foreign ships trading with natives and interceded in various wars with the Indians. In 1860, the Russian American Company rejected a new charter from the czar that removed its monopoly over trade and required more direct supervision by the Russian government. Russia now had only three options to deal with the Alaskan territory—administer Alaska herself, let the territory decline, or sell it.

Negotiations with the United States resumed in 1866, this time with Secretary of State William H. Seward in charge. Seward was an expansionist. As a member of Congress, he had backed the building of the transcontinental railroad, promoted California's admission to the Union, pushed the idea of building a telegraph line across the Bering Strait to China and Europe, and encouraged trade agreements with China and Japan. As secretary of state, he realized that any trading empire that the nation developed would require naval protection, which in turn required naval bases strategically placed around the world—including Alaska.

Russia's negotiator was Edouard de Steockl, who was authorized to accept no less than $5 million for the territory. The negotiations between Seward and Steockl moved swiftly and within two weeks a draft treaty for $7.2

million in exchange for 570,373.6 square miles was presented to President Andrew Johnson. Johnson, whose mind was on more pressing Reconstruction issues, gave the treaty his approval and sent it on to the U.S. Senate, which by law is required to approve all treaties. Within a fortnight the Senate passed the treaty 73 to 2. The more difficult fight would be getting the House of Representatives to approve the $7.2 million appropriation.

By spring 1867, Congress and the president were at an impasse on major Reconstruction legislation, with Johnson blocking almost everything that came from Congress. Therefore, the House was not predisposed to approve just anything sent by Johnson, especially a treaty that gave away more than $7 million in exchange for a frozen wasteland. The House wanted simply to deal Johnson another defeat—payback for the many times that he had vetoed their Reconstruction legislation. The House delayed hearings on the appropriations several times. In the meantime, the territory had been ceded to the United States and formal possession had occurred in October 1867. Only after the impeachment trial of President Johnson did the House vote to approve the expenditure—113 to 43, with 44 abstaining. On July 28, 1868, the Treasury Department issued a draft for $7.2 million.

By the time the deal had been struck, Seward had come in for a great deal of criticism. Newspapers referred to the purchase as "Seward's Folly" and "Seward's Icebox." Most considered Alaska worthless, although gold and oil had been discovered by Russians. Following congressional approval of the $7.2 million payment to Russia, speculation abounded in the newspapers that the House vote had been "paid for." Massachusetts representatives Thaddeus Stevens and Nathaniel Banks were accused of having received bribes for their support, although both had always supported the purchase. A contemporary congressional investigation, and historians, have found no proof that such bribery occurred. However, Steockl was given money by the Russian government to help "grease the skids," which he did. Recipients of Russian money included the U.S. lawyer who acted as Russia's lobbyist and John Forney, editor of the *Washington Chronicle*. Perhaps small amounts also reached the pockets of other newspapers, but there is no documentation of such payments. Purchasing "friendly" articles was not considered unethical at the time.

Congress did not initially provide for a local government in Alaska, so the War Department controlled Alaska from its headquarters in Sitka. Between 1867 and 1877, the army's job was primarily to resolve disputes between the few Americans and native Indian tribes. The army was withdrawn in 1877, and administration was transferred to the Treasury Department.

It was not until 1896 that Alaska's true worth was realized when gold was discovered in the interior in Canada's Yukon Territory. Thousands of miners sailed to Alaska and crossed the mountains into Canada to stake claims around Dawson. Alaska's small port towns such as Skagway and Juneau became the jumping-off place for miners, and the wealth went to store owners who sold miners food, packhorses, shovels, and mining gear. Most of the gold adventurers failed in their quest when they realized how difficult it was to cross into the interior. In 1898, gold was discovered in Nome, along the western coast. This time, gold rushers were more successful.

The first editorial in the section favoring acquisition, by William W. Harding, underscores the point that Britain will not be happy when the United States acquires a territory north of Canada. The second editorial, by Henry J. Raymond, explains why having more than 1,000 miles of coastline facing the Pacific is an economic and political advantage. The last editorial in the section emphasizes that while not enough is known about Alaska, it is important to trust those who live in the West to evaluate its worth.

The section against the acquisition of Alaska starts with an editorial, by E.L. Godkin, that not only expresses a great dislike for Russia but also describes Alaska as a vast arctic wasteland. The remainder of the editorials argue that the purchase of Alaska is a waste of money, as there is nothing in the frozen north that will prove of any value in the future.

FAVORING THE ACQUISITION OF ALASKA

William W. Harding: "Russian America Ceded to the United States"

The United States had an uneasy relationship with England, going as far back as the war of 1812. The farther the United States stretched itself to the west and contemplated territories to the south, the more England worried.

Philadelphia Inquirer, April 1, 1867

On Saturday afternoon the telegraph rather startled the country with the announcement that Russia had concluded a treaty with the United States Government by which the latter, for the sum of seven millions of dollars, comes into possession of all Russian North America. Although a vast portion of the Russian Possessions is sterile and unfit for cultivation, yet other portions are valuable by reason of the furs which are yearly secured by traders for our own and foreign markets. . . .

Were it not for British Columbia our Pacific possessions would now extend from Lower California to Behring's Straits. As it is, the United States will control nearly the whole coast line lying between those two points. As intimated in the dispatch, Sir Frederick Bruce, the British Minister at Washington, has taken the alarm at this movement between Russia and the United States. England will not like it, and the old lion will undoubtedly growl, even if he does not roar. But his protest will amount to nothing. If Congress ratifies the treaty, there will be an end to his growling.

Henry J. Raymond: "A Large Territorial Acquisition"

This editorial, unlike others of the day, looks at the acquisition of Alaska as one more move in the game of Manifest Destiny—or the expansion of power through territory. Yet, the editor also takes a "wait and see" attitude, since so little was known about Alaska.

New York Times, March 31, 1867

It is announced that, by treaty with Russia, our Government has acquired possession of the large Arctic domain known as Russian America.

There are from four to five hundred thousand square miles in this new Territory—fully enough to make nearly a dozen States as large as New-York. Be the bargain what it may, it is big enough.

Its value, however, as a national acquisition is not likely to be measured by any theory of territorial expansion. The Russian ports on the coast, or rather in the islands bordering thereon, have had a small and diminishing fur trade for many years, and possibly this is susceptible of development under a new government and by means of American enterprise. But *that* at the best is a small matter. The great commercial advantages which would accrue to us from possessing a number of good harbors along a coast extending from latitude 55 to the Frozen Ocean hardly need to be pointed.

The Whale trade of the North Pacific would receive an impetus and encouragement it has never had before. Wherever our fast-growing commerce with Northeastern Asia extends the advantages of these Northern ports would be beneficially felt. The lines of commercial intercourse between our Western ports and China, Japan, &c., that we are now opening up, could hardly fail to profit by the additional feeders from a new quarter which this expansion of our political authority and commercial enterprise would necessarily supply. But the prime gain—if it is a gain at all for a leading Power to extend its sway beyond a certain limit—would have to be sought in the increased influence which our Government would acquire in all that affects individual States on this Continent, and the relations of the whole, alike with Asiatic and European Powers. If it is desirable to gain an influence thus paramount, there could be no more practical way of setting about it than by getting hold of a vast coast-line like this of Russian America. . . . The advantages of the acquisition may not be without something of a counterbalancing kind. Increased power and dominion bring increased responsibilities.

When we hear all about the terms of the treaty, and have weighed the question coolly and calmly, we shall know better how to value the purchase, and how to felicitate ourselves over having made it. Meanwhile we do not exactly see how it should have come to pass, as an evening paper has it, that in the precincts of the British Embassy at Washington the British lion should have been heard, yesterday, howling with anguish. Sir Frederick Bruce is supposed to be a man of some common sense; and if all the preliminaries of the treaty spoken of are fair and square, no Government—least of all that of Great Britain—need feel greatly demoralized over the transaction.

Anonymous Writer: No Title

At the time, probably only those who lived on the West Coast and had first-hand knowledge of Alaska truly appreciated the hidden wealth of the territory. This editorial is willing to take a risk that Californians have a better grasp of the situation.

New York Times, May 19, 1868

The House had before it yesterday two reports on the Alaska purchase—the majority report merely providing that the appropriation to fulfill the treaty stipulations be made, and the minority report arguing that the appropriation should not be passed, because Alaska is of no value to us, and has no productions of any kind that will benefit this country. In the meantime we learn from California, Oregon and all the Pacific region that the people are greatly troubled about the proposed repudiation of the treaty and the return of Alaska to the Russian Government; and the papers assert that if Congress carries out this policy, the Republican Party there will be utterly overthrown. This is certainly no reason for confirming the purchase: but the facts on which this feeling is based are good reasons for confirming it. The Californians consider Alaska of great value, and the latest advices say that trade with it is increasing. "If any man hauls down the American flag, *shoot him on the spot.*"

OPPOSING THE ACQUISITION OF ALASKA

E.L. Godkin: No Title

E.L. Godkin had covered the Crimean War, and this editorial is probably more influenced by his dislike of the Russian czar than any concern about Manifest Destiny.

The Nation, April 4, 1867

Russian America is inhabited by fifty thousand fishing, trapping, fur-bearing Esquimaux, and nine or ten thousand Russians, Russian Americans, and people whom the gazetteers call Aleoots and Kodiaks. They import a good part of their provisions, and export a yearly diminishing quantity of furs. The country is a frozen wilderness, better known to arctic explorers and whalers than to most other men, and probably of no possible value to any men but them, the semi-civilized tribes that support existence there, and the Russian sutlers who trade with them. The territory is rather larger than eight States like New York would be, its area being 894,000 square miles. What we want of it, unless to take a solitude and call it Seward by erecting it into a Territory, we do not know, but we can buy the privilege of flying the stars and stripes over a colony, and a worthless colony, by paying seven millions of dollars for it. This we suppose Congress will not do. There is no good reason for doing it, and several good reasons for not doing it. We do not want far-distance, detached colonies, nor ice and snow territories, nor Esquimaux fellow-citizens, nor Mt. Saint Elias, and there is nothing else to be had from Alaska and Barrow's Point, so far as we are informed. The Czar's intentions, aside from his design of getting the seven millions in gold, are doubtful. It may be that he thinks New Archangel not worth the powder and shot he may have to expend in its defense in case of a new Eastern war. It may be that he wants to impress Europe with the idea of the closeness of friendship that must exist between Russia and a country for whose sake Russia cuts off a limb. European statesmen, however, will hardly sleep the worse on account of the phantom of an alliance between this country and Russia, and the Czar himself probably knows that, not to put too fine a point on it, the people of the United States know little and care less about Russia. But with all these considerations we have no concern. We are to consider our own interests, say yes or no to Mr. Seward's chimerical project of saddling us with a frozen desert of a colony—and we imagine there will be little difficulty in choosing the right answer.

Horace Greeley: The Russian Humbug

Horace Greeley was an avowed enemy of William H. Seward and felt that the Alaska purchase was unwarranted and that Seward had exaggerated the benefits of Alaska.

New York Tribune, April 9, 1867

Mr. Seward's geographical discoveries continue to be telegraphed over the country. . . . The climate is delicious, and quite warm in Winter; yet the ice fields are inexhaustible, and in the burning heat of the Arctic Summer the Esquimaux take refuge in their shade. The country is covered with pine forests, and vegetable gardens flourish along the coast, whereon the walrus are also found in vast multitudes. Wheat, Seals, Barley, White Bears, Turnips, Icebergs, Whales and Gold Mines, are found as far north as the sixtieth degree. . . . All tastes are gratified in Mr. Seward's land, which is not Russian America, but Utopia. On paper it is a wonderful country; on ice it is what is generally called a big thing.

Carey Styles: "Alaska"

Like so many editorials from Southern Democratic newspapers, no matter what the subject, it was invariably linked to radical Reconstruction policies—even the Eskimos could not escape.

Atlanta Constitution, October 22, 1869

Sometime back, it will be remembered, that Mr. Seward gave a rosy account of the value of Alaska. This frigid spot is a pet of the statesman of the tinkling bell, and he is much interested in making it out great shakes.

Gen. Geo. H. Thomas has made a personal inspection of the country, and pronounces it good for nothing. It has some coal and iron, but we have plenty nearer home. It is worthless for farming. He advises as little expense as possible in governing it.

It would be a fine idea to make it the headquarters of Radicalism, and turn it over entire to the political heresy, with Seward as Grand Cyclops.

Anonymous Writer: "That Polar Paradise"

Following the purchase of Alaska, numerous expeditions into the territory brought back reports of Alaska's natural resources. The reports, curiously, were quite contradictory, and newspapers tended to pick up the report that best supported their own opinion of Alaska.

Chicago Tribune, March 20, 1871

At length something definite and apparently trustworthy concerning Alaska has been developed, in the reports of two United States officers and the census returns obtained by the government. The result is a most beautiful dissolving view not only of Mr. Seward's pretty picture of our polar possession, but of the $7,200,000 (gold) which he made us pay for the territory, and the $1,000,000 per annum which it takes to maintain possession of it. The only comfort or material aid to be got out of the territory is limited within the three lines, fur, fish, and lumber. The last is said by one authority to be "very valuable," but inaccessible, which qualification, it must be admitted, imparts a sarcastic force to the epithet "valuable." Another report denies that the lumber is good for anything after it is got at. This throws us back on the fish, which are very nice, but which, under the stimulus of American enterprise, have only yielded $14,400 per year, not exclusive of expenses. As to furs, the trade in them has been steadily diminishing ever since we occupied the country, until now it is less than $20,000 a year, in gross. Probably the profit—to somebody—is equivalent to that amount. The magnificent ice crop, which we were promised, turns out to be too porous to keep. The potatoes proving to be the opposite of the ice—that is, having too much water to be fit for use—there would still be some hope in onions; but alas! they lack that essential feature of a well-regulated onion, to-wit, the bulb, without which all stalks and blades are but vanity and vexation of spirit. Of Indians there is a very good crop—about 8,300, all told; but they can be put to no good use toward the development of the revenue. The stories about gold, copper, or even coal mines, prove to be of the genuine Munchausen type. Add to this the unfriendliness of the Russian population, the vileness of the Indians, and the demoralizing effect of their women upon our soldiers, and there seems to be a plenty of reasons to regret that we should ever have attempted to soothe our annexation fever with the icy compress of Alaska. . . .

QUESTIONS

1. What were the arguments in favor of the United States purchasing Alaska?
2. What were the major reasons against purchasing Alaska?
3. Why did Russia want to sell Alaska?
4. What effect did Reconstruction politics have on the purchase of Alaska?

NOTE

1. The information for this introduction comes from Ronald J. Jensen, *The Alaska Purchase and Russian-American Relations* (Seattle: University of Washington Press, 1975), and Paul Sothe Holbo, *Tarnished Expansion: The Alaska Scandal, the Press, and Congress, 1867–1871* (Knoxville: University of Tennessee Press, 1983).

CHAPTER 15

Impeachment of President Johnson, 1868

President Andrew Johnson was not an easy man to get along with—either socially or politically. He prided himself on his consistent and persistent adherence to a narrow set of political principles and rarely compromised on those beliefs. He also was not an astute politician. He could not "read" the public—either in the North or in the South—well enough to realize that as each day of his administration passed, he was losing the support of an increasing number of Republicans and Democrats.

Some of the more radical members of Congress wanted to oust Johnson from the first day he stepped into the White House. However, the majority of Republicans believed they could work with the president and convince him of the necessity of a strong Reconstruction policy. But Johnson refused to cooperate and at every turn found ways to disassemble Congress's work. For example, when he disallowed further confiscation of rebel lands, he took away the major source of financial support for the Freedmen's Bureau. By pardoning thousands of rebels, he enabled the old planter class to reassume leadership in the South. Johnson also used his presidential power of appointment to replace thousands of federal officeholders with men of his own political sentiments. As one contemporary said, Johnson "set back the work of Reconstruction . . . two full years."[1]

In 1867, Congress's patience was strained to the breaking point. Unless Republicans found a way to slow down the president's attempts to frustrate Reconstruction, the entire effort would be lost. The chance came with the Tenure of Office Act passed in March 1867, which required Senate approval if the president removed a cabinet member.

In August, when Congress was in recess, Johnson decided to challenge the Tenure of Office Act by asking for Secretary of War Edwin Stanton's resignation. When Stanton, the only cabinet member friendly with Republicans, refused to resign, Johnson suspended him and named General

Andrew Johnson receiving a copy of the summons from George T. Brown, *sergeant at arms, to appear for trial before the U.S. Senate.* Harper's Weekly. *Library of Congress.*

Ulysses S. Grant as interim secretary of war. The law allowed the president to suspend an officer when Congress was not in session. But when Congress reconvened in December 1867, the Senate refused to concur in Stanton's removal. In direct defiance of Congress and the Tenure of Office Act, Johnson fired Stanton and replaced him with General John Schofield. The removal of Stanton was the proverbial straw that broke the camel's back. The president had broken the law and had defied Congress. Within days of Johnson's actions, the House voted on an impeachment resolution, which accused the president of willfully violating an act of Congress.

Under Article II, section 4 of the U.S. Constitution, a president can be impeached, convicted, and removed from office if he is found to have committed "treason, bribery and other high crimes and misdemeanors." The impeachment process begins in the House of Representatives, whose members vote on an inquiry of impeachment and direct the Judiciary Committee to draw up articles of impeachment, specifying the charges. The committee can clear the president after investigation; otherwise, the full House votes on the articles—this is the actual vote "to impeach." The articles of impeachment are then sent to the Senate where the trial takes place. The Chief Justice of the Supreme Court presides and a member (or members) of the House acts as prosecuting counsel. The president, who is not required to attend, provides his own defense counsel. A two-thirds vote of the Senate is required for the president's conviction and removal from office.

On March 2, the House voted 126 to 47 on 11 articles of impeachment. Eight of the articles dealt with Stanton's removal, one dealt with the removal of a Southern military commander, one dealt with Johnson's behavior and actions against members of Congress, and Article Eleven was a catchall of the charges. The trial in the Senate began March 30.

Five weeks later, a vote was taken on Article 11. The two-thirds vote needed failed by one vote. The result was the same for Articles Two and Three. Seven Republican Senators had bolted the party line and voted with the Democrats to acquit. No further votes were taken. The effort to remove Johnson had failed, and he served out the rest of Lincoln's term. In 1926, the Supreme Court overturned the Tenure of Office Act, ruling that Congress could not pass a law infringing on the president's constitutional powers of removal.[2]

Depending on what side of the Senate aisle was sat on, a Senator saw one of two faces of the final vote. Either the vote maintained the principle that Congress should not remove the president from office simply because they disagree with him over policy, style, and administration of office or the acquittal was bought with bribes, and the vote of 35 men to convict condemned the president before the nation's eyes.

While the trial of Johnson did involve complicated issues of law regarding the interpretation of the Tenure of Office Act as well as what was and was not an impeachable offense, it was primarily a political trial. The real issue was the relationship between the presidency and Congress, and the question was whether Congress or the executive should oversee Reconstruction.

Impeachment was not a popular act, and only a handful of newspapers actually came out in favor of it. Even the staunchest Republican newspapers waffled around the issue, explaining why Johnson was in such trouble and how he could have behaved better to avoid his problems. The first reading in the section, by John Russell Young from the *New York Tribune*, was probably the strongest call for impeachment among Republican newspapers. The second entry, by George W. Curtis, explains why Johnson had no authority to break the Tenure of Office Act. The third entry, by Henry Raymond, describes all of the benefits that will come from the impeachment—although he states that he does not support impeachment. The fourth selection, by Samuel Bowles, believes that the relationship of the president to the people and to Congress was forever changed by the impeachment proceedings. The fifth selection by John Russell Young places the blame for all future problems with the president directly on the shoulders of the seven dissenters.

The section against the impeachment of Johnson begins with an editorial warning that should Johnson be convicted then impeachment would be a common tool to use against any president who did not toe Congress's line. The second selection, by Manton Marble, argues that the president has every right to break a law that he feels is unconstitutional, because he has taken an oath to uphold the Constitution. The next entry from *The Nation* admits that little was lost or gained by the acquittal, but praises the seven Republican senators who voted for acquittal for voting their consciences rather than their politics. The final selection from the *London Times* criticizes Republicans for trying to maneuver the Senate into convicting the president and believes that with acquittal the president will be stronger and the Republican Party weaker for their efforts.

In Support of Impeachment

John Russell Young: "The President Must Be Impeached"

Horace Greeley, editor of the New York Tribune, *did not support impeachment. In February, Greeley went on a lecturing tour and left the editorial page to John Russell Young, who had not always agreed with his mentor and boss. The editorial reversed the* Tribune's *stand on impeachment, and thereafter Greeley was a reluctant supporter of the impeachment movement.*

New York Tribune, February 24, 1868

We do not see how the House can refuse to arraign the President before the Senate for high crimes and misdemeanors. Impeachment is not a desireable proceeding. It is cumbersome and tedious. It may arrest legislation, and present a new issue to the country at a time when new issues are not wanted. It is not, perhaps, a wise precedent to make. It gives to power a temptation which passion cannot always resist. It is a high, solemn, sacred trust, only to be used, when absolutely necessary for the salvation of the country.

We believe the salvation of the country demands the impeachment of the President. We have all along felt that we might submit to Mr. Johnson's Administration, evil as it has been, rather than force an angry and doubtful question upon the country. With the Congress overwhelmingly Republican, there was no reason why we should not compel the President to pursue a wise policy. We reasoned upon the presumption that it was better to have impeachment held over him as a check than to begin a trial that might be as long as that of Warren Hastings. It was a debatable question. The evidence was far from being conclusive. Morally, there was no doubt that Mr. Johnson should be impeached. But impeachment is a question of law and evidence, not of moral belief. . . . Therefore we have constantly opposed impeachment, although at times we stood alone among the Republican press. There is no longer any doubt. The issue is as clear as it was when Gen. Beauregard opened his batteries upon Fort Sumter. Andrew Johnson, President of the United States, tramples upon a law, defies the authority of Congress, and claims to exercise absolute and despotic power. *Congress must impeach him immediately.* . . .

The time has come to cease trifling with Andrew Johnson. This man, who reeled into the Presidency; who has debased his high office by unseemly and indecent demonstrations; who has surrounded himself with the worst members of the worst phase of Washington life; whose retinue consists of lobbyists, Rebels, and adventurers; who has polluted the public service by making espionage honorable, and treachery the means of advancement; who has deceived the party that elected him, as well as the party that created him; who has made his own morbid and overweening vanity the only rule of his administration; who has sought to entrap illustrious servants of the people into ignominious evasion of the law, and who now claims to break that law with impunity—this most infamous Chief-Magistrate should be swept out of office. LET HIM BE IMPEACHED!

George W. Curtis: "The President and the Law"

Probably the strongest argument that the prosecution had was that President Johnson had taken it into his own hands to decide which laws to obey and which ones to disregard. See the New York World*'s (March 7, 1868) reply to this argument, provided below.*

Harper's Weekly, March 7, 1868

The Tenure-of-Office Act was passed by Congress, vetoed by the President, passed over his veto by the constitutional majority, and became the law. The President acknowledged it to be a law by conforming to its requirements, and explaining to the Senate why he had suspended the Secretary of War. The Senate did not approve the suspension, and there the matter should have ended. But by subsequently assuming to remove the Secretary the President deliberately and distinctly violates the law which forbids the removal of any civil officer appointed with the consent of the Senate without its concurrence if it be in session. There could not be a more flagrant defiance of law or usurpation of authority. If the President, as we have said, may do it in the case of one law, however constitutionally enacted, until the Supreme Court had passed upon it, and the consequent confusion and uncertainty would be intolerable. The argument . . . that a law may be held unconstitutional until pronounced otherwise by the court is subversive of the government and of civil order; and the question ought, therefore, to be distinctly settled whether the President has the power of dispensing with the laws a power which the English two hundred years ago dethroned King James II for claiming.

Henry Raymond: "The Impending Change in the Presidency"

In this editorial, editor Henry Raymond, who never came out in favor of impeachment, explains the benefits that would result from removing President Johnson.

New York Times, February 27, 1868

For our own part, we see no reason to change the views we have often expressed in regard to the wisdom or necessity of impeachment.

We do not think the President's acts as such demand the application of such a punishment—though we confess his whole course of action has been admirably calculated to provoke it. Nor can we fail to see that, while the impeachment and removal of the President will arouse party feeling and contribute somewhat to the excitement of the public mind, in other respects it will not be without its countervailing advantages. It will promote unity of action on the part of the different departments of the Government, and thus aid in the adjustment of questions that have greatly disturbed the public peace. The conflict between the President and Congress has been sharp, bitter and obstinate on both sides. There has been nothing whatever, on either side, of the spirit of conciliatione,—of mutual toleration and respect,—which is absolutely essential to the peaceful and harmonious action of the various departments of our Government. The President was firm, and we doubt not sincere, in his conviction that Congress was wrong; and Congress was equally sincere and frim in its belief that the President was wrong. Neither gave the other credit even for good motives. There has been no progress in the practical restoration of peace and prosperity to the disturbed and suffering sections of our common country.

The removal of the President, if it should be made, will remedy this, at all events. It will put an end to the conflict of authority and of action between Congress and the Executive. We shall have Congress enacting laws with the concurrence and approval of the President; and we shall have the Executive Department giving the full weight of its influence to their execution. . . . Instead of making Congress more extreme and violent in its action, it may, by increasing its sense of responsibility and removing exasperations to which it has been too ready to yield, have the effect of inducing a wiser and more judicious course of proceedings on the part of the law-making power. One thing is very clear:—so long as Mr. Johnson is President there can be no harmony of feeling and no unity of action between the two departments upon whose joint action the whole vigor and efficiency of the Government depend. The two will be at daggers' points so long as the incumbents of both remain. . . .

Samuel Bowles: "The Upshot of Impeachment"

The Springfield (Mass.) Republican *supported impeachment throughout the hearings. In this final editorial after the vote was in, editor Samuel Bowles still believes that President Johnson should have been convicted and sees the impeachment process as something to be desired rather than feared in the long term.*

Springfield (Mass.) Republican, **May 18, 1868**

Impeachment is as dead as Marley ever was, but it does not follow, that, like the old curmudgeon, it has lived wholly in vain. Nothing is more deceptive than the appearances of success or failure; and history has all and more than it can do, in reversing the verdicts of the times. "Another such victory would be fatal to our arms" is a saying attributed to an eminent English orator, upon the battle of Bunker Hill. . . . Such a measure as the impeachment of the president could not have been inaugurated and carried through such scenes to a full conclusion, without seriously affecting, for better or worse, the balance of governmental power, and exerting a considerable influence upon the destinies of the country. Up to the accession of Mr. Johnson, the right of impeachment was a mere sound and a mere name. It had no constitutional significance whatever. . . . It may fairly be said, that so far as our national life down to 1865 was concerned, this clause might just as well have been left out of the constitution.

It cannot be so in the future. The failure of impeachment in this case has established the possibility of its success at another time. There is no question that the great strength of the president's defense lay in the fact that it was an untried thing, and that the public mind shrank from its application. It was as new and strange to our people as war was before Bull Run. It never will be so again. The ice is broken. Impeachment has become a fact in our national life, a force among the forces of our government; and though it may and ought really to be employed but seldom, if ever, it must always hereafter exert a powerful influence upon the conduct of affairs. A new and tremendous possibility has been developed in our politics. We say possibility, because, though authorized by the constitution, it was an unknown and practically a non-existent thing before the extraordinary and almost miraculous cantankerosity, upishness, offishness, backwardness and forwardness at-every-wrong-time, of Andy Johnson worried a radical Congress for nearly three years into impeaching him.

We have previously given the reasons which induce us to believe that the executive power of this country needs some additional restraint under the prodigious enlargement and enforcement which it has received by the war, by the increase of federal patronage, by the extension of territory, and by the force and rapid consolidation and centralization of our republic during the past eight years. Nor is there any great practical danger of this power being perverted to party ends. There is less reason to apprehend its abuse than its disuse. So burdensome are the conditions with which conviction is coupled, so strong is the tendency to dissent and dissention in a court composed of politicians, as we have seen in the past week, so quick are the sympathies of the masses at any appearance of persecution or injustice, and so imminent always is reaction in politics, as to render it a great deal more likely that the country will suffer from lack than from excess of this constitutional remedy. . . . The presidents of the United States, equally with the ministers of England, are and should be held responsible in the language of Hallam, for the propriety and expedience, not less than for the legality, of their measures. It is easy to say that this makes it possible for impeachment to become a mere party weapon; but practically the danger is far less than that it will not be sufficiently employed to vindicate the responsibility of public officers.

We cannot, therefore, regret that such proceedings have been instituted, although it was found impossible to carry them out in the present case; nor that this mode of redress has now become familiar to the minds of the people. It is not even beyond reasonable expectation that this trial resulting as it does, will have a decidedly sobering effect upon Mr. Johnson. . . . If a man

like Andrew Johnson can be held to reason by the application of this constitutional remedy, who shall pretend hereafter to disparage its efficacy?

It appears to us a great mistake not to have convicted the president.
He was guilty. He deserved it: the nation needed it. The largest and best considerations of statesmanship required it. The spirit of the law and the constitution demanded it. And as a practical thing, notwithstanding the many and
serious objections against it, the country would have been better for it. . . .

John Russell Young: "The President's Future Course"

After the Senate voted to acquit the president, the New York Tribune *asserted that the Republican Party could not be held responsible for President
Johnson's future actions. Salmon Chase, chief justice of the Supreme Court,
presided over the trial, and Robert Fessenden, senator from Ohio, was one
of the seven Republicans who voted against the impeachment articles.*

New York Tribune, May 18, 1868

The Republicans who initiated and have sustained this prosecution have
relieved themselves from a grave responsibility. For years, Andrew Johnson
has been the terror of the Southern loyalists and the chief obstacle to the
rapid progress of peaceful and loyal Reconstruction. Thousands have impa-
tiently murmured—"Why is he not impeached and removed?" It was in vain
that we urged that this was a big job—that it was likely to fail if attempted;
and that such failure would only increase his power for evil. . . .

So we have tried and not succeeded; but the result is quite other than
failure. The Republican party stands forever relieved from all responsibility
for Mr. Johnson's future misdeeds. Let him now wrest the command of the
Army from Gen. Grant—let him wield the Military as well as Civil power of
the Government in the interest of Rebellion and Aristocracy—let him obstruct to the utmost the return of the Southern States, free and loyal, to the
councils of the Republic—the country and the world will hold us wholly
blameless. Messrs. Chase, Fessenden & Co. have taken the Old Man of the
Sea upon their shoulders—we shall see how they bear up under the load!
They have nine months ahead of such responsibility as we do not covet—we
shall be agreeably disappointed if that does not break them down.

Thanks to Infinite Mercy, there is an ordeal before us in which a concurrence of two-thirds is not required to insure a righteous verdict. Let Messrs.
Chase, Fessenden & Co. take care of their man Johnson, while we organize
for and make certain the joyful advent of GRANT and VICTORY.

AGAINST IMPEACHMENT

Anonymous Writer: "Impeachment"

The perils of impeachment were not lost on the more reasonable people of the time. Many newspapers expressed the fear that should the president be removed, impeachment would become a common remedy.

Boston Daily Advertiser, March 3, 1868

Let us not feel, however, that this is to be a habitual remedy. If it is a simple one, it is a heroic one, and used to meet a great disease. Let us feel that the pass to which we have been brought is really a crisis, and see to it that we do not come to such crises again. When this medicine becomes a daily food, the people can scarcely be said to have any Government at all. When it can be administered without passion, and for good cause . . . it serves the legitimate purpose and enables the Government . . . to move on according to the law. But the internal struggle and suffering for which it is the relief should be remembered and studied, and should become more familiar to us than the process of cure. *If we come to like this process we shall be victims of a disease which will require sterner remedies, if indeed, any can be found.*

Manton Marble: "Resistance to Void Laws Is Obedience to the Supreme Law"

This editorial is the New York World*'s answer to a* Harper's Weekly *editorial of the same date that argued that it did not matter if the president believed the Tenure of Office Act to be unconstitutional; he was bound by law to obey it. The* World *counters that the president should disobey any law that is unconstitutional and then let the courts decide the issue.*

New York World, March 7, 1868

An unconstitutional law is void from the beginning. It is void till adjudged unconstitutional, and after. It is not more void after than before. It is void from its enactment till its erasure. That is the sound doctrine of all governments with a written constitution, which is the supreme law. The supreme law permanently exists and controls. The inferior law conflicting therewith (that is, unconstitutional) cannot also control, else there are two supreme laws, both of which it is impossible to obey by the hypothesis; else law are only made not to guide the obedient, but to make obedience impossible. The inferior law cannot control, nor can it even exist as law. It exists as the pretence of law. But conflicting with the law which permanently exists it is not only void, it cannot but be void. The courts but declare its character and affix the brand, they do not make it that which it is. They declare not merely that [it] is not law, but declare also that it has not been law. Therefore an unconstitutional law is void from the beginning.

This applies to the Tenure of Office law. It is an unconstitutional law. It is plainly such, as sixteen Presidents, thirty-nine Congresses, and the Supreme Court have practically adjudged. It concerns the President's right of removal of the officer by whom he is to take care that the laws be faithfully executed. It is void from the beginning. It violates the supreme law. Both laws cannot co-exist and be obeyed—this Tenure of Office law and the Constitution, which is the supreme law, and with which all inferior laws must be in conformity. To violate the void law is to "preserve, protect and defend" the supreme law, which the President is sworn to do. Not to violate the void law, the unconstitutional Tenure of Office law namely, would have been to violate the supreme law. Void laws should always be broken, never obeyed. Resistance to an unconstitutional law is obedience to the supreme law.

President Johnson has no choice but to violate one or the other law—the supreme law or the usurpation which was disguised as a law. . . .

It is absurd to say the President must execute all laws without regard to their constitutionality. His very highest duty is to defend the Constitution. Suppose the Rump, overriding the President's veto, establishes an order of nobility. Shall he not question that?—and if that, why not this? On the contrary, no man from President to policeman, has a right to execute an unconstitutional and therefore void law. Every man, and first of all the Chief Magistrate, has a right to resist a void law, to question it before the courts at least, subject only to the hazard of having erred in his judgment on the very point of constitutionality. So, that again we say, void laws should always be broken, never obeyed, and the sooner the better, that the brand of the courts may be at once affixed and their quality known to all man; and as resistance to tyrants is obedience to God, so disobedience of an unconstitutional law is obedience to the supreme law.

E. L. Godkin: "The Result of the Trial"

The Nation was lukewarm, at best, regarding the impeachment of President Johnson. This editorial notes that while it would have been nice to have a guilty verdict, nothing was really lost by not finding the president guilty.

The Nation, May 21, 1868

The vote on the verdict, even if it has not resulted in conviction, has abundantly justified the House in impeaching the President. When thirty-five out of fifty-four senators pronounce him guilty, it would be absurd as well as unjust to say that there was not "probable cause" for instituting the prosecution, and one may take this view of the matter even after making some allowance for the influence of party feeling and political excitement. . . .

The failure to convict is to be regretted for several reasons, but that it leaves Mr. Johnson in the Presidential chair we no longer include amongst the number. In the first place, it is not unlikely that during the remainder of his term he will behave well; in the second, even if he should desire to do mischief, his powers of mischief now, as we have already pointed out, are almost nil; and in the third, if he should commit fresh follies and extravagances, although the scandal will be great, it will be more than compensated for by the fact that they will help the Republican party during the coming campaign. . . . But the acquittal, although the largeness of the vote for conviction may justify the House morally, is not likely to strengthen the confidence of the country in the judgment of the majority. Moreover, it has some tendency to create a certain amount of confidence in the President's judgment. It leaves him less hopelessly in the wrong than he seemed six months ago, and it leaves him in possession of the honors of the field. His escape, to be sure, has been very narrow, but in politics, as in war, an inch of a miss is as good as a mile. He was, before the trial, in the position of a man whom Congress might crush, but would not; now, he is in the position of a man whom Congress tried to crush, but could not. It is certainly not Congress that has gained by this change. . . .

We believe, for our part, that the thanks of the country are due to Messrs. Trumbull, Fessenden, Grimes, Henderson, Fowler, Van Winkle, and Ross, not for voting for Johnson's acquittal, but for vindicating . . . the dignity and purity of the court of which they formed a part, and the sacred rights of individual conscience. They have afforded American young men an example such as no politicians have ever afforded them in the whole course of American history, and at a time, too, when the tendency to put party claims above everything is rapidly increasing. . . .

Anonymous Writer: No Title

Even in London, politically savvy editors knew that the radicals' fury and President Johnson's obstinacy led to the impeachment trials.

London Times, **May 29, 1868**

The acquittal of President Johnson on three articles of the Impeachment has been accepted as decisive in the United States. Though a single vote transferred from the minority to the majority would have turned the scale against him on any one of the eight remaining articles, the verdict already delivered by the Senate practically closes this memorable State trial. . . .

From first to last the grossest and most barefaced attempts have been made to force the Senate into conviction, and public meetings have been held all over the Union to "resolve" that President Johnson must at all hazards be found guilty. . . .

It may be said, indeed, that in such a trial as that of President Johnson questions of law and politics are so mingled as to be almost inseparable, and that any intelligent citizen had as good a right to form an opinion upon them as the fifty-four Senators who sat as Judges. . . .

No one who has read even the briefest abstract of the elaborate arguments on both sides will be disposed to accept this view, but, whether sound or unsound, it avails nothing to excuse these unscrupulous efforts to bias or intimidate a Court of Justice. Nor was there even the semblance of a patriotic motive to render them less disgraceful. On the contrary, it was notorious that most of this clamour for conviction proceeded from hungry office-seekers, who looked to Mr. Wade for their reward. . . .

If the undoubted courage of Mr. Johnson were combined with a statesmanlike capacity of seizing upon rare opportunities, it is possible that he might even yet rally and consolidate a powerful Conservative party. Upon his first accession to the Presidency, accidental though it was, he occupied a vantage ground from which he might have guided, without assuming to dictate the reconstruction of the South. His failure to do so, and the present ascendancy of Jacobinism in Congress, are due to his obstinate self-reliance and his strange blindness to the limitations of his Executive authority. . . . Not satisfied with passing acts over his veto, and imposing their own terms on States seeking re-admission, the dominant majority in Congress resolved to push matters to extremes by deposing him, and they have incurred a defeat not the less signal because they came within a hair's breadth of success. The consequence, so far as we can foresee, will not be so much a reaction in the President's favor as the development of a rupture long impending among the Republicans. . . .

The calmness, not to say the apathy, which has characterized the attitude of the non-political classes in the United States at this crisis is very remarkable. While professional demagogues, wirepullers, and lobbyists have been almost beside themselves with excitement, the great American public has maintained its self-possession, not without symptoms of a desire to get the whole affair over.

QUESTIONS

1. What was the real reason behind the impeachment effort?
2. What would have been gained by Johnson's impeachment, according to Henry Raymond of the *New York Times*?
3. Why did editors believe that Johnson's intemperate speeches against Congress should not be cause for impeachment?
4. What reasons did *Harper's Weekly* give for why the president should not be allowed to break a law?
5. How might you counter the argument that the seven Republican senators who voted for acquittal did so because they were cajoled and bribed?

NOTES

1. Michael Les Benedict, *The Impeachment and Trial of Andrew Johnson* (New York: Norton, 1999), 47.

2. Brooks D. Simpson, *The Reconstruction Presidents* (Lawrence: University Press of Kansas, 1998), 175.

CHAPTER 16

Creating the Carpetbagger Myth, 1867–69

Come South to boast and swagger
With an empty carpet-bag
To rob the Whites of green-backs
And with the black go bunk
And change my empty satchel
For a full sole-leather trunk.[1]

The myth of the carpetbagger was a Southern propaganda tool to convince both the North and South that the carpetbag-led Reconstruction policy was a conspiracy against white supremacy. They were successful, and by the late nineteenth century a caricature of the Northern carpetbagger had been engraved on the American mind: low class, corrupt, cunning, and dishonest adventurers who came South carrying all their belonging in a suitcase made of carpet and who took advantage of blacks and plundered the helpless white Southerner. In the South, carpetbaggers were described as "the larvae of the North," "vulturous adventurers," and "vile, oily, odious."[2] More generous writers described the carpetbagger as a shiftless wanderer looking for a handout from radical governments.

These images became standard not only in history textbooks but also in fiction and movies with such constancy over the past century that they have become part of the American mythology. Not until the 1970s did scholars begin to redeem the carpetbagger by using demographic and census information, voting records, and statistics from state conventions, state legislatures, and Congress. With these tools, scholars have given us a very different picture from the one first proposed by Southern Democrats.

Rather than being low-class scoundrels, most of these men were young, educated, middle-class Northerners. Some were doctors, lawyers, and

The Man with the Carpet-bag. *This is one of Thomas Nast's most famous cartoons depicting the stereotypical carpetbagger with his bag made of carpet heading South.* Harper's Weekly. *Library of Congress.*

bankers. Others were teachers and ministers, and many were artisans, journalists, and small business owners. These young men were enticed to go to the South by advertisements encouraging Northerners to set up factories, establish small businesses, and buy cheap and plentiful land. Some went to the South as agents of the Freedmen's Bureau or as teachers for bureau schools. While a few immigrated to the South for political adventures, most wnt to become part of the economic life of the South.

The carpetbagger first became visible during the early months of congressional Reconstruction, when blacks were voting for the first time and Southern states were calling constitutional conventions to vote on new constitutions. For the first time in U.S. history, political decisions were being made by a biracial coalition of Republicans from the North and South. Despite the charges by Southern whites that these "black and tan" conventions were dominated by "unscrupulous Northern adventurers," only 16 percent of the delegates were actually carpetbaggers. State by state, the percentage of carpetbaggers in conventions ran from a high of 26 percent in Florida to a low of 7.5 percent in Georgia. The typical carpetbagger delegate was young (about 36 years old); from the Northeast; had served in the Union Army, Freedmen's Bureau, or both; was a farmer, professional, or laborer; and had arrived in the South immediately after the war.[3]

Despite their small numbers in the conventions, carpetbaggers received the brunt of Southern invective. The Southern press called these "radical interlopers" a "second army of invasion" that had given the balance of their power "to ignorant and debauched negroes" and created legislation "as unintelligible as the drunken brains in which it was conceived." Black delegates most often were characterized as dupes of the carpetbaggers who, like sheep, "follow their leaders, and whenever, wherever he goes, all go together, whether into green fields or over a precipice."

Because they had more political experience than blacks or Southern loyalists did, carpetbaggers played an increasing role in the new state governments they helped create. Stepping into the leadership vacuum left by the disfranchisement of the former Confederates, they served as governors, legislators, and judges, and they headed state offices from agriculture and railroad commissioner to treasurer.[4] But despite their political participation, carpetbaggers rarely dominated any one state's government. That role went to their Southern-born counterparts—the scalawags.

The one place where carpetbaggers did hold a more than fair share of influence was in federal positions such as judgeships, marshals, revenue agents, postmasters, and collectors of customs. Carpetbaggers also held many of the South's congressional seats. One study shows that from 1872 to 1875, 23 percent of the Southern delegation in the House were carpetbaggers, 6 percent were black, 34 percent were scalawags, and 37 percent were Southern Democrats.[5]

But numbers alone do not necessarily reflect power and influence. The power was in the men themselves—the ability of the carpetbag politician to know when to compromise, create coalitions, reach across political lines, pull Republicans of divergent views together, and build a broad base of popular support. The carpetbagger did all of these things well.

But with power also came corruption. Studies have shown that during the early 1870s the amount and severity of corruption was no higher in states dominated by Democrats than in states dominated by Republicans.[6] Nor were carpetbaggers any more likely to be rascals, thieves, robbers, plunderers, and cheats than any other politician was. Corruption was endemic to postwar politics in the North and South. Nevertheless, carpetbag corruption in the South played a significant role in the downfall of the Southern Republican Party in part because of the powerful rhetorical forces at work in the press. In other words, carpetbaggers received enough "bad press" that they were blamed for everything that went wrong in the South.

In the North, most voters believed in the concept of the two-party system as one that celebrated and strengthened democracy by allowing for a robust but civil discussion about differences. It was a game that grown men played with great relish and enthusiasm. And at the end of the day, they met their political enemy at the men's club or saloon to share a drink and a smoke. In the South, politics was life and death, as witnessed by riots, massacres, lynchings, and bulldozing. On politics depended the fate of the "white South," whether whites would be dominated by "Sambo—mounted and booted and spurred by white devils to ride over their own race" or by "intelligent white men" who would create a white government for white men.[7]

Consequently, when Southern newspapers reported on Southern corruption or when Southern correspondents wrote Northern newspapers about corruption, the descriptions and facts were embellished with damning accusations and venomous harangues to create a picture of "carpetbag rule" that not even the most loyal Republicans could ignore. No one looked at individual carpetbaggers but instead treated them as a "mass" of meddling Northern interlopers. Even Horace Greeley, editor of the *New York Tribune* and staunch radical, bought the picture of the carpetbagger that the South was selling. In a speech given in New York in 1872, he described them as men who "crawled down South in the track of our armies . . . " and "stand, right in the public eye, stealing and plundering, many of them with both arms around negroes, and their hands in their rear pocket, seeing if they cannot pick a paltry dollar out of them. . . ."[8]

The section titled "The Southern View" begins with a reading from the *New York Times*, which criticizes carpetbaggers for doing more harm than good by interfering with the relationship between whites and blacks and promoting agitation. In the next reading, W.M. Elliot declares that blacks do not need carpetbaggers because carpetbaggers use and cheat the freedmen. The third editorial, by Carey Styles, is typical of the kind of Southern rhetoric that created the carpetbagger myth, and it describes carpetbaggers as thieves, pests, and vagabonds. The last selection, by Horace White, accuses carpetbaggers, particularly those who have been elected to Congress, of being tools of radical tyranny.

The selections under the heading "The Northern View" do not praise carpetbaggers but attempt to defend the activities of the honest carpetbaggers. The first reading, by Horace Greeley, suggests that the best way to get rid of carpetbaggers is to do away with the inequality of blacks, much as abolitionists disappeared when slavery ended. The second selection, also by Greeley, refuses to believe that all carpetbaggers are bad and declares that 99 out of 100 are "honest and true men who do their duty faithfully...." The third editorial, by Parke Godwin, believes that carpetbaggers have been made the scapegoats for the misdeeds of the military and Southerners. The last entry, by George Jones, was written in the final year of Reconstruction and notes with some dismay that Northern men are no longer welcome in the South, particularly if they are Republicans.

THE SOUTHERN VIEW

Correspondent: "How to Do It"

The Northern newspapers relied heavily on Southern correspondents to inform them of the day-to-day vexations of the post–Civil War South. This correspondent voices the typical complaints about carpetbaggers' being meddlesome agitators. Captain John Emory Bryant was the editor of the Augusta Loyal Georgian, *an agent of the Freedmen's Bureau in Georgia, and organizer of the Georgia Equal Rights Association. He often was put before the public as the stereotypical carpetbagger.*

New York Times, **May 21, 1866**

No little mischief is being done by men who are infesting the State at present in the capacity of "friends of the freedmen," founders of colored savings banks, colored seminaries, equal rights journals, and other kindred enterprises. These men are working diligently to make the negro discontented with his condition, to persuade him that he is grossly wronged by the white man and that he is entitled to a position of perfect social and political equality with the whites. There is a 'Capt. Bryant' in this State, the self-constituted Head-Center of an 'Equal Rights Association,' who is going about making speeches in this line; and while he may be earning a very comfortable income at small expense, he is doing much harm to both races.... So far from offering any obstacle to the education and improvement of the colored population, the people were ready and willing to promote them by every means in their power; and so far as the civil rights of the negroes were concerned, the Legislature recognized and secured them in the most effective manner, by placing them on the same footing with white men in everything relating to person and property. He is no friend to the negro who comes here now to induce him to agitate for more than he has got. His efforts, if successful, can only work serious injury to the whites, and surely result in the ruin of the blacks. Those emissaries are nothing but *chevaliers d'industrie,* gathering into their pockets the postal currency of the poor blacks-walking gift enterprises, exchanging pinch-beck equal rights notions for the sweat-earned dimes of the gullible savages who desert their plows and hoes to listen to the white man who is going to make gentlemen and ladies of them all. I have watched the operations of these peripatetic philanthropists, and a more pestilent set of knaves I never met. They are a nuisance which ought to be speedily abated.

W.M. Elliot: "The Negro Throwing Off His Fetters"

This editorial, meant as much for the black reader as for the white, warns blacks not to trust carpetbaggers, who use and abuse the black man in politics.

Richmond (Va.) Whig, **April 14, 1868**

The relations between the white and black Radicals are not altogether pleasant and harmonious. The whites exact too much and concede too little. They claim the spoils while the negroes are expected to do the service. This all appeared fair to the negroes at first, but now they begin to look upon it as unjust. Elated with their suddenly acquired freedom, and regarding the Northern whites as their liberators and benefactors, they worshipped them as superior beings. They then saw through a glass darkly, and did not discriminate between good and bad men and between good and bad motives. All Northern or white men who claimed to be their friends were placed upon the same footing and regarded with the same gratitude and admiration.... Under this influence they filled the Convention with carpet-baggers and other mean whites and surrendered themselves to their guidance. These men thus obeyed, trusted and worshipped, came to think that the negroes as much belonged to them as if they had bought them with money....

The negroes have at last begun to find out the true character of these men and their real aims and objects. They call them carpet-baggers and adventurers who want to use them as the mere instruments by which to acquire office. Dull and sluggish as the negroes are, we have been surprised that it took them so long to make this discovery. It has been a common expression in the South that there is no better judge of a gentleman than your negro, and it perplexed us all when we saw Sambo receiving to his embrace the white trash that crowded around him. But poor Sambo found himself in the new situation, and he was disconcerted and thrown off his balance. We are glad that his obfuscation is coming to an end, and that his old instinct is about returning to guide him.

He is beginning to say to himself these people have imposed upon and cheated me. They are not my true friends—they are not my liberators—they are not the soldiers who fought the war. No; they are camp-followers, cow-boys, bummers, skulkers, jackalls, plunderers, and unprincipled money hunters.

Sambo begins to think, and while his thoughts are not very clear, they are in the line of truth. He says to himself, I am a native Virginian and a voter; without me the carpet-baggers, squatters, and other white trash could do nothing. All told, they are but a handful. I have measured intellects with them, and find myself their equal. They acknowledge my equality, and yet, under one pretence or another, they carry off all the honors and offices. They say I can vote, but I ought not to aspire to office. . . . "Why is this thus?" He cudgels his dull brain for an answer, but cannot strike out one, and with the savage resolve of a man who suddenly discovers that he has been griev-ously duped and wronged, he says to himself, I will no longer submit to these carpet-baggers, adventurers and "trooly loil" natives; I will set up for myself. By me the battle is to be fought.—Without my votes none of these white vermin can get an office. I am the grand elector, and will elect myself. I'll show that a "Virginny nigger" is not only the equal but the superior of the white trash.

Such is the train of thought into which the negro mind has fallen, and we may expect a negro candidate for every office—from Governor and Con-gressman down to Constable.

Carey Styles: "Carpet-Baggers Not the Class We Want"

Colonel Carey Styles hated anything that smacked of radicalism and was in part responsible for creating the myth of the carpetbaggers as pests, thieves, and vagabonds.

Atlanta Constitution, July 17, 1868

Under the changed condition of affairs, feeling the necessity for a new system of labor, industry and enterprise, the people of the South, ever since the close to the war, have been exceedingly anxious to induce immigration from all quarters into their midst. Their arms have been open to receive and their hands extended to welcome the right kind of new comers from Europe and the North. They have no disposition whatever to proscribe any one coming from abroad, provided he comes among them as a citizen in good faith. A contrary policy applied to the right kind of immigration they know full well would be suicidal to their best interests. But in the name of their own self respect, and in behalf of every thing they hold dear, they do protest against being made a Botany Bay for the filthy swarm of jail thieves, pardoned convicts, bummers, abandoned men and prostitute women, who, like foul birds of prey, have settled over all her domain. From such the South has withheld her hand. She scorns their fellowship as she would the embrace of leprosy, and their polluting touch as a stain no purification could erase. They are simply pests in the shape of prowling wolves seeking to destroy her peace and tranquility, to break the mutual bond of relation between the races white and black, and to sow the fire-brands of mischief broad-cast in the land. This motley swarm of thieves and vagabonds following in the desolated track of war came South with no better purpose than to rob, to plunder and to steal. The negro they have converted into a useful tool, and wielded him to the promotion of their fiendish purposes. They have in thousands of instances inflamed his ignorant passions against his old and his best friends. To lie, to steal, to cheat, to swindle and defraud is their chief stock in trade. They have that interest in the South which the filthy cormorant has in the decaying carcass. Like a set of barbarians they came upon us with no other motive than that which prompts the robber and plunderer. They go about over the land like famished mastiffs scenting for power and pelf. Wherever they find an opening to steal, or the negro element in the majority, there they swarm like bees. Their instincts are sharpened with fiendish lusts, and their vandal appetites are such as theft, robbery and rapine only will appease. With no respectability at home, bankrupt in character and outcasts from society, they are scorned and repudiated by the good people of the North. As adventurers coming South, and self-convicted of their own baseness and mendacity, they dare not seek admittance into the society of respectable white people, whose doors, they know by an instinctive sense of their unworthiness, are closed against them. In the companionship of negroes and the lowest class of whites they meet and mingle with their kindred element. A majority of these people, had they their dues, in punishment of the crimes and misdemeanors of which they are guilty, instead of seeking through fraud, corruption and rascality to represent the Southern people, or by their base misrepresentation of facts to bring upon them the vilest species of oppression and tyranny, would to-day be serving their time in penitentiaries, and in other modes propitiating their crimes. Away with such foul birds. They have already cursed the South with calamities worse than a pestilence.

We repeat, the South is anxious for immigration from the North. Let it come in the shape of honest, industrious, bona-fide citizens, and she will extend to it a welcome hand. She wants labor to build up her waste places and to develop her vast resources, but she asks to be delivered from the pestilent adventurers with whom she has been inundated since the close of the war. But for the disturbers of her peace—intermeddlers with her private and public relations—the country would have long since been restored to law, order and harmony. . . .

Horace White: "The Carpet-Bag Despotism"

Editorials such as this in Republican newspapers helped spread the myth of the Southern carpetbagger—a man who used political connections with the Republican Party to plunder the Southern states. It was also such editorials that did much to end Northern support of Republican rule in the South and to bring a rapid end to Reconstruction.

Chicago Tribune, August 26, 1872

The *Nation* . . . says, virtually, that the election of Grant will not affect the South in any way, except by preventing the accession to office of "unrepentant Rebels." . . . The *Nation* seems to have closed its eyes lately to the most vital element of American politics affecting the internal affairs of the States and the condition of the people,—the element which has been more shamefully abused than any other—the element upon which the issues in this campaign mainly turn. We refer to the use of Federal patronage. It was this element which fastened the carpet-bag *regime* upon the Southern States; which opened the way for the plunder of State Treasuries; which interfered with the right of the States to control their internal affairs; and which has, by corruptions and frauds almost innumerable, impoverished the Southern people. . . . In communities where poverty and ignorance prevail, and especially where as a race, all their lives bound down in servitude, and brutalized by oppression and ignorance, are suddenly enfranchised, and pass at one step from gross darkness into the arena of politics, the use of this patronage is well nigh omnipotent. No measures of honesty or virtue, no efforts for good government, can prevail against it. It debauches the ignorant; it buys the vicious; it menaces the timid; and it paralyzes the honest. Without its power, the Grant party in the Southern States would fall to pieces like a rope of sand. The Administration has no considerable influence upon the South, except such as it exerts by the employment of patronage. . . . It is by virtue of this very ignorance, supineness, and connivance that the carpet-baggers flourish. These are the very qualities upon which patronage exercises itself. Without patronage, carpet-bagism could not exist. Without carpet-bagism, intelligence, enterprise, and honesty would soon be in the ascendant. Of what use is it to say that the control of the Southern States has passed into the hands of their own people, and therefore Grant is not responsible, when the Administration, working upon ignorance, poverty, fear, and viciousness, with patronage, controls enough of those people to keep carpet-baggers in power, to plunder for themselves and to plot for the re-election of that Administration, and, by virtue of plundering and plotting, keep each other in office? . . .

THE NORTHERN VIEW

Horace Greeley: "How to Do It"

This is Horace Greeley's answer to the New York Times *correspondent's (May 21, 1866) criticisms of carpetbagger interference. Greeley compares the carpetbagger with the prewar abolitionist.*

New York Tribune, May 22, 1866

We do not doubt the truth of this picture as it presents itself to the ex-Rebel mind. It is "a nuisance" to have strangers telling those who have for forty years done your work for nothing but the coarsest food and clothes, that they ought to be paid for their labor, ought not to be flayed with a cowhide at your discretion, and ought to be accounted as good as you are, so long as they behave as well. We do not believe the genuine Southron will ever get so used to this as to like it; and we wouldn't have him such a hypocrite as to pretend to like it when he doesn't.

We are only vexed that the Southrons don't see, and that their Northern sympathizers don't try to make them see, the short, sure and easy way to abate this nuisance at once and forever. There is no excuse for their failure to see it, in view of a kindred deliverance both recent and striking.

For thirty odd years, the South was annoyed and convulsed by the acts and inculcations of Northern Abolitionists. These long-haired, gaunt-visaged, canting, sniffling rascals were as "peripapetic" [*sic*] and as "pestilent" as the "friends of the freedmen" now are—in fact, far more so. They kept both the South and the North in hot water, despite all the hemp that the former could grow, and all the rotten eggs that the latter could discover. There was no end of the "nuisance" they created. But the South has done for them at last. They may cant and snuffle to their heart's content, but nobody hears nor heeds them. No Southerner would waste a rope on the lot: and, as for stale eggs the boys of the North would grudge them a bare half-dozen.

In short, they are completely "played out." If they don't go to work for a living we can't guess how they are to get on hence forth.

Now, why shouldn't the South extinguish the new brood of busybodies in the same way? Why not block the game of Capt. Bryant and his tribe, by asking the colored people of your respective States to choose delegates to meet delegates chosen by the Whites and let the chosen representatives of the two classes or races settle amicably all questions that now divide or are likely in the future to alienate them? Just extinguish the interlopers and mischief-makers by taking away their trade, as you easily and surely can do. . . . Equal Rights is the true antidote for equal rights journals' and there isn't a negro in all the South willing to give his "postal currency" for the removal of grievances which no longer exist. Why not give this simple sovereign remedy for the deprecated "nuisance" a fair trial?

Horace Greeley: "The Thieving Carpet-Baggers"

After touring the South in the spring of 1871, Horace Greeley gave a speech in New York in which he described Republican rule in the South. Although Democratic newspapers picked up on his denunciation of carpet-baggers, Greeley did not believe that all Northern men were thieves.

New York Tribune, July 19, 1871

In the hasty survey given in our Lincoln Hall Speech of the Southern situation, the persistent Democratic outcry against "the carpet-baggers"—their hypocrisy, their venality, rapacity, &c.—claimed attention. No statement of the Southern problem would be complete or candid which ignored this complaint. "Carpet-bag" villainy was often urged as the provocation and excuse of Ku-Klux atrocity. Did such villainy exist? If so, what was its nature and extent?

We answered these questions frankly and truthfully. All those stigmatized as "carpet-baggers" are not rascals; many of them are worthy, upright men, who are obnoxious to the old planting aristocracy and its satellites only because they are earnest, efficient Republicans. If they would support and vote the Democratic ticket, they would not be accounted "carpet-baggers" at all, though fresh from New-England or Ohio. But *there are* "carpet-baggers" who are knaves and hypocrites—who, making loud professions of zeal for Republican ascendancy and Negro enfranchisement and elevation, are mainly intent on filling their own pockets from the spoil of an impoverished, unthrifty people. And this kind of "carpet-baggers" have been prominent and powerful in the legislation and administration of several Southern States, as their bloated public expenditure, taxation and indebtedness, abundantly, deplorably attest. Such is the naked truth, exaggerated, very naturally, by partisan hostility and bitterness, but bad enough when reduced to its real dimensions. This rapacity has embittered the ex-Rebels, who were bitter enough already, and too willing to believe that every Republican was of course a canting knave. It has alienated and repelled many who would have been Republicans ere this had the new State governments been thoroughly upright and frugal, as it was imperative, on many accounts, that they should have been. It has impeded Reconstruction, and is this day, the chief impediment to the triumph of Republican principles at the South. So we said in substance in our Lincoln Hall speech, and every intelligent person in the reconstructed States knows it to be substantially true.

Of course, the Democratic journals picked out so much of our statement as could be made to serve their purpose, and were quite willing to give the impression that we denounced all "carpet-baggers" as knaves and robbers. This was not fair, but it was smart, and excited no surprise.

Parke Godwin: "The Carpet-Baggers"

The New York Evening Post, *like the* New York Tribune, *was reluctant to believe that all Northerners who immigrated to the South were adventuring carpetbaggers. Instead, most of the problems blamed on carpetbaggers can be blamed on others.*

New York Evening Post, August 8, 1872

If some one were to make for all the South such an examination into the Constitution of the state governments as has been done for Alabama, the result undoubtedly would be some curious revelations. Never was the force of the proverb—"give a dog a bad name"—more perfectly exemplified than in the case of the "carpet-baggers." They are, we have no doubt, a "bad lot," who are responsible for a good deal of evil; but we do not believe, heterodox as it may sound, that all the Northerners who have gone South can properly be classed as "carpet-baggers," or that those who may be so classed are responsible for all the evil that has been done at the South. Indeed, we know of young men who have emigrated thither for legitimate and praiseworthy purposes, and whose identification with the interests and the people of that part of the country could only be to its great benefit. . . .

Still more is it true that much of the wrong that has been perpetrated there for the last half-dozen years is not the work of northern men. The wrong may, perhaps, have been done under the pretence of a northern or Republican origin; sometimes even the presence of military rule has been taken advantage of to commit outrages under form of law, which would not otherwise have been ventured upon. But there has doubtless been great exaggeration as to the share that Northern men have had in the enormities of legislation, the infliction of intolerable taxes, the creation of enormous public debts, in all the gigantic swindles from which southern people have been made to suffer, and to which they point as reason enough for the discordant condition of the country and their reluctant submission to the order of reconstruction.

There can be no doubt that the "carpet-bagger," assumed to be a northern adventurer, has been made the scape-goat of other sins than his own. . . .

George Jones: "The 'Carpet-Bag' Bugaboo"

By January 1877, all but two Southern states had thrown off Republican rule. Nevertheless, the carpetbagger was still feared and no longer welcome in the South. George Jones assumed the editorship of the New York Times *after Henry Raymond died.*

New York Times, January 1, 1877

It is not a little singular that while other portions of the Republic are endeavoring to allure settlers and new citizens, the South should persist in a policy of exclusion. Exactly how far this is true of a majority of the Southern people it is difficult to say. But those who are most conspicuous in public affairs in that section of the Union do lend themselves to schemes of proscription. We should prefer to believe that, as is usual in politics, those who make the most noise are the least influential. Rightly or wrongly, however, there is a general impression that the South has practically put up a sign warning all persons off the premises. It seems to be considered in the South that there is some peculiarly sacred quality in the soil which resents the presence of a stranger as an intrusion. And a stranger is one who was not born on the soil. He who first drew breath north of the Potomac is an alien. . . .

Perhaps it is not because these "strangers" are Northern, but because they are Republicans, that they excite the ire of the so-called leaders. It is said that all Southern men are politicians. We should be sorry to believe that they are such in the bad sense in which that word is usually applied. But if Southern politics are proscriptive of any class of citizens, so much the worse for the State thus afflicted. And if Northern men, Republicans or otherwise, are to be warned off the premises when they seek opportunity for the investment of capital, so much the worse for the whole country. The people of the South cannot afford to give their section of the country over to the domination of men who make politics a trade—men whose policy it is to drive out all whose presence may seem to menace their own supremacy.... If that region of country is to recover all that it has lost in industry and wealth, it must at least tolerate the presence of men who come with the honest intention of performing all the duties of good citizens.

QUESTIONS

1. According to conservatives, how did carpetbaggers treat blacks?
2. What was the primary difference between carpetbaggers and "honest and industrious" immigrants from the North?
3. Why were carpetbaggers hated so much in the South?
4. What does Horace Greeley recommend as a solution to the carpetbagger problem?
5. How effective was the *Atlanta Constitution*'s negative portrait of carpet-baggers?

NOTES

1. In Richard L. Hume, "Carpetbaggers in the Reconstruction South: A Group Portrait of Outside Whites in the 'Black and Tan' Constitutional Conventions," *Journal of American History* 64 (1977): 313–30, 316.

2. See Richard Current, *Those Terrible Carpetbaggers: A Reinterpretation* (New York: Oxford University Press, 1988).

3. Hume, 320.

4. John Hope Franklin, *Reconstruction after the Civil War*, 2d ed. (Chicago: University of Chicago Press, 1994), 98.

5. Peter Kolchin, "Scalawags, Carpetbaggers, and Reconstruction: A Quantitative Look at Southern Congressional Politics, 1868–1872," *Journal of Southern History* 45 (February 1879): 63–76.

6. See Current.

7. Quoted in Donna L. Dickerson, " 'Got no Souls . . . ': Racism in Southern Reconstruction Newspapers," *Proceedings of the Association for Education in Journalism and Mass Communications, Southeast Colloquium* 1 (March 1992): 18–26.

8. *New York Tribune*, 19 July 1871, 4.

CHAPTER 17

The Battle for Woman Suffrage, 1867–70

Although women had been active politically since before the American Revolution, the woman suffrage movement did not formally begin until 1848, when the first women's convention met in Seneca Falls, New York. The convention, called by Lucretia Mott and Elizabeth Cady Stanton, adopted a Declaration of Sentiments calling for equal rights in education, property, voting, and other matters. This first convention and all those that followed received no support from American men, the great majority of whom opposed the movement, believing that women were less intelligent than men and did not understood all the nuances of the ugly business of politics. Men also argued that women's participation in politics would ruin the family and result in higher divorce rates. After all, if men wore the pants in the family they should also be the ones to represent their families at the polling booth.

What opponents failed to understand was that women had been involved in politics as long as men—only in less formal ways. For more than a hundred years, American women had marched and picketed to protest everything from the military draft, high food prices, unsanitary conditions to slavery and children's work laws. In fact it was the abolitionist movement throughout the Northeast that served as a training ground for women's political participation. The women's movement saw the plight of the slave and the plight of women as the same cause.

At a Women's National Loyal League meeting in New York City in 1863, resolutions were adopted in support of the Union, Lincoln's Emancipation Proclamation, and furthering the equality of blacks. However, debate centered around one resolution that supported the "civil and political rights of all citizens of African descent *and all women*." The resolution did not pass because many women believed that their focus should be on supporting the end of slavery and not muddying the waters with women's issues. But one of the resolution's supporters noted, "I rejoice exceedingly that this resolution should combine us with the negro. I feel that we have been with him. . . . True we have not felt the slave holder's lash; true, we have not had our hands manacled, but our hearts have been crushed. . . . I want to be identified with the negro; until he gets his rights, we never shall have ours."[1]

Women took advantage of the Reconstruction debates in Congress to insist that women should receive the same civil, political, and social rights that blacks were demanding.[2] For example, women hoped that the Fourteenth Amendment would afford an unprecedented opportunity to help not only black men but also black and white women. But when it was clear that only men would be counted by the amendment's representation clause, many activist women campaigned against the Fourteenth Amendment. They felt that women had been betrayed not only by men but also by the abolitionists who were backing the amendment. Horace Greeley, a strong proponent of black suffrage, explained that combining woman suffrage and black suffrage was "an innovation so revolutionary and sweeping, so openly at war with a distribution of duties and functions between the sexes" that it would never receive approval.[3]

When Congress deliberated on the Fifteenth Amendment, which granted black men the right to vote, leaders of the women's movement once again saw a chance to broaden Republican principles to include women. But debates in Congress made it imminently clear that the amendment would guarantee only what was absolutely necessary to get it ratified in the North. Thus, the amendment did not grant suffrage to Indians, the foreign born, or women. While several Republicans endorsed woman suffrage in principle, they believed that the exigencies of the moment made giving women the vote an impracticality.[4]

Once again betrayed by Congress, Stanton's anger flared into unabashed racism when she argued that the vote should go to only those who were literate. "Think of Patrick, Sambo and Hans and Ung Tung who do not know the difference between a Monarchy and a Republic, who never read the Declaration of Independence . . . making laws for Lydia Maria Child, Lucretia Mott or Fanny Kemble."[5]

In 1869, Stanton and Susan B. Anthony founded the National Woman Suffrage Association, whose goal was to lobby for an amendment guaranteeing universal suffrage and against the Fifteenth Amendment. The same year, another group of women, led by Lucy Stone and Julia Ward Howe (the founder of the Girl Scouts) formed the American Woman Suffrage Association in Boston. The American Woman Suffrage Association also worked for the vote, but it did so by lobbying individual states to give the vote to women. In 1869, Wyoming became the first territory to pass a woman suffrage law. The next year, Wyoming's women were allowed to sit on juries. When Wyoming sought statehood, Congress threatened to withhold admission unless the state legislature rescinded women's voting rights. The governor sent a stinging telegram to Washington stating that Wyoming would remain out of the Union 100 years rather than join without woman suffrage. Wyoming was admitted to statehood in 1896 with woman suffrage intact. In 1870, Utah joined Wyoming in giving women the right to vote.

In 1872, Anthony and a group of women voted in the presidential election in Rochester, New York. In a trial that attracted nationwide attention, Anthony was fined for voting illegally. The same year, Sojourner Truth, black abolitionist leader, was turned away from a polling booth in Grand Rapids, Michigan.

In 1878, Anthony succeeded in having a proposed constitutional amendment introduced in Congress. Although it failed, the same proposal would be introduced each year for the next 41 years. In 1920, the Nineteenth Amendment to the U.S. Constitution was ratified, extending the vote to women.

The section against woman suffrage begins with an editorial by Manton Marble that points out that if radicals are going to argue that blacks are fit for the vote then they are hypocrites not to insist on the same privilege for women. The second entry, by William W. Harding, uses the most common argument of the day—that women really do not desire the vote and until more women begin demanding it, it is a nonissue. The third reading is a humorous piece by Mark Twain pointing out all of the reasons why men do not want women to vote. The last entry is a letter from a "Grandmother" confirming that women like her do not want the vote because it would interfere with their domestic duties.

The selections favoring woman suffrage begin with Stanton's plea to Congress to include women in any measure that might enfranchise blacks. The second entry, by Samuel Bowles, argues that it is no longer logical to exclude women from the vote when blacks and foreigners are included. The third editorial, by George W. Curtis, counters the argument that women will vote when the majority of women desire it, pointing out that it is not the women who will make the decision about suffrage; instead, it will be the men. The final selection, by Miriam M. Cole, criticizes the patronizing tone of the Republican Party's 1872 platform, which gave only lip service to woman suffrage.

Opposing Woman Suffrage

Manton Marble: "Woman Suffrage and Negro Suffrage"

This is not an editorial in favor of woman suffrage. Instead, it is an argument against black suffrage. The two issues were inextricably intertwined, but few men could see that the next logical step after giving blacks the vote was to give women the vote.

New York World, **November 9, 1866**

Mrs. [Elizabeth Cady] Stanton and Miss Susan B. Anthony, and their associates in the American Equal Rights Association, have begun their next campaign already, so to speak. They invite the lecture lyceums to invite them to lecture. Miss Anthony raises her flag with "Bread and the Ballot" inscribed upon it, and goes forth to conquer for her sex with that formidable weapon, the ballot, "equal place and equal pay." Mrs. Stanton will proclaim in her itinerancy "The duty of Congress, now, to guarantee universal suffrage, the only true republican form of government, to the thirty-six States of the Union." We bid these two apostles in petticoats, or in trowsers, as the case may be, good speed. One of these days we may have something to say on the enfranchisement of women; but just now we are chiefly interested in the success with which these earnest-minded women follow the Radical logic to its conclusion. The Radicals with beards do not do it. Let us see if these Radicals without beards can teach the bearded ones what their own arguments prove. . . .

If Congress can give Southern negroes the ballot, it can give Northern and Southern women the ballot. The arguments for the former are good for the latter. If it is essential to a Republican form of government, that male negroes should vote, it is essential to a Republican form of government that white and black women should vote. If Congress has power to do the one, it has power to do the other. The argument on intelligence, too, is as good for Mrs. Stanton as it is for Sambo. The white women of the South and the white women of the North are fitter for the intelligent use of the ballot today, and are more susceptible of its educative influence than the male blacks of the South. If Mr. Greeley's argument is good, Mrs. Stanton's argument is better; and in the interest of openness, honesty, and candor in politics, therefore, we wish Mrs. Stanton all possible success in forcing the Radicals to accept at once the consequences of their arguments and utterances, and the logic of their situation. Far more safely can the ballot be given to Northern and Southern women than to the mass of adult male negroes; far more wisely can the former be entrusted with political power. But the arguments which the negro-suffrage people use are either worthless or else they prove every doctrine of Miss Anthony and Mrs. Stanton. And what is more, all the arguments of the negro-suffrage people, who call themselves impartial suffrage people, are either worthless or else they too prove the doctrines of the woman-suffrage advocates. As for universal suffrage, the phrase is inaccurate; nobody believes in it, for nobody, as yet, declares for giving babies, boobies, or prisoners a vote.

But let these bold champions of woman-suffrage compel the friends of negro-suffrage to accept the whole consequences of their own logic.

William W. Harding: "Women as Voters"

Even a radical Republican like William W. Harding, who forcefully es-
poused equal voting rights for blacks, could not bring himself around to the
idea of allowing women to vote. The argument that women really did not
want to vote was a common one in contemporary editorials.

Philadelphia Inquirer, **November 22, 1866**

One of the annual or semi-annual conventions of the Woman's Right advocates is now being held in the State of New York. Mrs. Elizabeth Cady
Stanton, candidate for Congress in New York city the other day, who received four votes, is among the orators present at the convention, which
contains many old women of both sexes, together with wearers of the
bloomer costume and long haired philosophers. The convention has resolved solemnly that women ought to have equal political rights with men,
and ought to be allowed to vote and to hold office. The injustice of man in
arrogating political affairs to himself is inveighed against, and, altogether
the parties concerned make out a very strong case. In regard to this question
of extending the elective franchise to women, we have no doubt that they
can obtain it whenever they ask for it. But, with the exception of the fifty or
one hundred strong-minded women who take part in these conventions,
there is no evidence whatever that the sex desires the privileges of participating in the excitements, controversies and demoralization of politics.
When delicate women desire equal rights in voting with their fathers, brothers, husbands and lovers, they can easily obtain it. Their influence is irresistible. But there is no evidence of any such desire on the part of the female
sex, and the agitations and complaints of the few women who unite with
Mrs. Stanton in her lamentations is the exception which proves the general
rule.

Mark Twain: "Female Suffrage"

This editorial is an early example of Mark Twain's humor. At the time this
piece was written, Twain was a reporter for the Buffalo (N.Y.) Express
and just gaining recognition as an American humorist.

Springfield (Mass.) Republican, **August 3, 1868**

"Mark Twain" writes to his "Cousin Jennie" on the subject of "female
suffrage," as follows:—

There is one insuperable obstacle in the way of female suffrage, Jennie.
I approach the subject with fear and trembling; but it must out. A woman

would never vote, because she would have to tell her age at the polls. And even if she did dare to vote once or twice when she was just of age, you know what dire results would flow from "putting this and that together" in after times. For instance, in an unguarded moment, Miss A. says she voted for Mr. Smith. Her auditor, who knows that it is seven years since Smith ran for anything, easily ciphers out that she is at least seven years over age, instead of the young pullet she has been making herself out to be. No, Jennie, this new fashion of registering the name, age, residence, and occupation of every voter, is a fatal bar of female suffrage.

Women will never be permitted to vote or hold office, Jennie, and it is a lucky thing for me and many other men that such is the decree of fate. Because, you see, there are some few measures they would all unite on—there are one or two measures that would bring out their entire voting strength, in spite of their antipathy to making themselves conspicuous, and there being vastly more women than men in this state, they would trot those measures through the Legislature with a velocity that would be appalling. For instance they would enact:—

1. That all men should be at home by 10 p.m. without fail.
2. That married men should bestow considerable attention on their wives.
3. That it should be a hanging offense to sell whisky in saloons, and that fine and disfranchisement should follow drinking in such places.
4. That the smoking of cigars to excess should be forbidden, and the smoking of pipes utterly abolished.
5. That the wife should have a little property of her own, when she married a man who hadn't any.

Jennie, such tyranny as this could never stand; our free souls could never endure such degrading thraldom. Women, go your way! Seek not to beguile us of our imperial privileges. Content yourselves with your little feminine trifles—your babies, your benevolent societies and your knitting—and let your natural bosses do the voting. Stand back; you will be wanting to go to war next. We will let you teach school as much as you want to, and we will pay you half wages for it, too; but beware! We don't want you to crowd us too much.

Letter to the Editor: "From a Grandmother"

One common argument against woman suffrage was that, if given the vote, women would for some reason be forced to use it and be required to be politically active against their wishes.

Chicago Times, February 18, 1869

To the Editor of the Times.

Will you allow a grandmother to occupy a small space in your paper, to express a few thoughts on the "woman suffrage" question, suggested by some remarks of its most prominent advocates, as reported through the press?

We are told that Mrs. Stanton said, not long since, in Washington, that woman did not wish for the rights of suffrage; that, if she did, she would obtain it. Now, as far as my observation extends, *that is so;* and I think that I have had opportunity to ascertain the views and feelings of very many Christian women in the various walks of life. More particularly in the older states of the union, one in an hundred of the intelligent Christian mothers in Illinois desire the right of suffrage. Nor do I believe that our law-makers will be so heartless as to inflict it on those who do not desire it, but who are to be driven to vote in self-defence, or, what amounts to the same thing, in defence of what they think is right; for we are distinctly told by the lady who claims to know the "wants of women"—*some* women, if you please . . . "that, to prevent the worst classes from exerting a controlling influence at the polls, the rest will have to bestir themselves." Allow me to say that it is my belief that a majority of our best wives and mothers do not desire "to bestir themselves" in that way; and, however respectable the minority may be, we do not feel that they ought to petition for suffering to be inflicted on us, that they may enjoy the right of suffrage.

Most of us who are mothers and grandmothers, have home duties that would be neglected if we mingled in the political arena. But in the quietude of home, we read the daily papers, watching the progress of events, and, if need be, though we should shrink from the notoriety, we, too, may petition congress that it will not add to our cares and responsibilities by making it necessary for us to attend caucuses and go to the polls.

Grandmother

FAVORING WOMAN SUFFRAGE

Elizabeth Cady Stanton: "This Is the Negro's Hour"

This letter to the editor is Elizabeth Cady Stanton's response to a speech by abolitionist Wendell Phillips at the May antislavery meeting in which he declared that "this is the Negro's Hour"; women's rights would have to wait. The letter mirrors the profound strain between male and female abolitionists after the Civil War.

National Anti-Slavery Standard, **December 26, 1865**

Sir, By an amendment of the Constitution, ratified by three-fourths of the loyal States, the black man is declared free. The largest and most influential political party is demanding Suffrage for him throughout the Union, which right in many of the States is already conceded. Although this may remain a question for politicians to wrangle over for five or ten years, the black man is still, in a political point of view, far above the educated women of the country.

The representative women of the nation have done their uttermost for the last thirty years to secure freedom for the negro, and so long as he was lowest in the scale of being we were willing to press *his* claims; but now, as the celestial gate to civil rights is slowly moving on its hinges, it becomes a serious question whether we had better stand aside and see "Sambo" walk into the kingdom first.

As self-preservation is the first law of nature, would it not be wiser to keep our lamps trimmed and burning, and when the Constitutional door is open, avail ourselves of the strong arm and blue uniform of the black soldier to walk in by his side, and thus make the gap so wide that no privileged class could ever again close it against the humblest citizen of the Republic?

"This is the negro's hour." Are we sure that he, once entrenched in all his inalienable rights, may not be an added power to hold us at bay? Have not "black male citizens" been heard to say they doubted the wisdom of extending the right of Suffrage to women? Why should the African prove more just and generous than his Saxon compeers? If the two millions of Southern black women are not to be secured in their rights of person, property, wages, and children, their emancipation is but another form of slavery. In fact, it is better to be the slave of an educated white man, than of a degraded, ignorant black one. We who know what absolute power the statute laws of most of the States give man, in all his civil, political, and social relations, do demand that in changing the status of the four millions of Africans, the women as well as the men should be secured in all the rights, privileges, and immunities of citizens.

It is all very well for the privileged order to look down complacently and tell us, "this is the negro's hour; do not clog his way; do not embarrass the Republican party with any new issue; be generous and magnanimous; the negro once safe, the woman comes next." Now, if our prayer involved a new set of measures, or a new train of thought, it would be cruel to tax "white male citizens" with even two simple questions at a time; but the disfranchised all make the same demand, and the same logic and justice that secures Suffrage to one class gives it to all. . . .

This is our opportunity to retrieve the errors of the past and mould anew the elements of Democracy. The nation is ready for a long step in the right direction; party lines are obliterated, and all men are thinking for themselves. If our rulers have the justice to give the black man Suffrage, woman should avail herself of that new-born virtue to secure her rights; if not, she should begin with renewed earnestness to educate the people into the idea of universal suffrage.

E. Cady Stanton

Samuel Bowles: "After the Boston Convention, What?"

In 1868, Boston hosted the largest women's convention in U.S. history. The luminaries of the suffrage movement as well as its opponents were present. In this editorial, Samuel Bowles, who had only a year and a half earlier written against woman suffrage, now finds that most of the old arguments no longer stand up. A central issue at the convention was a constitutional amendment giving men and women the right to vote in federal elections.

Springfield (Mass.) Republican, **November 22, 1868**

And let no man smile at the idea of a clause in the United State constitution allowing women to vote. A little reflection will convince all who can reflect that this is more likely to be carried now than any of the recent amendments were ten years ago; and a good deal of reflection will not furnish us with any sound reasons against it, drawn from our political system. The real difficulty will be to convince women themselves that they ought and need to take an interest in government, and that to the extent of voting and holding office. For—down with it all, ye conservatives, at one dose—we must not only allow them to elect but to be elected to office, low and high. . . .

But is this the time to press a constitutional amendment giving to women the ballot? We are about to try one confirming the already declared right of the negro. . . . Yet, is it, after all of any consequence to the negro whether the claim of woman is urged now or postponed? . . . We allow the negro to vote because his vote is needed to restore the balance of government at the South, and the fact that it is so needed will secure its being granted not only there, but at the North. . . .

Woman's claim to suffrage rests upon a different and broader basis. We need her vote not to tranquilize and balance, but to purify our elections. We cannot refuse to her what we have just granted to the undisciplined negro and what we have long permitted the rude foreigner to abuse. But in admitting her to the ballot we may also insist that citizenship shall mean something more than it now does, or has ever done in the United States. We can then impose such tests and restrictions as . . . shall rid the franchise of a vile and festering mass of voters who degrade the ballot, and defile and endanger our institutions. The sooner women are allowed the vote, the sooner can this be done, and we see no possible harm in pressing forward the new movement. There is an instinct in mankind that selects the right time for such political changes, and the sudden and general favor with which the intelligent, of all parties, look upon woman suffrage, is an indication that ought not to be neglected.

George W. Curtis: "The Reason Why"

Away from the editor's desk, George W. Curtis was a strong supporter and active participant in the woman suffrage movement. However, as an editor, he knew that the issue would not receive favor from his predominately male readers. This editorial is the only one Curtis wrote supporting woman suffrage.

Harper's Weekly, December 11, 1869

In the course of some remarks upon the late Convention at Cleveland to form a National Woman's Suffrage Association, the New York *Times* remarks: "The vast majority of men are really indifferent to the whole matter, and very willingly stand aside to leave women to settle it among themselves." The article is an amplification of this amusing statement, and its moral is, that if women do not vote it is because they do not wish to. But, if the *Times* really supposes that this is the fact, it should inform itself a little. If it imagines that some women do not vote because other women do not wish to, it would perhaps be useful for the *Times* as a public teacher, to know that the reason no woman votes is that men will not permit it. The fundamental law of the State is made by men, and it restricts the political franchise to men. It is merely absurd to say that they would carefully establish so immense an exclusion if they were wholly indifferent to it.

The *Times* repeats the old remark, that when the majority of women wish to vote they will be admitted to the suffrage, as a matter of course. But this is not the manner in which such changes of fundamental laws are made. Were the newly admitted voters in England polled upon the subject before the Reform bill passed? Were the majority of the colored citizens in the Southern States asked to express a wish before the suffrage was given them? And is it also to be gravely urged that when the majority of women wish that the women who have a genius for any profession or art should devote themselves to it, they will of course be allowed to do so? The question must be decided upon quite other considerations. If there be no objection to the voting of those women who wish to vote except that certain other women do not wish to, the argument is suddenly shifted, and it becomes the duty of those who make the assertion to show why the disinclination of one person should disqualify another.

If, as is alleged in the article of which we speak, the present voters, who are men, "stand aside to leave women to settle it among themselves," why do they not remove the restriction? It is idle to speak of awaiting the demand of a majority of women, not only because it is ridiculous that an intelligent woman should be deprived of such a power by the whim of a possibly indifferent and foolish woman, but because there is no way of ascertaining the wishes of such a majority. The only sensible and practicable policy upon the subject—since even the *Times* concedes that men are indifferent, and that there is no serious objection—is to remove the barrier and let women decide for themselves. . . .

Miriam M. Cole: "Our Ohio Letter"

The Fourteenth Resolution of the Republican platform that was adopted at its convention in Philadelphia was written, in part, by Susan B. Anthony. But, Miriam M. Cole, coeditor of the Woman's Advocate *of Dayton, Ohio, does not believe it goes far enough. Her honesty of opinion as well as her wit is refreshing in a period when writing was pedantic and filled with verbal cacophony. Lucy Stone and Julia Ward Howe edited the* Woman's Journal *for the National Woman Suffrage Association in Boston.*

Woman's Journal, July 6, 1872

DEAR JOURNAL:—Have you any faith in the notable Fourteenth Resolution to spare? If so, please forward some to my address, C.O.D. In the absence of the applause and enthusiasm which greeted it at Philadelphia, it seems to me a dead letter, without hope of final resurrection. Who is the wily diplomat who can write an article so carefully worded that friends and foes can adopt it without fear of compromising themselves? Why Horace Greeley may pipe it from the *Tribune* roof and not go back on his record! The "True Woman" may touch it and live! The Republican party of the United States, assembled in national convention in the city of Philadelphia, again declares its faith and announces its position upon the questions before the country. Its fourteenth position is one to be proud of—it is of vital importance to every woman, that is, if said woman can see anything in it of vital importance. It is one of those curious documents capable of supplying millions with *inferences*. Draw an inference to suit yourself and invite your neighbor to do the same. The original is inexhaustible.

It says, "The Republican party is mindful of its obligations to the loyal women of America for their noble devotion to the cause of freedom." Let not the Republican party dream it is monopolizing gratitude—why even publicans and sinners (ycleped democrats), are mindful in like degree and manner. Doubtless said party is grateful to woman for being born with unlimited capacity for cooking, sewing, and raking up the loose straws, and picking up the chips. It is not yet too late for a resolution to that effect to be embodied in Church or State platform. If it had not been for a few Woman Suffrage Republicans who called it to mind, women to-day, the loyal ones I mean, would be living without a single "thank you" from any political party. It is so gratifying and mollifying to know that who scraped lint, and bound up wounds, and gave her mite, and her son, and her husband, and wrought early and late in fields and mills, and stores, is at last publicly rewarded by the Republican party! "It is much obliged to her!"

Said resolution also confessed its "satisfaction" in women being "admitted to wider fields of usefulness"! "The heathen Chinee" may not cut off his pig-tail in despair over such an innovation! . . . Let us see how far beyond him this Fourteenth Resolution stretches. It continues its benevolent language thus: "And the honest demands of any class of citizens for additional rights should be treated with respectful consideration!" Ye gods! That is, in words we have heard from the beginning, "When all women ask for the ballot they shall have it." I admit we have gained an inch, inasmuch as our demands "should be treated with respectful consideration." Lucy Stone thought, twenty-five years ago, that her demand for political equality *should* be treated respectfully, but it was not. Will it be now? We fear not, unless the framers of the resolution can be induced to put the verb *should be treated* in the indicative mode and first future tense, *shall*,—we have not unlimited confidence in the potential. May, can, might, could and should, do not declare positively. These auxiliaries leave a man too much a free agent. I cannot see that women have any hold on the Republican party by the Fourteenth Resolution. It promises just nothing. It is polite—it touches its hat to woman—it expresses moderate joy in seeing her out of the kitchen—it acknowledges obligation to her, for her devotion to freedom, as if she were a being not personally interested in freedom and all her labors in its behalf, just disinterested benevolence—it winds up by saying that her honest demands for additional rights should be respectfully considered. It might have added with truth, "but owing to the selfishness of men, they will not be so considered."

If we are ever enfranchised, we shall cut our way thither as through solid stone. In one day or ten days we may not see the mark of our chisel and yet we know every stroke tells. To this end we have got to work slowly, patiently, and hopefully, not looking to a Fourteenth Resolution for help. . . . To insert in a party platform, a resolution *pretending* to favor a class of people is a gross indignity. Every other resolution gives a certain sound—it plants itself fairly and squarely on every question, but this fourteenth hovers and flutters but don't slight. . . .

Miriam M. Cole

Questions

1. What role did humor—like Mark Twain's—play in the effort to prevent woman suffrage?
2. What danger did women present to the male-dominated political status quo?
3. Was the argument that not enough women wanted to vote a convincing one?
4. Why did Congress not want to include women in the Fourteenth and Fifteenth Amendments?
5. Why did it take until 1920 for women to be given the right to vote?

Notes

1. *Resolutions and Debate* (presented at the Woman's National Loyal League Meeting, New York City, 14 May 1863).

2. Joan Hoff, *Law, Gender, and Injustice* (New York: New York University Press, 1991), 148.

3. Ellen Carol DuBois, *Feminism and Suffrage: The Emergence of an Independent Women's Movement in America, 1848–1869* (Ithaca, N.Y.: Cornell University Press, 1978), 87–88.

4. Xi Wang, *The Trial of Democracy, Black Suffrage and Northern Republicans, 1860–1910* (Athens: University of Georgia Press, 1997), 31.

5. Eric Foner, *Reconstruction: America's Unfinished Revolution, 1863–1877* (New York: Harper & Row, 1988), 448.

CHAPTER 18

Indian Policy in the West, 1867–76

During the first half of the nineteenth century, the relationship between whites and Indians in the East and West were relatively peaceful, with only a few minor scrapes, mostly with the Plains Indians. But, when gold was discovered in California in 1848 and hundreds of thousand of speculators, settlers, and miners began moving West, the peace quickly ended and 40 years of Indian wars ensued.[1]

In 1850, approximately 360,000 Indians lived west of the Mississippi. Some of the tribes, such as the Hopis, were peaceful shepherds and farmers; others, such as the Apaches and Sioux, were nomads and warriors. But as far as most Americans were concerned, the distinction was meaningless.

In 1851, a policy was adopted to clear Indians from the trails and the settlements and to restrict them to reservations. This policy of "removal and concentration" reflected America's approach to Indians since 1834, when 84,000 Indians were removed from southeastern states and resettled in the Oklahoma territory. Using the pretext of meaningless treaties, Indians were forced to resettle on less desirable land, away from hunting grounds and ancestral homes. Many of the Indian chiefs who signed treaties probably had little idea what they were signing, lured instead by cartloads of blankets, food, rifles, and ammunition that were waiting for their signed X. Nevertheless, in the 1850s, hundreds of treaties were signed. No sooner were they signed than either the army or the Indians broke them. The Indians had plenty of cause to break the treaties: corrupt Indian agents, miners who trespassed on tribal lands, the slaughter of buffalo, and the building of immigrant trails and the transcontinental railroad lines that cut through traditional hunting grounds. But the government had little sympathy with these complaints. To ensure that the treaties were kept and that Indians who broke the treaties were punished, the army concentrated the vast majority of

A SCHOOL FOR SAVAGES; or, Teaching the Young Idea not to Shoot.

BIG INJUN. "White man, hold on; we want to Big Talkee."
GENERAL SHERIDAN. "No, no. I'll Whip you first, then you can Big Talkee afterward."

A School for Savages. *General Phillip Sheridan is depicted beating civilization into an Indian. In the background is a map showing how the West has been sectioned off into small reservations.* Harper's Weekly. *Library of Congress.*

its forces in the West, building a string of military posts along the Oregon, Santa Fe, and Bozeman trails.

The Indian Wars—"wars of concentration"—escalated after the Civil War as the army was assigned to protect the railroads, cattle drives, immigrant trains, and miners. Massacres perpetrated by the army and by Indians fill history textbooks with names like the Fetterman Massacre, Sand Creek Massacre, the Sioux outbreak, the Battles of Big Meadows, and the Yakima War. As more and more whites pushed west, it became imperative to move the Indians into smaller and smaller territories, concentrating them on reservations where they could be controlled and made dependent on the Indian agent and trading post.

For those Indians who refused to be "concentrated," the only recourse was war. For example, on December 21, 1866, Indians attacked a group of wagons hauling wood from Fort Phil Kearny. Captain William J. Fetterman, who had once boasted he could defeat with 80 men the whole Sioux nation, led a column of 80 cavalrymen against the Indians. Indian decoys lured the column over a nearby ridge where more than 1,500 Sioux rose up from the tall grass and massacred the entire column and two civilians.

The Fetterman Massacre and the massacres led by the army in retaliation were of great concern in the East, where many people saw the Indian policy as a huge drain on resources that had no end in sight. In 1867, a peace commission was created, whose purpose was to encourage the Indians to sign new treaties and to move onto reservations. The government designated new reservation areas closer to tribal lands and agreed to establish trading agencies closer to where the Indians lived. More than 70 treaties were signed, and new and larger reservations were set aside in South Dakota, Oklahoma, and Montana. But it was one thing to negotiate and another to carry it out.

Some tribes moved onto the reservations and accepted government rations during the winter months, returning to their tribal lands in the milder seasons. Many bands refused to accept the treaties, forcing the army to beat them into compliance. Even before his inauguration in 1869, President Ulysses S. Grant, recognizing the ineffectiveness of the current Indian policy, announced a new "peace policy" for dealing with Indians. Those Indians who stayed on the reservations would be Christianized, educated, provided with rations and clothing, and taught to farm. For those who chose to raid and massacre whites, there would be war. Grant even asked the Indian Bureau to hire Quaker Indian agents, who were well-known for their pacifist ways and strong Christian beliefs. But Grant's "peace policy" had little staying power. Hostilities reached their peak between 1869 and 1878, when more than 200 battles were fought. By the mid-1870s, the majority of Indians were on reservations—moving on and off of them to hunt and raid. But the more warlike tribes continued to resist—the Apaches in the Southwest, the Cheyenne and Sioux on the Great Plains, and the Nez Perce in the Rocky Mountains.

The beginning of the end was the Battle of the Little Bighorn in 1876. In 1868, a treaty was signed that allowed the Sioux to occupy all of present-day South Dakota, west of the Missouri River. Sitting in the middle of the new Sioux reservation was the Badlands, aptly named because the territory was the most inhospitable in all of the West and white men had no interest in the barren and mountainous terrain. However, all that changed in 1874 when gold was discovered in the Badlands, and thousands of miners poured into the Sioux reservation in violation of the treaty. At first, the government tried to buy the land, but the Sioux chiefs would not sell. Then the government ordered all Sioux to report to the agency in January 1876. When the Indians—who were spread across Montana, Wyoming, and Nebraska—did not come, the army set out to "pacify" them. The army's operation ended when General George Custer and 230 soldiers of the Seventh Cavalry were killed at the Little Bighorn River in eastern Montana. Custer had underestimated the cunning and strength of a coalition of Sioux, Oglalas, and Cheyenne. "Custer's Last Stand" became one of the worst defeats in U.S. military history. Back East, Americans were shocked and outraged. New commissions were formed, new treaties were drawn up that decreased the size of reservations, and more soldiers were sent to the West to take revenge.

By the late 1880s, there were 243,000 Indians on 187 reservations occupying 181,000 square miles. The last major Indian defeat was the Massacre at Wounded Knee in 1890, when the Sioux nation finally succumbed. The Seventh Cavalry moved to Wounded Knee Creek on the Pine Ridge Agency where, on December 29, 1890, the regiment attempted to disarm the chief of a small band of Sioux. An Indian's rifle was discharged into the air as two soldiers disarmed him, precipitating a battle in which more than 150 Indians, including women and children, and 25 soldiers were killed. Wounded Knee was the last major Indian engagement, and as the century drew to a close so did the traditional nomadic life of the Indians.

U.S. newspapers were just as befuddled about what to do with the Indians as was the government. The first section includes editorials favoring a strong military stand against the Indians. The first entry in this section, by E.L. Godkin, explains the tremendous cost of the Indian wars and the corruption in the Indian Bureau, and it concludes that slow extermination of Indians is the only solution. The second and third reading advocate extermination as the only way to prevent the killing of more white settlers. The fourth editorial, by Charles de Young, encourages the government to give the military the full power to deal with "bad" Indians. The last selection calls for the military to avenge the massacre of General Custer at the Little Bighorn but fears that Washington may return to its former inept and lenient policy and leave Custer's murder forgotten.

The section favoring a peaceful, moderate policy toward the Indians begins with a reading, by Samuel Bowles, that places great hope in the peace commission, because any act of extermination would be an inhumane act. The second editorial, by John Mcleod Keating, denounces the military incursions against the Indians and calls for resettlement, education, and Christianizing of Indians. The third selection, by Wilbur F. Storey, sees

Washington's treatment of Indians as another radical policy and accuses Republicans of covering up corruption with more raids against Indians and of promoting a negative view of Indians as brutes. The next selection, by George Jones, uses sarcasm to describe the dilemma of the Indians as they are forced to deal with the duplicity and illogic of the white man's Indian policies. The final editorial, by George W. Curtis, argues that the best tribute to the fall of General Custer would be a humane and reasonable Indian policy that would treat Indians with humanity and prevent the loss of more white soldiers and settlers.

FAVORING A STRONG MILITARY APPROACH TOWARD INDIANS

E. L. Godkin: "Our Indian Policy"

This editorial was written within a year of the end of the Civil War and is a summary of Indian affairs to date. It points out the tremendous cost of keeping an army in the West and of unscrupulous Indian agents. It also hints that slow extermination of the Indian is the only solution.

The Nation, January 25, 1866

Standing by itself, the war waged during the rebellion with the Indians would have seemed of huge and striking proportions. Not less than twenty-five thousand men have been and are now operating against the aborigines.
. . .

The advance of civilization here, as elsewhere, is literally "upon a powder-cart," for this large army holds open the great overland and Santa Fe mail routes, two thousand miles in length, with their daily and weekly service, which costs the country annually upwards of a million of dollars. It protects two thousand miles of navigable waters above Omaha, by which the adventurous pioneer may reach the El Dorado of that region. It guards the overland telegraph from the Missouri to Carson Valley. Under its aegis a hundred thousand emigrants go thronging annually toward the Pacific, while our scattered settlements that jut from east and west out into our vast pastoral plains, once familiar to us only as the "Great American Desert," and the growing overland commerce whose profits are reckoned by scores of millions, owe their prosperity and stability to the same military police.

How great are the interests thus fostered, and how important it is that they should remain for ever undisturbed, is evident to all. It is also pretty generally understood that our past policy toward the Indians and our present conflicts with them have effected little for the desired security. The cost of this warfare is appalling. . . . "It is estimated," says the report of Secretary Harlan, "that the maintenance of each regiment of troops engaged against the Indians of the plains costs the Government two million dollars per annum. All the military operations of last summer have not occasioned the immediate destruction of more than a few hundred Indian warriors." Indeed, it is an axiom in the Department that it is much cheaper to feed than to fight Indians. But it has only recently begun to be asked whether it is necessary to do either; whether savage warfare will not largely cease when treaty stipulations are strictly fulfilled, when honest trading shall be the rule, when agents forbear to grow rich on moderate salaries, and when justice shall be visited promptly and impartially on the lawless white man who boasts of shooting an Indian whenever seen, as on the latter when he madly runs a muck. . . .

Now, our policy towards this people has been . . . to acknowledge by treaty their primitive title to the soil, and then purchase it by paying them in annuities of money and goods, reserving suitable tracts on which to place the various tribes, and there instruct them in agricultural and other civilized pursuits. The system has not worked well in any one of its three aspects. The treaties have given the Indians an exaggerated idea of their own importance. . . . There is the same objection . . . to the payment of annuities, which is even more disastrous in its effects, inasmuch as it has served to make paupers of the tribes. . . . To the rascality of the [agents] in debasing or withholding the promised supplies, money, or presents, are attributable many of the worst Indian outbreaks. Finally, the reservation plan is almost an entire failure. . . .

Anonymous Writer: "Indian Hostilities: The Probable Extermination of That Race in Our Territories"

Every army victory brought with it prognostications that the Indians would soon be exterminated or starved.

New York Herald, **July 31, 1867**

There was a battle with the Indians on the 25th and 26th of the present month at Platte River Bridge, on the telegraph road, in which about a thousand men of the Sioux, Cheyennes, Comanches, Arrapahoes and Blackfeet were beaten by two hundred and fifty United States troops. The Indian loss was perhaps large, and they retreated, tearing down the telegraph as they went, and swearing that they were now making war "for all time." This was, therefore, in all probability, the first of a series of fights, that will result in the extermination of that race in the limits of the United States Territories—the first combat of an Indian war that will prove the last we will be troubled with. . . . Every train of emigrants that crossed the plains, carrying the arts of civilized life with them, reduced the self-supporting power of the Indians, and the great development of the gold bearing regions did the same to a greater degree. Settlements of whatever character injured their hunting grounds, and so inevitably increased their dependence upon annuities. Then the war broke out, and its demoralizing influence upon the savage was very great. They were easily led into war from any cause; they lost their annuities, and suffered considerable distress, and thus were made ready to go to any extremity. What will make all this still worse is that we must expect, now that our greater war is over, a more extensive emigration, and development of the gold fields, and a consequently greater pressure than ever upon the Indians.

The circular from the Commissioner of Indian Affairs, which we give elsewhere, shows the temper in which the government regards these hostilities. The Indian Bureau . . . orders the immediate cessation of all intercourse with hostile Indians. Thus the Indians, dependent in a large degree upon the government for support, have that support at once entirely withdrawn, and cannot even purchase the necessaries of life from traders. Then the immense present power of the government will, no doubt, be used against them with proper vigor, and the resistance that their fifty or sixty thousand warriors can offer—even if all are brought into the struggle—will soon be overcome. The Indian has accomplished his part in the development of one portion of this continent, and must make way. . . .

Horace Greeley: No Title

In the late summer of 1868, Horace Greeley toured the West, writing letters back to the New York Tribune *during the trip. Although Greeley was never a friend of the Indians, he and his position toward the Plains Indians were significantly and negatively affected by the tour.*

New York Tribune, **September 23, 1868**

I have hinted at an Indian war. What to do with the Indian is a question which you have freely discussed in your columns. The western men have but one answer—kill him. I have found only one man in all the western country—I speak of the country west of the Missouri—who holds a contrary opinion. That one man advocates kindness and conciliation; everybody else argues nothing but extermination by the quickest method. They see in the redskin only a false, treacherous, fiendish animal and denounce the author of "Lo, the poor Indian"[2] as a malignant enemy of every settler upon the plains. They listen to your theory of kindness and admit that it would be more humane, more Christian, and perhaps more potent than the system they advocate, if you had now to begin dealing with the Indian people; but, to take the fact of today and deal with a race which now sees in every unprotected pale face a victim to be tortured and murdered, they declare nothing but vigorous war will do. . . .

Charles de Young: "The Latest Batch of Indian Murders"

Most newspapers in the West advocated a strong-arm policy against Indians, since one of the major impediments to western immigration was Indian raids and massacres.

San Francisco Chronicle, September 27, 1872

We are every day more strongly convinced that the only effective way to restrain the ill-disposed Indians, and to secure the punishment of those who commit crimes, is to make the military arm all-powerful in dealing with them—to teach them a series of lessons which they will long remember. It is worthy of note that no hostile tribe has been subjugated in Arizona within the last decade. A temporizing policy has been pursued, and the results have been deplorable.

General Crook, by experience elsewhere, has learned how best to treat the Indians. His men, as well as the entire people of Arizona, have complete confidence in him; and we earnestly urge that the Government will consult the true interests of all concerned by authorizing the General to inaugurate a vigorous aggressive policy and to pursue marauders relentlessly. Let us have all the bad Indians well whipped first, and then we may talk of reservations, which will be well enough, if properly guarded. Let us cease crying peace, when there can be no genuine peace until we win one. Let us give Crook *carte blanche* to pacify Arizona. He will do it, if we let him.

Anonymous Writer: "Massacre"

The Battle of the Little Bighorn was a significant turning point for public opinion regarding the government's Indian policy. This editorial calls for a harsher policy but at the same time doubts that it will happen.

Fort Wayne (Ind.) Weekly Sentinel, July 12, 1876

Yesterday a thrill of horror passed over the country when the news was received of the brutal and bloody massacre of Gen. Custer and his brave command by the Sioux Indians. The story seemed too terrible to be true, but the circumstantial details which accompanied it sufficiently attested its accuracy, and effectually forbade any hope that the news might be false.

In the death of Gen. Custer the country has lost a brave, noble, intrepid, honest officer. Although under thirty-seven years of age, he was one of the most distinguished military men in the United States, and had successfully led over sixty cavalry charges. . . . The butchery of Custer and his three hundred brave soldiers calls for instant and swift retribution. It is time that imbecility and corruption should cease to be the marked features of the government's Indian policy. If the country is to be shocked at regular intervals by tales of such butcheries; if the Fort Phil Kearney massacre, the betrayal and murder of Gen. Canby, and the butchery of Gen. Custer are to be duplicated in future, the people will rise *en masse* and demand that a war of extermination be carried on against the savages. It is true, that alternative is repulsive to all civilized people, but if it becomes a choice of evils, the people will prefer the least, and would rather see every redskin banished from the face of the earth, than to have our bravest and noblest sons fall victims to the blood-thirstiness and cruelty of the savages.

The Quaker peace policy is a failure. The management of Indian affairs by the interior department has been notoriously and grossly corrupt and inefficient. . . .

In reference to the war with the Sioux, every candid person must admit that the government was in the wrong. She has made herself as ridiculous in making treaties with nomadic bands of savages as she has shown dishonestly in recklessly breaking and allowing the treaties to be broken. But having become involved in a war with the most powerful, brave and skillful Indians of the plains, the government should have adopted no half way measures. A large force should have been pushed at once to the front, and the most vigorous offensive course pursued.

We presume, after the first interval of excitement is over, Gen. Custer and his brave comrades will be forgotten, and matters will move along as heretofore. Howling demagogues of both political parties will stand up in congress and demand the reduction of our paltry, feeble army. . . . And when the next cold blooded massacre takes place the old story of Fort Phil Kearney and the Lava Beds and the Little Horn will be repeated.

FAVORING A MODERATE POLICY TOWARD INDIANS

Samuel Bowles: "A True Indian Policy at Last"

Samuel Bowles and many others in the East placed great hopes in the peace commission's ability to bring about a peaceful solution to the Indian problem.

Springfield (Mass.) Republican, July 20, 1867

The new bill for the settlement of the Indian difficulties, which passed the Senate on Thursday and is pretty certain to become a law, provides for a commission to consist of three army officers not below the rank of brigadier general, to be appointed by the president, in connection with Senator Henderson of Missouri, Representative Windom of Minnesota, and Mr. John B. Sanborn, commissioner of Indian affairs. It is made their duty to call together the chiefs and headmen of the hostile Indian tribes, and endeavor to make peace with them, on the basis of the permanent settlement of the tribes upon reservations. The commissioners are authorized to select one reservation north of Nebraska, west of the Missouri river, and south of the southern Pacific railroad; and another south of Kansas and west of Arkansas, including a portion of the present Indian territory, but these reservations are not to be occupied by the Indians until the selection of territory has been approved by Congress; and not only the hostile tribes, but those that are peaceful who have no permanent reservations are to be located upon them. If the tribes refuse to make peace the war is to be vigorously prosecuted.

This is the first step towards a fixed settlement of the Indians and our difficulties with them. The extermination of the Indians by war, so freely threatened, is next to an impossibility, and would be a great national crime if it were possible. But the government has the clear right to compel their settlement in territories by themselves. The extension of the Pacific railroad and the safety of settlers and emigrants on the route makes it imperative that the Indians be removed at once from the great belt across the continent which must be kept open for emigration and travel. The hostilities of the Indians are in many cases provoked by outrages committed upon them by unprincipled white men, there is no doubt; and the reports of Indian atrocities that come from the West are often false and generally exaggerated; nevertheless there is enough that is known to be true to show the necessity of getting the Indians off the track of the grand march of civilization towards the setting sun....

John Mcleod Keating: "Lo, the Poor Indian!"

Some Southern editors accused the army of excessive brutality and com-pared the Indian policy with the Republican's Reconstruction policy.

Memphis (Tenn.) Appeal, December 4, 1868

On Tuesday we published in the Appeal the facts of the programme laid down by Gen. Sheridan for the wholesale massacre of the Indians who dis-turb our military and render frontier garrison life irksome and dangerous. . . .

In reading over the dispatch of Gen. Sheridan, we were struck by the ab-sence of any regret for a course rendered necessary by the conduct of the white men whose robberies of the Indians incite his hostility to our race. . . . No quarter, no peace, nothing but extermination awaits the Indians under the joint management of Sherman and Sheridan, both whom believe in the contradictory and untenable policy, for a Christian people, of mitigating the horrors of war by the infliction of a punishment that is in itself the sum of all its horrors. If anything were needed to prove the correctness of the position of the Indian Commissioner, Mr. Nat. Taylor, that the military should not be entrusted with the management of our Indian affairs, surely this massacre that threatens annihilation ought of itself to be sufficient.

Peace and the influences of Christianity have made of the Indian nations on our Arkansas frontier a community possessed of all the ennobling in-stincts and qualities of their white brethren. Among them will be found men of high intelligence, well educated, possessed of wealth directed by cred-itable energy in avenues of profit, lawyers, journalists, mechanics and farm-ers. What has been accomplished with these Indians in less than two generations, may be with those who now infest the highways of the plains and make travel, even upon our great Pacific Railroad, very dangerous. Con-gress should legislate upon this matter promptly, and profiting by the lesson we suggest, should initiate a policy for these people such as that which has resulted so well for the Indian Nation.

Wilbur F. Storey: "What to Do with the Indians"

This editorial is as much a slap against the radical Republicans in general as it is against Washington's Indian policy. Nevertheless, it does reflect a more humane approach to dealing with Indians than many of the editori-als of the day did.

Chicago Times, June 25, 1870

It is quite evident that the Indian negotiations lately conducted at Wash-ington have been a signal failure. If the thing is possible, the result was more disastrous than simple failure. In other words, not even the *status quo ante bellum* was preserved. What was done was to convince the Indians that they may expect no change in the policy of the government; and that their only resort is to obtain such satisfaction as they may be able to obtain by the use of the scalping knife.

However, this visit of these Indians has not been without a moral benefit. For the past ten years, the outrages of the party in power with reference to the Indians has been excused by assertions that the Indian is a mere brute, a blood-thirsty animal, without gratitude, intellect, or faith; and that the only possible method of dealing with him is to exterminate him. The Indians have been provoked into depredations in order that, under the clamor of Indian wars and Indian cruelties, the real difficulty—radical mismanagement—might be kept from public view. And thus it has somehow always happened that, no sooner has the public attention been directed toward the abuses of the Indian system, than straightway there has sprung up an Indian "war," or some hideous account of Indian cruelties, by which public attention was withdrawn from the point at which it was originally directed. . . .

The moral effect of Red Cloud's visit is, that it has furnished a most emphatic contradiction of the frontier literature in regard to the nature of the Indian. This chief showed himself something beside a mere savage, who cares only for beads, whisky, warpaint and scalps. His various speeches prove him not only capable of a high order of reasoning, but of a more than average order of eloquence. In other words, he showed himself a human being capable of doing creditably, without education, many things upon whose accomplishment we pride ourselves. . . . Henceforth whatever may be the fate of the Indians, there will be an influential and thinking class of people who will believe that to a great extent, it was our own wickedness, and cruelty, and rapacity which led to their persecution. . . .

We freely admit that Indian or negro has no right to impede the march of our civilization; and that whenever he is an obstacle to its march, he must either stand aside or be annihilated. But there are only 300,000 of these Indians—scarcely more than the population of Chicago. Now, with all our enormous territorial resources, we have ample room for the bestowal and support of this limited number of men and women. We can spare the land for their residence, and we can and should guarantee it from the encroachment of white men. . . .

George Jones: "Preposterous Pagans"

On first read, this editorial—written 10 days before the Battle of the Little Bighorn—appears to support a heavy-handed approach—even death—toward Indians. But, a more careful reading will reveal that it is in fact a parody of the United States's blundering Indian policy. Many of the descriptions of Indians as depraved, dirty, heathen, lying vagabonds come from a speech delivered by Minnesota senator William Windom several months earlier in which he said that the Black Hills should be opened to miners regardless of any treaty.

New York Times, June 12, 1876

It is generally conceded that a war with the Sioux is inevitable. The Indians have killed so many of the Black Hills gold-hunters that their conduct cannot be over-looked, and before many days we shall probably hear of a sharp battle between the troops and the savages.

The conduct of the Indians who claim to own the Black Hills country has been characterized from the first by treachery and turbulence. They began their systematic outrages by signing a treaty with the United States by which they secured exclusive possession of the Black Hills. Of course, we should never have made any such treaty if we had had the least idea that the Black Hills region was worth anything. . . . The Sioux took a base advantage of our ignorance, and actually induced the Government to guarantee that no white man should enter the Black Hills. Having extorted this treaty from us, they fancied that they would have undisturbed possession of their homes, and that the guarantee would be faithfully carried out. These absurd ideas occasionally enter the minds of savages sunk in ignorance and vice, and it is seldom that an Indian can be made to comprehend that, when he makes a treaty with a white man, he, and not the latter, is bound by its provisions.

Some time after the treaty had been made, a military exploring party was sent into the Hills under the command of Gen. Custer. The Sioux impudently claimed that the explorers were white men, and that their presence in the Black Hills was a violation of the treaty. Of course, it is not necessary to discuss this atrocious claim, since it was avowedly based upon the false theory that white men are under obligation to keep their engagements with Indians. . . . The exploring expedition returned in safety, and announced that the Black Hills country was not only a delightful region, but that it was full of gold, which could be easily mined if the Indians were only driven out.

Of course, this announcement was followed by an immediate rush of gold-hunters, who were determined to work the mines in spite of the Indians. The Government warned the miners that they would probably be scalped, and made a few efforts to turn back parties of emigrants. The absurdity of forcing American citizens to observe a treaty with Indians was, however, so manifest that it was resolved to compromise the matter by buying the Black Hills and placing the Indians on a reservation which no white man would covet. The Sioux chiefs were therefore summoned to Washington and asked to sell their land. They were offered $25,000 for a region which was supposed to contain an enormous quantity of gold and which was large enough to make a good-sized State. . . . The Indians pretended that the price offered was far too small, and they declined to leave a country abounding in game, in order to go on a reservation stocked with prairie dogs and rattlesnakes. It is this spirit of grasping covetousness which renders it so difficult to do anything with an Indian except to kill him. A naked Sioux will refuse to sell a few thousand acres of land for a blanket and twenty-five cents. . . .

It is for these unprovoked attacks upon the inoffensive men who had taken possession of the Sioux hunting grounds, merely in order to dig a little gold and build a few trifling cities, that the copper-colored miscreants are now to give an account to the United States Army, and however stubbornly they may resist, there is no doubt that in the end they will be taught that savages who insist that white men should be bound by treaty stipulations have only themselves to blame if they meet with their proper punishment. . . .

George W. Curtis: "A National Disgrace"

It did not take long for Americans to begin creating a new myth out of "Custer's Last Stand." But rather than Custer's death influencing a more peaceful policy, it in fact resulted in a harsher policy that soon saw all Indians pushed onto reservations and their way of life deeded to the Bureau of Indian Affairs for the next century.

Harper's Weekly, August 5, 1876

The fate of the brave and gallant Custer has deeply touched the public heart, which sees only a fearless soldier leading a charge against an ambushed foe, and falling at the head of his men and in the thick of the fray. A monument is proposed, and subscriptions have been made. But a truer monument, more enduring than brass or marble, would be an Indian policy intelligent, moral, and efficient. Custer would not have fallen in vain if such a policy should be the result of his death. It is a permanent accusation of our humanity and ability that over the Canadian line the relations between Indians and whites are so tranquil, while upon our side they are summed up in perpetual treachery, waste, and war. When he was a young lieutenant on the frontier, General Grant saw this, and, watching attentively, he came to the conclusion that the reason of the difference was that the English respected the rights of the Indians and kept faith with them, while we make solemn treaties with them as if they were civilized and powerful nations, and then practically regard them as vermin to be exterminated. The folly of making treaties with the Indian tribes may be so great as treating with a herd of buffaloes. But the infamy of violating treaties when we have made them is undeniable, and we are guilty both of the folly and the infamy.

We make treaties—that is, we pledge our faith—and then leave swindlers and knaves of all kinds to execute them. We maintain and breed pauper colonies. The savages, who know us, and who will neither be pauperized nor trust our word, we pursue, and slay if we can, at an incredible expense. The flower of our young officers is lost in inglorious forays. . . .

It is plain that so long as we undertake to support the Indians as paupers, and then fail to supply the food; to respect their rights to reservations, and then permit the reservations to be overrun; to give them the best weapons and ammunition, and then furnish the pretense of their using them against us; to treat with them as men, and then hunt them like skunks—so long we shall have the most costly and bloody Indian wars, and the most tragical ambuscades, slaughters, and assassinations. The Indian is undoubtedly a savage, and a savage greatly spoiled by the kind of contact with civilization which he gets at the West. There is no romance, there is generally no interest whatever, in him or his fate. But there should be some interest in our own good faith and humanity, in the lives of our soldiers and frontier settlers, and in the taxation to support our Indian policy. All this should certainly be enough to arouse a public demand for a thorough consideration of the subject, and the adoption of a system which should neither be puerile nor disgraceful, and which would tend to spare us the constant repetition of such sorrowful events as the slaughter of Custer and his brave men.

QUESTIONS

1. What factors were to blame for the failure of the government's various Indian policies?
2. What were the main arguments for dealing harshly with Indians?
3. Compare and contrast the depiction of Indians with that of blacks and Chinese.
4. Why was Grant's peace policy popular with newspapers but unpopular with the army?
5. What effect did corruption have on the United States's relationship with Indians?

Notes

1. The information for this introduction comes from Robert M. Utley and Wilcomb E. Washburn, *Indian Wars* (New York: Mariner Books, 2002), and Dee Brown, *Bury My Heart at Wounded Knee* (New York: Henry Holt, 2000).

2. From *Essay on Man, Epistle I,* by Alexander Pope: "Lo, the poor Indian whose untutor'd mind / Sees God in clouds, or hears him in the wind; / His soul proud Science never taught him to stray / Far as the solar walk or milky way." Alexander Pope, *Selected Peotry* (New York: Viking Press, 1985) 130. Newspaper editors often used the term "Lo" as a derogatory name for Indians, much as they used the term "Cuffee" for blacks.

CHAPTER 19

Violence and the Ku Klux Klan, 1867–72

The Ku Klux Klan was founded in 1866 in Pulaski, Tennessee, by a group of young ex-Confederate officers opposed to Reconstruction, in general, and blacks, specifically. Initially, the Klan was a quasi-military band of vigilantes. But it quickly took on the trappings of other popular secret organizations and thereby gained not only a wider audience but also a more broad mission—to be an avenging, yet invisible, angel for the Democratic Party. With its night meetings, secret oaths, white robes, and mysterious rituals, the Klan attracted men from all stations of life, but particularly from the rural and poorer educated segments.

In less than a year, more than 200 local Klans had organized in Tennessee, and dozens were appearing in neighboring states. A national convention of the Klan was held in Nashville in 1867, at which time the organization became known as the "Invisible Empire of the South." The convention elected General Nathan Bedford Forrest as grand wizard, supported by a complex hierarchy that rivaled any government. Under Forrest's influence and leadership, the Klan spread quickly.

In the summer of 1867, blacks throughout the South were preparing for their first elections. The Union League, an unofficial educational arm of the Republican Party, spent months organizing the black vote, and by election time more than a half million blacks had registered. When it was apparent that the black voters were not lining up behind the Democratic ballot box, white supremacists launched a counterrevolution. But despite the intimidation and violence, black voter turnout throughout the South was strong. New constitutions were approved, black and white delegates were elected to state legislatures, and the business of Reconstruction began to move forward.

But, seething below the surface was an undisguised hatred of the new "black and tan" governments. Throughout the presidential campaign

Ku Klux Klan. *This Thomas Nast cartoon depicts a hooded member of the Ku Klux Klan clasping hands with a member of the White League over a shield depicting a black couple holding a child. In the background is a burning schoolhouse and a man hanging from a tree.* Harper's Weekly. *Library of Congress.*

season of 1868, bands of well-armed whites patrolled public highways intimidating blacks and warning that if they did not vote Democratic they would be killed. At first, the Klan's activities were confined to intimidation such as posting broadsides that threatened blacks, night visitations, and whippings. But pranks and vandalism quickly turned to murder.

By Election Day in Louisiana, more than 2,000 blacks had been killed. In Bossier Parish, 125 bodies were found in the Red River after a Klan raid. In St. Landry Parish, the white editor of a black newspaper was driven out of town and night riders invaded local plantations, killing more than 200 blacks. In South Carolina, two state legislators were killed, as was the president of a local Union League, who was murdered in his front yard. Plots to kill the governor, attorney general, and other prominent South Carolina Republican leaders were later uncovered.[1]

The Klan's campaign of terror was a success. Although Grant won the presidency, it was a slim victory. Klan terror had reduced black voter turnout by almost 20 percent, compared with elections a year earlier. In 11 predominately black Georgia counties, not a single Republican vote was cast. General Forrest, grand wizard, was so pleased with the work of the Klan that in February 1869 he declared the Klan's work finished.

But, the Klan was out of control. Emboldened by its success during the past two years, the Klan and other similar organizations such as the White Brotherhood, White League, Red Shirts in South Carolina, White Liners, and Knights of the White Camellia escalated their violence. During the 1870 election season, the Klan destroyed ballot boxes, and blacks were dragged from their homes and beaten. In Laurensville, South Carolina, 13 blacks were murdered, along with a white judge and a black legislator. Grant ordered troops to remain in South Carolina during the elections, but there were not enough troops to control the violence throughout the state. In Eutaw, Alabama, 4 blacks were killed and 54 wounded when a group of armed whites broke up a Republican campaign rally.[2]

With the support of the Klan and its terror tactics, Democrats increased their control over the statehouses in the South. Grant appealed to Congress to provide legislation that would protect not only voting rights but also basic civil rights of blacks. When Congress asked for evidence that such legislation was needed, Grant produced the report of a grand jury investigation documenting more than 5,000 cases of floggings, lynchings, and other acts of terrorism. The answer from Congress was the Enforcement Act of April 20, 1871—also known as the Ku Klux Klan Force Act. This law, aimed directly at the activities of the Klan, prohibited any person or any conspiracy to deprive citizens of their rights and privileges under the Constitution. The law also gave the president authority to suspend the writ of habeas corpus and use military force to suppress the violence.

In June 1871, Congress initiated its own investigation of "the condition of affairs" in the South. Hearings were held in the summer of 1871 in Washington as well as throughout the South. Despite 13 volumes of eyewitness testimony detailing Southern violence and calls for help from Southern governors, President Grant was cautious about using the extraordinary powers that the new enforcement laws had given him. Many Republicans believed that federal intervention was an overreaction and an overreaching of federal authority. They also blamed the violence on inept state administration. Trying to find that perfect balance between protection against violence and protection of state sovereignty was not easy for Grant.

The first major assault on the Ku Klux Klan Force Act occurred in South Carolina in 1873 when 533 Klansmen, arrested for various acts of violence and intimidation against black and white Republicans, were tried under the new law. But the mere logistics of trying so many men soon stalled the machinery of justice. It was almost impossible to prove a conspiracy, since no one would testify against compatriots. Only 102 men were actually convicted or pled guilty. In the spring of 1873, the attorney general ordered prosecutions to be suspended.

A handful of cases from other Southern states made their way through the federal courts, and at each turn judges tore down the Ku Klux Klan laws as an unconstitutional usurpation of state power by the federal government. Congress tried to correct the laws with more laws, but this too was doomed. With fewer cases and fewer convictions, the policy of enforcement had failed, the black vote had been effectively neutralized, and white supremacy was the victor.

Although Klan activity—at least reported activity—subsided somewhat after 1873, violence continued through the end of Reconstruction and beyond. Both President Grant and President Rutherford B. Hayes were forced to use military intervention, but sparingly. By the end of 1874, most of the South was under Democratic control, and the U.S. Supreme Court and other federal courts had eviscerated the Fourteenth and Fifteenth Amendments as well as the enforcement acts. States were now free to disenfranchise blacks. The reign of violence had succeeded.

The Northern press would have been slow to connect violence with the Klan had it not been for the reporting of black Republican newspapers in the South. Newspapers such as the *Mobile (Ala.) Nationalist* and the *New Orleans Tribune* informed the nation about the rise of the Klan and kept stories of violence in front of Americans. *Harper's Weekly* also drew attention to the Klan through Thomas Nast's cartoons, which portrayed the sheet-clad Klansmen as cowardly, ignorant, and evil.

The first section challenging the Klan begins with a description, by J.R. Young, of how the Klan uses hoods, rituals, and violence to intimidate blacks and Republicans, all for the purpose of regaining the South for whites. The second entry, by Albert Griffin, warns readers to pay no heed to the printed warnings of the Klan that appeared in newspapers and posters but to be prepared to protect themselves in case of real violence. The third entry is an essay by Mark Twain that uses humor and sarcasm to decry lynchings by the Klan. The next entry, by George W. Curtis, accuses the Klan of being an unofficial arm of the Democratic Party, and should the Democrats wish to get rid of the Klan it could do so very easily. The final editorial in this section, by William W. Harding, supports federal intervention and the Force Acts as the most appropriate means to stop the violence and protect blacks and Southern Republicans.

No newspaper dared to come out in support of the Klan and its tactics; instead, Democratic newspapers took the stance that the violence was exaggerated or that the Klan was a figment of Republican imaginations. The first two selections in the next section, by W. M. Elliot and Carey Styles, blame all violence on Republicans, carpetbaggers, and the Union League. The third entry, by Albert Pike, accuses the Northern newspapers of lying about the atrocities of the Klan and blames the violence on radicals and the Freedmen's Bureau. The last reading, by Elliot, declares that as election time rolls around, Northern newspapers exaggerate the violence in the South and make every small incident a national tragedy.

AGAINST THE KLAN'S ACTIVITIES

John Russell Young: "Ku-Klux Klan"

This editorial is one of the best descriptions of the work and aims of the Klan. See the response of the Memphis (Tenn.) Daily Appeal, *provided below.*

New York Tribune, April 13, 1868

Not only the ordinary hatred of loyalty, but the remote hope of political advantage, has led to the establishment of the order here referred to, known generally as the Ku-Klux Klan. Their leading idea is, of course, the defeat of reconstruction, and the postponement of anything like admission to the Union until they may realize the very remote contingency of a grand Democratic triumph in the North. Such a triumph, they seem to believe, would restore the now silent South to its old potency in the national councils; then they could "reduce the nigger to his normal sphere;" the bugbear of negro voting would vanish under a summary disfranchisement of the entire race, and although absolute slavery might not be restored, the old aristocracy would be able to hedge the negroes and poor whites within such labor regulations as practically to restore the patriarchal institutions in all things except auction sales of human being.

To this end work the K.K.K. They get up a mysterious fellowship; adopt a frightful disguise; scatter abroad horribly worded proclamations; make sudden forays at midnight; and do all fantastic tricks that may suit their purpose. The purpose is to frighten and annoy loyal colored men (and white men, too, if they can,) so that they will leave the Southern States. Thus, some time ago, in Mississippi, they circulated a ridiculous story about some horrible monster in the swamps, a dreadful demon that had an insatiable appetite for negro flesh; a similar monster was seen in Arkansas, and scarcely a week passes without producing a startling account of another of the blood in some neighboring quarter. This does very well for the credulous colored people, but white men must have stronger doses, and so the K.K.K. favor peaceful and hard-working Union men with cloudily-worded warnings, and emphasize the warnings by midnight visitations, threats of violence, and sometimes actual assault.

What shall be done? Is it to be tolerated that in a land of civil government an irresponsible gang of ruffians shall spread terror far and wide over a third of the national domain—or even over a square mile of that domain? That, there is a powerful organization, composed of the very worst men in the South, and aiming at the ends we have described, no one can doubt. . . . The loyal press of the South give facts that prove the great strength and base purposes of the Klan, while the faint attempts of the rebel press to laugh at the affair are equally substantial proof of its reality and importance. . . . But when, in any section of the country it is possible for armed men to ride abroad in disguise, their faces closely concealed, and order this man to move, that other to stay; drag forth and flog one for loyalty; burn the house of another; drive unoffending schoolmistresses from their homes, and spread terror over the whole State, it is high time to pull off the gloves.

It is significant of trouble that the more violent of the rebel press favor the growth of this society. Some of them pretend to laugh at the fears of the loyal citizens, but there is a "covert devil in their sneer," that betrays both knowledge and approval of the Klan. Let them all—members and supporters—recall the fate of the Knights of the Golden Circle, or Sons of Liberty, and, whatever flush of success may now encourage their efforts, they may be sure that swift and speedy destruction will fall upon them should their operations fulfill the promise that the few attempts already on record appear to justify. . . .

On the whole, we judge that this Klan is a reality, and means dangerous mischief. It has spread, in an incredibly short time, from Eastern Tennessee to every nook and corner of the Southern States. It is petted in an indirect way by the most of the rebel press, and hints are given here and there of the great deliverance from Congressional rule that the South is to have at some future day through its operations. If it is really another secession snake, the sooner its fangs are drawn by the judicious exhibition of Loyal power, the better it will be for all of us, more particularly, however, for the Southern people.

Albert Griffin: "The Ku Klux Klan"

Mobile, Alabama, saw its share of Klan violence throughout the late 1860s, and the Mobile (Ala.) Nationalist, *a Republican newspaper for blacks, filled its columns with stories of Klan violence.*

Mobile (Ala.) Nationalist, March 26, 1868

An organization by this name, having for its object the perpetration of outrages on white and colored Unionists, has for some time had an existence in Tennessee. Of its strength in numbers and purpose we have no positive knowledge, but many cowardly outrages have undoubtedly been committed in its name.

Considerable gasconade has appeared of late in the city papers, (or rather in the *Tribune,* which seems to have gone "clean daft" on the subject,) concerning the advent of this organization in Mobile, and circulars of sanguinary portent, printed in red ink, and liberally sprinkled with typographic daggers, have been served upon many gentlemen distinguished for their fidelity to the cause of their country.

To those timid people who have been alarmed by the bloodthirsty threatenings, ghastly warnings, and melodramatic tomfoolery about the "bloody moon," "white death," "rattling skeleton," and "serpent's den," . . . contained in these circulars, we would say that men who are bent on the shedding of blood do not usually go about warning their intended victims in this fantastically absurd fashion. Our advice is that every one go about his business peaceably and quietly as usual; giving no heed to this direful claptrap. If attacked, it is your right and your duty to defend yourself; but don't fret about danger until it makes its appearance.

On the other hand, we would say to the mover, in this matter that in playing with the superstitions of the ignorant and the passions of the depraved—more especially in the present condition of public feeling—they are tampering with the peace of the community in a manner that demands the immediate attention of the military authorities. Whatever violence may be committed, whatever blood may be shed, whether by the members of this band or in its name, justice will point to the men who are bent on stirring up strife as the real criminals.

The military are placed here to maintain the peace, and it is their duty to suppress with the strong hand any movement that is willfully and wantonly intended to lead to a breach of the peace. And the authorities here will be strangely recreant to their duty if they do not at once ferret out and punish the scoundrels who under the vail [*sic*] of burlesque, are furnishing ruffians with arguments for assassination.

Mark Twain: "Only a Nigger"

This short satirical essay was published while Mark Twain was co-owner and editor of the Buffalo (N.Y.) Express. *It appeared unsigned but has been attributed to Mark Twain. The essay is a protest against lynching, a subject Twain deals with in the* Adventures of Huckleberry Finn, *published 16 years later. Twain uses the word "nigger" in this essay to indicate that it is the dehumanizing word used by Southern gentlemen for whom lynching is yet another sport.*

Buffalo (N.Y.) Express, August 26, 1869

A dispatch from Memphis mentions that, of two negroes lately sentenced to death for murder in that vicinity, one named Woods has just confessed to having ravished a young lady during the war, for which deed another negro was hung at the time by an avenging mob, the evidence that doomed the guiltless wretch being a hat which Woods now relates that he stole from its owner and left behind, for the purpose of misleading. Ah, well! Too bad, to be sure! A little blunder in the administration of justice by Southern mob-law; but nothing to speak of. Only "a nigger" killed by mistake—that is all. Of course, every high toned gentleman whose chivalric impulses were so unfortunately misled in this affair, by the cunning of the miscreant Woods, is as sorry about it as a high toned gentleman can be expected to be sorry about the unlucky fate of "a nigger." But mistakes will happen, even in the conduct of the best regulated and most high toned mobs, and surely there is no good reason why Southern gentlemen should worry themselves with useless regrets, so long as only an innocent "nigger" is hanged, or roasted or knouted to death, now and then. What if the blunder of lynching the wrong man does happen once in four or five cases! Is that any fair argument against the cultivation and indulgence of those fine chivalric passions and that noble Southern spirit which will not brook the slow and cold formalities of regular law, when outraged white womanhood appeals for vengeance? Perish the thought so unworthy of a Southern soul! Leave it to the sentimentalism and humanitarianism of a cold-blooded Yankee civilization! What are the lives of a few "niggers" in comparison with the preservation of the impetuous instincts of a proud and fiery race? Keep ready the halter, therefore, oh chivalry of Memphis! Keep the lash knotted; keep the brand and the faggots in waiting, for prompt work with the next "nigger" who may be suspected of any damnable crime! Wreak a swift vengeance upon him, for the satisfaction of the noble impulses that animate knightly hearts, and then leave time and accident to discover, if they will, whether he was guilty or no.

George W. Curtis: "The Ku-Klux"

Harper's Weekly *ran numerous stories, editorials, cartoons, and wood engravings about the Klan and its activities in the South. In this editorial, George W. Curtis accuses the Klan of being an arm of the Democratic Party, as demonstrated by Democrats' consistent denial of Klan brutality.*

Harper's Weekly, November 4, 1871

That the bitter hostilities of the war would survive it, was to be expected. That the hatred of the government and of the influences which were victorious would long continue, was only natural; and that its consequences should be turned upon the race whose slavery was the cause of the war, and whose freedom was the sign of the victory, was not surprising. The terror which prevails in certain parts of the late rebel States, under the name of the Ku-Klux, is undeniable. Yet how strong party feeling upon the subject is at the North may be seen in the fact that when the statement of a just man from one of the Southern States was read in the Senate, that fifty thousand persons had been murdered by the Ku-Klux since the war closed, it was asserted by an opponent that there had not been one. And we are still, despite railroads and telegraphs, so far from the Southern States, that few persons who have not carefully read or heard the unquestionable reports are willing to believe in the confusion and terror that still prevail in many parts of that region. If any one, however, will talk with quiet and careful observers from the interior of the Southern States, who are really friendly to the government, yet who would live peaceably with their neighbors, he will find that the stories of the Ku-Klux are true. . . . The masked blow of the Ku-Klux always falls upon some loyal man, black or white, and always upon a Republican. Democrats are unharmed. It is not a terror for those who attempted to destroy the government during the war, but for those who sustained it. The conclusion is irresistible that it is an organization of Democrats. This fact is made still more unquestionable by the denials and sneers of Northern Democrats. They call it rawhead and bloody-bones, a bugaboo of scared radicals, and a device invented to authorize military coercion of Democratic districts. But if every victim in the Southern States who is taken from his home and scourged, or mangled, or murdered were a Democrat instead of a Republican, how the land would ring with the cry that a radical Administration abandoned innocent citizens to the tender mercies of savages!

Of course the darkness and the mystery with which the Ku-Klux is enveloped serve both to exaggerate and to conceal the truth. . . . If the Democratic party were resolved that the Ku-Klux should disappear, it would be heard of no more. If it were as anxious to restore and confirm the tranquility of the Southern States as it is to throw the odium of military despotism upon a government which seeks to protect innocent citizens from cruel lawlessness, that lawlessness would cease. The country will not forget that the Democratic party sustains the Ku-Klux by affecting to deny its existence; that the terror which is undeniable in certain parts of the Southern States is Democratic; and that the party whose leaders refuse to assist the authorities in maintaining order hopes to elect a President and obtain control of the government.

William W. Harding: No Title

This brief editorial comment praises the government for stepping in with the Ku Klux Klan Force Act of 1871 and using it to dispose of Klan activity in South Carolina.

Philadelphia Inquirer, October 18, 1871

With its usual forbearance, the National Government has suffered the illegal and murderous associations of assassins and incendiaries, known as Kuklux-Klans, to spread terror throughout most of the Southern States. Congress, at its last session, clothed the President with full powers to punish the Klansmen and crush out their power in the most summary manner. The Executive was chary of proceeding to extreme measures, trusting, no doubt, to the moral effect of the anit-Kuklux act. In her old spirit of insolent defiance, South Carolina mistook forbearance for fear, and her Klansmen plied the pistol, knife and torch more vigorously than ever. And now mete punishment has overtaken these persistent evildoers. Under the provisions of the act approved April, 1871, the President has suspended the writ of habeas corpus in nine counties of South Carolina, embracing the region where Kuklux outrages most abound. The swift, stern, unsparing processes of martial law will soon put an end to organized assassination and incendiarism, and save not only South Carolina but the entire South from anarchy.

REFUSAL TO ACKNOWLEDGE THE KLAN'S VIOLENCE

W.M. Elliot: "Inflammatory Appeals, &c., &c."

In April 1868, after numerous stories of Klan intimidations surfaced, General George Meade, military commander over Georgia, Alabama, and Florida, issued the following order. Democratic newspapers argued that the order should have been aimed at such Republican organizations as the Union League, which was described as "quiet, silent, secret and dark in its movement . . . and deep, dangerous and deadly."[3]

Richmond (Va.) Whig, April 21, 1868

In Paragraph IV, of his order against the Ku Kluxes, General Mead employs the following language:

> All public writers and speakers are enjoined to refrain from inflammatory appeals to the passions and prejudices of the people, and from publishing or saying anything calculated to produce breaches of the peace, or to intimidate any persons from the exercise of the political privileges.

This is a harder blow to the Radical slang whangers and editors than to any other class. If all of the military commanders in the South had commenced their administration with such an order and enforced it rigidly up to the present time, the public tranquility would never have been under the fancied necessity of issuing any order against such imaginary organizations as the Ku Kluxes. From the moment that negroes became suffragans and the dispensers of offices, Radical emissaries and carpet-baggers and demagogues have made it their constant business to stir them to mutiny and rage. Their passions and prejudices have been inflamed by incendiary speeches and writing, and all the arts that black-hearted white men, traitors to their race, could employ have been put in requisition to array them against the whites and precipitate a conflict between the two races. We do not exaggerate when we say that nine-tenths of the trouble experienced by the military commandants has been hatched by these miscreants.

Carey Styles: "Should an Outbreak Occur, Who Will Be Responsible?"

According to the Atlanta Constitution, *the carpetbaggers were more to blame for violence than was the Klan. The* Constitution *never acknowledged the Klan on its editorial page, although it did publish stories of Klan violence as well as of Klan meetings.*

Atlanta Constitution, August 19, 1868

Were we to undertake to correct all the false statements made by Radical Speakers and papers, we would be guilty of a reckless waste of time. But a late issue of a Radical sheet contains some statements so palpably false that we cannot permit them to go uncorrected. It charges that the "hue and cry raised by the Democratic press against alleged organizations of armed men, is a trick of bad men to bring about a rupture which they evidently desire." Now this charge bears the mark of falsehood upon its face. It refutes itself. There is not an intelligent man in the whole country but knows the Democrats personally and politically would be losers by a war of races. The Radicals know that a conflict of any kind at this time would damage the cause of the Democratic party, hence, the eagerness with which they labor to bring it about. Had the Radicals the honesty to confess it, they would admit that the Democratic is the peace party—that it preaches peace, counsels peace, and practices peace. It is false and dishonest to charge them with a desire, much more an attempt, to produce a war of races. We do not wonder at the alarm of the black man, when Radical incendiaries are daily and nightly firing him with the most inflammatory speeches, by intensifying his hatred against the whites, and by telling him that the object of the Democratic party is to re-enslave him. The Democratic party makes no complaint against the negro; he has done well, remarkably well, in view of the evil influences surrounding him. It is willing he should exercise the franchise right undisturbed. But to the white scoundrels who are doing every thing in their power secretly to produce a conflict, it offers no compromise. They are enemies of the human race, and as such, we can never look upon them with feelings other than of loathing and disgust. They are remorseless hyenas, seeking to sacrifice both races at the South that they may feast upon their putrefaction. No: if a conflict of races is inaugurated, the fearful responsibility will not attach to the negroes nor the Democrats. The sin of it will attach like a leprous sore to a few miserable Radical creatures who have nothing to lose in any event, but whose cowardly instincts would prompt them to desert the negro in the conflict, whilst their thieving propensities would be turned to plunder and repine. We confess that such men are very "dangerous to the country;" but why not go further and frankly give these dangerous men their true identity. No one would have the hardihood to deny that the Radicals are wholly responsible for these threatened outbreaks. . . .

So long as men sent here in the capacity of peace preservers-men, as we are informed by eye-witnesses, who disgrace the uniforms they wear, by making violent appeals to the passions and prejudices of the negroes against the whites—men who counsel them to arm themselves for the fight, declaring when once begun, that it will not close until the whites, from the innocent infant at its mother's breast, to the gray-haired sire, shall be exterminated. So long as such men and such conduct is tolerated, we can have no peace.

May Heaven protect us from the calamities these outlaws would bring upon us. But should they come, the vilest will not live to charge the responsibility to the Democrats.

Albert Pike: "The Ku-Klux Klan"

This is the Memphis (Tenn.) Daily Appeal*'s answer to the* New York Tribune*'s description of the Klan's work, provided above. Not only is the Klan's work exaggerated, according to the* Appeal, *but even worse offenders are the Freedmen's Bureau, blacks, and Republicans.*

Memphis (Tenn.) Daily Appeal, April 16, 1868

The New York *Tribune*, after, "a careful study of facts and sifting of testimony," concluded that there is "solid reality under the stuff and nonsense with which the Southwestern paper mask this rapidly spreading organization."

It admits that it is not *unnatural* at any time, that secret societies should exist; and that men *will* unite for protection or for congenial association. . . .

It is useless to expect the *Tribune* to be honest or veracious in its accounts of anything in the South. It has a monomania for lying. Everything is in the plural, with it. A single outrage, reported from Tennessee, one warning, probably got up by some devilish boys to scare some one not braver than Bob Acres or Ancient Pistol, gets multiplied or breeds a whole litter, while the account of it is transmitted by wire or by letter of some Dugald Dalgetty of falsification, to the *Tribune* columns.[4] It was intended that everyone who might read the [editorial] should understand that the warnings, visitations and threats spoken of have been matters of constant and multitudinous occurrences; because even actual assaults have been *sometimes* committed. Intended to be so understood, it is, slightly an exaggeration, after the *Tribune's* happiest manner. . . .

We do not suppose that the Ku Klux-Klan, with its masks and devices to scare superstitious negroes, and other extravagances, was any thing more than a local organization, got up for fun and frolic; and we were of course inclined to laugh at it, until it seemed about to be abused for discreditable and lawless purposes. Associations of that sort give a power to individuals, which there is always too much temptation to use improperly; and they will, moreover, be made use of by those who do not belong to them, who, committing excesses, cause them to be imputed to this or the other suspected order. . . .

We do not know what the Ku-Klux organization may become, if it ever becomes anything. It is quite certain that it will never come to much on its original plan. It must become quite another thing to be efficient.

The disfranchised people of the South, robbed of all the guarantees of the Constitution—aye, hell-kite! *all*, "at one fell swoop,"—can find no protection for property, liberty or life, except in secret association. Not in such association to commit follies and outrages; but for mutual, peaceful, lawful, self-defense. If it were in our power, if it could be effected, we would unite every white man in the South, who is opposed to negro suffrage, into one great Order of Southern Brotherhood, with an organization complete, active, vigorous, in which a few should execute the concentrated will of all, and whose very existence should be concealed from all but its members. That has been the resort of the oppressed in all ages. To resort to it is a right given by God; and the Brownlows and Meades would find it idle to attempt, by any threats or denunciations, to prevent it, if the people were not so entirely sunken in the apathy of hopeless despair as not to have energy enough to unite for *any*thing.

W.M. Elliot: "Twelve Days Off"

This editorial is a typical denial of violence. The real culprits are Northerners who believe the exaggerated tales of imaginary outrages.

Richmond (Va.) Whig, October 23, 1868

The Presidential election is but twelve days off, and no imagination; however active and fertile, is equal to the task of conceiving the vast amount of fraud, fabrication and misrepresentation that will be perpetrated within that brief space of time. Most of this will be at the expense of the South, for it has been found that the manufacturer of southern outrages upon negroes and northern men has proved the most "profitable of all the various electioneering agencies." We had hoped that the Radical victories in the late elections would put that party in a better humor, and that, inspired with confidence in their ability to carry the Presidential election without further trouble, they would rest from their labors. But their mills grind as actively as ever. Indeed, the near approach of the critical period has imparted more activity to their operations, and there is reason to believe that as the opportunities for refutation are diminished by the shortness of time, the number of calumnies, inventions and outrages will be proportionally increased. Already, and within the last few days, an unusual number of Southern atrocities have been telegraphed northward from remote Southern localities, and it is gravely assumed by leading Radical newspapers that the long talked of "renewal of the rebellion" is at last actually impending. Every sparrow that falls at the South will be magnified into a Northern man or a negro, and the urchin, who killed it, into a terrible and blood-stained rebel, bent upon the subversion of the Government. Every death by accident will be represented as a rebel murder, and scores of Northern men and negroes will be mercilessly slaughtered, who never had any existence save in the prolific imaginations of Radical letter writers. These imaginary outrages will not only be published, but they will be gotten up on the most artistic manner, with the utmost minuteness of detail, and with every circumstance of horror. Even in old Virginia, where there is, as far as we have learned, no expectation of participation in the election, the lie manufactory has been started. The New York *Tribune,* under a sensational caption, publishes a telegram stating that very recently, at Suffolk, Virginia, "the Democratic party ran up the rebel flag and saluted the same."

It is, in truth, but a waste of time to attempt to arrest this current of falsehood, or to refute any calumny however unfounded. The accusations go North and are believed, while the refutations never find their way beyond the limits of the South, where they are not needed. Perhaps the shops will be shut up when the election is over, and the falsehoods will cease when there is no longer a motive for telling them. It is to be hoped so at least.

QUESTIONS

1. Why was the Ku Klux Klan considered an arm of the Democratic Party?
2. How did the Klan use cloaks, masks, rituals, and symbols to help it do its work?
3. How effectively does Mark Twain use his humor to get his point across?
4. Why did Southern newspapers blame violence on carpetbaggers and radicals rather than on the Klan?

NOTES

1. Stetson Kennedy, *After Appomattox: How the South Won the War* (Gainesville: University Press of Florida, 1995), 89; Eric Foner, *Reconstruction: America's Unfinished Revolution, 1863–1877* (New York: Harper & Row, 1988), 342; Richard Zuczek, *State of Rebellion: Reconstruction in South Carolina* (Columbia: University of South Carolina Press, 1996), 54.

2. Brooks D. Simpson, *The Reconstruction Presidents* (Lawrence: University Press of Kansas, 1998), 151–52; Xi Wang, *The Trial of Democracy, Black Suffrage and Northern Republicans, 1860–1910* (Athens: University of Georgia Press, 1997), 82–83, 94; Foner, 427.

3. *Mobile (Ala.) Advertiser and Register,* 8 April 1868, 2.

4. Bob Acres, a cowardly country squire, is a character in *The Rivals,* a 1775 play by Richard Brinsley Sheridan; Ancient Pistol is a bullying coward in Shakespeare's *Henry IV, Henry V,* and *Merry Wives of Windsor.* Dugald Dalgetty, from a character in Sir Walter Scott's *Legend of Montrose,* refers to someone who is paid, in this case, to lie.

CHAPTER 20

Sunday Liquor Laws, 1866–73

As early as the 1580s, there was a growing movement among Puritans in England to restrict activities on Sunday to only those that were spiritual. Puritans took quite literally the fourth commandment to "remember the Sabbath day to keep it holy," believing that the entire day from sunrise to sunset should be set aside for public and private religious observance. In other words, there was to be no work, no play, and no idleness.

These Sabbatarian observances were transplanted to the U.S. colonies and were particularly strong where Protestant—as opposed to Catholic or Anglican—colonies were established. The colonial Sunday laws (or blue laws) could be extreme, restricting even the most ordinary and innocent activities on Sunday and meting out harsh physical punishment for those who disobeyed. Others were merely admonitory, like the 1623 blue law enacted in Virginia, which merely required citizens to "repair to their churches" and that "the Sabbath day be not ordinarily profaned by working in any employment."

New York's 1695 Sunday law forbade traveling, laboring, working, shooting, fishing, sporting, playing, horse racing, and frequenting of "tippling houses."[1] As the influence of these theocratic colonies declined after the American Revolution, so did many of the Sunday laws. Where they did remain on the books, they were not enforced. But, various religious movements during the eighteenth and nineteenth centuries would spur the revival of Sunday laws, as would the temperance movement during the late 1800s. For example, in 1810, evangelicals lobbied against a federal law requiring post office workers to distribute mail on Sunday. The Sabbatarians argued that the law was a blatant disregard for the ancient custom and biblical laws, and they prevented 10,000 postal clerks and mail handlers from observing the Sabbath. The federal law was not changed.

Sunday liquor laws, also known as Sunday closing laws, were an outgrowth of Sunday laws and an important part of the effort by Protestant reformers to "cleanse" society of what they believed were the ills plaguing a society, namely drinking and gambling. The restrictions were aimed directly at the working class, who were seen as mere children who needed to be protected from the temptations that society placed before them. Sunday closing laws banned the sale of alcohol and tobacco and closed restaurants and drinking places. Theoretically, the intent of these laws was to keep the sober workingman at home with his family on Sunday.

Sunday liquor laws were hardly noticed in the rural areas; however, in the cities they quickly became the bane of saloon keepers, brewers, and "regular folk." The tavern, inn, or saloon had become a social institution, a place where men gathered with friends to talk about sports and politics and to get away from the family. On Sundays, particularly in the German and Jewish communities, the whole family would gather at bars and beer gardens—working-class social centers.

Consequently, Sunday closing laws and their enforcement became a highly emotional and important issue in the large cities. On one side were reformers, typically middle- and upper-class Republicans, who wanted to clean up the city and get rid of gambling, drunkenness, and prostitution by closing down their places of business. On the other side were the saloon keepers and brewers, who often created protective associations to lobby against Sunday laws and pay off police and judges.

In 1866, New York not only passed a new Sunday closing law but also increased the liquor license (excise) fee and mandated that police search out and identify—for licensing purposes—every business that sold liquor. Trying to identify everyone who sold liquor was an awesome undertaking in New York City. Boston also had a Sunday closing law that some of that city's major hotels decided to break. The Tremont, Revere, and Parker Houses as well as other hotels were arrested and convicted of selling liquor in violation of the Sunday closing law. Each hotel was sentenced to pay a fine of $50, and the managers were sent to prison for three months.

The Sabbatarian movement often became an anti-immigrant movement. In 1855, the mayor of Chicago decided not only to enforce the state's Sunday closing laws but also to increase the liquor license fee from $50 to $300 and to shorten the period that a license was valid. Most Chicago saloon keepers defied the new laws, but only the Irish and Germans were arrested. Angry immigrants marched in protest on city hall but were met by police. At the end of the day, 15 people were dead. The Chicago law remained on the books, and although it was rarely enforced, it continued to be the subject of debate by the German community every time the city council decided to change the license fees or the period for renewal or to otherwise tinker with the law. In 1871, the German community once again protested an attempt to try to enforce the Sunday liquor law. But, there simply were not enough Germans on the city council to vote down the ordinance. One councilman suggested an amendment to the ordinance that would replace the word "Sunday" with "February 29." The ruse did not work. However, protests from the growing German community resulted in a compromise whereby the police would not enforce the law in the German beer gardens or family taverns.[2] But, that compromise did not last long.

After the Chicago fire in 1871, thousands of single men flooded into the city to work for construction contractors. Saloons and gambling houses sprang up in the areas where the construction workers lived, and they became targets for reformers. In October 1872, Mayor Joseph Medill (one of the owners of the *Chicago Tribune*) ordered his police chief to close all saloons on Sundays. Meanwhile, the Germans and Irish on the city council again organized to overthrow the reformers' agenda by proposing an entire revision of the city code. Each ordinance was reviewed, including the Sunday liquor ordinance. In an initial meeting of the council, with six members absent, the ordinance was revised to require that only front doors and windows of saloons be kept closed on Sunday. Medill eventually vetoed the entire revision of the city code. In the summer of 1874, Medill abandoned his position as mayor and opened the way for the Germans and Irish to organize and put forward a more liberal candidate for mayor. They mounted an antiprohibition campaign and elected a new mayor. The city council finally passed an ordinance that required all saloon doors that faced the street to be closed on Sundays. The police would not interfere with what went on behind the closed doors.

The issue of liquor regulation—whether closing laws or licensing—split down party lines, with Republicans taking the role of reformers against alcohol and Democrats supporting the rights of immigrants and workingmen to enjoy their drink whenever they wished without excessive state interference. Horace Greeley, editor of the *New York Tribune* and a temperance advocate, once announced, "I never said all Democrats are saloon keepers; I only said all saloon keepers are Democrats."[3]

As can be seen from the editorials supporting Sunday liquor laws, there is an assumption that in the United States, Christian doctrine holds a privileged position and Christianity and civil behavior are synonymous. The first reading in this section, by Greeley, argues that if laws are going to be on the books, they should be adhered to by everyone. And if the liquor sellers want to rebel, they should take a lesson from the late war. The second entry, by Samuel Bowles, does not ask that all men go to church rather than the saloons on Sunday but only that those who do wish to observe Sunday may do so peacefully. The third editorial, by Wilbur F. Storey from the *Chicago*

Times, argues that the law should ignore the cultural differences that exist in the city and apply the Sunday liquor laws equally to everyone. The fourth entry, by Horace White, examines the enforcement of the liquor laws in Chicago and finds that the police have not overenforced the law; quite the contrary, they have been lax, especially in the German neighborhoods. The final entry is a letter from the Temperance Bureau in Chicago that argues that when the Sunday liquor laws were not enforced, arrests for drunkenness on Sunday almost doubled.

The editorials on the other side of the issue begin with one by Ben Wood from the *New York Daily News* that argues that Sunday liquor laws not only are a policy of radical Republicanism but also are artifacts left over from the past that cannot work in a booming metropolis like New York. The second selection is a letter from a workingman who wants to be able to enjoy his day off from work doing as he pleases, including going to the saloon after church or a beer garden after a Sunday walk with his family. The final selection from the *London Times* pokes fun at the religious conservatism of the United States and notes that anyone who wants to have a drink on Sunday just has to take the ferry to New Jersey.

SUPPORTING SUNDAY LIQUOR LAWS

Horace Greeley: "Law and Liquor"

Horace Greeley was well-known as a temperance man who supported any and all efforts to control the sale of liquor. This is the New York Tribune *'s answer to the* New York Daily News *'s editorial, provided below. The comparison of the "rebels" against liquor with the rebels of the Civil War is an example of the "waving the bloody shirt" tactics that Republicans used.*

New York Tribune, April 28, 1866

There is just a spice of truth in the main inculpation of *The News.* We certainly do believe that, if there were less drunkenness, less riot and debauchery of all kinds, there would be fewer Democrats, according to the classification of *The News.* Hence, we do not care to deny that we consider the new Excise act politically as well as morally wholesome. Stop the manufacture of drunkards, and we shall confidently look for a diminunition in the numerical strength and absolute power of negro-hating Sham Democracy.

As to the "storm of indignation," it amounts exactly to this: The laws of our State have always prescribed that you must be licensed in order to retail intoxicating Beverages; but the lower grade of rumsellers in our City have been accustomed to defy the law. The law says no one must sell on Sunday; but they defy this also, with many other restrictions. Now, the new Excise act undertakes to make these ostentatious law-breakers haul in their horns and respect the laws of the land; which (we are told) excites their "indignation." We can assure them that apprehension would be a more wholesome labeling.

The News assumes that the Liquor Traffic may be regulated and restrained in the rural districts, but not in this great, dissolute City. We shall see. It may be that Avarice and Appetite will "rebel," as *The News* predicts; but, if so, their strength cannot be more formidable than that of the recent Rebellion, which *The News* fomented and upheld, but which came to a bad end, as did many of its inciters. If any one is tempted to "rebel," let him ponder the fate of the slaveholding rebels, and forbear. There will be liquor enough sold, and it will be easy enough to get liquor, under the Excise laws as they stand, but let the rumsellers "rebel," and Rumselling may fall into the pit where Slavery is now hissing out its final curse. Better let rebellion alone.

Samuel Bowles: "Sunday and Liquor Laws"

Springfield, Massachusetts, was a small community with a strong religious history and "a church on every corner." This editorial reflects a strong Sabbatarian belief that those people who observe Sunday as holy have more rights than those who do not.

Springfield (Mass.) Republican, July 18, 1867

In the heated controversy as to Sunday laws, now going on in some of the western cities, the question is unfortunately discussed upon theological grounds almost exclusively. Unfortunately, because this throws an unnecessary burden on those who desire to be protected in the enjoyment of the Sabbath as a day of rest and of worship. It is not essential to this purpose that they should demonstrate that the Sabbath is a prescribed Christian institution, and the opponents of Sabbath laws are able to quote many names of weight in the church against this view....

The proper object of such laws is not to compel all men to observe Sunday as a sacred day, whether they believe in it or not, but simply and solely to protect in the observance and enjoyment of the day those who do believe in it. This is the limit of the legitimate efforts of the government to protect Sunday, and it should be the limit of the argument for such protection, otherwise its advocates imperil their own cause by claiming too much. The Jews, the Quakers, the German infidels, the irreligious Americans, or whoever for good or bad reasons may disregard the Christian Sabbath, have the right to devote the day to business or pleasure, so far as the government is concerned, but they have no right to disturb the worship or the repose of the Christian portion of the community. This is an obviously just and proper limitation of the rights of the anti-Sabbatarians. It should also limit the demand and argument of the Sabbatarians.

Wilbur F. Storey: "The Sunday Liquor Traffic"

The Chicago Times *did not much care for the Sunday liquor laws, but it did insist that if a law existed it should be enforced equitably and not selectively across all groups in the city.*

Chicago Times, **February 24, 1870**

The demonstration in Farwell hall, on Tuesday evening, in favor of executing the law against the liquor traffic in Chicago on Sunday, was an expression of public sentiment that it would be very unwise to ignore or misunderstand. . . .

There is a law in this city prohibiting the liquor traffic on Sunday, and every liquor license issued prescribes the condition that the party licensed shall obey the law. Now, either the law ought to be executed, or it ought to be repealed. It is a notorious fact that it is not executed, and has not been for years. If it be wrong to execute the law, it must be because the law itself is wrong. Then let it be at once removed from the statute book.

Hitherto, the officers whose positive duty it is to execute the law have framed for the public conscience, whenever its execution has been demanded, some such absurd excuse as this; The Germans celebrate Sunday as a holiday, and a holiday means beer. It is a national custom with them; it is, in fact, their religion; religion in this country is free; therefore those temples of religious worship, the lager-beer saloons, ought not to be shut up on Sunday. And it would be unjust, unfair, and outrageous to shut up the whisky-saloons, and thus turn all their Sunday customers to the beer saloons. It would be equivalent to recognizing the religion of lager as the state religion in Chicago, which would not do.

Of course it would be a gross violation of equity and justice to execute the law against one class of saloon-keepers and not against another class. It would be a great deal worse than not to execute it at all.

But it is about time that the miserable, hypocritical, and contemptible cant about the "national customs" of a class of people who are supposed to be American citizens, should be discontinued. America is sometimes called, in the Blatherskite language, "an 'asylum' for the oppressed of all nations." However that may be, America is certainly not a asylum for the habits and customs of all nations. The laws of America are made for Americans, and not for Germans, or Irishmen, or Scandinavians, or men of any other foreign sort (excepting niggers). When immigrants come to our shores, they bring not with them the laws of the countries from which they come; nor yet any of the customs or usages of those countries which our own laws forbid. . . .

Whatever custom the laws of America forbid, the foreigner who becomes an American citizen must give up, no matter how freely he might enjoy it in the country he came from. The German saloon keepers can neither excuse themselves nor be excused for disobeying the law which prohibits the Sunday liquor traffic, upon the pretence that Sunday carousals are a national custom with them. They constitute a custom which our laws forbid. It is simply a question whether American laws shall prevail in America. There is no moral or religious aspect that is at all essential to the subject. Let us execute our laws or repeal them.

Horace White: "The Sunday Difficulty"

The Republican Chicago Tribune *was a steadfast supporter of Sunday liquor laws. This editorial does not rely so much on the Sabbatarian argument as it does on the necessity to keep down drinking and disorder on Sunday, when men are idle.*

Chicago Tribune, June 11, 1871

Some of our German citizens are raising a good deal of a ferment among the representatives of their nationality in Chicago over the subject of Sunday liquor ordinances. The resolutions of their meeting, held at Turner Hall a few evenings since, have been published in our columns. But the agitation is by no means stopping there. They propose to have "vigilance committees" appointed in each ward, the obvious intent being to prevent the execution of any Sunday ordinance, if the City Government shall insist upon keeping such a law on the books. The German papers are all "broken out" with calls for meetings, announcements of committees, and appeals to "our fellow-citizens" to rise and shake off the yoke of oppression. . . . Calls are issued for meetings this evening in all the wards of the North Division, and a warm time may be expected at each of the "antitemperanzversammlungen," as they are called. The saloon-keepers and theorists directly interested are arousing the national feeling of other Germans to a considerable extent, the fact being that the ordinances, *if rigidly enforced,* would prove very distasteful to a large proportion, perhaps the whole, of the German population. . . .

The Council has not recently passed, nor proposed to pass, any laws upon the subject which are more stringent than those already existing. . . .

The ordinance, as it has stood for several years, absolutely forbids the vending of spirituous, vinous, or fermented liquors on Sunday; the Mayor, who grants the license, being empowered to revoke the same, and also to declare forfeit the bond of the saloon-keeper upon becoming satisfied that the terms of the license have been violated. . . .

Mayor Mason was known to be a temperance man when he was elected. He has, we believe, acted as such to the utmost extent justified by popular sentiment and the spirit of our institutions. And the Germans cannot say that they have gone thirsty on account of any attempts on his part to force his views upon them. They cannot say that the turn-halls, the beer-gardens, and other places to which Germans love to resort on Sunday for music, and recreation, and lager beer, have ever been closed on them, or that the keepers of those institutions have in any way been prosecuted. The columns of the *Staats Zeitung* and other German papers have been filled on Sunday mornings with notices of innumerable festive occasions to be observed on those days. . . . It is not unusual to see members in regular attendance upon good orthodox sermons on Sunday forenoons dropping into Turner Hall on an evening or afternoon, to hear the music and sip a glass of beer. Their wives, even, have gone, and, not having been struck dead for Sabbath-breaking, have made bold to repeat the operation.

Indeed, looking at the matter from a German point of view, we should say that things were working as favorably as could be reasonably asked. The agitation against Sunday recreation has become measurably silent. The opponents of impertinent legislation are increasing rather than diminishing in number. Wherefore, then, the need of such violent agitation and threats of forcible resistance? The laws which prohibit the general opening of saloons and vending of intoxicating liquors on Sunday have not, eventually, any relation to anybody's religion. They are made, or at least they are enforced, mainly because more people being idle on Sunday than on any week day, it becomes necessary to enforce more stringent laws against those excesses and disorders toward which idleness tends. This being the case, nothing is more assured, in this community, than that the privilege of orderly Sunday recreation will continue to be freely allowed. It will not be interfered with, because public sentiment would not justify such interference. . . .

Temperance Bureau: "Sunday a Day of Rest, or a Day of Crime"

When the Chicago city council began revising and consolidating existing ordinances, including the Sunday liquor ordinance, the Temperance

*Union and Temperance Bureau in the city launched an all-out informa-
tion war against proposed changes that would allow saloons to sell liquor
on Sunday. The kind of information collected in this letter to the editor was
important in the battle to retain Sunday liquor laws.*

Chicago Tribune, January 1, 1873

To the Editor of The Chicago Tribune:

SIR: The nature of the conflict in the Common Council over the Sunday
ordinances is not fully appreciated by those members favoring their repeal,
or even by that portion of their constituents who are earnestly opposing
them. That it is a direct question between the orderly and disorderly elements in society is conclusively proved by a comparison of the results of
open or closed saloons for the 11 Sundays from Oct. 20, 1872, to Dec. 29,
1872, with the 11 preceding Oct. 20, 1872, when they were in full blast on
Sunday, and murders, deadly assaults, and other crimes of violence were of
almost daily occurrence. On the contrary, since the closing of saloons on
Sunday, no murders have been committed, until this week the murder of
Lars. G. Larsen occurred, which was perpetrated by the son of a drunkard,
thus showing that intoxicating liquors are primarily responsible for nearly
all crimes. From Aug. 11 to Oct. 20, 1872, there were arrested on Sundays
for drunkenness 403 persons; for drunk and disorderly, 402 persons; for
disorderly, 727 persons; total, 1,532. From Oct. 20 to Jan. 1, including same
number of Sundays, the number of arrests for drunkenness were 285; for
drunk and disorderly, 203; and for disorderly, 345; total, 833,—a difference
of nearly one-half in favor of closed saloons; and it must also be borne in
mind that the saloons have only been partially closed for want of an energetic enforcement of the law, the observance on the North Side being partial and hypocritical in the extreme; but these facts are sufficient to show
that if the law was thoroughly enforced, drunkenness and disorderly conduct would almost entirely disappear, the lives of our citizens would be safe,
and the Police Courts adjourn for want of business. These facts being in-
controvertible, every citizen and voter should scan the records of the Common Council next Monday evening, and remember the names of those
Aldermen who are willing to plunge the city again into the state of criminal
terrorism which prevailed in August and September last. Remember the
men who are willing to endanger lives and property in order that the business of liquor-selling may flourish and prosper. The issue is sharply drawn,
and, should they succeed in repealing the ordinance, we shall, doubtless,
have cause to remember their vote, written, perhaps, in blood, before they
present themselves again for our suffrages.

Temperance Bureau

Opposing Sunday Liquor Laws

Ben Wood: "Law and Liquor"

The Sunday liquor law caused a split right down political lines. Democratic papers argued against the laws, and Republicans supported tighter licensing of liquor. And, as so often happened during this period, if a Democratic editor did not like something the Republicans did, the issue was painted with a "black Republican" brush. There was no way to escape Reconstruction politics, even in the most mundane of the day's issues.

New York Daily News, April 27, 1866

The State Legislature seems determined to *govern* the City of New-York into Black Republican traces. The evil effects of unwise central legislation appear to concentrate upon the Metropolis, and of all the unjust inexpedient, unpopular and probably unconstitutional measures adopted by the Radicals at Albany, the Excise bill is the most unjust, the most inexpedient, certainly the most unpopular and probably the most unconstitutional. It has already created a storm of indignation that we do not think any legislation can withstand, and the spirit of popular opposition thus evoked will defeat the purposes of the bill and will help to destroy the party with which it originated. The provisions of the bill might be enforced in the rural districts, but not in the great commercial emporium of the Republic, the center of commerce, travel and social life, whose conveniences and very necessities rebel against the spirit of this arbitrary act. A community like this, whose welfare and advancement depend upon the free action of its machinery of business intercourse, cannot endure the restrictions of trade contemplated by the Excise bill; and when the people, in addition to the material injury threatened to their pecuniary interests, appreciate the fact that the object of the bill is to secure political power to the Black Republicans, they will find some means to rend asunder the means of the ingenious net that has been cast over their city.

T. Doremus: "Sunday—How to Be Honored"

This letter to the editor expresses the viewpoint of many immigrants and workingmen in New York against laws that would prohibit selling liquor on Sunday.

New York Tribune, April 27, 1866

SIR: I see in to-day's TRIBUNE an article, "Another Excise Sunday," wherein you speak of the success of one brewer in disturbing the temperance of one section of the city.

I find in all that you speak or write about temperance or this Excise law, that you are *no friend* of the poor workingman and his family. Six days in the week are for work; the seventh day is a day of rest. Now, Sir, if you would be a workingman, wouldn't you like, after six days of hard work, to have a walk with your family in the free, open air, and then be undisturbed in taking some refreshments, and enjoy your life? I tell you, Sir, this would be a far better and truer religion than yours, and the religion of the American people in general. Our God and Father did not wish that his creatures should be hypocrites, and go to church all Sunday. No, sir; he wants them to enjoy their life on a Sunday. Go to other parts of the world, where people are more enlightened in religious matters—go to France, Germany, even to Russia—and you will see how the Sunday is celebrated there. All theaters are open; there is dancing, singing, and enjoying life, everywhere on a Sunday. But, in this country, where the parsons have got hold of the people, there will be no enlightenment as long as this hypocrisy is not overthrown by enlightened men.

And so God wills that this time must come, and will come, sooner or later.

Yours, T. DOREMUS.

Anonymous Writer: No Title

This observation comes from a visitor from London, who saw Sunday liquor laws as a peculiarly American interpretation of Sabbatarianism.

London Times, October 3, 1867

Sunday is a terribly dull day within the boundaries of the city, but the dullness results from an application of teetotal rather than of Sabbatarian principles. Tobacconists' shops are even more generally open than in London, and newspapers can be purchased at street stalls as freely on Sunday as during the rest of the week; but all bars for the sale of intoxicating liquors are peremptorily closed throughout the sacred day. The law by which this extensive operation is effected falls with especial severity on the keepers of lager-bier saloons, and is therefore horribly offensive to the Germans, who are the chief consumers of the beer and have not a particle of Sabbatarian feeling in their constitutions. It likewise annoys the proprietors of the restaurants, who may supply their customers with any comestibles they please, but cannot vend them any beverages besides icewater and a few non-exhilarating drinks.

One of the effects of the Sunday law is to send crowds of people to Hoboken, in New Jersey, where teetotalism is unknown, and which is much nearer to New York city than Greenwich is to London. The scenes that occur when the cars and ferries bring home the revelers from the site of their day's debauch furnish inexhaustible material to the police reporters of the newspapers.

QUESTIONS

1. According to supporters of Sunday liquor laws, what was to be gained by prohibiting the sale of liquor on Sundays?
2. What groups were most affected by the Sunday liquor laws?
3. What role did compromise play in creating Sunday liquor laws that everyone could live with?
4. To what extent does Sabbatarianism still affect laws in the United States?
5. What were the main arguments against Sunday liquor laws?

NOTES

1. *Maryland v. McGowan*, 366 U.S. 420, 434n10 (1961).

2. *Chicago Tribune*, 11 June 1871, 4.

3. William Harlan Hale, *Horace Greeley: Voice of the People* (New York: Harper-Bros., 1950), 326.

CHAPTER 21

Mormons and Polygamy, 1870–77

The Church of Jesus Christ of Latter-day Saints (Mormon Church) was founded by Joseph Smith, who as a teenager had a vision in which God and Jesus told him that he was chosen to restore on earth the true Christian Church. Later, Smith reported that he was visited by the angel Moroni, who showed him a place near his home in Palmyra, New York, where he unearthed golden tablets that turned out to be the *Book of Mormon.* According to the tablets, Christ himself had come to the United States before his ascension. Several days after the publication of the *Book of Mormon* in 1830, Smith organized his first congregation of the Mormon Church.[1]

Between 1830 and 1850, the United States experienced a period of tremendous religious revival, and Smith's new church captured the attention of those who were looking for a connection between religion and nationalism. The church also attracted people who were seeking stability, authority, and security against the growing secularism that many believed was taking over the country.

But so different were their beliefs that wherever Mormons gathered, gentiles (as non-Mormons were called) became fearful and hostile. Smith first moved his followers to Kirtland, Ohio, where the church grew into a large congregation with a governing body of 12 men who were the restored Apostles. In 1837, a split in the church forced Smith and the majority of members to move to Missouri. So large was the Mormon community in Missouri that mobs attacked Mormon businesses and harassed church members. Even the governor of Missouri declared Mormons enemies who "must be exterminated or driven from the state. . . . " In the middle of winter the Missouri Mormons crossed the Mississippi River into Illinois, where they established the town of Nauvoo.

Once again, violence followed the Mormons. Smith and his brother were killed in 1844 when a mob stormed the jail where they were being held. In

President Ulysses S. Grant, *served as president, 1868–76. Library of Congress.*

the spring of 1846, Brigham Young, Smith's successor, led 16,000 Mormons across the western plains to the Great Salt Lake Valley, where they founded Salt Lake City. Young was elected governor of the State of Deseret, and the church's Council of Fifty became the legislature.

Many Mormon practices disturbed non-Mormons. One was the idea of allowing only Mormon leaders to participate in civil government—courts, city councils, and so forth. The idea of a theocratic state ran counter to traditional democratic notions of freedom of religion. But, it was the practice of polygamy—multiple marriages—that was the most disturbing. Originally, polygamy was not part of the Mormon doctrine. In fact, the *Book of Mormon* forbids the practice. But, Smith is reported to have had further revelations from an angel who stood before him with a drawn sword and told him that it was God's will to restore the Old Testament practice of polygamy. It was not until years later that Smith announced his revelation to the Council of Fifty. Smith is reported to have had 30 wives, 2 of whom were 14 years old when they married him. Brigham Young had 50 wives.

Newspapers criticized the doctrine as simply a theological justification for adultery. But proponents countered with God's commandment to "multiply and replenish the Earth." Despite the public outcry, polygamy was openly practiced by the church leadership and by an estimated 20 percent of the Mormon families in Utah.

Not only did non-Mormons consider polygamy blasphemous but they also viewed it as inherently undemocratic. Taking cues from the abolitionist movement, antipolygamists criticized Mormons for being no better than Southern slaveholders with their breeding quarters for slaves. Mormon men were often pictured as barbarians who enslaved women. In 1856, the Republican Party adopted a national platform calling for the abolishment of the "Twin Relics of Barbarism, Slavery, and Polygamy." The Mormon lead ers responded to these associations with slavery with the common rejoinder of slaveholders—leave us alone. Like slavery, polygamy set off debates of states' rights versus national authority, and it created bitterness and misunderstanding.

In 1862, President Abraham Lincoln signed the Morrill Anti-Bigamy Law, which was aimed directly at the Mormons. The law made bigamy punishable by a $500 fine and imprisonment not exceeding five years, and it annulled all laws passed by the territory of Utah "pertaining to polygamy and spiritual marriage," and limited churches from owning more than $50,000 of real property in a territory of the United States. Lincoln never enforced the Morrill Act. When asked what he intended to do regarding the Mormons, Lincoln in his backwoods style is supposed to have replied, "When I was a boy on the farm in Illinois there was a great deal of timber on the farms which we had to clear away. Occasionally we would come to a log which had fallen down. It was too hard to split, too wet to burn and too heavy to move, so we plowed around it. That's what I intend to do with the Mormons. You go back and tell Brigham Young that if he will let me alone, I will let him alone."2

Young, the first territorial governor, was replaced by a non-Mormon in 1857 when Mormons deliberately and openly rebelled against federal marshals, judges, and other federal officers. Thereafter, until statehood was granted in 1895, every governor was a non-Mormon. In 1869, two bills—the Cragin and Cullum bills—were introduced in Congress to counteract the power of the Mormon Church over civil affairs. The Cullom Bill, which did not pass thanks to extensive lobbying by Mormon leaders in Washington, would have allowed the territorial governor to appoint all local officials and make the governor the financial head of the church.

Throughout the 1870s and 1880s, the church continued to seek statehood at the same time that it became more adamant about its doctrine of polygamy. Congress reacted by passing more laws to force the Mormon Church to give up polygamy. Between 1880 and 1885, 23 bills were introduced in Congress dealing with polygamy.

It was not until 1890 that church president Wilford Woodruff issued what became known as the Woodruff Manifesto, calling on Mormons to

"refrain from contracting any marriage forbidden by the law of the land."
This manifesto served to pave the way for statehood, and Utah was admitted
into the Union in 1896.

The dilemma for those who opposed the practice of polygamy was that
the Mormons, unlike blacks, Indians, or Chinese, were whites and could not
be easily tamed or confined by laws. Consequently, many people simply
chose to advocate patience, believing that polygamy, if not all of Mormonism, would eventually die out. The first reading in the section, by Louis J.
Jennings, warns that the Cullom Bill might bring about a war with Mormons and advises patience, because eventually the press of western immigration would push Mormonism out of the picture. The second entry, by
Wilbur F. Storey, argues against any measure that would put the military in
conflict with the Mormons and instead advocates strict enforcement of antipolygamy laws. The third selection, by William W. Harding, predicts that
democracy will eventually win over theocracy as more immigrants move
into the Utah Territory. The final editorial in this section, by Horace White,
suggests a number of ways in which Mormonism can be diluted by immigration, the transcontinental railroad, and merging the Utah Territory with
the non-Mormon state of Nevada.

The section advocating a harsher approach to Mormons begins with an
editorial by Horace Greeley, who supports a bill to prohibit anyone who en-
gages in a polygamous marriage to hold office or to work for the federal
government. The next two entries, by Charles de Young and William W.
Harding, call for strict enforcement of existing antipolygamy laws in the
courts and support enforcement by military force if necessary. The last reading in this section is a review of a very popular book by a Mormon wife that
graphically describes the life of Mormon women in Utah.

ADVOCATING PATIENCE WITH MORMONS

Louis J. Jennings: "Shall We Have a New Conflict with the Mormon?"

*The one solace that antipolygamists had was that Salt Lake City could not
continue to exist in a vacuum separated from the rest of civilization. The
nation was becoming smaller with every mile of railroad track, and soon
Mormons would find themselves outnumbered by new immigrants.*

New York Times, **February 27, 1870**

Mr. Cullom's bill for the suppression of polygamy in Utah has evoked
from the Mormons a fierce protestation that they will fight sooner than sub-

mit to it. The whole temper of Brigham Young and of his people upon the subject is defiant and belligerent. To all appearance it must soon become a practical question whether the measure is to be pushed to a bloody issue.

This question could be settled forthwith if it could rest only on the two fixed points that polygamy is a monstrous evil, and that the authority of the Government ought to prevail within its own territories. But these are not necessarily the controlling considerations. They do not control in respect to our wars with Indians, who murder, scalp, pillage and burn, and practice other evils quite as bad, perhaps, as polygamy, and who, though living within the national territories, are equally defiant of the national authority. . . .

It is as certain as anything can be, that Mormon heathenism is as short-lived as Indian savagery. We have only to wait for that great inlet of civilization, the Pacific Railroad, to get at its full work, when we shall see the beginning, in Utah, of a quick assimilation with the life, habits and laws of the rest of the country. Polygamy and every other relic of barbarism would soon melt away. We have already seen much of this operation, even before the road has attained its development. . . . There can be no doubt that the increasing contiguity with civilization is producing a solvent effect upon Mormonism. But even apart from that, the nature of its own system is necessarily short-lived. It is too rotten, inherently, to last. Like every other system opposed to divine law, it carries within itself the seeds of its own destruction, and in due time must perish, whatever man does, or fails to do. They every way miss the point who argue against Mormonism as a foul stain which must endure forever unless exterminated by the strong arm. We must not forget that, if let alone, it cannot at the worst, survive another generation. . . .

Wilbur F. Storey: "The Radical Treatment of Mormonism"

A number of congressmen believed that the best solution to polygamy and Mormons was armed intervention. But in the end, the solutions listed in this editorial became the crux of the government's Mormon policy.

Chicago Times, **January 30, 1870**

The territorial committee has agreed to introduce a bill into the lower house of congress to abolish polygamy in Utah; and, also, authorizing the president to use military force, if necessary, to enforce the law. Very fortunately, the bill is, at present no more than the work of a committee. It has not yet passed the house; and should it succeed in getting thus far, it would almost certainly fail in the senate.

What the country wishes in this matter is a philanthropic cure of this evil of polygamy. While determined that the evil shall be remedied, it does not propose to accept remedies which, while their efficacy is doubtful, are bloody, uncalled for, and outrageous to the last degree.

What will reach polygamy is a provision forbidding its further extension. Let its spread be stopped, and it will speedily die out. To attempt to extirpate by force what now exists, would be inhuman, and, possibly, a failure. We seem to forget, in our eagerness to aim a blow at Mormonism, that the sinning ones are the men, and not the wives. And yet the remedy of force would touch lightly the real culprits, and fall with crushing weight upon the majority, which is composed of innocent women.

The wives of Mormondom became such in good faith. There may be many of them who desire relief from the position in which they find themselves, and for such cases there should be afforded adequate relief, but for thousands of others, the forcible disruption of their marriage relation would be starvation, or worse. For the sake of this class should the government forbear coercive measures.

The true method of treating the Mormon difficulty can be thus briefly summarized:

Provide by law that after the date of its passage, polygamous marriages may no longer be contracted;

Make provision for throwing ample protection about every Mormon wife who may wish to sever her relations with a husband who has more than one wife;

Let existing polygamous marriages die out in the natural course of time, or provide that, say in twenty or thirty years from date, such marriages shall expire by limitation. . . .

William W. Harding: "Ulysses and Brigham"

This editorial personifies Mormonism and the U.S. Government in the form of President Ulysses S. Grant and Brigham Young and transforms the issue into one of two very powerful men.

Philadelphia Inquirer, July 26, 1871

The Mormons expect to be favored next month by a visit from President Grant, who will stay upon them, so it is supposed by the Polygamists, on his way to California. It is true that he will have to make a detour in order to reach the many-wived city, but the attractions are so great that the Mormons believe that he cannot pass the other way and must stop in to see them. Salt Lake City they consider one of the wonders of the country, equal to Yo-Semite or any other great curiosity. It will be interesting to witness the meeting of President Grant and Brigham Young. Each a potentate in his own way. One the ruler of a Democracy, acting according to the spirit of republican institutions, believing in the rights of the people and professing to govern only in their name and according to their views. The other the head of a Theocracy, claiming to be, by divine appointment, the special ruler over a people, admitting no right in the people to control or influence his actions, and being, in all respects an infallible autocrat, from whose decision there can be no appeal. Young claims to be the vice-[regent] of God; Grant is merely the instrument of man. Young's government ought to endure forever; Grants' government has no other security than in the good will, confidence and esteem of the people. And yet, as the two men look upon each other, the one must feel that, inasmuch as he represents doctrines alike hostile to Christianity and to civilization, his power cannot endure, while the other knows that time only, and the opening of the Western wilds to civilization, is needed to sweep away every vestige of the spurious system which has been temporarily fastened upon a few misguided followers of a base imposture.

Horace White: "The Mormons"

The Chicago Tribune *suggests that the Mormon problem will be solved politically when the transcontinental railroad brings more non-Mormon immigrants into the Nevada and Utah territories.*

Chicago Tribune, August 1, 1871

The effect upon the Mormons of building the Pacific Railway is beginning to show. The oligarchy is becoming shaky. Before the opening of the railroad the Gentiles in Utah were few, and were not, generally speaking, of a class likely to disturb the confidence of the people in their semi-religious government. The first effect is the rapid growth of Mormon seceders. There was a time when these come-outers would have perished by assassination at the hands of the "avenging angels." But the influx of Gentiles has given them a physical and moral support, which was impossible in past days.

The discovery and opening of silver mines in the Territory have drawn to it a large anti-Mormon population, which will be heard from politically in time. The introduction into society, in Salt Lake City, of respectable women, other than Mormons, has had a serious influence upon Mormon society. The young women, the second generation of those born in Utah, cannot see these Gentile wives, each the sole mistress of her household, without making comparisons. Religious fervor may blind many to their real condition, but the first break down in Mormonism will be the marriage of the Mormon girls to Gentile husbands. These candidates for matrimony are rapidly filling the Territory, and gradually the coils are drawing around the great abomination.

Politically, there is no reason for continuing the Territorial organization of Utah. The Territory ought to be annexed to the State of Nevada, which has now a very small population. The population of Utah added to that of Nevada would give the latter about enough to entitle her to one Representative in Congress. In the reorganized State the Gentiles would have a majority, and the union of Church and State would be abolished. Mormons would be emancipated, particularly the women, and then the fabric of Mormon superstition will fall. The strength of the institution is the rigorous absolutism with which the Church controls the personal action of its members.

The union of Utah and Nevada would make the latter a very large State, but not larger than California. It would make Nevada a comparatively respectable State in the number of its population; it would lessen the taxation in both places, and rid Utah of its useless set of Federal officers. Salt Lake would rapidly become the center of a new civilization, and the country be relieved of the present disgraceful institution of wholesale polygamy.

Advocating a Harsh Policy toward Mormons

Horace Greeley: "Mormon Marriages"

The bombast and lack of patience that Horace Greeley displayed years earlier against slavery are once again seen in this editorial against polygamy and the attempts by Mormons to lobby against anti-Mormon legislation.

New York Tribune, February 11, 1868

It seems to us that polygamy itself is respectable in comparison with the stolid impudence of those who practice and defend it. Whenever an attempt, like that now pending in Congress, is made to repress this belated abomination, this moral anachronism, this rejected system of all Christendom, its Mormon champions invariably adopt a tone of injured integrity, and irritate us by dogmatically assuming that they are the angels, and that we are the beasts. Claiming for their social anomaly a religious sanction, there is no limit to the latitude of their nonsense. They are the modern patriarchs. They are the restorers of primeval purity. They are about to bring back to our world the golden age of human innocence. In the mystery of many marriages they have discovered a truth which, though now professed in a corner, is destined to change the character of the continent. Having read everything which has been published by these self-canonized saints in vindication of their repulsive domestic arrangements, we are prepared seriously to assert that we have never seen any defense of them worthy of the least consideration, and hardly any which touched the points at issue at all. . . .

We are glad that another attempt is to be made to put this public mortification under the ban of the law; and should Mr. Cragin's bill, now pending, be passed, we trust that some way may be found to rigidly enforce its provisions. . . . The promoters of the bill will not, we trust, be frightened by this gasconade into an abandonment of a measure which is to be commended even if practically it should prove to be no more than an official protest against the legal establishment of concubinage. Salt Lake City is a long distance from the Capitol, but the distance has already been considerably diminished, and the arms of the Government are growing longer and longer every day. If polygamy cannot be put down in one year or in two, it may in five or in ten. If we place these promiscuous and left-handed marriages under the ban of national law, and then treat every Mormon who violates it, and who comes to Washington, as a criminal incapable of holding any office of honor or of profit, we shall then at least have made a beginning. The Republican party once thought this a matter of sufficient importance to be noticed in their National Convention and in their Declaration of Principles; there has thus far been no change in its universal opinion, which we trust is about to find an authoritative and sufficient expression.

Charles de Young: "The Mormon Plague Spot"

Westerners did not like Mormons and felt that Brigham Young posed a threat to western immigration, trade, and the peace of the entire West.

San Francisco Chronicle, February 1, 1870

It is a notorious fact, in regard to which there is no dispute at all, that polygamy is extensively practiced in Utah, and that it is a recognized and cherished institution of the Latter Day Saints. It is also a fact that the Congress of the United States has passed a law prohibiting polygamy in the Territories. Brigham Young and the Mormons defy the law and trample upon it, thus heaping contempt upon the authority of the Federal Government. This is a condition of things not creditable to a nation that ranks so high among the great Powers of the earth as the United States. It is indeed a humiliating spectacle for an American citizen to see a coarse and brutish tyrant like Brigham Young, with his handful of wretched dupes and murderous fanatics, openly setting the Federal Government at defiance. . . . General Grant is now in a position to turn his attention to the subject, and we think the people have a right to expect that he will do so. By grappling with this too-long tolerated abomination and sweeping it away with the strong hand of righteous power, he can earn for himself a fresh title to the gratitude of posterity and to a lofty niche in the temple of fame. Brigham Young is a tyrant and an oppressor; if not himself an actual assassin, he is the instigator of assassination and the friend and protector of assassins. This is no rash charge made in the heat of passion. The proofs of his complicity in deeds of bloodshed and murder are abundant. . . .

We trust that the present Congress will find time, amid their political discussions, to give some share of their attention to this most urgent matter. No surface remedy should be attempted, no kid-glove handling of the apostles or assassination resorted to. Let a bold, stringent and rational measure be adopted, which will bring the whole question to a prompt and definite issue. In such a measure we are confident that the Administration will be sustained by the entire American people.

William W. Harding: "The Choice of the Mormons"

While some people believed that civilization might eventually overrun Mormonism, many still argued that the law and the army ought to put an end to the illegal practice of polygamy.

Philadelphia Inquirer, September 29, 1871

Brigham Young has returned to Salt Lake, and his friends announce that, while he is willing to submit to be called as a witness touching the question of polygamy about to come before the grand inquest in Utah, or to obey a warrant of arrest, he will not endure imprisonment. In this connection it will be well to remember that information has been recently given to the country that the Mormons are still drilling, notwithstanding the law is against their doing so.

There is no reason why Mormonism should be disturbed so long as it submits itself to the law of the land, but it has not done this; on the contrary, it has set up within the jurisdiction of the General Government a distinct and autocratic authority, and assumed to act outside of the fundamental laws of the States. This it has done for good many years past without meeting with the interference of the Washington administration. Congress has frequently had the subject of polygamy in Utah before it, but, while it provoked very acrimonious discussion in and out of the two houses, it all ended in discussion. And we think very properly so. There are enough laws on our statute books to settle in the most conclusive manner the disturbing elements of Mormon faith and practice. A plurality of wives is as much a crime in the Territory of Utah as it is in the Territory of the District of Columbia. There are courts and juries in both places, and they should deal with the offense in one Territory precisely as they deal with it in another.

There is nothing in Mormonism so far as it is related to government that gives it rights, wrongs or privileges not permitted to other sects. There is nothing in the condition of Utah that renders it independent of the control of the United States courts.

For many years past the Christian community of the country have protested against the worse practice of the Mormons. They felt that it disgraced the cause of morality everywhere and shamed the government that countenanced it. But the mistake they made consisted in hammering at the doors of Congress, instead of invoking the power of the courts. This power is now about to assert itself in Utah, and any show of resistance made by Brigham Young or his followers will only more quickly and certainly put an end to polygamy. The Mormons may drill to their hearts' content, but they are no longer an isolated people hedged about by the impenetrable wilderness. The Pacific railroad can carry troops to their very doors, and extirpate Mormondom quite as effectually as the courts can destroy polygamy. The Mormons can now take their choice, either to voluntarily abandon their offenses against the laws of the country or be compelled by force to do it. They have no choice beyond that.

Anonymous Writer: No Title

This is a review of what would become a very popular book decrying Mormonism and polygamy. The book was written by Fanny Stenhouse, the first wife of T.B.H. Stenhouse, a prominent Mormon businessman and lobbyist for the Mormon Church in Washington. Stenhouse was a member of the Godbeites—a group of intellectual Mormons who separated from Brigham Young's ironclad rule. The Stenhouses were popular speakers on the lecture circuit in the Northeast.

Harper's Monthly, November 1874

A Woman's Life in Polygamy, by Mrs. T.B.H. Stenhouse (A.D. Worthington and Co.). The volume is what its title indicates, not a comprehensive history of the system, but a personal autobiography of one who has suffered the effects of its despotic sway over body and intellect and conscience. In her pages the physical tyranny and brutality of Mormonism are less prominent than in her husband's book, but the degrading effects of this singular superstition on mind and heart, the struggle of the woman's better nature against a perverted conscience, a false religion, a poisonous social influence, all tending irresistibly to her own self-degradation, are far more effectively described. The pitiful feature of Mormonism is that woman is compelled to perform a moral *hari-kari,* to assist in her own moral and social sacrifice. The wife-burning of India is merciful and ennobling when compared with the immolation, the living sacrifice, which Mormonism has required of its victims. The blasphemous travesty of Scripture, the hideous anthropomorphism which it has evolved out of the Bible, is a fitting foundation for such a system. It begins by degrading God; it ends by destroying the family and corrupting both man and woman. . . . Educated under such a system, the woman is taught to practice a religious asceticism that has no parallel in the history of the world. She is required to crucify not merely her body, not merely her affections, but her womanly self-respect, to her superstition. With a refinement of cruelty that seems well-nigh incredible, the first wife is compelled to join the hands of her own husband and his second wife, and thus to ratify the ceremonial that is the funeral service of her own heart. . . .

Yet Mrs. Stenhouse writes without bitterness, without vituperation. The calmness and candor of her narrative render it the more terrible an indictment. To the psychological student, to whom Mormonism is a mental problem insoluble, and the seemingly stolid acquiescence of woman in her own shame an inexplicable mystery, not the least interesting feature of this volume will be the fact that it traces so clearly the process by which superstition gained, first an influence, then an absolute control, over a mind originally intelligent and over a will originally independent. . . .

QUESTIONS

1. Was Congress right to make polygamy unlawful in the Utah Territory? Are such laws a violation of freedom of religion under the First Amendment?
2. What were the characteristics of the Mormon culture that made it a theocracy?
3. What effect did the railroad have on Mormonism?
4. What were the arguments against allowing Mormons to continue practicing polygamy?
5. Why did some believe that the practice of polygamy would eventually fade away?

NOTES

1. Unless noted otherwise, the sources for this introduction are Sarah B. Gordon, *The Mormon Question: Polygamy and Constitutional Conflict in Nineteenth Century America* (Chapel Hill: University of North Carolina Press, 2002), and Ronald Walker et al., *Mormon History* (Champaign: University of Illinois Press, 2001).

2. Gustive O. Larson, *The "Americanization" of Utah for Statehood* (San Marino, Calif.: Huntington Library, 1971), 60.

CHAPTER 22

Black Suffrage: The Fifteenth Amendment and Beyond, 1869–77

Not only was the Fifteenth Amendment the culmination of the work Republicans began with the Thirteenth Amendment, it also heralded the end of Reconstruction and any hope that Southern blacks would ever reap the benefits of those amendments that were written to safeguard their liberties. In effect, the Fifteenth Amendment was the beginning of the end.

In the election of 1868, Ulysses S. Grant won the electoral vote hands down by capturing 26 of the 34 states, but he barely won the popular vote. Grant squeaked out victories in most states, but his 300,000-vote margin (out of 5.7 million votes cast) was solely because of the black vote in the South. In the next presidential election, the Republicans would need the votes of blacks in the North and border states if the party was to stay in the White House. The election of 1868 also taught another lesson—that the alarming increase in violence against blacks by the Ku Klux Klan and other white supremacist groups had to be stopped or the Southern black vote would be lost by the next election.

In the face of these political exigencies, the Republicans moved quickly to pass the Fifteenth Amendment in February 1869. But the amendment was so pocked by compromise that it was, in the end, a very weak effort. During the congressional hearings, three viewpoints dominated—the Democrats and conservative Republicans who opposed any federal guarantee of black suffrage; the radical Republicans who wanted to enact universal male suffrage, with no educational or property-holding tests; and the moderates who wanted only to prohibit racial qualifications in determining who could vote.[1]

The moderates prevailed, and the result was an amendment that prohibited race, color, or "previous condition of servitude" to be used to deny the right to vote. The amendment also gave Congress the power to enforce the amendment as it saw fit. The amendment did not guarantee an absolute right to vote, nor did it guarantee blacks the right to hold office. It also did not prohibit "racially neutral" tests or conditions such as ownership of property, poll tax, or literacy tests. And it did not include the right of women to vote. The purpose of the amendment was merely to save the Republican Party by giving the vote to Northern and border-state blacks—nothing more.[2]

Backed by Grant's approval, the amendment took 13 months to be ratified. However, the ratification was not a simple process. Two states—Indiana and New York—initially voted to ratify, but then withdrew their approval. But the secretary of state accepted only the first vote. Then Democrats argued that states not yet readmitted to the Union—Texas, Georgia, Virginia, and Mississippi—should not have their ratification vote count. The *Chicago Times* wrote, "The assertion that a state which is not in the union, and is not admitted to representation in congress, can ratify an amendment to the federal constitution, is so plainly at war with the clearest provisions of that constitution, that no man will make it who is not contemptuous of common sense and truth."[3] This argument also was ignored.

When the secretary of state reported on March 30, 1870, that the Fifteenth Amendment had been ratified, Grant told the country that the amendment "creates the greatest civil change and constitutes the most important event that has occurred since the nation came into life."[4] There was great rejoicing, and celebrations were held across the country. Blacks saw the Fifteenth Amendment as their salvation, Democrats saw the amendment as the instrument that would finally put the "negro question" to rest, and Republicans saw the amendment as the end of the their work for blacks. Even the antislavery societies began to disband, believing the amendment placed the finishing touch on the work they had begun 40 years earlier.

But President Grant knew that having the vote and keeping the vote were very different issues. No sooner had the new amendment been ratified than fresh outbreaks of violence marred the spring elections of 1870. State authorities dragged their feet in making arrests or pursuing prosecutions. Black witnesses were afraid to give testimony, white jurors would not convict, and jury and witness tampering were widespread. Aside from violence, Democrats used bribery, fraud, and trickery to throw elections. Democratic election officials in the North and South were not above moving, closing or even eliminating polling places, or refusing to accept poll taxes from blacks. State legislatures gerrymandered districts to neutralize the black vote, established literacy tests, and even shifted elected positions to appointive to control who held political positions.

In the face of escalating violence in the South and vote fraud in the North, a Republican Congress moved quickly to pass the first Enforcement Act of May 31, 1870. The law prohibited bribery, threats, and intimidation of voters; prohibited disguised groups from interfering with constitutional rights; and prohibited employers from withholding jobs in order to obstruct voting. The Second Enforcement Act of July 14, 1870, placed federal election supervisors at polling places in large cities and made it a crime for election officials to interfere with voting rights.

While Grant was strongly committed to enforcement of voting rights, he proved too cautious, concerned that the enforcement acts placed too much power in the federal government and eroded state sovereignty. The U.S. Supreme Court was given a chance to determine the validity of that charge in two significant cases heard in 1876—*United States v. Reese* and *United States v. Cruikshank*.

Reese grew out of an 1873 massacre of 60 blacks in Louisiana who tried to vote. *Cruikshank* came from Lexington, Kentucky, where a black man was denied the right to vote because he had not paid his poll tax. In both cases, lower courts convicted the white perpetrators under the Enforcements Acts. But the U.S. Supreme Court overturned the convictions and denied that the Fifteenth Amendment guaranteed any right to vote. The Court ruled that states may determine for themselves who may vote and under what conditions. The Court's decisions emasculated the Fifteenth Amendment and made it increasingly difficult to prosecute for racial violence, intimidation, and election frauds.

Also contributing to the collapse of enforcement was the Panic of 1873, which replaced race and Reconstruction as the central concern of Americans. Another issue was the mounting costs of keeping a federal presence in the South. Although the number of troops in Southern states was small, the government needed to move those troops to the West where Indian hostilities were escalating. When the U.S. attorney in Mississippi was asked to cut troops, he answered, "the removal of these troops from the state would be the most disastrous thing that could be done."[5]

The section supporting the Fifteenth Amendment begins with an editorial by Horace Greeley that argues against requiring education as a prerequisite to voting. Greeley states that like educated men, the uneducated also will vote according to their own interests. The second reading, by George W. Curtis, notes that the amendment is a fitting end to the work of Republicans. The third entry, by E.L. Godkin, argues that the South will always find a way to prevent blacks from voting. Until the black man is on the same economic footing as the white man, there will never be true equality. The next selection, by Louis Jennings, makes the proposition that while the acts of Reconstruction were extraordinary they were necessary, and in the end, the Fifteenth Amendment makes Reconstruction a national policy. The final selection is a congratulatory letter from the great abolitionist William Lloyd Garrison.

The editorials against the Fifteenth Amendment begin with one by Wilbur F. Storey that reminds readers that the amendment really did not give blacks political equality. The second selection, by John Mcleod Keating, is an appeal to defeat the amendment, because it is the odious work of radicals. The third entry, by Charles de Young, proposes that since the amendment finishes the work of Reconstruction, it is now time to reorganize both parties. The final editorial, by Storey, accurately predicts that not only will the amendment be held unconstitutional but that it will be ignored in the South.

Supporting the Fifteenth Amendment

Horace Greeley: "Grounds of Impartial Suffrage"

This elegant editorial puts the popular vote in perspective and argues that even uneducated men know their own interests and can match them to party policies.

New York Tribune, January 8, 1868

If suffrage could be made dependent on virtue, morality, intelligence, education, creed, or race, whom of us would our neighbors allow to vote? Virtues become vices when the vicious are judges. Morality is a moral stench in the nostrils of the depraved; and which are the depraved depends on who are the moral critics

We all have consciences keenly alive to the sins committed by others. And, as to intelligence, a fool always looks upon a philosopher as an ass. A knave instinctively holds a man of piety to be a hypocrite. A thief, whether in or out of our legislature, winks at honesty as to the last pretense of a scoundrel. And a drunkard hiccups in his maudlin stupor that the only difference between a saint and him is, that one gets drunk on rum and the other on religion. The slaveholders, whose property in the slave was a daily theft of his wages, honestly scorned the hero who gave the slave his freedom as on a moral par with the thief who steals a horse. None are so conceited in estimating their wisdom as the intensely ignorant; none so appreciative of the intelligence of the humblest in their sphere as the vary wise. . . . Contempt for men of any kind, class, or race, is never felt by the best men nor the highest races for the lower, but always by the lower for the higher. It is not the Christs who crucify the rabble, not Socrates who administers hemlock to the dunces, nor Galileo who imprisons the bigots, nor the reformers who burn the sensualists at the stake. So it is not the higher classes of the American or English nation who object to universal suffrage, but they whose right to the suffrage is as doubtful as that of those to whom it is proposed to extend it. Ask the first man you meet who cannot read whether the right to vote ought to be limited, and he will answer Yes! Not of course expecting the limitation will exclude him. . . . But ask the Chief-Justice of the United States if all men ought to vote without limitation, either as to education or property, and he answers "Certainly: voting is the simplest of all matters; men do not vote for measures, nor even for principles, but only for one of two political parties, and the most ignorant man knows with which party his immediate interests lie." The popular vote is not designed to teach statesmanship, nor to solve intricate questions of any kind; for those are never submitted directly to the mass of voters. It is designed to tie statesmen and politicians to the people's interests, not to supply them with the knowledge how those interests can best be served. . . . But all men know what their personal interests demand. All poor men want freedom to labor, and the power to recover their wages, protect their families, educate their children, sue in the courts, sit on juries, and enjoy the benefits of the government which taxes them. Whatever party most liberally and sincerely offers these benefits, not to others, but to their own class, workingmen will vote for. . . .

Voting, therefore, though very important, is a very simple right, and one which requires neither learning nor ability to exercise without harm, and with real advantage to the country.

But the principal use of the ballot is to secure for the humblest citizen the respect of officials, and kind and just treatment at the hands of courts. Deprive a race of the ballot and every agency of the Government which ought to protect will combine to oppress them. Deprive the Southern Freedmen of the ballot, and oppression, resistance, and a war of races, are inevitable. Leave them the ballot, and peace and ultimately prosperity are assured.

George W. Curtis: "The Suffrage Amendment"

George W. Curtis praises the Fifteenth Amendment as a significant step toward political equality and a barrier to the South's attempts to disenfranchise blacks.

Harper's Weekly, February 13, 1869

The Republican Congress has just adopted another of those great measures which commend it to the confidence of all thoughtful men, and to the gratitude of posterity. Down to the year 1860 this country had been subject for more than a generation to the party whose chief aim was the utter degradation of a seventh of the population. The purpose of the party that succeeded it has been the elevation of every individual to a perfect equality of right and opportunity. The one sought prosperity and power by the most revolting tyranny; the other aims at permanence and peaceful progress by the most enlightened justice.

Mr. Boutwell, in introducing the amendment of equal suffrage, well said that it was a necessary and logical act for the Republican party. It gives the express guarantee of the United States to the political equality of all its citizens, and secures the principle of the reconstruction policy. The objection that it infringes the right of the people to settle the suffrage precisely reverses the fact; for the amendment provides that no local law shall deprive any citizen of a fundamental right secured to him by all the people.

There is, as we believe, no sound doubt of the authority of Congress to establish equality of suffrage by law. But a law is repealable by a majority in Congress; a constitutional amendment can be disturbed only by three-fourths of the State Legislatures. It is certainly better that a provision of such importance should be intrenched [*sic*] in the fundamental law; and the general feeling of the country would undoubtedly prefer that it should be so. . . .

The amendment is also a measure of wise consolidation. It touches no right of which any State can justly be jealous, or which it can reasonably deny to the United States. The first essential condition of a popular national government is the equality of its citizens equally secured. Ours, indeed, is not a national government in the simplest form; but, on the other hand, it is not a league nor a confederacy of States. It is a national Union. It has a national substance and necessity, and the attempt to regulate a national policy upon the theory of State sovereignty as hitherto maintained is futile. The adoption of the amendment will be the declaration of the people that they perceive the legitimate conditions of a truly national Union. . . .

E.L. Godkin: "The Constitutional Amendment"

E.L. Godkin has little faith that the South will honor the amendment, and he is fully aware that enforcement will be needed even into the next century to protect blacks in their suffrage. The real solution is acquisition of wealth, which is the badge of respectability—something that would also not happen until the next century.

The Nation, **February 18, 1869**

The Amendment is an attempt to restrain (or rather to eradicate) the passions of a dominant and hostile race, not by punishment, not by the effect of terror, but by a simple declaratory resolution. We say declaratory, because although the power be given to Congress to enforce it by appropriate legislation, the legislation will always be difficult of execution, and therefore inefficient.

It is very true that the idea of the extreme members of the Republican party is, that until the negro is educated to the point at which he can compete evenly with the white he is to be protected by such legislation as may from time to time prove necessary; that this new article, for example, will enable the North to deal summarily with any State which violates its provisions. . . . This method of dealing with the South is that which one section of the Republican party has long advocated, the policy of extending the arm of the Government over the black until he was quite able to hold his own. . . .

We may be sure that for a very considerable length of time the Southern whites will find means by which to override any restriction we may impose upon their love of domination. No amendment can exclude the possibility of intimidation such as that which lately rendered the black vote useless in Louisiana. Cases like these will be occurring continually, and unless public attention can be riveted upon the negro question during the next century, we do not see any way in which political outrage of that sort is to be hindered by protection. . . . The moment is fast coming when the negro will disappear from the stage of national politics. The last thing we can do for him is to pass the Fifteenth Amendment and establish on paper the principle that his right to vote shall not be taken away from him by State restrictions, and that neither an aristocracy of color, nor of race, nor of property shall enslave him. . . .

But *the ballot is no panacea for political ills*. It has been proved as well as anything can be proved in politics that a whole class or a whole race may be enfranchised, and yet injustice and oppression remain in force as before. . . . But, slight protection as the ballot affords the freedman, it is the only protection in our power to give, and we have always maintained that such value as it might yield was justly his. But we repeat that very little good will come to him from laws or constitutional amendments unless supplemented by what in other cases has given newly-enfranchised classes influence among the communities which gave them the suffrage. What makes the German and Irish emigrant a dreaded if not a respected member of society in America? It is certainly not the ballot, but the fact that he uses the ballot intelligently as a weapon against all who would trifle with his liberties. . . . The ballot does not protect him, but the semblance of power which it gives makes him facile in the hands of his oppressors. If the negro will work and earn money, if he will put it away in banks and not squander it in riotous living, if he learns to make as sharp a bargain as his white neighbor, then the ballot will be of some use to him, but not otherwise. Every deposit in a savings-bank is worth ten votes to him. His color will be forgotten as soon as he is "respectable," and to be "respectable" in modern times means to exhibit the faculty of acquiring independent wealth. He must find some means of making his Southern fellow-citizens look upon him as an equal, and this he will never do by merely being able to produce a copy of the Constitution of the United States and refer the usurper to the Fifteenth Amendment.

Louis Jennings: "Reconstruction Nationalized"

Many people hoped that the ratification of the Fifteenth Amendment would be the last chapter of Reconstruction. In this editorial, Louis Jennings makes the proposition that Reconstruction had affected every state in the nation, not just the South. The Fifteenth Amendment had removed the taint of slavery from the nation as a whole, and it had done so with measures that at times seemed harsh but were in fact necessary.

New York Times, February 21, 1870

Hitherto the Republican policy of Reconstruction has been essentially sectional. It has been the means employed by the major power in the Union to extinguish the last signs of the rebellion, and to establish order and authority in the Southern States, in accordance with the principles and purposes which triumphed in the war. The measures employed for the attainment of this object were necessarily exceptional in their nature, and resulted in a reorganization of States on a basis fundamentally different from that which previously existed. The change, though arbitrary, was not unjust,—though radical, it was not illogical. The fact of resistance to the National Government was a sufficient reason for exacting guarantees against the recurrence of conflict. The fact of emancipation introduced a new element into citizenship, imposed upon a race new obligations, and entitled them to new privileges, and rendered inevitable the measures necessary to protect them in the exercise of the power conferred upon them. The proceedings incident to this policy may sometimes have looked harsh and objectionable. But the harshness, wherever it appeared, was simply the exercise of an absolute authority in a case which had resisted milder methods of treatment. And the features most objected to have really been the natural developments of a revolution begun in hostility to the Union, and ending practically, in the revision of some of its conditions, and the consolidation of its power.

The Fourteenth Amendment invested the colored man with citizenship, and the Reconstruction acts gave him his share of political power. The citizenship was national, the suffrage was restricted to the States to which those laws applied. Thus the anomaly was presented of a race enfranchised in certain States by virtue of Federal authority, and disfranchised in others by reason of local law. . . . The Fifteenth Amendment therefore became necessary, not only to harmonize the conditions of suffrage throughout the Union with the conditions imposed upon the South, but to guarantee those at the South who had cooperated with National Government against possible political vicissitudes in their own States. The Amendment does this without impairing the control of States over the question of suffrage. It neither enacts universal suffrage, nor forbids the application of tests, whether of education or property, as qualifications for voters. It simply forbids unjust discrimination in the enforcement of tests. In providing that "the right of citizens of the United States to vote shall not be denied or abridged by the United States, or by any State, on account of race, color, or previous condition of servitude,"—it secures political equality. The measure was the completion of the work of which emancipation was the commencement. It purges the Union of the last taint of slavery, and makes Reconstruction national.

William Lloyd Garrison: "Letter to Baltimore's 15th Amendment Celebration Committee"

William Lloyd Garrison, considered the nineteenth century's greatest abolitionist, was not only responsible for the antislavery movement but also was seen as the man who gave blacks hope that they would eventually live in true freedom. At the time of this celebration in Baltimore, Garrison was 65 years old and in poor health.[6]

Baltimore American and Commercial Advertiser, May 20, 1870

Dear Sir—I am very reluctantly obliged to forego the pleasure of participating in the celebration of the adoption of the Fifteenth Amendment, by the colored citizens of Maryland, excepting this expression of my feelings as a substitute for my presence. How supreme that pleasure would have been, and, consequently, how great is my disappointment, I have no language to express seeing that it was in Baltimore where I began my advocacy for the immediate liberation of all who were then groaning in bondage; and now that all yokes are broken, and citizenship is accorded to the entire colored population of the country it would seem to be peculiarly fitting that I should join in this particular commemoration in the very city in which I dedicated my life to the cause of universal emancipation. . . .

O ye ransomed millions; rejoice and give glory to God that not a slave remains in the house of bondage; that there is to be no more buying and selling of human flesh on the auction block, no more hunting of fugitive slaves, no more rending asunder husbands and wives and parents and children, no more forcing to unpaid toil under the lash of a driver, no more abrogating the marriage institution, no more punishment for attempting to learn the alphabet! Freedom is yours to enjoy and maintain yours by natural right and the grace of God as well as by the decree of the nation constitutionally secured, yours with all its responsibilities and duties, its manifold blessings and sublime possibilities, yours without bloodshed, or violence or any disorder whatever or any desire for retaliation, yours to advance in wisdom and knowledge in skill and enterprise, in wealth and prosperity.

Citizenship is yours, with political enfranchisement whereby you are to help decide what shall be the laws for the common defence and the general welfare, and ultimately to obtain a fair share of the honors and emoluments of public life. In this hour of jubilation I will not pause to give you any counsel as to your future course. I have no misgiving on that core. You have been the best behaved people in the past under the most terrible provocations, and why should any doubt as to your behavior hereafter, under all the favorable conditions of freedom and equality? I rejoice that the South will now have unlimited means for growth in population in education, in enterprise in convention in literature, in the arts and sciences in material prosperity. Henceforth may every blessing be vouchsafed to her through the removal of slavery so that as her depression has been deplorable her exaltation shall be glorious! Such has ever been the desire of my heart and the aim of all my labors.

Yours, rejoicingly, WM. LLOYD GARRISON

OPPOSING THE FIFTEENTH AMENDMENT

Wilbur F. Storey: No Title

The weakness of the Fifteenth Amendment was that it did not specifically guarantee anyone the right to vote. The right had to be granted by the states, and once granted, it could not be denied or abridged. This was a difficult concept for most Americans—black and white—to grasp.

Chicago Times, February 27, 1869

If the negroes of the country clearly understood the tactics of the Jacobin party in dealing with them, they would have no other feeling toward it than aversion and contempt. . . .

Suppose this amendment be ratified by three-fourths of the states, negroes will not acquire the right to vote by such ratification. What is meant by "the right to vote"? It is the privilege to cast a ballot granted by the respective states. . . . The proposed amendment merely provides for impartial suffrage. Those who have been ranting about it, in congress, have talked as if it would of itself give the negro the ballot. They have endeavored to delude the blacks of this idea, and that it would give them equality of political privileges in all things. Under the amendment, they can be permitted to vote and be denied all other political privileges.

John Mcleod Keating: "The Fifteenth Amendment"

Several states attempted to defeat the Fifteenth Amendment by delay, but none of the tactics worked. The Fifteenth Amendment was ratified a year after it was proposed.

Memphis (Tenn.) Appeal, March 9, 1869

Already this amendment has received the endorsement of Nebraska, Nevada and Illinois. Indiana, by the adroit management of the Democratic members, all of whom resigned and have gone home, cannot pass upon it until the next session of its Legislature. Our own Legislature, having adjourned, it cannot therefore be passed upon by us until next fall. Much opposition is manifested to it in Republican quarters, but it is thought that since Grant has pronounced for it all that will be overcome, and the odious and usurping act of an usurping Congress be engrafted upon the organic law by the consent of the desired two-thirds of the States. Yet we hope the Democratic party, following the example of the legislators of Indiana, will everywhere endeavor to defeat it. The people should be thoroughly aroused to the enormity of a measure the final adoption of which by them will seal the doom of State rights, and pave the way for a disruption of our system of Government.

Charles de Young: "The Next Deal of the Cards— Reconstruction of Parties"

For the young Democratic editor of the San Francisco Chronicle, *the Fifteenth Amendment did not just toll the end of Reconstruction; it presented an opportunity for a complete political reorganization of both parties that would take the focus away from the South, Reconstruction, and blacks.*

San Francisco Chronicle, March 25, 1870

Now that the Fifteenth Amendment is passed, and Sambo has become a voter; now that the last vestige of slavery has been removed from our sight, it would seem as though a reconstruction of parties were in order. Has not the Republican party fulfilled its mission? Is not its work finished? Is there, in short, any further need of a Republican party? These are questions which in one shape or another are just now occupying the attention of many reflecting men who have hitherto acted with the Republican party, and who are the chivalrous and loyal friends of progressive and humanitarian ideas. The reconstruction process being happily over, and all the old issues between the Democrats and Republicans being fairly fought out and definitively settled, why should these political organizations in their present shape be continued? Would it not be better that both should be dissolved, and party lines be drawn anew, leaving the members of each of the old organizations free to take a fresh survey of the situation, and to define their position anew? The great and momentous issues that divided the Democrats and the Republicans from 1852 to 1868 are settled and removed from the field of contemporary politics. Other and fresher problems now confront us. . . . Republicanism, so far as it represented the irrepressible conflict between free labor and slave labor, between Southern institutions and Northern institutions, is now *functus officio*. Democracy, so far as it represented the barbarism and devilishness that justified the ineffable enormities connected with the "patriarchal institution," is also played out. Why then should not both the old parties be disbanded, and party lines drawn anew upon fresh and living issues? . . . There are men who have long acted with the Democratic party, and who are ranked as Democrats, who as a matter of fact entertain Republican ideas. There are also men who have trained with the Republicans who are disgusted with the Fifteenth Amendment. By all means let us have a new deal, and a new drawing of party lines. . . .

Wilbur F. Storey: "The Fifteenth Amendment"

This editorial accurately predicts that the South will obey the word, but not the spirit, of the Fifteenth Amendment by restricting the ballot to only a small portion of blacks.

Chicago Times, February 5, 1870

Under such a state of facts, it must be evident that the Fifteenth amendment will not be regarded as a part of the constitution by a large portion—perhaps a majority—of our citizens. The secretary of state may proclaim its adoption, and the federal government may recognize and enforce it as law, but it may be overthrown by the judiciary, or by a political revolution which will place men in power who interpret the constitution differently from those who now have possession of the government.

The probabilities are that the country will unwillingly accept the amendment, and thus pass a quietus on the negro question. Were the political disabilities of the whites in the south removed, and the ballot restored to them, they could easily frame laws within the amendment which would take the ballot from the great body of the blacks. Were what is known as intelligence and property qualifications required from voters, not one negro in a hundred could vote. The amendment simply requires that the suffrage shall be impartial.

When the southern states shall all be admitted to representation in congress, we may expect such sweeping changes as have occurred in Tennessee. Her constitutional convention can to-day assume that the Fifteenth amendment is valid, and yet exclude negroes from holding office, and take the ballot from such of them as ought not to vote because of ignorance and vicious habits. . . .

QUESTIONS

1. Maryland, a border state, did not ratify the Fifteenth Amendment until 1973. Why do you believe it took Maryland so long?
2. Why was the Fifteenth Amendment seen as the "completion of the work of emancipation"?
3. How many of E.L. Godkin's predictions in his editorial "The Constitutional Amendment" eventually proved correct?
4. Why did the Fifteenth Amendment have to be enforced by additional laws?
5. Why were education and economic independence factors in blacks keeping the vote? Were blacks in the South able to achieve either of these conditions? Why?

NOTES

1. Xi Wang, *The Trial of Democracy, Black Suffrage and Northern Republicans, 1860–1910* (Athens: University of Georgia Press, 1997), 57–68.

2. William Gillette, *Retreat from Reconstruction, 1869–1879* (Baton Rouge: Louisiana State University Press, 1979), 19.

3. *Chicago Times,* 11 June 1870, 4.

4. Gillette, 22.

5. Stephen Cresswell, "Enforcing the Enforcement Acts: The Department of Justice in Northern Mississippi, 1870–1890," *Journal of Southern History* 53 (August 1987): 421–40.

6. Garrison had stopped most of his abolitionist work after the Thirteenth Amendment was ratified, believing that the work of the movement was complete. But others, namely Wendell Phillips, insisted that the work continue until black suffrage was guaranteed. Phillips dissolved the American Anti-Slavery Society after the ratification of the Fifteenth Amendment.

CHAPTER 23

Chinese Immigration, 1867–72

When word of the California gold strikes reached China in 1848, thousands of Chinese men spent what little money they had for transportation to the United States. Their lives in China had been so devastated by wars, floods, drought, famine, bandits, corruption, heavy taxes, and economic depression that many Chinese felt the only way they could support their families was to strike it rich in California and send the money back to their families. These earliest Chinese immigrants, from the southern part of China, found passage on U.S. trading vessels headed back to San Francisco and Monterey. In 1848, there were only three Chinese in California; by 1852, almost 20,000 Chinese had arrived to find economic freedom in the gold fields.[1]

When they arrived in California, Chinese immigrants were immediately ostracized by the white miners. They were not allowed to live near the white miners and in many places were not allowed to file claims. In areas where they could not file their own claims, they worked abandoned claims. By 1850, the number of Chinese in the mining business had grown so large that a white backlash resulted in more than a dozen riots in which Chinese miners were killed and their homes destroyed.

Despite the violence, entrepreneurial Chinese established laundries, restaurants, and bathhouses to service white miners. Chinese also built mining roads and the giant water flumes that carried water to the gold-mining areas. By the mid-1850s, the heyday of California mining was quickly coming to an end, and white and nonwhite miners moved to the cities to find jobs.

Other Chinese moved to the South and to the East. In the South, planters experimented with using Chinese labor to replace black laborers. Some planters found the idea of Chinese labor so attractive that they formed the Mississippi Valley Immigration Labor Company to bring 5,000 Chinese contract laborers to work on Southern plantations. The plan never was implemented. In the East, Chinese worked in a variety of manufacturing areas including ironworks, woolen mills, shoe factories, and clothing factories.

Many Chinese laborers arrived through the "coolie"[2] system. The contract worker was credited a passage, but upon arrival his credit ticket was sold to a broker and the laborer became the property of the broker. It would take anywhere from 7 to 10 years for a worker to buy his freedom. The system, considered another form of slavery, exploited poor Chinese workers and filled the pockets of California recruiting agents and labor contractors. In 1862, the U.S. Congress prohibited importation by U.S. vessels of contract laborers except where certified by a U.S. agent. The new law was meant to stop the practice of "Shanghaiing" men off the streets of cities in China and forcibly bringing them to the United States to work under arduous labor contracts.

The first major employer of contract laborers was the Central Pacific Railroad Company, which was building the western half of the transcontinental railroad. Between 1863 and 1865, Irish men were used, but when the work moved into the mountains the Irish workers refused to do the more dangerous jobs such as scaling mountains, setting off explosives, and living in tunnels for weeks at a time. Chinese laborers proved themselves to be hardworking, tireless, and fearless and to be willing to work for less pay than the white men were. By the time the Central Pacific Railroad was completed in 1869, almost 11,000 Chinese had been employed in its construction.

When the Central Pacific Railroad was completed, some Chinese railroad workers moved on and built other railroads throughout the West and South. But most of them went back to San Francisco and other California coastal cities, where they were willing to do work that no one else would do. Although work in the cities was scarce, enterprising Chinese established businesses of their own—laundries, restaurants, and produce stands—or worked in factories. But the competition for even the most menial jobs became fierce. Because Chinese were willing to work for very low wages, white accused Chinese of taking jobs away from white workers.

In March 1867, the Anti-Coolie Labor Association held its first meeting to devise ways to eliminate the Chinese from labor competition. This meeting quickly got out of hand, and men and women spilled into the streets, attacking Chinese with rocks, knocking down Chinese women, and burning laundries and other Chinese-owned businesses. One of the worst anti-Chinese riots occurred in Los Angeles in October 1871. A quarrel between two Chinese men who shot each other attracted a large crowd of whites. One of the white spectators was accidentally shot and killed, setting off a riot that ended with the death of 19 Chinese and with Chinese homes and businesses burned. No one was punished.

California cities passed city ordinances that discriminated against Chinese. In San Francisco, the Sidewalk Ordinance forbade the use of poles that Chinese traditionally used to carry heavy bundles. The Queue Ordinance required any Chinese arrested to have his queue—long braid of hair—cut off. Other ordinances placed higher taxes on Chinese laundries than others. Some of these ordinances were eventually overturned because they were prohibited by the Civil Rights Act of 1866 or by the Fourteenth Amendment.

San Francisco also became one of many cities to force Chinese into separate "Chinese Quarters" within the city where there typically was no police protection or sanitary system. Through their own organizations, Chinese established San Francisco's Chinatown as a safe haven from violence where Chinese families could live in relative safety, establish businesses, organize benevolent societies, and build schools and hospitals—all without the help of city or state money.

Many Chinese had no intention of staying in the United States; instead, once they had saved enough they would return to China. They even sent the bodies of their dead back to China for burial. They lived and worked in close-knit "clannish" communities, typically bought their food and clothing only from Chinese merchants, and spent very little money on the "necessities." Chinese men continued to wear their traditional dress, kept their queues, and often refused to learn English. All of these factors plus Americans' general suspicion and fear of anything foreign produced a significant anti-Chinese attitude among whites that eventually led to the legal exclusion of Chinese from the United States.

As the economic depression continued and the anti-Chinese agitation grew, Congress held hearings in San Francisco on the question of Chinese immigration. This committee and others recommended that Chinese immigration be stopped. But the recommendations were not acted on because of treaties between China and the United States. Meanwhile, Congress did pass some general immigration laws that affected Chinese immigration. The immigration laws of 1875 required physical examinations of immigrants and excluded convicts, polygamists, prostitutes, persons suffering from loathsome or contagious diseases, and persons liable to become public charges.

It was not until 1882 that the Chinese Exclusion Law was passed that prohibited the immigration of Chinese laborers for 10 years. The law allowed the immigration of students, families of Chinese merchants (but not of laborers), teachers, merchants, diplomats, and tourists only. The federal law became a pretext for communities and counties throughout California to expel Chinese and send them to San Francisco. In 1892 and again in 1902, exclusion was extended for another 10 years, and in 1904 exclusion was extended indefinitely. Restrictions against Chinese immigration finally began to relax in 1930, and in 1943 President Franklin D. Roosevelt signed a law repealing the exclusion acts. The law, however, did not repeal the quotas, and in 1943 only 105 Chinese were allowed to immigrate to the United States. The immigrant quotas were finally lifted in 1965.

The first set of readings is favorable toward Chinese and Chinese labor. The first reading is from a Southern newspaper that clearly finds Chinese more acceptable than blacks and believes that with good treatment they can become economically valuable. The second piece, by Frank H. Norton, describes the positive attributes of Chinese and declares that the United States needs Chinese laborers. The next selection is critical of the congressional investigation of Chinese immigration and blames much of California's labor problems on whites' prejudice and intolerance of foreigners. The last entry in this section, by Murat Halstead, praises the Chinese culture and urges Californians to be more open-minded about Chinese. If Chinese are excluded, the country risks the loss of lucrative trade with the Far East.

The section against Chinese immigration and labor begins with an editorial, by Samuel Bowles, critical of the coolie trade, comparing it with slavery and calling for legislation to stop the importation of involuntary Chinese immigrants. The next entry is from a Southern newspaper that sees Chinese as another inferior race that the South does not need. The last reading urges California to take an anti-Chinese stance, even if it means giving up cheap labor.

FAVORING CHINESE IMMIGRATION AND LABOR

Anonymous Writer: "Coolie Labor"

There was a good bit of talk in the South after the war about how to provide the necessary labor for plantations, since Southerners were convinced that black men would not work. Some wanted to bring in Eastern European immigrants, others suggested poor families from the North, and others seriously considered contracting for Chinese, who had already proved themselves in California (and China) to be farmers at heart.

Baton Rouge (La.) Gazette, reprinted in the *Mobile (Ala.) Advertiser and Register,* October 25, 1868

In California, the only portion of our country where the Cooley has been imported as a laborer, he has been treated by the sanctimonious Yankee more like a beast of burden than a human being. Civilized man is only a child with pantaloons on, and it is one of the traits of the savage to hate for-eigners and to persecute them; but with all this hatred and persecution, the Cooley has been found so serviceable, and so superior to other kinds of la-borers, that the Californians continue to import him, and there are now some fifty thousand of them in that State—some twenty or thirty thousand being employed on the great Atlantic and Pacific Railroad alone. One of the peculiarities of this people is their great docility and gentleness of character. They make the best body servants in the world, and a stout Chinese man will nurse an infant with the tenderness and care of a woman. It is only nec-essary to state this to show what effect good treatment would have upon them. If, instead of deriding their peculiarities of race or religion, depriving them of their civil rights, and kicking and cuffing them about generally, as the Californians have done, and are doing, we should receive them kindly, lodge them comfortably, and treat them like human beings, there is no doubt that they would become here, as they are in the English colonies under similar treatment, a respectable, as well as useful class.

Frank H. Norton: "Our Labor-System and the Chinese"

This is an excerpt from a long article that describes the labor conditions in the West that made Chinese labor not only necessary but also a bargain for U.S. businesses.

Scribner's Magazine, September 1871

From what we know of the Chinese, we can fairly say they are neither ig-norant nor brutal. Without the advantages which we possess, with few of the aids which these advantages have given to us, they have reached a high con-dition of civilization; while in many of the arts they have advanced far be-yond any of the more liberally-endowed peoples. . . .

The Chinese are expert tillers of the soil, and with only the rude appli-ances that have been in use in their country for centuries, will get more out of an acre of ground than we do, with all our new machinery and improved methods of working. Yet, when placed in charge of labor-saving machines, they are found quick to learn and intelligent to operate. Personal observa-tion and the experience of travelers justify us in considering them among the most intelligently industrious people of the world. They are, too, faith-ful to a remarkable degree to those for whom they labor. Experience is daily proving this in the few instances where they are employed among us: while in California they have long been noted for their just and upright dealings. . . .

In every capacity in which the Chinese laborers have been tried in this country, they have proved a success. In the mines of California and New Mexico they have worked, and worked faithfully, where Americans and Europeans have given up in despair, either from unremunerative returns or unhealthy conditions in the locality. In their little market-gardens in California, in their laundries, and in their own peculiar manufacturing avocations, they have ever been found earnest, industrious, and persevering.

The Central Pacific Railroad would be today a thing of the future had it not been for the labors of the Chinese. And in the few manufactories in the Eastern States where enterprise has been found sufficient to press their employment, they have proved themselves to be diligent workers and sober, temperate human beings. . . .

Of late, renewed efforts have been made in San Francisco to discountenance not only the employment of the Chinese, but their immigration; and these efforts, sustained by unfaithful servants of the law, have been so far successful as to occasion a great falling off in the arrivals of Chinese emigrants in that city. The only result of such action will be the changing of the depot of reception for the Chinese emigrants from San Francisco to some other port. If their labor is needed in this country, not all the feeble stragglers of our present laboring class can prevent its reception. . . .

Among the objections which are frequently made to the employment of Chinese laborers, and particularly to their employment as domestic servants, are their personal habits. . . . The truth is, that while they are excessively unclean in their private domestic arrangements, they are scrupulously neat in their personal appearance, and attend carefully to their personal cleanliness. Chinese women are the dirtiest people conceivable; and the effect which a slatternly woman will produce on a household over which she has jurisdiction is too well known to need comment. But it has been noticed that where Chinese men are employed to perform the menial duties usually given to female servants, they perform them with a rigid exactitude of order and care really remarkable. . . .

The Chinaman works for a motive, the strongest possible to his race; his sole wish and design is to obtain sufficient money by his savings to enable him to return to his family, and live in comparative comfort and ease for the rest of his days. He is therefore economical and abstemious. A few hundred dollars in gold will accomplish all his needs and his desires, and if he can save this amount in three or five years he is satisfied. Again, he is content with the current market price of labor, and such an idea as a combination or "Union" to enforce a higher standard of wages, is not only unknown to him, but is foreign to all his instincts and repugnant to his feelings. . . .

Accustomed to be governed, and to have no word or voice in the laws or their execution, they have only a desire to be allowed freedom to pursue their own avocations, and personal safety while engaged in the pursuit. Of votes, and candidates, and caucuses, and primary elections, torch-light processions, nominations, jobs, and rings, they are in blessed ignorance. And since we know them to be intelligent, there is the less fear of their influence, when they do arrive at this height of learning and experience, then if it were accompanied by that condition of ignorance which cannot discern the difference between right and wrong, except when a greenback is placed between them.

The present condition of our labor-system is to be feared of all men. That any improvement can come to it, except by means of the freest competition, is impossible. . . .

As no great event can take place in this world without a wise ulterior design, it may be that the final solution of the labor-problem will be found in the advent into the West of "Heathen Chinee."

Anonymous Writer: "The Chinese Question in Congress"

Once the Chinese workers had built the Central Pacific Railway, it was time for them to go home and stop competing with white men for jobs. Protecting jobs for whites often was used as an excuse for racist government policies.

New York Times, March 1, 1877

It was to be expected that the Joint Committee of Congress on Chinese Immigration should find in California and elsewhere a great diversity of opinion. This they acknowledge at the outset, and their report seems to have been prepared with an amiable intention to meet the views of all parties to the controversy. On the whole, however, we should say that the report made to the Senate on Tuesday will be more acceptable to the extreme "anti-coolie" party in California than to anybody else. That party outnumbers any other in the State. The conclusions arrived at are violent, to say the least. It is asked of Congress that legislation for the Pacific States, peculiar in its character and at variance with the general spirit of our laws, shall be considered. . . .

The Congressional report will not please those who insist that Chinese immigration to California is an unmixed evil. The committee agree that the resources of the State, (of which we hear so much,) have been more rapidly developed by the cheap and docile labor of the Chinese than they could have been without it. But it is further argued that this apparent prosperity is deceptive; it benefits the capitalist and depresses the white laborer. A sound social prosperity, argue the committee, is based on adequate wages, the family, and education of the young. None of these elements are found among the Chinese. Therefore the wealth which their labor produces is unwholesome or fictitious. This means, we must suppose, that it would have been better if the Pacific Railroad, the great water-ways in the mining districts, and other works requiring the investment of considerable capital, had cost more, or had not been built so soon, or had never been built. They were constructed by Chinese labor when the cost of white labor would have made their completion impossible. This seems like a very thin argument. Public improvements which facilitate the movement of goods, passengers, and industrial products, and others which hasten the development of natural resources are not desirable if they are the work of an alien race. Why? Because, it is answered, these aliens not only do work which white men could not or would not perform, but they also compete with them in other fields of activity. Not only so, but they are objectionable because they are unclean in habit and in all their associations.

Competition in labor, says the committee, might be endured. But when the successful competitor is helped by a cheapness which is secured at the cost of personal comfort and decency, he is an unendurable interloper. This is precisely the conclusion to which the committee are forced. It is complained that the Chinese in San Francisco "live in filthy dwellings, upon poor food, crowded together in narrow quarters, and disregarding health and fire ordinances." We are surprised at this confession of the weakness of the Municipal Government of San Francisco. . . . If it is true that this small fraction of the total population of the city cannot be controlled, more shame to the weak local Government. If the Chinese quarter is a deadly spot, and if the influence spreading therefrom is fatal to the rest of the people, where are the statistics to prove it? It may be admitted that crowded tenements and narrow streets are unsightly, but there is nothing to show that mortality among the Chinese denizens of these quarters is any greater than in the densely-populated area of San Francisco where other foreigners live and die. . . .

Murat Halstead: No Title

This editorial is a particularly fine example of Murat Halstead's penchant for human liberty. It might well have been written 70 years later, when newspapers were lobbying to lift the ban on Chinese immigration.

Cincinnati Commercial, June 7, 1877

There has been sufficient pandering in California to the anti-Chinese prejudices of the common people to encourage the formation of a secret society, the purpose of which is to drive the Chinese out of the country or exterminate them if they refuse to go. A letter of the President of this organization leaves no doubt whatever of the intentions of those who have conspired to work the destruction of the adventurous Asiatics. There seems to be some alarm among decent and intelligent people lest there be a sudden outbreak and a massacre. . . .

At the time when this foolish agitation began it was possible for the politicians of California to have modified it, had they been disposed to do so; but rather than face the excitement they preferred to intensify it, going with the prejudices of the populace, and encouraging its violent manifestation. It has come to pass that a Chinaman in California has no rights that a white man is bound to respect, and the murder of a Coolie goes as unpunished as the assassinations in the Pennsylvania mining districts, when the Molly Maguires controlled affairs, or a midnight murder by the Ku-Klux when they raided about Central Kentucky. The consequence is a formidable secret organization of men in San Francisco, who contemplate the massacre of the Chinese, if they do not leave the State, and who are sworn to exterminate them.

In the Philadelphia Exposition the Chinese have one of the most interesting departments. It is filled with the products of their industry and marvelous skill. It testifies to the intelligence, the civilization, the enterprise of this ancient people. It is possible to cultivate a vast and profitable trade with them—a trade in which the people of the Pacific coast are especially interested. Gradually China is opening her ports to foreigners, and the wall of commercial exclusiveness is broken down like that stupendous structure which once defined the boundaries of the Empire on one side and kept out the Tartars and other warlike nomads, who made continual forays into the cultivated districts, to the ruin of their peace and prosperity.

If the anti-Coolie organization of San Francisco is to have its way, the progress made in establishing commercial relations with China will be checked. Its outrages will be followed by retaliation; the doors opened to our own merchants and shippers will be closed against us, and it will not be for us to say that such treatment would not be merited. It is of the first importance, therefore, that the Chinese in California be protected, and if the authorities of the State are not equal to the emergency, the general Government should interpose to save the lives of the immigrants and the name of American civilization from a National disgrace.

OPPOSING CHINESE IMMIGRATION AND LABOR

Samuel Bowles: "Coolies to Take the Place of Slaves"

Many Chinese workers were exported to the Caribbean to do the work formerly done by black slaves. The use of Chinese in the South was experimented with but only in a limited way. Fewer than 5,000 Chinese worked on Southern plantations.

Springfield (Mass.) Republican, July 29, 1867

A cargo of coolies has lately arrived at New Orleans from Cuba, to be used as laborers on the Mississippi sugar plantations, and it is stated that Ah Yuc, a commissioner from the Chinese government, has concluded a contract with a number of Louisiana, Alabama and Texas planters, to bring 5000 Chinamen to this country for their use, and that they will soon arrive. We suppose, as in the West Indies and other places, these laborers are bound out to serve for a term of years, for stipulated wages, which are of course very low, and under certain conditions. What the conditions may be in this case we do not know, as the only one announced is that, in case of death of any of the laborers, their remains shall be returned to China at the expense of their employers. What the other conditions of the service are, however, we do not care; whatever they may be nominally the coolie system is only a modification of slavery, and even worse in some of its features, and we protest in advance against its introduction into the United States.

The experiment of coolie labor has been thoroughly tried in the West Indies, and some of the South American states, in Australia, and elsewhere. Everywhere it is found as bad as slavery, both for the masters and the laborers, who are brought across the ocean much as cargoes of slaves were in old times, and when they reach their destination they are regarded as chattels, without any rights that anybody is bound to respect. We want none of the odious system here. . . . It is not to be wondered at that the southern planters, being deprived of slave labor, seek for something that may come as near it as possible, and choose the coolie system rather than employ their former slaves in their new character as American citizens. But the rest of the country has an interest and a voice in the matter, and one that must be heard and heeded. The attention of the government should at once be directed to stopping this coolie traffic; or, if there is no legal means of putting an end to the nefarious business, Congress should devote to it its earliest attention on reassembling. The United States must be a free country in reality as well as in name, hereafter.

Anonymous Writer: No Title

According to the writer of this editorial, the South already had one "inferior race" to contend with and did not need another, especially one that acted so much like a white man.

Mobile (Ala.) Tribune, reprinted in the *Mobile (Ala.) Advertiser and Register*, October 25, 1868

The Chinese, so far as they have come in contact with Europeans, are industrious, skillful, polite, provident; but also deceitful in trade, corrupt, wily, revengeful, irritable, cowardly, libidinous and intemperate, on the whole a kind of "white man" much more objectionable as servant, neighbor, or relative, than the negro himself. Let us rather be poor for several generations to come, than selfishly saddle posterity with another inferior race; that will surely bring upon their heads such wars and fanatical hatreds as we ourselves have experienced. . . .

Anonymous Writer: "The Chinese Riot—Its Lessons"

San Francisco experienced numerous Chinese riots during the 1870s—most provoked by white laborers. The San Francisco Chronicle *urges California's employers to stop hiring Chinese and hire white men instead.*

San Francisco Chronicle, May 24, 1870

The Chinese riot on Sunday will go far to convince many of our citizens who have heretofore been inclined to look with favor upon a class of people whom they considered a timid and much abused race, of their true character. It is but an earnest of what may be anticipated when this "timid and law abiding race" shall become strong enough, numerically, to oppose the authorities. The riot was caused, not by great injustice or long suffering, which might be palliated or glossed over by the popular designation of "revolution," but in consequence of a simple difference of opinion on a matter of business. . . . The whole affair illustrates a dangerous element in the Chinese character. They are cunning, vindictive, cruel, and unscrupulous; caring little for life and regardless of consequences in their insatiate fury. Experience confirms the general opinion that the Chinese are an undesirable and turbulent element in a community such as ours; they are now restrained by the police authorities, but will soon attain numbers sufficient to defy any force. Shall they be permitted to increase their numbers? The people of California have it in their power to settle the question in the negative. By earnest and united effort; a little sacrifice here and there; a preference for white Labor over Chinese, and the whole matter can be settled within a year. Let the people discard Chinese employees and rely upon white labor and their own energies. Many Chinese are employed at low wages as luxuries which can be easily dispensed with. Some such united effort on the part of the people, who should prefer the advancement of their own race, would effectually prevent the rioting of Chinese, in competing for patronage that should in every case be denied them.

QUESTIONS

1. Why was it so difficult for Chinese to integrate into U.S. society?
2. What qualities about Chinese did Americans like and dislike?
3. Compare and contrast the way that Chinese were treated with the way that blacks were treated in the South.
4. What are the economic factors that breed racial tension?
5. What were the arguments against using Chinese "coolies" in the South as a substitute for blacks?

NOTES

1. The information for this introduction comes from William Tung, *The Chinese in America* (Dobbs Ferry, N.Y.: Oceana Publications, 1974), and Thomas W. Chin, ed., *A History of Chinese in California* (San Francisco: Chinese Historical Society of America, 1969).

2. The term "coolie" is a Hindi word for peasant laborers or slaves in India. In the United States, the word became a pejorative term for Chinese, along with "Yellowjack" and "John Chinaman."

CHAPTER 24

Boss Tweed and His New York Ring, 1870–73

I n 1876, American poet James Russell Lowell wrote the following tongue-in-cheek ode in celebration of the nation's 100th birthday and its accomplishments:

Show your legislatures, show your Rings;
And challenge Europe to produce such things
As high official sitting half in sight
To share the plunder and fix things right;
If that don't fetch her, why you only need
To show your latest style in martyrs,—Tweed!

Lowell was alluding to the widespread graft and corruption that gripped U.S. politics from the end of the Civil War well into the twentieth century. Fueled by greed, incompetence, and apathy, corruption found its way into almost every city, legislature, and federal agency.

Probably the worst among corrupt city politicians was William Marcy "Boss" Tweed who, through his political ring dominated state, city, and county governments in New York. Estimates are that from 1867 to 1871, the Tweed ring pilfered between $75 million and $200 million from the citizens of New York. He worked his corruption through padded bills, false receipts, protection rackets, unnecessary repairs, renting to nonexistent tenants, letting high bid contracts in exchange for shoddy work and large kickbacks, and an extensive patronage system that bought favors with bribes.

Tweed entered the world of corrupt politics when he served as a volunteer fireman, a highly politicized brotherhood that ruled New York City's wards. His active involvement in ward politics in turn earned him, at age 28 years, a seat on the powerful New York Board of Alderman. In 1857, Tweed was elected to the New York County Board of Supervisors, one of the most powerful positions in New York and one that provided many opportunities

"WHAT ARE YOU LAUGHING AT?   TO THE VICTOR BELONG THE SPOILS."

"Boss" Tweed. *Tweed is depicted as a debauched Caesar who has been "whipped out of his boots."* Harper's Weekly. *Library of Congress.*

for graft. The Board of Supervisors was responsible for auditing city expenditures, appointing election supervisors, and supervising public improvements. Tweed also purchased his own printing company, and through his various public offices he gave himself lucrative city printing contracts.[1] Tweed continued to accumulate political positions until he was one of the most powerful men in New York City. One contemporary described Tweed as "a vulgar good fellow by nature, a politician by circumstances, a boss by evolution, and a grafter by choice."[2]

By 1869, the all-Democratic Tweed ring consisted of Tweed, city chamberlain Peter Sweeny, city comptroller (treasurer) Richard B. Connolly, and Mayor A. Oakey Hall. Between these four men, the ring owned New York City. One of their most successful political tools was the befriending of new immigrants. Tweed welcomed the newcomers with food baskets, jobs for the men, housing, and emergency relief. In exchange for this largesse, the immigrants voted—legally or illegally—as a block for the ring.

New York was a statutory city chartered by the state legislature. Under this form of government, the legislature made the major decisions for the city, from running the most essential services to deciding the tax rates, salaries, building rules, and welfare budget. The mayor of New York City had very little power. Therefore, anyone who wanted to "boss" New York City needed to be influential at home and at the state capital. Tweed accomplished this feat by being elected to the State Assembly in 1868, a position that linked Albany to New York City, and completed Tweed's ring.

His greatest accomplishment as assemblyman was passage of a new city charter that significantly reduced the number of legislative commissions and replaced them with city departments run by mayoral appointees—Tweed, Connolly, and Sweeny.[3] With the new charter, the ring had complete power over the city council, the mayor, and many of the judges. And, if anyone tried to disturb this comfortable position, untold largesse was used to silence dissent from within and without.[4]

Democrats and Republicans soon became outraged at the ring's open corruption, but Tweed's ability to maintain a very broad base of support as well as to compromise even his detractors made it difficult to bring him to justice. For example, many of the city's newspapers were in Tweed's pocket, because they either received payments for city printing or held lucrative contracts to run legal advertising for the city and county or their reporters were on the city payroll. According to the *North American Review,* no fewer than a dozen staff on the *New York Herald* held city jobs.[5]

The Republican papers in the city were less likely to be in Tweed's debt. *Harper's Weekly* kept up a constant barrage of cartoons by Thomas Nast, depicting Tweed as a large-bellied rogue. As early as 1868, the *New York Times,* the *New York Tribune,* and the *New York World* regularly took jabs at the ring and carefully chronicled Tweed's efforts to get the city charter through the state assembly. However, without concrete evidence of fraud and bribery, the newspapers made little headway in bringing Tweed down.

In January 1871, evidence of fraud finally was uncovered when the city auditor, who had been killed, was replaced with an accountant who was secretly working for one of Tweed's political enemies, James O'Brien. O'Brien turned over to the *New York Times* extensive records from the comptroller's office that covered three and a half years of graft and corruption.

Beginning July 8, the *New York Times* ran several installments detailing extensive fraud in the building of the New York County Courthouse and in the renting and maintenance of armories to National Guard units. The records revealed that from 1868 to mid-1871, more than $12 million had been spent on the construction of the yet-to-be completed courthouse. According to the *New York Times,* enough money had been spent to build 16 courthouses.

Most of the money went to businesses operated by or on behalf of the Tweed ring. These businesses, acting as contractors on the courthouse, either endorsed payments to subcontractors who did not exist or padded the bills as much as tenfold. For example, payments of more than $750,000 for enough carpet to cover four courthouses were made to J.A. Smith, a fictitious carpet dealer. When the *New York Times* investigated why Robert G. Griggs, another carpet dealer, was being paid $20,000 a month for carpeting city buildings, Griggs replied, "Carpets in public offices wear out very quickly." It was later determined that much of the carpeting ended up in a hotel owned by Tweed's son.

Andrew Garvey, dubbed the "Prince of Plasterers," received payments of $62,000 for plastering work done by subcontractor R.J. Hennessey, who later stated that he never did any plastering work for Garvey. James W. Smith, an awning maker, charged the city $150 each for awnings that normally cost $12.50.[6]

With these revelations, *Harper's Weekly* cartoonist Thomas Nast took up his pen to campaign alongside the *New York Times* against the ring. In fact, Nast's cartoons often have been credited as being the most effective instrument in bringing down Tweed and his ring. Tweed is reported to have told *Harper's Weekly* editor George Curtis, "I don't care a straw for your newspaper articles, my constituents don't know how to read, but they can't help seeing them damned pictures." Nast was offered a half-million dollar bribe to end his campaign of editorial cartoons. When Harper Bros., publishers of *Harper's Weekly,* refused to fire Nast, the publishing company lost the lucrative contract to print textbooks for New York schools.

Tweed was arrested in October 1871. His trial ended in a hung jury. He was rearrested and tried in 1873 and convicted of 204 counts of fraud, fined $122,500, and sentenced to 12 years in prison. On appeal, his sentence was reduced to 1 year and a $250 fine. He was released from jail in January 1875, only to be rearrested and placed in debtor's prison, charged by the state with $6 million in debts. While in prison, Tweed was allowed to visit with his family, and on one such outing Tweed fled to Cuba then to Spain where he worked as a seaman. He was arrested after being identified from one of Nast's cartoons. He was returned to jail, where he died in April 1878.

Meanwhile, Sweeny and Connolly fled to Europe. Although Hall was tried twice, he was never found guilty.

With the exception of a few small Democratic "ward" papers that owed their existence to the ring's generosity, the New York press was not kind to Tweed, and the newspapers outside of the city were generally similar in tone.

The selections against the ring begin with editorials that show the give and take between the *New York Times* and the *New York World*—with the former challenging the latter to clean up its party before the next election. The *New York World* takes up the challenge and pledges to work to remove the Tweed stench from the Democratic Party. The third selection, by Louis Jennings, was published on the day that the *New York Times* revealed the first documentation supporting the charges of fraud. The fourth entry, by George W. Curtis, condemns the corruption but warns that rings are everywhere—in the federal government and in other cities—and it is the public's duty to get rid of the various rings. The next selection is a letter, by Charles Nordhoff, describing the new courthouse as a shabby building lacking little evidence of plastering, carpets, repairs, or other expenses reportedly paid for by the city. The final selection is a poem accounting the history of the Tweed ring.

Few editorials appeared in defense of the Tweed ring. Those that did were probably written by Tweed or for Tweed and planted in local newspapers to refute the charges of the large city newspapers. The first entry in this section, by A. Oakley Hall, appeared in a newspaper owned by Tweed and attempts to refute the charges by denouncing the *New York Times's* source for their information as being dishonest and unreliable. The second selection insists that the exorbitant charges for work on the courthouse were the accumulation from the past 10 years and that they were paid by the old city government not the new. The final reading, by William Cassidy, takes a step back and reminds readers that the frauds happened because politicians from both parties profited. Tweed's money was just as likely to end up in the hands of Republicans as it was in the hands of Democrats.

AGAINST THE TWEED RING

Louis Jenning: "The Sorrows of Tammany"

The New York Times *recognizes that not all Democrats are corrupt, but they have allowed the ring to take over. Once inside, they cannot be moved.*

The New York Times *challenges respectable Democrats to do something before it is too late.*

New York Times, January 25, 1870

There is fresh trouble in the ranks of the City Democracy. Some of the leaders have come to the conclusion that it is extremely desirable to take the advice we have more than once given them, and get rid of the reproach which the government of this City has long been to the whole party. It is not too much to say that the flagrant corruption and profligacy exhibited in New-York have made the Democratic Party a by-word all the world over. It has injured it almost irreparably in the eyes of the great body of the American people. Nothing can be more natural than for thoughtful persons to say, "We can judge what a Democratic rule would lead us to from the condition of New-York. The Democrats are the masters of that City, and see what they have made of it. . . . " The City is, in fact, a standing warning to the nation against permitting itself to fall into the hands of the Democrats. The example makes a greater impression upon the public mind than all the argument or invective of political adversaries. . . .

The title of "Alderman" or "Deputy Sheriff" became too often synonymous with the worst terms of opprobrium. To call an honest man by either title is to take away his character. The guardians of the City make themselves common in the lowest places of resort, or act as ringleaders in disgusting orgies, where women are thrown out of boxes at the theatres, and men drink themselves into a state of frenzy. . . . The "shoulder-hitters, ballot-box stuffers and repeaters" do not want to be "respectable." It is a luxury which they do not understand, and could never be brought to admire. Is it at all likely that our present Aldermen, Sheriffs, and the like, will voluntarily relinquish the prizes they have seized? They must undergo a strange transformation before they are capable of any single act which honorable citizens would be likely to approve. The tiger which has once tasted human blood, cannot afterwards be put on a milder diet. We are sorry for the Governor and his friends, but after all they alone are to blame for their present afflictions. They who sow the wind must reap the whirlwind. . . .

Manton Marble: "War to the Knife"

The New York World, *New York City's most prominent Democratic newspaper, had been critical of the ring for several years, but it kept its criticism just short of creating problems for the party. Here Manton Marble takes up the* New York Times*'s challenge and agrees to lead the fight within the party to clean house before the upcoming elections.*

New York World, **February 16, 1870**

The Democrats of New-York and of the United States are entitled to know from us what the *World* is about in breaking down the power of the organization and the men who for many years have held sway in the politics of the City. In the first place, the *World* calls its friends here and elsewhere to witness that it has not attacked the Ring of corrupt Democrats in New-York City at a time when to break down their power would have broken down or divided the strength of the Democratic Party, and surrendered the City or the State to the worse alternative of Radical rule. It has contented itself with maintaining an attitude of simple independence of the Ring. . . .

But next Fall a Governor of New-York is to be elected, and two years thereafter a President of the United States.

In our deliberate judgment not New-York State itself can possibly be carried again by the Democracy handicapped with this millstone of the "Ring." What is more, the Democracy would not deserve to carry the State next Fall if here, where their power at the ballot-box is supreme, and while at Albany they control every branch of the State Government, they shall not also proceed to sweep from power these men who have debauched our politics and defiled the name of Democracy. And if with this "Ring" mill-stone about our necks the Democracy cannot keep control of the State of New-York, much more can they not get control of the United States. . . .

Handicapped with the "Ring" millstone about our necks, the Democracy of the Union can no more win in that contest than they could win in 1864, upon the peace platform of Chicago, or in 1868, upon the greenback and revolution planks of Tammany Hall. The millstone may drown those who prefer it. We prefer free air to the bottom of the sea. And so do the honest Democrats of New-York City, who are uniting with the *World* to cast it off. . . .

But the Democracy of the State and of the United States are entitled to demand of the *World*—What is your prospect? Can you win? . . . Can this island be the culminating point of the enterprise, the culture, the wealth, and the power of the continent, yet its people be incapable to shake off the rule of the dozen sordid men of selfish hearts and narrow brains who have plundered us to millions yearly, obstructed our material growth, made our markets, our wharves and piers and streets mere monuments of their rapacity, our elections a farce, and now have put up Judges in our very Court Houses to sell injustice for a price? Assuredly not.

The friends of the Ring throughout the State are purchased friends. They are few and powerless with the people. Here their dependents are numerous, and their friends are intrenched in every place of profit and of power. But out of every place they will be expelled. The honest Democracy have most to fear from being incumbered with the Ring's deserters. That the *World* has waited patiently and long before calling on this fight for honest government in New-York City must be our only present guarantee that it has not called it an hour too soon for final victory.

Louis Jennings: "The Rings and the City Armories"

This is the lead editorial for the issues of the New York Times *that revealed for the first time specific examples of Boss Tweed's graft.*

New York Times, July 8, 1871

We lay before our readers this morning a chapter of Municipal rascality which, in any other city but New York, would bring down upon the heads of its authors such a storm of public indignation as would force them to a speedy accountability before the bar of a Criminal Court, or compel them to take refuge in flight and perpetual exile. Here, however, it will, doubtless, be laughed at by some as a good joke, and an evidence of "smartness" on the part of our City officials, be discredited by others as unworthy of "outrage," but, like other outrages of the same character, to be quietly submitted to because of the supposed impossibility of obtaining redress. Nevertheless, we trust that all our readers will give the article a careful perusal, and that the facts it contains will be treasured up as part of the accumulated mass of official corruption which is being piled up against the Tammany Ring, and which is destined, at no distant day, to descend like an avalanche upon their heads and crush them beneath its weight.

The source from which the facts and figures relative to the renting of armories in this City have been obtained are of the most reliable character, and a large portion of the statements can easily be verified by any citizen who chooses to take a little personal trouble. If there is a single mistake in any of the statements or figures contained in the article, we shall be most happy to publish the correction, provided Mr. Connolly, or any other official concerned will send it to us duly verified. The Times has been often charged by those whose interest it is to belittle its exposures of the frauds of the Ring, with making random charges unsupported by facts and specifications. This charge comes with a bad grace from men whose master-stroke of policy for the last three years has been the concealment of all their official transactions from the public eye. These men are in the position of a gang of burglars, who, having stolen all your silver-ware and jewelry and placed them under lock and key, turn around and challenge you to identify your property. In the case of ordinary burglars, you could summon the Courts to your assistance, arrest the thieves, break open the locks and get a sight of your stolen goods. But the Tammany Ring are a law unto themselves; they are the government; they control the machinery of justice, and own a large share of the Judges. Hence they defy your efforts to detect their villainy, and laugh at the idea of restitution. But, notwithstanding all these drawbacks and difficulties, the Times has succeeded in exposing many frauds upon the City Treasury, and has furnished better vouchers for its bills of indictment than Controller Connolly has furnished for the bills he has drawn on our tax-payers. We apprehend that no one will complain of a lack of facts and specification in the article to which we now call the reader's attention; and that not even the Tribune or any other of the eighteen daily and weekly papers that have been gagged by Ring patronage, will be able to find an excuse for ignoring the startling record presented elsewhere, on the ground that it is not sufficiently definite.

George W. Curtis: "Frauds and Parties"

The Tweed ring is described as just another example of the fraud and corruption that existed across the country and that will eventually bring the country down.

Harper's Weekly, August 26, 1871

The fact of very general corruption in our politics has been long alleged. That elections are carried by fraud, that the whole civil service is a vast system of virtual bribery, that politics have become a profitable trade, and that places in the Legislature and elsewhere are sought for the money to be made out of them, are assertions by men of both parties with which we have all been long familiar. But not before has there been such a clear and conclusive exposure of immense official corruption as in the recent disclosures of the financial management of the city of New York. The country will have observed that there has been no denial of the frauds, while the pretenses of defense or apology have been utterly contemptible. As a last and desperate resort it was promised that the accounts would be published, as if that were an indisputable proof of innocence, although the law requires a financial statement every year, and none has been made for more than a two years and a half. But even the promise to publish them has not, up to this writing, been fulfilled. . . .

The situation, therefore, is this. Enormous frauds are charged, and the figures and other details are given. . . . Corruption so vast, so confessed, so general, is a peril to this country as deadly as slavery ever was. The city is cheated that the State may be bought. Then, under the same auspices, the city will be cheated that the country may be bought. And still further, the city will be cheated that the national elections, as well as State, may be carried. But when the country believes that a Presidential election has been decided by fraud, a civil war is just as inevitable as it was when slavery tried to sever the Union. . . .

The corruption now exposed in the city of New York is not, of course, confined to that city. It is known elsewhere, even if not upon so large a scale nor so distinctly revealed. Its object is the security of party ascendancy. Now it is a very grave question for the consideration of every American citizen who can lift himself above the mere partisan view, how long our system is safe and our peace assured when, every four years, this corruption is invited to struggle for the possession of a hundred thousand offices and the raising and spending of three or four hundred millions of dollars. . . . If Republicans are guilty, let them be exposed as these Democrats have been, and let both suffer. . . .

Charles Nordhoff: "A Visit to the New Court-House"

Charles Nordhoff wrote this letter to the New York Times *shortly after leaving his position as editor of the* New York Evening Post *following a fallout between himself and William Cullen Bryant over the* New York Evening Post*'s reticence in covering activities of the Tweed ring. This description of the New York City courthouse was widely quoted.*

Reprinted in *New York Evening Post,* July 26, 1871

To the Editor of the New York Times:

Having some idle time on my hands, I took the liberty this morning to visit the new Court House, which you have lately made famous.

New Yorkers are such busy people, that I suppose not a great many, except politicians and the lawyers who practice in the city courts, have seen the inside of this costly piece of their property; and I can tell them that a shabbier place they could not well find, unless they should visit the old City Hall, which seems to me dirtier and more dilapidated than even the new Court House. . . .

In Mr. Andrew J. Garvey's little account, which you printed on Monday, there are dozens of entries of "repairs." About these I can tell you nothing, except that he seems to have done his repairing in such a manner as to necessitate more; for the walls are in a disgraceful condition. They are not only dirty, but in the lower halls and elsewhere pieces of the plastering have peeled off, leaving ugly blotches, which give the famous New Court House the appearance of a dilapidated and neglected ruin.

Now, you can imagine, perhaps, my amazement when I discovered that there is really, considering the styles of the building, very little plastering in the New Court House. The interior consists largely of iron. I think I could find you a good many plasterers in town who would gladly do all the plastering in the New Court House for $20,000. But the taxpayers of New York were obliged by Mayor Hall and Comptroller Connolly to pay for this work more than $268,000, to say nothing of hundreds of thousands of dollars' worth of "repairs." . . .

When I had done with the plastering I began to look at the furniture of the rooms. Here I naturally thought I should see something fine. Many insurance offices and banks are nowadays furnished with great magnificence, and I have read that even Mr. Tweed's stable is a marvel of fine wood and costly furniture.

Well, I assure you the new Court House is very plainly furnished. The wood-work is of black walnut, true, but it is all common in style, a little shabby. If it had been of oak or some high-colored wood, the rooms would have been less gloomy. It is not easy for one to guess at the actual value of this furniture, but it consists largely of common black walnut chairs, and seventy-five thousand dollars would be an extravagant estimate of the real value of all the furniture in the new Court House.

But you say that $1,476,908 were paid to one firm by Mayor Hall and Comptroller Connolly. I should say they had paid $1,400,000 too much. . . .

I must defer to another day some account also of the old City Hall, and of some of its surroundings. But I advise every citizen whose taxes have been raised to meet the furniture, curtain and plastering bills of the new Court House, to go and look at it with his own eyes.

Yours truly,
Charles Nordhoff

Anonymous Writer: No Title

New York Evening Post, 1874

In eighteen hundred and seventy
The Charter was purchased by W.M.T.
By eighteen hundred and seventy-one
The Tweed Ring's stealing had all been done.
By eighteen hundred and seventy-two
The amount of the stealing the people knew.
By eighteen hundred and seventy-three
Most of the thieves had decided to flee.
By eighteen hundred and seventy-four
Tweed was allowed his freedom no more.

In Defense of the Tweed Ring

A. Oakey Hall: No Title

The New York Leader *was a Democratic newspaper owned lock, stock, and barrel by Tweed and Tammany Hall and edited by Mayor Hall. It was the organ that Tweed used to refute charges by the* New York Times *and other city newspapers. This editorial is typical of the type of story the* New York Leader *ran at Tweed's bidding.*

New York Leader, July 21, 1871

Recently the Times has found a clerk who was discharged from the Comptroller's office for dishonesty, and who, claiming afterward to have keyhole information to sell, was politely shown the door and mentally kicked out by at least three officials. He found, however, ready purchase money in the Times office, and from that tainted source comes the publication of immense claims which the Times says have been divided between the Mayor and the Comptroller! It is enough for the friends of these gentlemen to know that they cannot pay any claims unless these have been first audited by either the Board of Supervisors or former boards of audit, and that they never have paid claims without such statutory audit; and that both of them deny the charges of the Times of Friday in the language of the old answer in chancery, and say they are "as false in substance as they are scandalous in form."

"Progress": "The Quarrel over the City Accounts"

In all likelihood, this letter was written by a member of the Tweed ring and is one of many sent as part of a letter-writing campaign by the ring to air its side of the story in the larger New York newspapers, which were almost 100 percent critical of the ring and its corruption.

New York Evening Post, July 24, 1871

New York, July 23, 1871

To the Editors of the Evening Post:

(1.) Why do you not tell the whole truth about the malicious attacks the *Times* is making upon Mayor Hall and the Comptroller?

(2.) Why do you not expose the obviously low motives which actuate it, and the weakness and pointlessness of nearly all its charges, even if the facts and figures which it pretends to have were admitted to be true?

(3.) Suppose that before the county supervisors were abolished, they did order the payment of a great many claims which had been accumulating ten years and which were extravagant in amount; and that they were paid upon their order; and suppose that this was but the culminating point of their extravagance and fraud under which the public money has been wasted for many years, and which compelled the legislature to abolish them and to pass the new charter, giving the Mayor and Comptroller full power to regulate expenditures; and suppose that the extravagance and fraud in question were stopped by them as soon as they had the power. Does all this, which the *Times* story, if true, would indicate, make the present city government responsible for the corruption of those abolished officers?

(4.) The *Times* takes the dates at which bills were made up, and pretends that all the work charged for in bills running back for months and years must have been done on the one day on which they are dated. It lays great emphasis on the payment of $20,000 in one day, and asks: 'Is it probable that this amount was ever actually paid for *one day's work* done to armories and drill rooms?' It finds bills of $636,000 made up on Sundays, and calls it the account for "Sunday work." Nearly all the inferences and specific charges it makes are equally absurd and meaningless, even if its figures are admitted; can they have any weight with sensible men?

(5.) Why will you not go through these charges in detail, if you take any notice of them at all, and expose their weakness? and, above all, why not point out the fact that the *Times* has not at any time brought forward one single charge or specification which affects in any way the honesty or economy of the new city government under the new charter, but that every word it says bears upon the old system of mixed boards and commissions, which the Evening Post so ably opposed, and which it helped so much to destroy?

"PROGRESS"

William Cassidy: No Title

The Albany (N.Y.) Argus, *a Democratic newspaper, explains that much of the money stolen by the Tweed ring ended up in the hands of Republicans, who controlled New York's legislature. Tweed had to grease palms in Albany to gain the control over New York City.*

Albany (N.Y.) Argus, August 2, 1871

A radical editor recently went through the New York Court House, and asked, where is all this plastering, all this furniture? We can tell him. The hands of radical politicians at Albany had to be plastered annually before the New York tax levy could become a law. To one man, a saint of St. Lawrence, sixty thousand dollars had to be paid; to another, a white neck-clothed scoundrel from Madison, a sum nearly as great. Garvey's plaster whitens walls and fertilizes farms in the west of the state. Ingersoll's furniture decks respectable mansions in the interior, and the neighbors wonder how the wealth and taste of the owner were so suddenly developed.

Does any one suppose that that old Republican firm of plumbers, the Keysers, were let off with furnishing a New York courthouse? No; their lead pipe ran into Herkimer, and tapped the politics of Montgomery. Indeed, the sewerage of Cayuga and Chatauqua, it is believed, found their machinery and equipment at this good old Radical establishment.

There is a drainage from New York into the interior, under the laws, which amounts to millions annually. The school law and the system of appraisement in New York, as contrasted with the ratio in the rural districts, gives an advantage to the state or against the metropolis of several millions a year. But this equality under the law is nothing compared with the secret subterranean drainage which exhausts the vitality and the strength of the metropolis for the benefit of radical politicians in the interior. . . .

Questions

1. Why did it take so long for Tweed's frauds to be stopped?
2. Why did the *New York Times* believe that it was the responsibility of the Democratic Party to clean up the Tweed mess?
3. Just how independent was the press of New York City?
4. In what ways were Republicans responsible for Tweed's corruption?

Notes

1. See Seymour J. Mandelbaum, *Boss Tweed's New York* (New York: John Wiley, 1965; reprint, Chicago: Ivan Dee, 1990); Alexander B. Callow, Jr., *The Tweed Ring* (New York: Oxford University Press, 1966).

2. Samuel P. Orth, *The Boss and the Machine: A Chronicle of the Politicians and Party Organization* (New Haven: Yale University Press, 1921), 65.

3. Mandelbaum, 75.

4. Orth, 65–67.

5. Charles Wingate, "An Episode in Municipal Government (Part II)," *North American Review* 120 (January 1875): 119–74, 173–74; Mark D. Hirsch, "More Light on Boss Tweed," *Political Science Quarterly* 60 (June 1945): 267–78, 270, 277.

6. "How New York Is Governed: Frauds of the Tammany Democrat," *New York Times,* 1871.

Chapter 25

The Crédit Mobilier Scandal, 1872–73

A s early as the 1840s, merchants and entrepreneurs had dreamed of being able to cross the United States by railroad, tying the commerce of the East with the growing western seaboard. The first person to consider seriously the idea of a transcontinental railroad was Asa Whitney, who had made a fortune in the Chinese tea trade. His dream was to connect the Eastern United States with the Far East through a combination of merchant vessels and railroads. To realize his dream, Whitney asked Congress to grant him the land for the railroad right of way. His plan was rejected by Congress in 1848 and again in 1850 and 1851.

However, with the gold rush and the economic boom in the West, Congress finally authorized the survey of a possible transcontinental railroad.[1] In 1862, President Abraham Lincoln authorized the Union Pacific Railroad to be built from Nebraska west to the Nevada-California border. Another line to be called the Central Pacific Railroad was to be built east and west from Sacramento, with one end in San Francisco and the other at the terminus of the Union Pacific. For both railroads, the Pacific Railroad Act provided 6,400 acres of land for each mile of railroad built for a total of 20 million acres and guaranteed 30-year bonds at 6 percent interest. The total value of the bonds was more than $60 million—half of what was needed for the project. The balance was to be raised from private investors. And, finally, the law required 100 miles of track to be finished and operational by July 1, 1866, and the entire road completed by January 1, 1874.

As soon as the transcontinental railway bill passed, a convention was held in Chicago to organize the Union Pacific Railroad. The law required 2,000 shares to be subscribed at $1,000 a share (for a total pledge of $2 million) before the Union Pacific could elect a board of directors and be on its own. However, there was very little enthusiasm for the new venture. During wartime, there were certainly more lucrative ways to speculate with one's money than a railroad that crossed uninhabited plains and deserts and reached across treacherous mountains.

Thomas Durant, a railroad investor, stepped forward and put up the cash necessary to get the board of directors installed and the company running on its own. But, the company still needed $1 million to build the first 40 miles. In 1865, Durant and seven other directors of the Union Pacific Railroad purchased a defunct Philadelphia holding company and named it after a prestigious French credit firm. As a holding company, Crédit Mobilier purchased Union Pacific stock at face value, and then sold it at below face value to get the cash needed to begin construction. Finally, with loans and capital of more than $2.5 million, construction began.

All of the construction of the Union Pacific was done by a group of seven contractors—all directors of Crédit Mobilier and the Union Pacific Railway Company. In effect, the Union Pacific Railroad directors paid themselves through Crédit Mobilier to build the railroad. The most prominent among these contractors were Durant and Oakes Ames, a U.S. congressman from Massachusetts who had become rich manufacturing shovels and who owned one-third interest in a steel company that made rails. Now, he would become even richer, selling himself shovels and rail to build the Union Pacific. Crédit Mobilier's operations were typical of nineteenth-century railroad building because investors had long since learned that they could make more money from building the railroad than from operating it. But there were those who were critical that so much federal money was ending up in the hands of only a few men. One of those was Charles Frances Adams, a young lawyer turned journalist who had a good understanding of the railroad industry. In an 1869 article for the *North American Review*, Adams described the Crédit Mobilier:

> The members of it are in Congress; they are trustees for the bondholder, they are directors, they are stockholders, they are contractors; in Washington they vote the subsidies, in New York they receive them, upon the Plains they expend them, and in the Crédit Mobilier they divide them. As stockholders they own the road, as mortgagees they have a lien upon it, as directors they contract for its construction, and as members of the Crédit Mobilier they build it.[2]

Here is an example of what Adams was describing: Durant, who owned a construction company received a contract from Crédit Mobilier, of which he was a director, to build a certain amount of track. Durant would give Crédit Mobilier an inflated estimate of what it would cost to lay the track. As manager of Crédit Mobilier, Durant would accept the inflated estimate from Durant the contractor and pass it on to the Union Pacific for approval. As vice president of the Union Pacific, Durant would write the check to Durant's construction company.

The first rails were laid at Omaha in July 1865, and by January 1866, the requisite 40 miles of track had been approved and $640,000 worth of government bonds released. Bonds are like loans, and each time the Union Pacific sold a bond it was actually taking out a loan that had to be repaid with interest. All cash from the sale of the bonds was held by Crédit Mobilier, which paid the contractors. In other words, Crédit Mobilier got the cash, and the Union Pacific kept the debt.

Durant and his cohorts intended to pay off the debt with freight surcharges and taxes on use of the railroad. Durant had even managed to grease enough palms to get Congress to amend the first Pacific Railway Act (which gave free transportation to the mail services, federal freight, and the military) to require the government now to pay one-half of its freight charge. On its face there is nothing wrong with using future profits to pay off the debt. However, because the cost to build the railroad had been inflated, the users, including the federal government, would be paying for a debt that was four to five times what it actually cost to build the railroad.

When the Union Pacific Railroad reached Promontory Point, Utah, in September 1869, it had a $74 million bonded debt. At the same time, Crédit Mobilier, through overcharges on construction costs, use of inferior building materials, and substandard construction, had earned between $16 million and $23 million for its stockholders.

This scheme could not have worked without Congress's help. Beginning as early as 1867, Crédit Mobilier, through Ames and Representative James Brooks of New York, transferred to certain congressmen and public officials shares at three to four times below market value, with guaranteed returns of 100 percent per year. Among those who received the stock were Speaker of the House Schuyler Colfax (vice president in President Grant's first term), Representative Henry Wilson (vice president in President Grant's second term), Representative James Blaine (later speaker of the house), and future president Ohio representative James Garfield.

Rumors of congressional pay-offs had been circulating for several years, but evidence of the bribes was not made public until September 1872, two months before the presidential election. A.M. Gibson, editor of the *New York Sun,* began investigating rumors of bribery more than a year earlier, when a disgruntled stockholder brought a civil suit against Crédit Mobilier. Testimony in the suit included letters written by Ames, listing congressmen who had been offered stock. No sooner had the *New York Sun* publicized the fraud than the implicated congressmen sold off their stocks at hardy profits. The *New York Sun* never obtained solid proof of bribery taking, and many

Republican papers either refused to run the story or called it an exaggeration or a mean-spirited last-minute attack by Democrats. Consequently, the release of the story right before the 1872 elections had little if any effect on the election's outcome.

After the election, the House of Representatives impanelled two investigative committees—one to look into the Crédit Mobilier–Union Pacific dealings; the other, the Poland Committee, to determine the guilt or innocence of congressmen accused of taking bribes. After several weeks of closed hearings and hundreds of witnesses, the Poland Committee found no evidence that the accused were influenced in their action by the stock. Only Ames and Brooks were censured. Brooks, who was a government director for the Union Pacific, knew all of the workings of the Crédit Mobilier and, according to the committee, allowed the government to be defrauded. Brooks died within weeks of the censure; Ames died several months later. A resolution to impeach Colfax, based primarily on perjured testimony, failed to pass by a mostly party-line vote of 106 to 109 (Brooks and Ames being two of the votes to acquit). Colfax retired to South Bend, Indiana.

While the committees investigating the railroad and Crédit Mobilier amassed a huge amount of testimony, their report was shelved and no action was taken against any of the Union Pacific or Crédit Mobilier directors.

Both the Union Pacific and Central Pacific railroads were nearly bankrupt, despite the fact that the federal government had given them 44 million acres of free land and $61 million in cash loans. Also, a lot of shoddy railroad had been built, and both companies were forced to rebuild much of the track. In 1874, Congress required the Union Pacific to allot 25 percent of its earnings for loan repayment and to allow its books to be inspected regularly. The Union Pacific finally went bankrupt in 1893.

The entries critical of the Crédit Mobilier scandal begin with a review by Louis Jennings of Charles Adam's article in the *North American Review* in which he describes the way that the Crédit Mobilier worked and how it was peddling shares to congressmen in return for favorable legislation. The second entry is a poem that makes fun of Representative James Blaine, who allegedly received some of the Crédit Mobilier shares. The next two readings criticize Congress for not coming down harder on the congressmen who took bribes. The entry in *The Nation* by E.L. Godkin sees the reticence to sanction fellow congressmen as an indicator that the Republican Party is outdated and no longer responsive. The entry in the *New York Times* by Jennings believes that the investigators begged the question when they concluded that the congressmen under investigation did not know they were being bribed.

The entries skeptical of the Crédit Mobilier charges are led by an editorial, by Godkin from *The Nation,* which initially refused to believe that the good men of the Republican Party could be so base as to accept bribes. *The*

Nation quickly changed its editorial mind when the investigations revealed more of the scandal and bribery. The second entry is from another newspaper that also would eventually change its mind. However, in this editorial by Parke Godwin, the *New York Evening Post* saw the charges as an attempt by Democrats and Liberal Republicans to injure the reelection of President Grant. The last two selections are by George W. Curtis from *Harper's Weekly*. The first entry accuses the press, particularly the newspapers supporting Horace Greeley for president, of being malignant and licentious in spreading the false rumors against Republicans. The final entry, written after the investigation was complete, insists that the congressmen accused of taking bribes were innocent because they did not know the shares they were given were in exchange for votes.

CRITICAL OF THE CRÉDIT MOBILIER CHARGES

Louis Jennings: "Railway Problems"

In 1870, Charles Adams warned the public about the operations of the Crédit Mobilier and the giving of shares to congressmen.

New York Times, January 23, 1870

Few blows more direct and powerful have been dealt, of late, in public discussion, to the vicious and monstrous subsidy system in constructing railroads than the paper which Mr. Charles F. Adams, Jr., contributes to the current number of the *North American Review*. It is a direct blow, because it deals with names and figures, not with generalities; it is a powerful blow, because it thoroughly exposes the intrigues of past, the iniquities of present and the perils of future legislative manipulation. The evil, too, is one that afflicts alike national and State legislation. When, for example, we are told that during the twenty-six working days of the session of Congress last Spring, no less than twenty-three bills were introduced into the Senate for aiding railroads that unaided private capital shrank from building, we may appreciate the extent of the evil. When we learn that this modest array of bills proposed to construct over fourteen thousand miles of road, and to appropriate for the purpose more than two hundred and twenty-four millions of acres of the public domain, or more than one-half of the territory now unoccupied, we may concede that it was a pretty good month's work for the subsidy beggars. Nor was that all since three out of these twenty-three bills additionally asked the Government to become responsible for the interest on more than one hundred and sixteen millions of money indebtedness—an annual charge of nigh upon seven millions of dollars. . . .

Mr. Adams well says, that if the National Government goes on for twenty years at simply the same rate and in the same path as Massachusetts, by the year 1890 it will be involved in the affairs of railroad corporations, two-thirds of them insolvent, to the extent of six hundred million dollars; and that it will have to complete and manage "the most hopelessly bankrupt and unpromising roads," while by that time, with subsidy jobbing in full sweep, "the moral condition of the Government will have become unendurable." For, besides the question of money, there is a great question of morals, considering the enormous power and patronage of railroads, the sums they lavish on legislation and the lobbying and log-rolling to which so many of them resort in buying or bullying their schemes to success.

But, vast as is the subsidy question, the question of railway consolidations is, in Mr. Adams's view, still more important. And this, too, connects itself with the Pacific Railway problem, because every prominent road in the East, we are told, has been hard at work securing, through consolidation, perpetual leases, or close contracts, a connection with the single trunk road. . . .

All that can well be said, however, on this subject, as on that of subsidies, is that, knowing well the tendency, and surely forecasting the result, we must throw the weight of public opinion against the efforts to combine and consolidate. . . . We have sometimes heard the possibility discussed of carrying consolidation to the extent of making one railway corporation control all the rest. In that case it is clear that a single powerful man could have at command a treasury representing two billions of money and apportioning their means of livelihood to half a million of men. It is no chimera which Mr. Adams creates—it is rather the tracing of actually working causes to their probable effects. What counteracting causes will in their turn be set at work remains to be seen.

Anonymous Writer: "The Crédit Mobilier Frauds"

Cincinnati Commercial, reprinted in *New York Sun,* September 23, 1872

The good Mr. Blaine
Came up out of Maine
As poor as the proverb's church mouse is,
But when he returned
His pockets all burned
With riches in gold and in houses.

How came Mr. Blaine,
So poor down in Maine,

In Congress to fatten so quickly?
Why, Mr. Oakes Ames
Had a long list of names
With shares written down to them thickly.

And poor Mr. Blaine,
Well knowing that Maine
Could seldom her church mice enrichen,
Made a trade of his wares
For some sheaves of those shares,
And fed on the Oakes like a lichen.

E.L. Godkin: "The Republican Party and the Credit Mobilier Scandal"

This powerful editorial not only condemns the House of Representatives for not doing enough to sanction the bribe takers but also blames this reticence on a corrupt and aging Republican Party.

The Nation, January 30, 1873

The House of Representatives has dealt with the Credit Mobilier affair very much as might have been expected. As we ventured to predict some weeks ago, it has refused to expel anybody; but it has censured Messrs. Brooks and Ames, which we did not think it would do—not because we did not believe those gentlemen deserve censure, but because we thought censure simply too ridiculous a penalty even for the House to inflict. Why the penalty is ridiculous of course hardly need explanation. If Oakes Ames, in his dealings with the members in Credit Mobilier stock, did not mean to exert a corrupt influence on them, his transactions are no more matter for comment by Congress than his dealings with his customers at Easton. If he did mean to exert a corrupt or corrupting influence on them, of course he has been guilty of the gravest offence which a member of Congress, *qua* member, could commit. Censuring him, therefore, is very like finding a man guilty of willful murder, and then reminding him, by way of punishment, that his conduct has been culpable, and that he must be more careful in future. The same thing may be said, with still greater force, of Mr. Brooks's case.

There were scenes and incidents in the debate, too, which illustrated most powerfully the depth of the prevailing demoralization, and which explained pretty clearly how it is that the investigation has ended in nothing. Every step in the proceedings revealed clearly that widespread reluctance to punish anybody, or to apply to the vices of anybody in particular the disapprobation which we, in our books and sermons, inflict on vice in the abstract. . . . The whole debate reminded one of the efforts of a herd of sheep to find an opening in a fence through which they might escape a barking dog—the same scurrying to and fro, and the same frantic eagerness in front of all attractive-looking holes. . . . Honest men hang their heads in the presence of a rascal. They try him with great reluctance, pass sentence on him with sobs and groans, and then beg of him for God's sake to run away and leave them to their business. . . .

What effect [does] all this have on the Republican party? This is the question which everybody is naturally asking, because, whatever Congress may say or do, everybody who does not despair of the country believes that out of doors the sentiment about the Credit Mobilier affair is very different from that which seems to prevail in the House. . . .

We, on the other hand, maintain, and with increased confidence, that the shameful corruption in the Government which is showing itself side by side with overwhelming Republican majorities all over the country, is a fresh proof that the Republican party is a common human organization, for the ordinary political purposes—namely, the embodiment in legislation of a small cluster of ideas . . . and has for several years been kept in office by the popular dread of "reaction" and the force of the great patronage and enormous handling of money resulting from the war; and that in the absence of any great controlling ideas, or real work, and of a powerful and respectable opposition, its leading men, who, for all practical purposes, are the party and represent it, have grown careless, and insolent, and indifferent to public opinion, and finally corrupt. There is nothing ecclesiastical about them or it. It has no divine mission, and they have no personal consecration. It is simply the consensus of a large body of American people on a few points of home policy, and *they* are a number of not very remarkable gentlemen, whom the American people has put in charge of its affairs.

Louis Jennings: "Congressional Morals"

The New York Times *believed that the House committee that investigated the Crédit Mobilier scandal did not do its duty by the American people and should have handed down much harsher penalties or sanctions against everyone involved.*

New York Times, February 20, 1873

Was it right for Congressmen to share in the profits of this scheme? This is a question which cannot be avoided, and which the House of Representatives must answer if it hopes to retain the respect of the public.

The Poland committee does not meet it at all satisfactorily. It says that there is no evidence that the Congressmen knew of the nature of the stock. This is begging the question. Congressmen ought to have known of the nature of the stock before investing in it. It was their business to inform themselves, and they could very easily have done so. The character of the Credit Mobilier was no secret. The source of its profits was very well known at the time Congressmen bought it. Though Oakes Ames may have succeeded in concealing his own motive, which was to bribe Congressmen, their acceptance of the stock was not on the account innocent. The dishonor of the act, as a participation in an obvious fraud, still remains.

Moreover, the account is not settled, even if it is assumed that the members who took the stock knew neither its character nor Oakes Ames' bad motive in offering it. Some of them have indulged in testimony with reference to the matter which is contradicted. The committee errs gravely in not probing such cases to the core. It distinctly rejects the testimony of several of the members. This can only be done on the ground that it is untrue. But untrue testimony given under oath is morally, if not legally, perjury. The committee finds members guilty of this offense, but does not see its way clear to recommend any punishment for it. Either the committee is mistaken as to its facts, or it falls far short in its recommendations.

It is the plain duty of Congress to visit with punishment all who took Credit Mobilier stock from Oakes Ames. Ames himself is justly recommended for extreme treatment because he acknowledges an intent to bribe. A similar treatment of Mr. Brooks is required, by the fact that he was a Government Director, and was intimately acquainted with the character of the scheme. For the rest a resolution of severe censure is the least they deserve, and this is demanded, not only as the act of justice, but in order that a definite standard may be established for the future. . . .

SKEPTICAL OF THE CRÉDIT MOBILIER CHARGES

E.L. Godkin: No Title

E.L. Godkin was among those Republican editors who initially found it difficult to believe that the leaders of the Republican Party could be involved in accepting bribes. However, after more information was revealed and the hearings in the House of Representatives were completed five months later, Godkin chastised these "good men" for their indiscretions.

The Nation, September 26, 1872

We have refrained from noticing the scandal concerning the Credit Mobilier to which the *Sun* first gave currency, until all the parties to the controversy should have had a chance to speak for themselves. This is always a prudent course to take in dealing with the *Sun*'s charges, but especially so when, as in this case, the witness on whom it relies has not a reputation for entire trustworthiness. It was, too, a little difficult to believe, on the mere evidence of a pencilled memorandum of Col. M'Comb's—incorrectly reproduced, as it now appears, by the *Sun*'s reporter—that the very cream of the Republican party, including Speaker Colfax, Mr. Blaine, and Senator Wilson, have been bribed by Mr. Oakes Ames into lending their support to the schemes of the Union Pacific Railroad Company. Mr. Boutwell, moreover—nor was he the only one of those implicated—had on several occasions notoriously opposed the company both in Congress and as Secretary of the Treasury. There were other inconsistencies and improbabilities which would have been sufficient to justify the Congressmen named in taking no notice of the accusation, except that Mr. Ames's letters fairly warranted the inference that he contemplated using the stock of the Credit Mobilier in the manner alleged. . . . Mr. Blaine was the first to give a flat denial to the charge against himself, and he has been followed by Messrs, Dawes, Wilson, Colfax, and Garfield with equal explicitness. Mr. Ames, on his part, has publicly assured his constituents that he "never gave a share of stock of that or any other company, directly or indirectly, to any member of Congress," and that he, as well as all the executive officers of the Credit Mobilier and several of its largest stockholders, had already answered to the same effect under oath, in the suit which M'Comb is now engaged in prosecuting against them in Pennsylvania. He does not, however, deny the authenticity of the letters attributed to him, as, we suppose, he cannot; and he does not, as he might easily have done, and as, we must say, he ought to do, explain away the appearance in them of a readiness to procure legislation corruptly.

Parke Godwin: "The Swarming of Falsehoods"

The New York Evening Post *was another Republican newspaper that initially believed the scandal was deliberately advertised before the election to hurt the Republican Party. However, after the Poland Committee began its investigations in January 1873, Godwin changed his mind. When the report was issued, he criticized it for its leniency.*

New York Evening Post, September 15, 1872

The Times published the other day a long list of atrocious lies that had been invented and circulated during the present canvass, in order to injure the President or his immediate friends. . . .

As another instance of the shameless recklessness of the Press, in its assaults upon reputation, take the story of Oakes Ames' scheme for the bribery of certain members of Congress, to which we alluded yesterday. In a suit at law, now pending in Pennsylvania, one McComb produces a letter purporting to be written by Mr. Oakes Ames, in which he proposes to distribute a large number of the shares of stock in the Credit Mobilier among members of Congress "where they will produce the most good." Accompanying this letter is a memorandum, indorsed by Mr. Ames, containing the names of those whom he is going to bribe, with the number of shares attached to each. . . .

Now, who are the men who are said to have been purchased in this way? Obscure, insignificant, doubtful characters? Not at all: but the foremost men of Congress and of the nation. Judge Bingham, Gen. Garfield, Speaker Blaine, Mr. Dawes, Mr. Boutwell, Mr. Wilson, Mr. Colfax, &c., have been before the public for many years; their integrity as men has never been questioned by anybody that knew them; if they are scoundrels, then there are no honest men any more. . . . Yet there are journals which do not scruple to publish, day by day, charges against such men that are preposterous on their face, wholly unsupported by any evidence beyond the merest conjecture, and which, if true, would consign them to the lowest depths of obloquy, and disgrace the whole country in the person of its most distinguished representatives.

Some of the gentlemen maligned have not thought it beneath their dignity to give a formal contradiction to these infamous libels. Mr. Ames himself, in an address to his constituents, yesterday, showed that these charges had years ago been met and answered, and that they were not only absolutely false, but preposterous. Mr. Blaine, Mr. Dawes, Mr. Wilson and Gen. Garfield pronounce them to be without the shadow of a foundation: but, for our part, we think they are only properly treated with scorn. The very denial of them give occasion simply for fresh devices of scurrility and insult. How, for example, could a mercenary charge be impugned in more comprehensive, pertinent and satisfactory words than those of Mr. Dawes, that "neither Oakes Ames, nor any other man, dead or alive, ever gave me, directly or indirectly, a penny of the stock of the 'Credit Mobilier,' or of any other corporation in this world. I never owned a dollar of any stock or any

property of any kind that I did not pay the full value of, with my own
money, earned with my own labor." And yet the retailers of calumny cry, "It
will not do; it is evasive; it is disingenuous;" and go on repeating their lies
without end.

George W. Curtis: "Mud as an Argument"

The following articles from Harper's Weekly *show just how intransigent
George W. Curtis was regarding the scandals. He saw the charges as an attempt to undermine President Grant's bid for a second term as well as another example of the "licentiousness of the press."*

Harper's Weekly, **October 5, 1872**

We speak elsewhere of the slander of this campaign. There is a storm of
the most reckless falsehood, incessantly repeated after the most constant
exposure. But the spirit in which they are told is one that does not care for
the truth. Aiming to wound, it is indifferent to every thing else. Nothing illustrates this spirit better than the story about the Crédit Mobilier which
was leveled at the Republican candidate for the Vice President and some of
the most eminent Republicans in Congress. They were charged with having received money, directly or indirectly to favor certain legislation. The
charge needed no answer. Their characters were their sufficient defense.
But they nevertheless made a formal, explicit denial. The Greeley papers
thereupon told them that it was not enough. They must prove that they told
the truth. They were evading. In fine, they were guilty, and they need not
try to deny it. Nothing could be baser, nothing more degrading than such
journalism. . . .

It is this reckless licentiousness of the press which is one of the most
powerful foes of political morality in this country. Men may be very able and
very patriotic and very willing to serve the state upon fair conditions. They
may be perfectly willing to encounter opposition to their opinions and arguments and policies. But few men care to expose themselves to the most
malignant and ingenious falsehood. . . . Moreover, the press injures itself by
such conduct, like all falsifiers. It teaches the readers to disbelieve it. The
perilous truth which ought to be known about men and affairs will not be
credited when told by a paper which has shown that it does not care for the
truth, but only for the plausibility of its statement. There are papers which
never correct an assertion which they have made. They call it good journalism. But that is precisely what it is not. . . .

George W. Curtis: "A Moral of the Crédit Mobilier"

Even after the investigation was completed, George W. Curtis never fully accepted that the congressmen charged knowingly accepted bribes in exchange for legislation.

Harper's Weekly, February 22, 1873

The investigation of the Crédit Mobilier is likely to have some unexpected collateral results. In speaking of the subject when the inquiry began we said, "If it shall finally appear that members owning stock voted favors to the company, then they must suffer in public estimation with the member who, being interested in any manufacturing industry, vote for its protection." The Crédit Mobilier investigation opens the whole question whether a member of Congress can honorably vote upon any question of favor to any enterprise in which he is pecuniarily interested. When the Tribune said that Mr. Blaine was "proved" to be guilty of fraud because, being a member of Congress, he had accepted stock in a company which Congress, with his assent, had subsidized, the accusation was totally untrue; but had it been true that he was an owner of the stock it would not have been a more flagrant offense than that which may now be correctly charged against hundreds of members of Congress from the beginning who are of the fairest reputation. We do not remember that the *Tribune* ever denounced those members as corrupt who, in voting for a high tariff, protected their own private interests. It rather considered them patriots, if we remember correctly, and supporters of a peculiarly "American system" and policy. . . .

The difficulty . . . is not that they consciously received a consideration for their votes, but that they received it unconsciously. . . . After the evidence before the Poland committee nobody seriously supposes that the Crédit Mobilier stock was accepted by members with an ill intent, whatever may have been the purpose of the distribution.

QUESTIONS

1. Why were more congressmen not censured for their part in the Crédit Mobilier scandal?
2. Why did some Republican newspapers believe that the Crédit Mobilier scandal was made up to embarrass President Grant?

3. What warnings did Charles Adams have regarding the subsidizing of railroads? Did the Crédit Mobilier scandal prove him right or wrong?
4. Why did some believe that a congressman could accept money but not know it was a bribe?
5. What role did federal subsidies play in the corruption surrounding railroad building? Would the railroad builders have been better off without federal money?

NOTES

1. Unless otherwise noted, the information for this introduction comes from David H. Bain, *Empire Express: Building the First Transcontinental Railroad* (New York: Penguin Books, 1999).

2. Charles Francis Adams, "Railroad Inflation," *North American Review* 110 (January 1869): 130–64, 148.

CHAPTER 26

The Trial of Susan B. Anthony, 1873

S usan B. Anthony, often referred to as the "mother of women's rights," was an active political figure during the Reconstruction period. Although she did not live to see the ratification of the Nineteenth Amendment giving women the vote, she along with her good friend Elizabeth Cady Stanton set the groundwork for woman suffrage.

Born into a Quaker family, Anthony was trained in hard work and education. Her parents believed in temperance and opposed slavery and taught their daughter benevolence and generosity, as well as independent thinking. As a young teacher, Anthony became involved in the local temperance organization, an activity that indoctrinated her into the ways of men's politics. She traveled the lecture circuit, presented petitions to the legislature, organized conventions, edited a newspaper, and lobbied Congress. She used these skills as well on behalf of the abolitionist movement, then for the woman suffrage movement.[1]

In 1872, Anthony hoped that the new Liberal Republican Party, which was created from a combination of Democrats and reform-minded Republicans, would take up the cause of women's rights. Horace Greeley, the Liberals' nominee for president, had supported women's rights, and although he did not go so far as supporting woman suffrage, he did admit, "When a sincere Republican is asked in sober earnest why we deny women suffrage, he must answer 'for no reason.' It must be acceded for it is the assertion of a natural right." Benjamin Gratz Brown, the new party's vice presidential candidate, also supported woman suffrage, as did other party leaders such as Theodore Tilton, the editor of the *Independent* and George W. Curtis, editor of *Harper's Weekly*. But when Anthony tried to convince the Liberal Republicans to include a platform in their campaign supporting the right of women to vote, they balked. Anthony then turned to the Republican Party.

Susan B. Anthony, *standing,* and **Elizabeth Cady Stanton,** *seated.*
Library of Congress.

With the help of Senator Henry Wilson of Massachusetts, Anthony wrote
a plank for the Republican convention in June 1872 that for the first time
recognized women in the official party platform. The Republican Party's
14th plank read, "The Republican party is mindful of its obligations to the
loyal women of America for their noble devotion to the cause of freedom.
Their admission to wider fields of usefulness is viewed with satisfaction,

and the honest demand of any class of citizens for additional rights should be treated with respectful consideration."[2]

Energized by this recognition for women's rights, Anthony began planning for Election Day by enlisting a group of 50 women in Rochester, New York, to register to vote. Several days before the election, Anthony and her three sisters entered a barbershop that had been set up as a voter registration office and demanded to be registered as voters. Her request was initially refused, but after a lengthy and loud debate among Anthony, the registrars, and their supervisor, the women were registered. In all, 14 women successfully registered that day in Rochester.[3]

On Election Day, Anthony and seven other women cast their ballots. That afternoon, Anthony wrote her good friend Elizabeth Cady Stanton: "Well I have been & gone & done it!!–positively voted the Republican ticket–strait this a.m. at 7 Oclock–& swore my vote in. . . . So we are in for a fine agitation in Rochester on the question."

For a few days everything seemed calm except for the editorials in the local Democratic newspaper calling for the immediate arrest of Anthony and the other women who voted. Finally, on November 14, a federal warrant was issued for Anthony's arrest. The charges were based on the 1870 Enforcement Acts, which made it a felony to willfully and knowingly cast a ballot "without having a lawful right to vote." If convicted, Anthony could pay a maximum penalty of $500 or spend three years in prison. Also arrested were the other 14 women voters and the election inspectors who had allowed them to cast their ballots.

At a preliminary hearing held before Christmas, Anthony was placed under arrest. She refused to pay bail and remained in jail. Finally, her lawyer paid the bail–much to Anthony's dismay. In January, Anthony was indicted for "knowingly, wrongfully, and unlawfully" voting "without having a lawful right to vote . . . the said Susan B. Anthony being then and there a person of the female sex." The trial was set for May 13, 1873.

The 52-year-old Anthony immediately set out on the lecture circuit, telling her story. Before the trial date she gave her speech "Is It a Crime for a Citizen of the United States to Vote?" at 29 different locations around Rochester. The prosecuting attorney complained that Anthony was attempting to prejudice potential jurors and persuaded the judge to grant a change of venue to another county. The motion was granted and the trial was rescheduled for June 17, 1873.

Meanwhile, troublesome news was coming from Washington. In April, the U.S. Supreme Court ruled in *The Slaughterhouse Cases* and *Bradwell v. Illinois* that states had legal jurisdiction over the civil rights of its citizens. If a state wanted to deprive women of rights held by men, it could. In *Bradwell*, the Court ruled that the state of Illinois was not required under the Fourteenth Amendment to admit a woman to the practice of law.

On the opening day of Anthony's trial, the courtroom was packed with spectators. The presiding judge was Ward Hunt, who had recently been appointed and sworn to the U.S. Supreme Court by President Grant.

Going into the trial, there seemed little hope that Anthony's attorney Henry Selden had much legal ground on which to base his arguments. He made the same arguments that Anthony herself had made regarding the Fourteenth Amendment's protection of the privileges and immunities of citizenship. But the U.S. Supreme Court had done such a thorough job of emasculating the amendment that the argument held little water. Finally, Selden pleaded that even if the amendment was not applicable, Anthony could not be prosecuted because she acted in the good faith belief that her vote was legal—she did not "knowingly, wrongfully or unlawfully" cast her ballot.

After the prosecuting attorney gave his summation, Judge Hunt pulled a piece of paper from under his robe and began reading his opinion, which he had prepared before the trial started. Hunt declared, "The Fourteenth Amendment gives no right to a woman to vote, and the voting by Miss Anthony was in violation of the law." The judge rejected the argument that Anthony did not knowingly cast an illegal vote. "Believing you have a right to vote is not the same thing as actually having such a right." Judge Hunt then directed the jury to return a verdict of guilty. But before issuing his sentence, the judge asked Anthony if she had anything to say on her behalf. Her reply—an eloquent plea for the political rights of women—was printed throughout the country and became an oft-quoted argument for woman suffrage.

Hunt set Anthony's fine at $100 plus court costs, which she refused to pay, hoping that she would be sent to jail, thus setting up a cause for appeal. But, Hunt refused to imprison Anthony, thus putting an end to the case. Anthony never paid the fine, and even though she petitioned Congress to remit the fine, that petition was never acted on.

Anthony described the trial as "the greatest judicial outrage history has ever recorded! We were convicted before we had a hearing and the trial was a mere farce."

Realizing that the courts were not the venue to promote woman suffrage, Anthony continued to write and lecture on the issue. She printed 3,000 copies of the trial proceedings, which she sent to congressmen, activists, newspapers, and libraries. Although men continued to reject the idea of woman suffrage, some believed the trial made Anthony a "martyr for the cause" and increased sympathy not only for her but also for the issue.

In 1878, Anthony succeeded in having a proposed constitutional amendment introduced in Congress. Although it failed, the same proposal would be introduced each year for the next 41 years. Anthony last appeared before the Senate's Select Committee on Woman's Suffrage in 1902. Anthony died in 1906. In 1920, 100 years after Anthony's birth, the Nineteenth Amendment to the United States Constitution, extending the vote to women, was ratified.

The first set of reading rejecting Anthony's right to vote begins with an editorial by E.L. Godkin from *The Nation*. Godkin relied on the Supreme Court's narrow interpretation of the Fourteenth Amendment to argue that Anthony had no legal ground to stand on, and the only hope for woman suffrage was an appeal to the public. The second entry, by George Jones, similarly argues that the Fourteenth Amendment does not support women's right to vote and it was not appropriate to trifle with the amendment's interpretation to arrive at a result contrary to its original intent. The last selection is a strong endorsement of the right of women to vote, but the writer believes the argument must be grounded in something other than the Fourteenth Amendment.

The section supporting Anthony's cause begins with a letter from Anthony's close friend Elizabeth Cady Stanton, who argues that while the Fourteenth Amendment may not speak directly to woman suffrage, the courts certainly have the power and the wisdom to interpret the amendment to be more inclusive. The second reading, by Parke Godwin, supports the Fourteenth Amendment argument and believes that women should be given the vote. The final selection is an oration to liberty, calling on the world to recognize the equality of all peoples.

REJECTING ANTHONY'S CAUSE

E.L. Godkin: No Title

E.L. Godkin was no great supporter of women's rights. In this editorial, he makes it clear that women should not try to find a safe harbor for themselves in the Fourteenth Amendment.

The Nation, June 26, 1873

Miss Susan B. Anthony has been tried in the United States Circuit Court at Canandaigua for violating the law in voting at the last Congressional election in the twenty-fifth district. She was defended by Judge Selden, who offered himself as a witness, and testified that she had consulted him as to her right to vote before doing so, and he had advised her "that she was as much a voter as he or any man." He made three points in his argument: that Miss Anthony was legally entitled to vote; that if she believed she was and voted in that belief, she was not guilty of a criminal offence; that she did believe it, and voted in good faith. Judge Hunt disposed of all this under the rulings in the Bradwell case. The right of voting is a right created by the State, and not by the Federal Constitution. The Fourteenth Amendment does not touch it, except to prohibit the denial of it on certain grounds, of which sex is not one, and the constitution of this State disqualifies women for voting. He also ruled, as might have been expected, that ignorance is no excuse for violating the law, and, as there was no dispute about the facts, directed a verdict of guilty, and sentenced Miss Anthony to a fine of $100, but, unfeeling man that he is, refused to commit her till she paid it. So she is left out in the cold, instead of enjoying martyrdom in jail. The opinion that the Fourteenth Amendment gave women the right to vote was originally propounded by Victoria C. Woodhull, though no credit for it has been given to that eminent jurist in any of the recent arguments. It must be clear to the friends of woman's suffrage now that there is nothing in it, that they had better give up reliance on quirks and technicalities, and devote themselves to working on public opinion. The change they seek is too momentous for them to hope that, even if made, it could long stand, if it were wrought by anything short of deliberate popular consent.

George Jones: "The Case of Miss Anthony"

The editor of the New York Times *sets out the various pitfalls of judicial lawmaking in Susan B. Anthony's case.*

New York Times, **June 25, 1873**

It is difficult to see how the most sincere friends of the "Cause" of women's voting can dissent from the logic, or seriously regret the decision, of Judge Hunt in the case of Miss Anthony. It must be remembered that the case does not involve, in the least degree, the merits of the question, Ought women to possess the right of suffrage? It does not relate to the end, but to the means. Any one who is entirely convinced that it is for the highest interest of the community that women should vote, and who also believes the concession of suffrage to women to be demanded by justice, might hesitate a long while before believing that the right should be claimed under the Fourteenth Amendment. Nothing can be more certain than that at no stage of its history was the Fourteenth Amendment intended to confer the right of suffrage upon women. The Congress which proposed the amendment expected no such effect from their proposition. No single one of the thirty State Legislatures which ratified the amendment intended any such result from their action.... Nor do we suppose that Miss Anthony herself would deny that if any such proposition had come before Congress, or before any one of the State Legislatures, or before the voters generally, in connection with the Fourteenth Amendment, it would have received little or no attention....

Miss Anthony believes, however, and has some very respectable legal counsel on her side, that the letter of the amendment does what its authors did not mean it should do, viz.: confer on her sex the right of suffrages.... The feature of our Government which gives it its greatest value is that the laws are in substantial harmony with public opinion. They are so because, if a very powerful public opinion can be created against them, they are changed, and they cannot be changed essentially in any other way. This fact gives them stability. The law is always reasonably certain, and, we may add, reasonably just. It is neither far above nor below the standard of most of those who are required to obey it, and it thus secures to them the greatest attainable security for their rights. But if it could once be demonstrated that the highest and most stable law of all, the Constitution ... could be altered in its most important regard by a slip of the pen, by ingenious construction of a verbal ambiguity, as the result of pure change, without any reference to public opinion, without any preparation of the public mind for the vast results involved—if this could be done, the value of the Constitution as an instrument of government would be instantly destroyed....

Of course women would suffer as much as men by such a wrench to our system of government. They would probably suffer vastly more, for if we were going back to the good old rule that "they shall get who have the power, and they shall keep who can," the women would hardly gain by the relapse. They ought really, therefore, even if they desire the suffrage, to be thankful that the courts are not likely to give it them on a quibble; that they will only get it, if at all, by the legitimate and recognized methods of changing the law.

Anonymous Writer: "Miss Anthony's Case"

The following editorial was written on the occasion of the publication of An Account of the Proceedings of the Trial of Susan B. Anthony, *a lengthy report of the trial and arguments plus diary entries and letters by Anthony. The editor of the Rochester paper, no matter how eloquent his plea*

*for universal rights, did not believe that Anthony could win on the Four-
teenth Amendment argument.*

Rochester (N. Y.) Democrat and Chronicle, April 23, 1874.

It must be conceded that Judge Selden makes a very strong argument,
as, indeed, does Miss Anthony in her addresses before the electors of this
and an adjoining county. Judge Selden's analysis of the term citizenship is
very exhaustive. He holds that the right to vote inheres in the citizen, and
fortifies his positions by the definitions of the lexicographers and the dicta,
if not the decisions, of the courts. If this be so, we cannot see how the conclusion is to be resisted that the fourteenth amendment includes in its
sweeping effect the prohibition of the states from making laws which shall
abridge the suffrage of any of their citizens. . . . The fourteenth amendment
to the constitution of the United States uses these express words: All persons born or naturalized in the United States, and subject to the jurisdiction
thereof are citizens of the United States and of the state wherein they reside.
If this does not include women, whom does it include?

Although not entirely convinced of the tenableness of the position taken
by Miss Anthony in asserting her right to vote under our present laws, we
are in full accord with the general movement in which she is engaged and in
which she has exhibited so much of courage and independence. . . . Woman
suffrage is only a question of time. It is coming for the republic, bringing
blessings in its train, so surely as the sun to-day illumines the earth. If the
law is against her it will be amended. If prejudices encompass her they will
vanish. If she is the victim of injustice she will rise superior to its thraldom.
Reason, equity and expediency are on her side; and, in the long run, they
will assert their power. . . .

One-half of the people of this nation to-day are utterly powerless to blot
from the statute books an unjust law, or to write there a new and a just one.
The women, dissatisfied as they are with this form of government, that en-
forces taxation without representation,—that compels them to obey laws to
which they have never given their consent,—that imprisons and hangs them
without a trial by a jury of their peers, that robs them, in marriage, of the
custody of their own persons, wages and children,—are . . . left wholly at the
mercy of the other half, in direct violation of the spirit and letter of the declarations of the framers of this government, every one of which was based
on the immutable principle of equal rights to all. . . . By the practice of those
declarations all class and caste distinction will be abolished; and slave, serf,
plebeian, wife, woman, all alike, bound from their subject position to the
proud platform of equality.

It was we, the people, not we, the white male citizens, nor yet we, the
male citizens; but we, the whole people, who formed this Union. And we

formed it, not to give the blessings of liberty, but to secure them; not to the half of ourselves and the half of our posterity, but to the whole people—women as well as men. And it is downright mockery to talk to women of their enjoyment of the blessings of liberty while they are denied the use of the only means of securing them provided by this democratic-republican government—the ballot.

SUPPORTING ANTHONY'S CAUSE

Elizabeth Cady Stanton: "The Fourteenth Amendment"

This is the answer of Elizabeth Cady Stanton, fellow suffragist, to a New York Times *editorial warning that no court would engage in the "subtle interpretation of a clause adopted for a wholly different purpose."*

New York Times, January 30, 1873

To the Editor of the New York Times . . .

Those who claim that women are "citizens" and already possessed of the right to vote, propose no further change in the Constitution. We think we have guarantees enough already to protect every citizen under Government.

We are not driven to the subtle interpretation of a clause, for the whole letter and spirit of the Constitution show that document to be our great charter of rights, made to secure the blessing of liberty to all the "citizens" of the Republic, and as it is the duty of the Supreme Court so to interpret its language, women are making earnest effort to have their claims adjudicated at this tribunal.

If women should be enfranchised by a judicial decision, it will not be the first time that justice has stood before us blind to caste and condition. Though England had held slaves for centuries, yet . . . by a judicial decision not only set the man free, but declared that no slave could breathe on the soil of Great Britain. . . . Thus you see, Mr. Editor, it is not a new thing we are asking of our sires and sons today; for the ablest judges have led the way. Neither is it an unimportant thing, for injustice to the humblest citizen involves the liberty of all. This is not simply a question of women's enfranchisement, but it involves the settlement of Federal and State rights and powers, constitutional law, and republican institutions.

Respectfully yours,

Elizabeth Cady Stanton

Parke Godwin: "A Change in the Woman Suffrage Question"

The editor of the New York Evening Post *was no particular friend of woman suffrage, but if the court were to rule in Susan B. Anthony's favor, he saw no reason to stand in the way of progress. After the case against Anthony was handed down the next day, the newspaper barely noted the judge's negative decision.*

New York Evening Post, June 15, 1873

The proceedings of the Circuit Court of the United States at Canandaigua, yesterday, before which Miss Susan B. Anthony was on trial for voting in Rochester at the late general election, were very remarkable. Hitherto the advocates of the right of our country-women to vote have hardly obtained a hearing but Miss Anthony has made an important step in advance. It is a great gain to obtain a judicial hearing for her cause—to have the merits of woman suffrage carefully considered by candid and able men. The appearance of so eminent and distinguished a lawyer as Henry R. Selden in her defence will give to the question a new aspect in the minds of many people. The position he took on the subject is still more encouraging to those who think that women have a legal right to vote. The distinction he made between the absoluteness of this right and the belief of Miss Anthony that she possessed such a right, since the distinction relates only to the legal guilt in this particular instance, is of no general importance; but his emphatic testimony, irrespective of the present case, that all women have both an absolute and a legal right to vote, is a fact to command attention.

So convinced was Judge Selden of the validity of this opinion that, for the second time in his professional life, as he himself said, he was compelled to offer himself as a witness in behalf of his client. . . .

It seems likely that the decision of the Court will be in Miss Anthony's favor. If such be the result, the advocates of woman suffrage will change places with the public. They will no longer be forced to obtain hearings from congressional and legislative committees for their claims, but will exercise their right by the authority of a legal precedent against which positive laws forbidding them from voting will be the only remedy. It is a question whether such laws can be passed in this country. A careful examination of the subject must precede any such legislation, and the inference from the result of Judge Selden's investigation is that the more the subject is studied the less likely will any legislative body be to forbid those women who want to vote from so doing.

Letter to the Editor: "Woman as a Citizen"

The case of Susan B. Anthony has given this writer an opportunity to express the great hope that, even if Anthony loses her case, a day may eventually come when all people of the nation are indeed equal before the law.

Boston Woman's Journal, January 25, 1873

An important question is likely soon to be settled by the approaching trial of Susan B. Anthony, for illegal voting at the last Presidential election. She claimed the right to vote by virtue of the Fourteenth and Fifteenth Amendments of the Constitution, and actually deposited her ballot, as did a dozen or more other women. For this act she has been arrested and found guilty, but the case is to go before a higher court for final settlement.

This is well; it is time we had an official interpretation of the laws, so that we may know whether or not Woman is a voting citizen. If she is not, as the law now stands, (and we expect to see the point taken decided against her) then all in favor of the movement can at once begin an agitation looking towards the modification of the laws, or the enactment of new ones, which shall give the women of America the same rights men now possess.

The world has not yet seen a real Republic, where all human beings stand on an equality before the law. The class in power has always quietly ignored whole races and sexes of human beings; has legislated, declaimed, prayed and fought, as if they were the saints of the earth to whom God had given special rights. The central idea of human society is one of caste, either resting upon race, color or sex. . . .

The quiet ignoring of human existence of whole races of human beings, and of the human rights of thousands who are conceded a human existence, has been going on all through the ages, and yet statesmen have planned, orators talked, and warriors campaigned for freedom. . . . Verily, if, as publicists and jurists have dreamed, society is intended to be an association of interests to protect the weak against the strong, then is society, as says Montesquieu, "a most magnificent failure," for it is, and has ever been in effect, a conspiracy of the strong against the weak.

Advancing civilization has, for the design of it, been nothing more than the perfecting of that machinery whose affair is to grind the faces of the poor. So long as human nature is essentially selfish, and essentially unenlightened, it is the impossibility of preventing the light of knowledge from permeating all ranks, not the benevolent purpose of the world's masters, that encourages the philanthropist to believe in progress, and reform to marshal its hosts. . . .

Fortunately, spite of our precaution, the great masses of the world, without distinction of race, color, condition or sex, are coming to know that they are all equally and inalienably men, entitled to, and claiming therefore—not as a concession or privilege, that may be granted or withholden—the rights, prerogatives and immunities, inherent in their common manhood and so, ushering in that glorious morn of the long-sung golden-age, when no narrow seas shall circumscribe the bounds of States, but when all shall be free men and citizens of the whole world.

FULLER-WALKER.

QUESTIONS

1. What were the main arguments against using the Fourteenth Amendment to support Anthony's cause?
2. What were the main arguments for using the Fourteenth Amendment to support woman suffrage?
3. How much did men's objections to woman suffrage have to do with the outcome of Anthony's case?
4. Did Anthony truly believe she had unknowingly violated the Enforcement Law?
5. Had Anthony won her case, what effect might that have had on the suffrage movement for the remainder of the nineteenth century?

NOTES

1. Elizabeth Cady Stanton, Susan B. Anthony, Matilda Joslyn Gage, and Ida Husted Harper, eds., *History of Woman Suffrage*, 2 (1881–1922; reprint, New York: Arno Press, 1969), 811.

2. *Boston Woman's Journal*, 6 July 1872, 1.

3. The information about Susan B. Anthony's trial comes from Susan B. Anthony, *An Account of the Proceedings on the Trial of Susan B. Anthony, on the Charge of Illegal Voting, at the Presidential Election in Nov., 1872* (Rochester, N.Y.: n.p., 1874), and Ida Husted Harper, *The Life and Work of Susan B. Anthony: Including Public Addresses, Her Own Letters and many from her Contemporaries during Fifty Years.* 3 vols. (Indianapolis and Kansas City: Bowen-Merrill, 1898–1908).

CHAPTER 27

The Civil Rights Act of 1875

Through the Fourteenth and Fifteenth Amendments and the Reconstruction Acts of 1867, a Republican Congress sought to provide emancipated blacks the basic rights of citizenship. They were guaranteed fair trials, the right to vote, the right to own land, the right to hold office, and the right to basic civil liberties. The next step, according to the "Father of Reconstruction" Massachusetts senator Charles Sumner, was social equality. In 1870 and every year thereafter until his death in 1874, Sumner introduced an amendment to the Civil Rights Act of 1866 that guaranteed all citizens equal access to public accommodations, transportation, public schools, churches, cemeteries, and jury service.

Sumner died in March 1874, and two months later the Senate passed his Civil Rights Bill, not because the Senators believed it would ever pass the House but as a tribute to the bill's author. Over the next nine months, the bill would be emasculated in the House by amendment after amendment. Democrats and conservative Republicans wanted to guarantee access on the basis of "separate but equal," others wanted to completely remove the sections about schools and cemeteries, and still others simply argued that the bill was unconstitutional.

When the Forty-Third Congress assembled for its final session in December 1874, the bill appeared to be dead in the House. However, the violence that had occurred during the fall campaign season breathed new life into the bill. Massachusetts congressman Benjamin Butler, who had kept the movement going after Sumner's death, revived the bill and put it at the top of Congress's agenda. Whether the Civil Rights Bill was a last ditch effort to secure black Republican votes after major Republican defeats in the South or one "last noble expression of Republicanism," Butler felt that the bill was the most important item on Congress's agenda.[1]

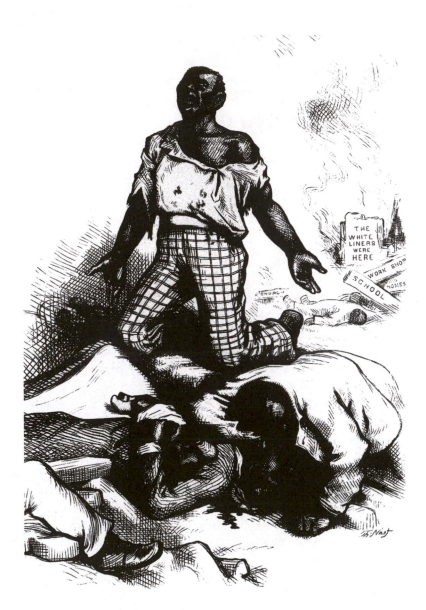

"Is This a Republican Form of Government? Is This Protecting Life, Liberty and Property? Is This the Equal Protection of the Laws?" *Thomas Nast illustration of a black man standing over the bodies of a murdered black family. In the background is another dead body against tumbled stones representing schools, workshops, and homes, and a larger monument declaring, "The White Liners Were Here." White Liners were a white supremacist group of vigilantes.* Harper's Weekly. *Library of Congress.*

However, with only 56 days left in the session, Butler had to move quickly if the bill was going to make it through the congressional gauntlet. Republicans refused to accept a bill that guaranteed separate but equal facilities; Democrats refused to accept a bill with integrated schools and cemeteries. A compromise was reached that guaranteed equal facilities but separate schools and that reduced the penalty for noncompliance from $5,000 to $500.

But it did not appear that a compromise bill would ever be voted on. Democrats used every parliamentary tactic they could think of to stall progress of the bill until the session was over. Every time the Democrats called for another roll-call vote or made another motion, Republican resolve was strengthened. Finally, Republicans practiced some dirty tricks of their own and kept the House in full session without recess for two days—filibustering with speeches, 75 roll calls on procedural points, and meaningless motions. But at the end of two days and two nights, the Republicans were the first to give up. Finally, the Democrats and Republicans reached a compromise, and the final House bill deleted all references to schools and cemeteries. While many Republicans believed that the removal of the schools section cut out the very heart of the bill, they were willing to take what they could get.

The bill, which had only a slight resemblance to the original bill passed a year earlier by the Senate, was sent back to the Senate, where it was expected to meet similar Democratic resistance. However, the Democrats in the Senate seemed to care little if the bill was passed, since they believed it was meaningless and would eventually be declared unconstitutional. Only two years earlier in the *Slaughterhouse Cases*,[2] the U.S. Supreme Court had taken a great deal of the wind out of the Fourteenth Amendment by separating national citizenship from state citizenship and declaring that most of the rights of citizenship that Americans desired and used on a daily basis— fair state trial, freedom of speech, right to sit on state juries, right to vote in state elections, right to hold state office, and protection from unreasonable searches by state authorities—were under the control of state law. Consequently, few believed that this new bill would survive legal scrutiny.

The Civil Rights Act of 1875, the most progressive of all Reconstruction era laws but also the most meaningless, was signed into law by President Ulysses S. Grant on March 8, 1875, without any comment from the president. It also received relatively little comment in the press. Many simply believed that it was "dead on arrival."

In 1883, in a series of five cases known as the *Civil Rights Cases*, the Supreme Court struck down the law.[3] The cases involved black citizens who were denied access to public accommodations and facilities. In an 8 to 1 decision, the Court held that the Fourteenth Amendment only prohibited state abridgement of civil rights and not abridgement by individuals. And in the infamous *Plessy v. Ferguson* case in 1896, the Court endorsed the "separate but equal" doctrine that kept enforced segregation alive for another 70 years.[4]

The *Civil Rights Cases* and the *Plessy* decision ushered in a new era in Southern racism—official segregation through Jim Crow laws. Unlike the earlier black codes that controlled the economic lives of blacks, Jim Crow laws were primarily to keep whites and blacks separated. States and cities passed laws establishing separate school systems, accommodations, and transportation—a U.S. system of apartheid that did not begin to die out until the 1960s.

The section containing editorials against the Civil Rights Act begins with one by Charles de Young from the *San Francisco Chronicle*, which declares that the animosity between blacks and whites is a fact and cannot be healed by forcing reforms such as common schools. The second entry, by E.L. Godkin, argues that not only is the South not ready for social equality but the law itself is unconstitutional since only the states, not the federal government, can create and enforce equality. The next selection is from a Southern newspaper, which uses racism and sarcasm to make the point that the Civil Rights Act will give blacks advantages not enjoyed by whites. The last reading in this section, by George Jones, argues that the Civil Rights Act will do great damage to the Republican Party, because it will make it impossible to attract any Southerners to the party—something that was needed for the party's survival.

The entries favoring the Civil Rights Act adhere to strong Republican principles that backed Reconstruction, namely the philosophy that all men should be equal in a democracy. The first two selections, by George W. Curtis from *Harper's Weekly*, support the notion of equality before the law. The first editorial notes that the law will benefit everyone in the country, including Jews, Irish, Catholics, and others who were the victims of discrimination. The second entry argues that by leaving out the issue of common schools, Congress pandered to the very notions of inequality that the law was supposed to combat. The last selection, by Charles de Young, accuses whites of being vulgar, narrow minded, and mean spirited when they will not even allow places of entertainment to be open to all.

Opposing the Civil Rights Act

Charles de Young: "Colored Children in the Schools"

During the Reconstruction years, many of the civil and social rights that radicals such as Charles Sumner wanted for the nation's blacks were tested in Washington, D.C. Washington enfranchised blacks in January 1867 and desegregated its schools in 1869. The issue of common or separate schools was a major issue in the debates over the Civil Rights Bill, and Washington's struggle to maintain common schools was often used by Democrats to demonstrate that integration did not work.

San Francisco Chronicle, **January 6, 1870**

Though we have no sympathy with the prejudices and antipathies that are based upon differences of race and color, we have quite as little with the fanatical spirit of humanitarianism that ignores those prejudices as existing facts and seeks to crush them violently by means of legislation, before they have been outgrown by the education of the popular conscience. Nature herself has made certain marked distinctions between the various races of mankind. She has placed an unmistakable and indelible imprint upon the so-called inferior races. The antipathy between the white man and the black man, however unreasonable it may be, is nevertheless a fixed fact, and as such must be recognized until it is outgrown. It seems to us that the radical reformers do not practically make sufficient allowance for this undeniable fact. Nothing is to be gained for the cause of progress by arbitrarily forcing reforms before the public are prepared to indorse them. . . . We can see no good reason for attempting to force the mixing of white and negro children in the common schools, in defiance of public sentiment. The colored children can be taught just as well, if gathered in schools of their own, as they can when thrust into the white schools. It is impossible to deny the existence or the strength of the prejudice, and it is equally impossible to deny that it is shared by a very large and respectable portion of our white citizens. Such being the case, we regard it as unwise and impolitic to attempt to crush it out arbitrarily. The people must be gradually educated into large and tolerant views on subjects like these, and the attempt to override and trample upon popular sentiment on such matters, however unintelligent it may be, is calculated to retard rather than to assist the march of liberal ideas.

E.L. Godkin: "The Civil-Rights Bill"

While many argued against the policy (social equality) of the Civil Rights Bill, E.L. Godkin and others argued that the bill was simply unconstitutional. Considerations of humanity aside, the Fourteenth Amendment did not authorize Congress to protect the civil rights of blacks within the states against anything but hostile state legislation. Many states were beginning to pass laws that segregated public facilities, and the argument was that it

made no sense to arrest citizens of a state under federal law for what was
permissible in a state.

The Nation, September 17, 1874

Towards the end of the last session of Congress, the Senate passed what was then usually spoken of as the Supplementary Civil-Rights Bill. It did not pass the House, although Mr. Sumner had, with great solemnity, on his death-bed bequeathed it as a sort of legislative legacy. . . . Its passage by the Senate did not at the time attract much attention at the North, except from the regular Republican newspapers, which seemed to regard it with a languid and perfunctory interest very different from the enthusiasm which had greeted the passage of the first Civil-Rights Bill. At the South, however, its fate has been very different. . . . Everybody in the South, Republican and Democrat alike, knows that the white children will not go to school with the black children, or be forced to do so by their parents and guardians, no matter what the latest civil-rights bill may be, and that the attempt to enforce a provision for mixed schools would only result in breaking up the whole school system. What is more than this, there is no evidence that the blacks themselves are particularly ambitious of social equality, or want either mixed schools or mixed hotels or cemeteries.

The Republicans in the Southern States, therefore, have found themselves in a very awkward predicament. They wish to conciliate the blacks, and it will not do for them to desert the party. At the same time, the last thing in the world that they want is to threaten the native white Southerners. The Conservatives of course denounce the attempt to pass . . . a measure subversive of the whole social order at the South, and the Republicans find it very difficult to make any reply which will not either involve them in the support of an odious bill, or make them seem to turn their backs on their party. . . .

Since the discussion . . . began, it is a singular fact that the constitutional power of Congress to pass any such bill as the Supplementary Civil-Rights Bill has hardly been questioned at all. It was discussed of course in Congress; but, since Congress adjourned, public discussion has been almost exclusively confined to the policy of the bill. . . . Yet there can be little doubt, if it were not for the fatal habit we have fallen into since the war of regarding the central Government practically above the law and the Constitution whenever the negro is concerned, that the mere suggestion of the constitutional points involved ought to have killed the bill for ever. It is plainly unconstitutional. . . .

The bill was passed in the Senate, it is to be presumed, under the impression that the power to pass it is somewhere given or implied in the Constitution, and the only clauses that have been cited in support of such a power are from the Fourteenth and Fifteenth amendments. The Fifteenth Amendment relates entirely to the right to vote, but the Fourteenth Amendment contains this clause (sec. 1) "No State shall make or enforce any law which shall abridge the privileges or immunities of citizens of the United States, nor shall any State deprive any person of life, liberty, or property without due process of law, nor deny to any person within its jurisdiction the equal protection of the laws." This is all there is. . . .

The first thing that strikes the mind with regard to the new Civil-Rights Bill, on comparing it with the Fourteenth Amendment, that one contains a series of provisions and prohibitions directed to *persons,* while the other contains simply prohibitions against action on the part of the *States.* The Civil-Rights Bill, stripped of its technical phraseology, amounts to this—that if any white man shall turn a negro out of a hotel, or school, or car because of his color, he can be sued and prosecuted criminally in a United States court by the negro. . . .

The Fourteenth Amendment has twice come before the Supreme Court at Washington, and on neither of these well-known occasions was the decision of the court of such a character as to lend much encouragement to those who believe the new Amendment to have introduced very revolutionary principles as to the relations of the States to the General Government. . . . In the light of those decisions, it may safely be inferred that the Supreme Court must look with extreme suspicion upon a law upsetting the domestic law of States on the subject of schools, of common carriers, of innkeepers, and substituting for them the new and strange system invented by the authors of this bill. In the interest of the negro, we trust that it may never reach the court. Deeply as we sympathize with his wrongs, we have no expectation or hope of seeing them righted by hounding on his old masters to acts of violence and lawlessness by the passage of equally violent and lawless acts of Congress. The Reconstruction period is ended, and the negro in future will occupy such a position as his industry and sobriety entitle him to. Such bills as the one we have been considering do nothing for him but turn his friends into enemies.

Anonymous Writer: No Title

This editorial is typical of the emotional and racist expressions found in Southern newspapers regarding the Civil Rights Bill.

Richmond (Ky.) Register, quoted in New York Independent, September 17, 1874

The graveyards you have selected, beautified, and adorned as a resting-place of those you have loved must be desecrated to satisfy the spite of those liberty lovers, and choice places given to the negro, even if it should require the exhuming of friends long buried. You must divide your pew in church, even if your wife and child are forced to sit on the floor, and no complaint must be made should Sambo besmear the carpet you have placed there with the juice of tobacco. Your children at school must sit on the back seats and in the cold, whilst the negro's children sit near the stove and on the front seats, and enjoy in every instance the money you toil for, whilst Sambo is sleeping and stealing. Or, as the darky explained to his less posted brother: "We's gwine to ride free on de railroads, smoke in de ladies' car, and put our feet on the percushions of the seats whenever we damn please. We's gwine to be al-lowed to stop at de hotels, and set at de head of de table, and habe de biggest slice of de chickens, and lay around in de parlors and spit on de carpets, and make de white trash hustled themselves and wait on us without grumblin'. We's gwine to be allowed to go to de white school and set upon the platform with de teacher. We's gwine to be buried in italic coffins on top of de white folks, and Gabriel shall call: 'All ob you colored gmmen rise furst.'"

George Jones: "The Civil Rights Bill"

This editorial sums up the dilemma of the Civil Rights Bill, believing that while it logically follows Republican policy, it could do more harm than good to the party.

New York Times, January 28, 1875

The House of Representatives has at last reached the point which has been anticipated from the opening of the session, where the tedious war over the Civil Rights bill is renewed. Yesterday Mr. Butler, from the Judi-ciary Committee, called up the substitute which the committee had re-ported for the Senate bill. . . .

The attitude of the Republican Party, as well as that of the Democratic Party, toward this measure is peculiar. Neither seems to us to be marked by very good sense. . . . We cannot perceive the necessity or the desirability of the passage of the bill. We do not believe that it is possible to administer its provisions effectively in any community where public opinion is strongly opposed to it, and we are convinced that any resolute attempt to enforce it would bring incalculable annoyance upon the class for whose benefit the bill is intended. It is, moreover, a bill of doubtful constitutionality. . . . We suppose that it will not be denied that the passage of the bill is regarded by many Republicans as a political necessity, and that it is pressed to some extent on that ground. It seems very clear to us that from the standpoint of party policy the measure is a mistake. The utmost it could do would be to preserve the adherence of the colored voters in something like the same degree that has hitherto been obtained. But that unanimity, especially if secured by such means, costs more than it comes to. It makes any considerable reinforcement of the Republican party from among the whites of the South a moral impossibility, and without such reinforcement the party is doomed to lose the Southern States which it already holds. The passage of the bill, therefore, can at best only retain strength, which will not prevent defeat, and cut off strength that is essential to victory.

If this act were necessary to secure and were likely to secure essential rights to the negroes, it would be the duty of the party to pass it at all hazards and at any cost, trusting results to the instructed conscience of the people; but, so far is this from being the case, it is an open question whether the bill will not do more harm than good to the negroes. It will certainly be of far less advantage to them than would be the existence of a strong, growing, healthy Southern Republican Party. . . .

On the other hand, however, the conduct of the Democrats is without the shadow of justification. It has no basis, so far as we can perceive, of principle or of intelligent policy. The Democratic leaders have made up their minds to block all public business in order to prevent the consideration of this bill. . . . If the bill is, as the Democrats assert, an unconstitutional one, let the majority pass it, and take the responsibility, especially as the bill itself provides that all cases under it shall be "reviewable by the Supreme Court," without regard to the amount involved. Unfortunately, however, the question has been merged in a bitter and obstinate struggle, which is likely to prejudice the larger interests of the country, without any advantage to either party.

FAVORING THE CIVIL RIGHTS ACT

George W. Curtis: "Mr. Sumner's Civil Rights Bill"

Senator Sumner introduced his Civil Rights Bill in every Congress beginning in 1870. George W. Curtis makes the point that the bill not only protects blacks but also protects Irish, Jews, and Catholics from discrimination. Harper's Weekly *was a steady supporter of the bill through its passage in 1875.*

Harper's Weekly, December 20, 1871

Mr. Sumner's supplementary Civil Rights bill receives the usual amount of smiles and wonder at its "fanaticism." But a man who has sat in the Senate of the United States for twenty years, and who, having seen Breckinridge in the chair, and having been smitten to the floor by the bullies of slavery, now sees Schuyler Colfax presiding, and in the chamber around him a vast majority of Republican Senators of a country in which war has abolished slavery, probably smiles compassionately at the contemptuous smiles of those who think principle fanaticism, and consistency impracticability. Mr. Sumner's bill contemplates the prohibition to all public institutions regulated by law in this country—such as hotels, railroad cars, etc.—of the recognition of distinctions which the law has abolished. Those who think that it is foolish to attempt to make people associate with those whom they dislike, and whose conclusive argument against emancipation and equal rights was, "How would you like your daughter to marry a nigger?" may, however, be comforted. They are not to be compelled to marry their daughters to any body, nor to invite distasteful guests to their tables. But those who hold certain grants under the law for the public benefit are not to be suffered to discriminate arbitrarily against a certain part of the public.

The keeper of a hotel, for instance, is bound to furnish entertainment to all orderly applicants, unless he has reason to suspect dishonest intention. He can not lawfully refuse a guest because of a whim against his blue eyes or his straight hair. He may, indeed, keep a temperance house, to which prohibitionists will naturally resort; or he may announce his preference of Baptists or Presbyterians as guests. But if a Methodist traveler applies in good faith for entertainment, the host can not turn him away because he is not a Baptist. Neither can he refuse a guest, because he is an Irishman or a German, because he is of a fair complexion or of a dark, if there be nothing suspicious in his appearance or conduct. But the Baptist and Presbyterian, the naturalized Irishman or the German, the man of fair or dark complexion, have no more rights under the law, as citizens, than the colored man.

Those who think that they have an antipathy to colored persons may be correct, but it is evidently not an antipathy which extends to the waiter who brings them their dinner. And there are many persons to whom the Irish citizen is not agreeable. And to the warm sectarian of any kind the Jew or the atheist is very repugnant. But we do not therefore permit them to be excluded from places of common public resort. If we did so, we should nullify our own laws and insult their spirit. Suppose that we had in all public places, in churches or in halls, a coop in a corner for the Portuguese or the West Indian foreigner who might stray to our shores? It would be a barbarous folly. And if it were the native citizen descended from Portugal or the West Indies, the folly would be only the more conspicuous. If it became a practice, so flagrant an outrage upon the equality of the citizen guaranteed by the fundamental law should be prohibited under penalties in the common interest. For the equality that we assert by law, the law must protect.

That is what Mr. Sumner's bill proposes. It forbids distinctions founded upon a system of caste which the law has abolished. It prohibits, within its sphere, making an American citizen a pariah because of his color. It aims to lift from the colored race as much as possible of the consequences of the curse which civilization has imposed upon it. If we meant to keep the people of that race an outcast class, we had no right to make them equal citizens. But having made them so, we can not keep them outcasts without infinite harm to ourselves. However, we need have no fear of appalling results. The colored citizens are not obtrusive. They are not disposed to go where they are not wanted. But what man of honor does not burn with indignation to see a polite and quiet colored passenger refused a place in a car or a steamboat from which a drunken and disgusting white traveler is not expelled? The fundamental principle of this republic is that every citizen shall be equal before the law. And whoever smiles at Mr. Sumner's bill smiles at the American principle.

George W. Curtis: "The Civil Rights Bill"

The most controversial section of the Civil Rights Bill guaranteed an integrated public school system. All mention of public education was dropped in the bill that was signed into law.

Harper's Weekly, March 20, 1875

The President has signed the Civil Rights Bill, and it is now a law. It is the bill which was reported to the House by the Judiciary Committee, and from which the school section was stricken out. As it stands, therefore, the bill recognizes and indirectly authorizes the very prejudice against which it is supposed to be directed. General Butler in supporting the Force Bill appealed to members to consider how they would feel when they heard the shriek of the widow and orphan fleeing from the Ku-Klux. And how does General Butler feel now that he has pandered to that very hatred of the Ku-Klux by authorizing it to recognize caste in the common school? If Congress is willing that colored children should be separated in the schools, why is it unwilling that colored parents should be separated in hotels and cars?

The principle of the bill is that in all public institutions, conveyances, and conveniences which exist in virtue of the law there shall be no discrimination on account of color. If the principle is correct—and of that there can be no question in a country where the Constitution expressly asserts the civil equality of all citizens—the inequality of application is absurd. If the equality fails to be enforced in the school, it is obstructed in the inn; and to say that half a loaf is better than no bread, upon the theory that the prejudice is stronger in the school than in the inn, is again absurd, because precisely the same arguments were urged against the emasculated bill as against its original form; and as it was said that equality in the schools would destroy the school system, so it is said that equality in the hotels will ruin them. The plea is as valid in one case as the other, and, as we believe, baseless in both. But if not baseless, if the enforcement of equality before the law of all citizens of the United States be fatal to the public school system in a large part of the country, the system which is one of the chief securities of free government, what shall be said of the policy that asserted and asserts that equality? General Butler and the Judiciary Committee, in striking the school section out of the bill, struck at the principle of the whole Republican policy of reconstruction. . . .

Charles de Young: "The Color Line"

The San Francisco Chronicle *began life as a staunch Democratic newspaper that decried anything and everything that smacked of liberalism. But by the mid-1870s, editor Charles de Young took a decided turn in his politics, becoming much more open. Compare this editorial with the one written seven years earlier, provided above.*

San Francisco Chronicle, **January 13, 1877**

At the Grand Opera House and at other theaters in San Francisco a rule is enforced excluding persons for the sole reason that they are colored. This rule results from a lingering prejudice growing out of the barbarism of slavery. It is an absurd prejudice, and is only entertained by the narrow-minded and ignorant. It is a curious fact that it is stronger among American people of Northern than of Southern birth, and of foreign nationalities the Irish is the one where it principally survives. . . . Hence, we say, that unless the vulgar and narrow-minded American or the prejudiced foreigner is superior in intelligence, pride, delicacy and social reserve to the more cultivated people of Europe, this feeling of opposition to the color of an individual is as absurd as it is baseless. It is absurd as tested by the course of events. It has abated almost everywhere in the North, and the prejudice has yielded to the laws of sense and decency here in our own city, except as to admission to theaters. So we suppose the inference is natural that the theater is the last and most impregnable fortress where illiberality and vulgar prejudice intrench themselves. The churches are open to the blacks, and we believe there is no religious sect in America whose teachings do not justify the colored person in hoping to enjoy with the whites the same heavenly paradise, or which does not allow the colored man or woman to taste from the same chalice the sacred wine at communion. In our street cars the presence of the colored man or woman is accepted, and we have never seen a shrug of discontent exhibited at the contact except by some individual of inferior manners, character and cleanliness. . . . The laws of our nation and the laws of our State give to the colored person equal recognition. The laws of God make them entitled to the same privileges. The rule of common sense and common decency should entitle them to equal accommodations at all places of public amusement, and the management which decides otherwise does it in obedience to a mean and narrow prejudice which the better sentiment of better people does not encourage or sustain.

QUESTIONS

1. Why did most Americans see the Civil Rights Act of 1875 as ill conceived?
2. What were the arguments for and against integrated public schools?
3. What were the arguments against the Civil Rights Act of 1875?

NOTES

1. William Gillette, *Retreat from Reconstruction, 1869–1879* (Baton Rouge: Louisiana State University Press, 1979), 261.

2. *Slaughterhouse Cases*, 83 U.S. 36 (1873).

3. *Civil Rights Cases*, 109 U.S. 3–26 (1883).

4. *Plessy v. Ferguson*, 163 U.S. 537 (1896).

CHAPTER 28

The Hamburg Massacre, 1876

Immediately after the Civil War, as provisional governments were installed in the South, governors filled the vacuum left by departing federal troops with state militia units. The militia units, acting as a state police force, were charged with enforcing laws and protecting persons and property. Militia units were typically formed at the local level by a former Confederate officer who recruited ex-rebel soldiers—still dressed in Confederate gray. Their targets were freedmen, and the laws they enforced were the old slave codes or black codes.[1]

These white militia that were loyal to conservative governors were disbanded when congressional Reconstruction was instituted in 1867, and federal troops were once again sent into the South. However, once a state reorganized, the job of policing the state and maintaining order fell back to the state. In 1869, Congress allowed states to create militia as long as they were composed of loyal men, that is, blacks or white Republicans. Consequently, the majority of militiamen were black.

The black militia, loyal to the Republican governments, was used during elections to protect the polls and also was called on to enforce martial law when violence escalated in various counties. At times, it also was called on to protect Republican governors and legislators whenever a disputed election resulted in violence. Wherever black soldiers appeared, however, their presence often did more to agitate the situation than to calm it, since white men did not like being ordered about by black soldiers. Resentment and hostility against the militia was encouraged by Southern newspapers, which spread stories—some true, some false—about outrages committed by the troops.

To counter the black militia, white paramilitary groups such as white rifle clubs, saber clubs, and artillery clubs were organized in almost every county in the Southern states, despite laws prohibiting any group, other than duly authorized militia, to organize, drill, or parade. Governor Daniel Chamberlain described their activities: "That they serve as the basis of political organization, and under the command and control of their officers engaged in political duties and work, is equally clear."[2] In many states, there was a running vendetta against black troops by the white rifle clubs, and clashes between black companies and armed whites were frequent and bloody.

In 1876, South Carolina was one of three remaining Southern states that still had federal troops posted to quell violence and oversee elections. One of those towns where racial tensions seethed was Hamburg, an impoverished and decaying town inhabited primarily by blacks. Before the war, Hamburg had been a thriving cotton port on the Savannah River, directly across from Augusta, Georgia. But when the railroads bypassed Hamburg in favor of Augusta, the town began to die out. The only activity of any note was the regular drills and parades by the "Doc Adams" Company of black militia.

On July 4, the black militia was going through its drills when two young white men—the sons of prominent white farmers—drove their buggy into town and ordered the militia to clear the way so they could pass. Since the road was wide enough for the buggy to go around the militia, Captain Doc Adams refused to move his troops. Heated words were exchanged between the white men until Adams finally relented and ordered his troops to step to the side so the buggy could pass.

The next day, General Matthew C. Butler, representing one of the white men, brought criminal charges against Captain Adams for blocking a public highway and ordered his arrest. The local magistrate, a black man, arrested Adams, who also pressed charges against the white men for interfering with a militia drill. Adams's trial was scheduled for the next day. Before the trial began, Butler demanded that the militia relinquish its arms. When Adams refused, Butler requested the magistrate to postpone the trial so he could cross the river to Augusta and bring back a cannon and several hundred white men to join him and Edgefield County's Sweetwater Saber Club. The saber club was commanded by Benjamin (later known as "Pitchfork Ben") Tillman, a 29-year-old South Carolinian, who would eventually be governor of the state and a U.S. Senator for 24 years.[3]

As more whites from Augusta, Edgefield, and surrounding communities began to arrive, tensions rose. The black militia refused to disarm and retreated to a small brick building where General Butler and the Sweetwater Saber Club attacked the militia. Fearing for their lives, the black militiamen escaped from the building and into the woods or into the river. Several hours after the shooting began, 25 black men had been captured. General Butler, according to black witnesses, selected the black militia officers out of the group and took them to a nearby hayfield where they were shot as they attempted "to escape." By the time the riot was over, six or seven black men were dead and two were wounded; one white man was dead and one was wounded.[4] The only white man killed in the riot was McKie Meriwether, one of the men Butler brought from Augusta. A monument was raised to him in North Augusta in 1916, where it still stands.

Governor Chamberlain immediately called on President Grant to send more troops to South Carolina to prevent similar incidents, but Grant refused. The president acknowledged that the massacre was "cruel, bloodthirsty, wanton, unprovoked, and uncalled for," but the solution was to be found at home, not in federal forces. He urged the governor to do his duty.[5]

Although Butler disappeared into history, Tillman built a political career on the event. As commander of the Sweetwater Saber Club, he boasted of his involvement in the Hamburg riot and used it to establish himself as a leader of the white South. Tillman later said that the white men of Edgefield County seized "the first opportunity that the Negroes might offer them to provoke a riot and teach the Negroes a lesson" by "having the whites demonstrate their superiority by killing as many of them as was justifiable." In a speech before the U.S. Senate in March 1900, Tillman was still defending his white supremacist viewpoints: "We of the South have never recognized the right of the negro to govern white men, and we never will. We have never believed him to be equal to the white man, and we will not submit to his gratifying his lust on our wives and daughters without lynching him."

In South Carolina, the Hamburg massacre strengthened the "Straight-Out" Democratic faction. To Republicans in the North, the Hamburg massacre became another symbol of the antiblack violence of an unreconstructed South. It was several months before any indictments were brought, and the case was not pursued after the Democrats assumed office.

THE VIEW FROM THE NORTH

E.L. Godkin: "The South in the Canvass"

This editorial warns against voting the "bloody" shirt and cautions voters to look at other issues before casting a vote. In effect, he is challenging the reader not to look at issues through party lenses.

The Nation, July 27, 1876

One of the saddest features in the condition of the South just now is the part it plays in the political contests at the North. We do not think we are at all uncharitable when we say that, during the next three or four months

[Republican leaders], and their subordinates and assistants in the canvass, will look for outrages and murders of negroes in their paper every morning as the most welcome bits of news on which their eye could light. To hear that a negro in Georgia or Mississippi was taken into the woods and whipped will make them smile; but to hear that several negro houses were burnt down, and the occupants pushed back into the flames, or that twenty negroes, arrested on a charge of chicken-theft, were taken from the custody of the sheriff on the way to jail and butchered in cold blood, will make them laugh and clap their hands, and run lustily to the nearest stump to improve and spread the story. We do not say that the Democrats are incapable of experiencing under like circumstances the same unseemly joy; but, luckily for them, the best news they can hear from the South at present is the news of peace and order. . . .

We are led to make these observations by seeing the great importance which the Republican orators and editors evidently attach to the Hamburg affair. Some of them, in fact, talk of it with as much gusto as if it were likely to exert a decisive influence on the Presidential election, or, at all events, as if one more good, substantial slaughter of negroes would make Hayes's election sure. Now, no language can well be too strong in condemnation of the state of manners which makes such occurrences as that at Hamburg possible. Nothing the negroes had done or tried to do, according to any version of the affair, could make the shooting of the prisoners anything but a piece of atrocious savagery. It is ridiculous for a community in which such things are either sanctioned or tolerated to talk of itself as civilized. . . . But then the atrocity of the affair, and of all such affairs, does not necessarily connect it with the general politics of the country. There is no sense in allowing it to determine how one will vote at the Presidential election if the vote is meant merely to be an expression of disapprobation. To vote for Hayes, for instance, without regard to other considerations, merely to show Southerners that we disapprove of such conduct, would be little short of folly. Southerners know already that the whole North, and the whole civilized world, disapprove of such conduct. They would not know it any better if we elected Hayes ten times over. Moreover, the election of Hayes would of itself not necessarily act as a deterrent from such acts. Stump orators and party organs talk as if it would, but they know it would *not*. Electing a Republican President, or keeping the Republican party in power, is not of itself sufficient to mend matters at the South. We have had a Republican President and a Republican House and Senate for eight years, and yet the South is, according to those who are most clamorous for a further trial of the remedy, in a terrible condition, as the Hamburg matter shows. . . .

We are, however, very far from asserting or insinuating that the condition of the South ought not to enter into the calculations of a voter who is making up his mind on which side he ought to cast his ballot at the coming election. On the contrary, we think it ought to engage his attention as seriously as, if not more seriously than, any other topic. But we do say, with all the earnestness at our command, that he is not the friend but the enemy both of Southern blacks and Southern whites who votes for the continuance of, or with the design of continuing, that form of protection which General Grant has extended to them. . . . If the success of the Republican ticket is going to perpetuate this shameful and demoralizing system, every honest and patriotic man ought to think twice before voting it; and if anybody infers from the occurrence of such incidents as the Hamburg tragedy that the system ought to be continued, he may be sure that his reasoning apparatus needs overhauling. . . .

George W. Curtis: "The Ku-Klux"

This editorial may be an answer to E. L. Godkin's editorial in The Nation, *provided above. Curtis advises voters not to ignore the "bloody shirt" and warns that under Democratic rule, violence against blacks will only be worse.*

Harper's Weekly, August 5, 1876

It is very easy, under cover of sneering at the bloody shirt, to do a very great and cruel wrong. Democrats like General M. C. Butler, of the Hamburg massacre, are very willing to hear any allusion to the brutal treatment of colored citizens in the Southern States reviled and belittled as a shaking of the bloody shirt, and Northern Democrats are very anxious to have no allusions made to it whatever, and to insist that the only question before the country is "reform." One reform is certainly indispensable, and that is reform of the spirit that displayed itself at Hamburg, as it has constantly shown itself in the Southern States for the last ten years. General Butler in his statement says that "the collision was the culmination of the system of insulting and outraging of white people which the negroes have adopted there for several years." These negro slaughters are undoubtedly very common and familiar in the late Slave States, and there may be those who believe that they are due to a negro system of insult and outrage. We believe, on the contrary, and from a careful study of many of the massacres, that the negro slaughters, and every kind and degree of Ku-Kluxery, are not due to negro insults and outrages, but to the deep and deadly contempt and hatred of the negroes upon the part of brutalized whites, intensified by the war and its consequences. . . .

The late Confederates seem, as a rule, to have abandoned themselves to awaiting the possible return of the Democratic party to power as an opportunity of "putting the negro into his place." The Southern States, of course, are full of such young men as the two who were "insulted" by the colored militia of Hamburg. They are supported by the general white sentiment of communities in which they live, and the natural consequences are such massacres as this. The victims "were murdered in cold blood after they had surrendered and were utterly defenseless," says Governor Chamberlain. Who murdered them? The spirit and the men that demand the election of Mr. Tilden—not because he would personally connive at any wrong, but because they are of his party. The country sees what crimes are possible when the friends of the colored race are in control of the national government. What would it be with the political friends of General M.C. Butler in control?

The situation, we repeat, is difficult. It demands both forbearance and firmness. We do not say that the negroes are always right; we insist only that they are not always wrong. Above all, we are sure that nothing could be more unfortunate for both races and for the whole country than the transfer of the national government to the party which the Ku-Klux spirit supports. Nor can there be found wiser, more generous, more timely, views upon the whole subject than those of Governor Hayes. . . .

Anonymous Writer: No Title

Like many Republican newspapers, the New York Times *not only censured the massacre but asks the question of the campaign season: Would things be any better under a Democratic administration?*

New York Times, July 17, 1876

It is useless to deny that such occurrences have political significance. There is no room for doubt that a large portion of the Southern whites are bent on depriving the negroes of all political power. They will not try to repeal the amendments to the national Constitution which guarantee equal rights to both races, for they know that would be impossible. They will not use their State Governments to accomplish their purpose, for they know that would bring them within the strictest interpretation of the prohibitory amendments of the Constitution. They will seek also to avoid the penalties of the "enforcements laws," by making it as difficult as possible to trace their acts directly to the motive of depriving the blacks of suffrage. Yet by such outbursts of violence as that at Hamburg, and by a general course of intimidations toward leaders and men of influence on the Republican side, they will do what they can to reduce the voting power of the negroes. How successful they may be can be inferred from the result in Mississippi, where the negroes were practically as much disfranchised as if the legal right to vote had been taken away from them. Now, the question which every American citizen is bound to ask himself is, Will this gross actual violation of the principles of free government be checked or sustained by the election of the Democratic President and Vice President? Granted that the constitutional means of preventing and punishing the offense are now small—as they are—what will be the consequence of placing in power a party that will not use the means which exist?

THE VIEW FROM THE SOUTH

No Author: No Title

The Democratic editor condones the use of rifle clubs to quell black violence, although Governor Chamberlain condemned the clubs as "neither peaceful, nor orderly, nor within the law. And yet they are perhaps the most prominent methods and agency employed by [Democrats] in this canvass."

Charleston (S.C.) News and Courier, June 28, 1876

This is not, in the usual sense of the words, "a call for troops"; it is rather the natural inquiry of a public officer who, at a critical time, desires to know what outside aid he can rely on, when his own resources shall have been exhausted. No attempt is made to attach to one race or party, more than another, the responsibility for the apprehended disorder; and no action on the part of the General Government is contemplated, unless the violence in question shall be "beyond the control of the State authorities." The state really has very little active power. In case that a band of negroes were engaged in a riot, the white rifle clubs could be called on by the Executive to repress the disorder; but there are no negro militia who could be, or dare be, moved against the whites, if they were riotous, and the white rifle clubs again would be the only reliance. Governor Chamberlain appears to think that a company of United States soldiers will have a more sedative effect than rifle clubs or civil *posses* . . . . We insist that the State, in every case, shall manage its own affairs in its own way, and we disapprove of the interference of soldiers, whether to put down a strike or to guard ballot boxes. This is a political principle with us, or we should not object to the sending of a company of United States soldiers to every courthouse in the State. The whites have no thought of killing anybody, or abusing anybody. The sympathies of the soldiers are with the whites, not with the blacks. . . .

Henry Grady: "The Hamburg Fight"

In this editorial, the Atlanta Constitution *is beginning to show the moderate tones that would distinguish it from the rest of Southern journalism over the next 90 years. Although this editorial places the blame on whites, several days later the paper wrote, "The outbreak was upon the part of the negroes, a defiant mob of drunken negro militia, who refused obedience to the civil process of the court. They are the parties first responsible."*

Atlanta Constitution, July 11, 1876

What interest [General Butler] had in the matter as between Rivers and the negroes, what authority to make demands upon a militia force and summarily punish refusals, and what he hoped to gain by organizing civil war in a community where no pressing necessity demanded it, are things which we cannot make out from the full accounts before us. Nowhere in the reports of the affair do we find warrant for the fighting which came on afterwards. There appears no evidence that the negroes intended bloodshed, opened hostilities, or could not have been induced, if properly approached and assured of right treatment, to lay down their arms and submit to legal adjustment of the question at issue.

In a matter like this we speak plainly and say that if the reports given of the affair are true an attempt has been madly made to repair a wrong by the commission of a greater one. There can be no question over the illegality and the gross outrageousness of the coercive warfare, as it was conducted by the outsiders.

These may be good and sufficient reasons for all that has been done. We hope those engaged in the affair will be able to show this, but until they make it plain that the safety of the people, the peace of the state and the interests of society demanded the killing of six negroes and one white man, the wounding of three negroes and one white man, and the other terrors of the occasion, the public will hold them guilty of a great outrage.

Apart from all party consideration and the danger to democratic success involved in these fearful affairs, there are higher questions of human rights, law and justice involved, and we hope that there will be no countenance shown to those who wantonly disregard them. While we deeply deplore the sad occurrence we trust it will be fully investigated to the relief of those who are not responsible for its calamities.

Anonymous Writer: No Title

It was typical of Northern Democratic newspapers to blame the Hamburg murders on the entire litany of radical abuses in the South, and in South Carolina specifically.

New York World, July 16, 1876

It is not easy for the resident of a State where the administration of law is reasonably certain and impartial, to understand the race conflicts which occasionally occur in those sections of the South where the Negroes, led by utterly reckless and scoundrelly whites, have control of the State and local Governments. Imagine New York under the conditions of South Carolina. Imagine the lowest and most ignorant, the most debased and servile elements of her population, controlled by still worse and more unscrupulous ruffians from other states, making and administering her laws—shamelessly plundering her treasuries; burning the houses of her citizens; outraging her women; riding roughshod over the country, with insult and robbery and murder everywhere in their track—with these thieves and murderers filling the bench and jury-box; even the chairs of the highest State offices and the halls of the Legislature itself. . . . It is the story of South Carolina since the war—the story of the "Prostrate State." It does not need that we should tell it here, as advocates of our party friends. It has been told in the columns of the bitter partisan press; it may not be denied in any detail. But there has been occasionally—so rarely as to excite wonder that long-suffering can so prevail without returning violence for violence—an outbreak of the people, and one bloody reprisal occurs for a long succession of not less bloody crimes. Forgetting the provocation, these reprisals are of a character to shock the country, and, of course, are eagerly seized upon by the partisan press to exhibit the bloodthirsty character of the Southern whites against their former masters. God save the mark! . . . This tragedy in South Carolina, shocking as it is, is to be referred directly to the misrule of the State for long years, marked by an uninterrupted reign of rapine in every form—of murder in every degree.

Anonymous Writer: "Correction"

On July 11, the Augusta (Ga.) Constitutionalist *criticized General Butler for his role in the Hamburg massacre, condemned the "excesses" and "disgraceful outrages" by the whites, and demanded "the perpetrators punished." The next day, the following "correction" was printed.*

Augusta (Ga.) Constitutionalist, July 12, 1876

In our report of the Hamburg riot yesterday, the typos made us say:

"While every honest and fair-minded man in South Carolina and Georgia, and the whole country, must condemn the course pursued by Gen. Butler and his men, &c."

What we really intended to say was that, "while every honest and fair-minded man in South Carolina and Georgia must regret the course of some of Gen. Butler's men," &c. Engagements elsewhere prevented a reading of the proof, and hence the error of the report. Paragraphs following the above relative to the noble gentlemen, Gen. Butler, whose kindness of heart is only equaled by his intrepidity, show that the sentence alluded to was simply a lapse which the best of us, in the midst of excitement and annoyance, may fall into. We make the earliest possible amends honorable.

Questions

1. Compare the editorials about the Hamburg massacre to those of the New Orleans riot (see chapter 11). What are the differences and similarities?
2. Why did the *Augusta (Ga.) Constitutionalist* correct its original story condemning General Butler?
3. How did the Hamburg massacre affect the redemption of Democrats in South Carolina?
4. Why did *The Nation* warn Republicans against using the Hamburg massacre as a "political tool" in the coming election?
5. What effect did such massacres have on national elections?

Notes

1. For an excellent description of the Southern militia, see Otis Singletary, *Negro Militia and Reconstruction* (Austin: University of Texas Press, 1952).

2. Walter Allen, *Governor Chamberlain's Administration in South Carolina* (New Haven: n.p., 1888), 383.

3. For the story of Tillman's involvement in the Hamburg massacre see Stephen David Kantrowitz, *Ben Tillman and the Reconstruction of White Supremacy* (Chapel Hill: University of North Carolina Press, 2000).

4. Richard Zuczek, *State of Rebellion: Reconstruction in South Carolina* (Columbia: University of South Carolina Press, 1996), 163–64; Eric Foner, *Reconstruction: America's Unfinished Revolution, 1863–1877* (New York: Harper & Row, 1988), 571.

5. Walter Allen, *Governor Chamberlain's Administration in South Carolina: A Chapter of Reconstrcution in the Southern States* (New York: Putnam's Sons, 1888), 325.

CHAPTER 29

The Compromised Election of 1876

For the first time since before the Civil War, Democrats were expected to win the White House in 1876. The Democratic ascendancy was foreshadowed two years earlier in the election of 1874, when reaction against corruption in the Republican Party was met with a resounding vote for the Democratic Party. The profile of the House of Representatives changed dramatically from a 110-vote majority for Republicans to a 60-vote majority for Democrats. Republicans barely maintained a majority in the Senate, and Democrats swept the gubernatorial elections in the North. There was no reason to believe that the sweeping Democratic victories in 1874 would not be repeated in 1876. The only problem was that when it came down to issues, the Democrats and Republicans did not differ that much.

Republicans, well on their way to abandoning Reconstruction, were looking toward a more conservative national fiscal policy that would be supported by a strong government reform movement. The Democratic platform also called for more reform and condemned fiscal policies that had resulted in hard times and depression. Since there was little of substance to separate the two campaigns, the campaign hinged on the differences between the two presidential candidates. Rutherford B. Hayes, three-time governor of Ohio, was an energetic and likeable politician. Samuel J. Tilden, governor of New York, was his opposite—uninspiring, impersonal, and almost pathetic looking.

Nevertheless, as early as June 1876, pundits were predicting that Tilden would win. But Democrats experienced a not uncommon setback when six black militiamen were murdered by white supremacists in Hamburg, South Carolina. Tilden refused to denounce the massacre, blaming the incident instead on a Republican state government that could not control its citizens. While the incident further united the Democratic South, it created

Counting the Electoral Vote. *This woodcut depicts Congress in joint session counting the disputed electoral votes in the election of 1876. From a sketch by Theodore Davis.* Harper's Weekly. *Library of Congress.*

divisions in the North and gained votes for the Republicans, who used the massacre as another example of why blacks in the South should not be abandoned.[1]

In the weeks leading up to the presidential election, Democrats in the North and South used fraud, violence, intimidation, and other devices to disenfranchise a significant majority of black voters. In some Northern cities, fewer than 10 percent of eligible blacks dared to show up at polls protected by armed Democrats. In the South, many counties with a majority of black voters registered no Republican votes. A week after the election, Hayes wrote in his diary, "If there had been neither violence nor intimidation nor other improper interference with the rights of the colored people, we should have carried enough Southern States to have held the country."[2]

Early returns on election night indicated a Democratic victory. By morning, while Tilden had won the popular vote by more than 250,000 votes, he was 1 electoral vote short of the necessary 185. Hayes had 166 electoral votes—19 short of 185. The only states that had not yet reported were South Carolina, Louisiana, and Florida. Immediately, party officials wired their counterparts in the three Southern states to urge them to "hold your state" for Hayes and "to look out for Democratic frauds." Several days later, all three Southern states returned for Hayes, giving him an electoral count of

185. However, Hayes lost an electoral vote when a Republican elector in Oregon was disqualified and replaced with a Democratic elector. Nevertheless, Hayes was declared the winner of the election.[3]

On December 7, Congress met in joint session to certify the electoral count, but it could not agree on a way to settle the 20 (19 in the South, 1 in Oregon) disputed votes. Tilden had 184 uncontested votes and only needed to keep the 1 Oregon vote or any one of the Southern states; Hayes had to win all four of the disputed states to win the election.

According to the Constitution, the president of the Senate opens the certificates of the electoral college before a joint session of Congress and counts the votes. But the Constitution says nothing about contested certificates. Republicans and Democrats agreed to establish an electoral commission consisting of five senators, five representatives, and five members of the Supreme Court. The commission would include seven Democrats, seven Republicans, and one independent. At first, it was believed that the independent member would be Justice David Davis. However, no sooner had the commission been established than the Illinois legislature elected Davis to a Senate seat. He was replaced on the commission by a Republican.[4]

The rules were simple: The commission's recommendation on each disputed vote was final unless both the House and Senate rejected it. The process of reviewing the electoral votes lasted from February 1 to March 2. In each of the disputed cases, the electoral commission accepted the state's official certificates, thus giving Hayes all of the questioned votes. The Senate accepted the electoral commission's recommendation; the House rejected each recommendation. The debates in the House were rancorous at best, hostile and violent at worst. There were even threats of another civil war. The Democrats engaged in various delaying tactics, including lengthy filibustering, knowing that if the joint session ended Hayes would be declared president. Finally, a compromise was reached in the early hours of March 2, 1877, and the Democratic-controlled House finally agreed to give all of the disputed votes to Hayes.[5] Hayes was sworn in during private ceremonies on March 3, just in case of problems on inauguration day.

What it had taken for the Democrats to give up Tilden and who was responsible for the compromise of 1877 did not become known until several years later. Negotiations had actually started in December when it was clear that the settlement would not be an easy one. Friends of Hayes, including a number of journalists, were able to work behind the scenes to convince Southern Democrats that if Hayes were elected, he would remove all of the troops from the South, recognize Democrats as the winners of the disputed gubernatorial elections in Louisiana and South Carolina, nominate a Democrat to his cabinet, and support the nomination of James Garfield as speaker of the house. Also, Hayes would support federal subsidies and credit to complete the Texas and Pacific Railroad that linked the South to California.

The final details of the compromise were worked out in a meeting at the Wormley Hotel[6] on February 26. No written record of the Wormley meeting exists, and to this day what happened remains a mystery. Some have argued that it was one of the most important meetings in U.S. history, as it resulted in quelling a potentially violent confrontation over presidential transition. Others maintain that the meeting did nothing more than lay out political issues already pledged by Hayes during the campaign. And still others believe the Wormley conference resulted in a travesty for the electoral process.

The Texas and Pacific Railroad never received its subsidy, and Garfield was not elected speaker of the house. A Southern Democrat was named postmaster general, South Carolina and Louisiana returned to home rule with Democratic governors, and Hayes did order troops in South Carolina and Louisiana to stand down.

Throughout his term, Hayes could not live down the compromise that put him in office. He was accused of stealing the office and was referred to as "Old Rutherfraud" and "His Fraudulency." Nevertheless, he was an honest and hardworking president. He worked diligently for civil service reform, and although not successful, his efforts were met with praise.

The first set of readings favor the work of the election commission and support the election of Hayes. The first selection, by Horace White, looks at the dispute from an economic viewpoint and urges a quick settlement so that the nation can return to economic good order. The second entry, by George Jones, describes the two candidates, with Hayes portrayed as honest and upright and Tilden as crafty and unscrupulous. The third reading, by Murat Halstead, explains that the compromise worked out between Republicans and Southern Democrats was nothing nefarious but only an attempt to settle the issue peacefully. The final reading in this section, by Charles de Young, praises the Democrats for giving up the fight and avoiding what could have become a disgraceful situation for the country.

The second set of readings challenges the necessity of the election commission and criticizes the tactics used by Republicans to steal the election. The first selection, by Whitelaw Reid from a Republican newspaper, charges the election commission with being an unconstitutional body with broad powers of investigation that will prolong the outcome of the election. The second entry, by Henry Grady of the *Atlanta (Ga.) Constitution,* takes its aim at the members of the election commission who "stole" 1 million white votes from the South.

FAVORING THE COMPROMISES OF 1876

Horace White: "The Compromise"

The Chicago Tribune *sees the proposal for an election commission as a good plan for getting on with the job of getting the nation back on its feet—no matter who is president.*

Chicago Tribune, January 21, 1877

Professional politicians generally will, as a matter of course, oppose the Electoral-count bill introduced as a compromise. All extreme partisans on both sides will criticize its object and denounce it. They have nothing to propose as a substitute; they prefer to act the part of the dog in the manger. What they want is a row, a civil commotion so dangerous that it will magnify them as leaders and great men. The officeholders want no compromise which will endanger their hold on the fat places they now have. The office-seekers can't bear the idea of a compromise plan of settling the dispute, because they think that Tilden is sure to be forced into the White House by some means. If by force and violence, so much the better for them. If the bill is carried it will only be in deference to the wishes and demands of the great business interests of the country. Unless the non-politicians insist on the passage of the bill, it will be ground to powder by office-holders and office-seekers, by the machine—men and political gamblers belonging to both parties. The country demands peace. It cares nothing personally for Hayes or Tilden, or this or that party, and when the means are offered for a prompt, final, peaceful adjudication of the whole difficulty by a majority of the Judges of the Supreme Court, it will hold every man and every party guilty of a great national wrong who shall defeat such an adjudication. While the Banks and Boards of Trade all over the country are unanimous in favor of this peaceful settlement, they are not so deeply interested in it as are the vast armies of men who are members of the labor unions, whose means of support for themselves and families are cut off and destroyed by the general prostration, from which there can be no revival and no recovery until this question shall be settled. With this question settled, the country will promptly recover. Our currency, paper, gold and silver wait only for peace to become equalized in value; our manufacturers only wait for peace and national security to enter upon a production for export to which the country has been a stranger since 1860. All things are ripe with abundance of capital for the general revival of trade and of production and the general employment of labor, which has been so largely idle since 1873. The politicians, the place men, the strikers and blowers in office and out of office stand in the way. Nearly all the disputes of life and the differences between men are settled by compromise or arbitration, but in this case the partisans are resolved that national peril shall not be averted by means of a Board of Arbitration, but that the quarrel must be fought out to the bitter end. They want office and plunder, and they prefer even war to a denial of their wants. Woe be unto those who overlook the suffering interests of the whole people and listened to the clamor of the howling mob of spoils-seekers.

George Jones: "Hayes and Tilden"

As often happens when candidates hold similar opinions on the issues, the election comes down to a matter of personality. This editorial is typical of the portrait drawn by Republican newspapers of the scoundrel Tilden and the upright Hayes.

New York Times, February 23, 1877

Never perhaps since the origin of the Government has there been such a striking contrast between rival candidates for the Presidency as between Hayes and Tilden. They represent two opposite types of political training. Each is the impersonation of the distinct methods or forces employed or at work in American politics since parties began to exist.

Hayes is all candor and openness; Tilden is all cunning and concealment. The former does directly and in the light of day what conscience commands; the latter, by indirection and stealth, what interest prompts. Tilden's methods of secrecy and deception never permit him to make known his real thoughts; Hayes' frankness never suffers him to make known anything else. The one utters aloud and in the presence of others his opinions on all proper subjects of discussion; the other confidentially, in whispers, and with many an aside, evasively insinuates what may be interpreted to suit the exigencies of the times. The one aims to be what he seems; the other strives to seem what he is not.

The methods of action of the two men are as opposite as their principles. Hayes believes that a sense of right and a love of justice sways the majority of mankind, and hence that to control them we must convince their reason. Tilden assumes that interest and passion move the majority, that money is the great motor, trickery the engine, deception the tender, and hatred and malice the fuel that propel the popular engine. Hence the unprecedented expenditure of money by a Presidential candidate, the evasiveness of his public utterances, the cipher dispatches, the secret agents traveling under assumed names, the attempts at bribery, and the fanning the fast dying out fires of civil strife. The electioneering methods of Tilden receive further illustration from the ballot-box frauds of 1868, for which he was held personally responsible by men of character and standing. Hayes' method of electioneering is to live an upright private and public life, to think and act up to the best thought and light of to-day, to build up the best character that he can, and then let that and his deeds plead his cause. This method of honor and truth renders unnecessary cipher telegrams, secret circulars or conferences, many-named agents, money in barrels or on draft or appeals to the lingering disloyalty of the land.

In the course of these two candidates we have had a fair test of the comparative worth of honesty and craft in a contest for the Presidency. Craft will gain points at the outset; honesty will gain honors and rewards at the end. Craft may be so cunning as to deceive for a time the very elect; honesty cannot be so guileless as to give the victor's crown to any but the veritably elected. Craft crops out too much and too soon to mislead the wary. Honesty bears fruit in time to make known to the wise the quality of the tree. Craft seldom wins success in the present and never in the future. Uprightness generally attains the highest success, and what is better, always deserves it. The machinations of Tilden, the politician, have not proved a match for the simple adherence to duty of Hayes, the unselfish soldier and upright citizen. Let aspiring men learn this easy, though paradoxical lesson—that the way to reach the Presidency is never to seek it, and the way to lose it is to scheme and plot for it, after the manner of the trading politicians.

Murat Halstead: "President Hayes and the Charge of Bargaining with the South"

After Hayes was declared the winner of the presidential election, charges surfaced that he had entered into a devil's bargain with the Democrats to stop the filibuster over the electoral votes. Charles Foster was a Republican congressman from Ohio, and Stanley Matthews was a boyhood friend of Hayes's who would later serve on the U.S. Supreme Court. Both men tried to reassure Southerners—through letters and meetings—that Hayes would look out for the South's interests.

Cincinnati Commercial, March 29, 1877

As soon as it was understood that Stanley Matthews and Charles Foster had no special objection to the publication of the letters written some weeks ago for the assurance of Southern men that there would be a new policy, the intense anxiety that the letters should appear lapsed, except in the case of the professional news men.

There is nothing mysterious about this affair. There is no secret history worth knowing. It is true that when the Southern members of Congress saw that the Electoral Commission would give Hayes a clear title to the Presidency unless there was filibustering, they sought friends of Hayes to gather from them if possible the measure of his meaning in his letter of acceptance, and that they were met with cordiality and pacific assurances, of a character with which the public are familiar.

Now all the friends of Hayes were not in such deep solicitude that the Electoral Commission should complete its labors, as was supposed in the Democratic camp. If the Democrats, after supporting the electoral Commission, had . . . throw[n] the country into a second Presidential election, the Democratic party would have been held responsible for the hard times of the summer, and it would have been smashed, Solid South and all.

Charles de Young: "Not a Party Triumph, but a National Deliverance"

There were many like Charles de Young who feared that the deadlock over the electoral count might lead to violence. The willingness of the Democrats to abandon their obstructive ways at the last minute was welcome relief for many.

San Francisco Chronicle, February 28, 1877

The abandonment by the Democrats of the dishonorable policy of obstructing the count of the Electoral vote in order to defeat the true intent and purpose of the compromise to which they had solemnly agreed is a matter far more important than the election of Hayes. While the mere partisans on the Republican side will rejoice over this event mainly because it secures the success of their candidate, all honorable and high-minded men of both parties will experience a profounder gratification in contemplating the defeat of the disgraceful tactics recommended by Tilden and others than could be derived by any mere party triumph. Had partisan spirit proved so strong as to bind the Democratic leaders to all considerations of honesty and good faith, such a fact would have been a baleful augury foreshadowing the speedy overthrow of our free institutions. It would have proved that the love of party among the American people is more powerful than the love of country, the love of fair dealing and the sentiment of personal honor which impels upright men who have deliberately made an agreement which results in loss to abide by it and accept the consequences. During the last few months the eyes of the lovers of liberty and the believers in free institutions in all the civilized nations of the globe have been watching the progress of events in the United States with profound interest and painful anxiety. Had they been called upon to witness the humiliating exhibition which would have been presented for their contemplation if the Democratic leaders had lent their sanction to a scheme designed to defeat the Republican candidate by such a flagrant act of dishonesty as the repudiation of the formal and solemn compact which created the Electoral Commission, they would have turned from the wretched spectacle in shame and despondency. But fortunately the leading men of the Democratic party could not bring themselves to sanction, in the face of the country and the world, the foul perfidy involved in the attempt to nullify the decision of the tribunal which they had assisted in creating, and to which they had bound themselves to submit all the issues of the contest. The act would have been stamped as infamous by all future generations. It is only a few weeks since the Joint Committee (composed in equal numbers of Democrats and Republicans) reported in favor of the bill. . . .

We will not at present pause to congratulate Hayes upon his election or the Republican party upon its triumph. We feel a stronger impulse to congratulate the country upon its escape from overwhelming disgrace. The event is to be hailed not as a Republican victory, but as a national deliverance.

Opposing the Compromises of 1876

Whitelaw Reid: No Title

Northern Republicans criticized the election commission as being extralegal. In fact, they simply wanted the official electoral certificates counted and the disputed certificates tossed out.

New York Tribune, January 19, 1877

We do not regard the question which candidate is to be declared elected as of so much consequence, since circumstances will, to some extent, make the victory of either a barren one; but we do not believe that this report provides a constitutional method of counting the Electoral vote, and shall regret its adoption as a precedent full of peril. First—It is revolutionary; it sets up a United States Returning Board, clothed with powers not conferred by the Constitution upon any man or body of men. Second—It involves the possibility of election either by cheat or by lot, as it is at least possible that the leaders of one party or the other have a private knowledge as to the position and probable action of some member of the contemplated Commission, which they believe will insure their success. Third—The Commission, if one is constituted, has power to investigate and to send for persons and papers like any one of the long-winded Committees now at work, but its duty will be to gather and pass upon all facts for which those Committees are searching, as to all questions at issue. Either these Committees are an impertinence or nuisance, or the task of this Commission will involve a labor of weeks or months. The Commission may or may not get organized, nor reach judgment before the 4th of March, but if it does, that judgment must still be considered and passed upon by the two Houses separately. In either case the same possibilities of unlimited delay exist, and it is altogether probable that either through failure to organize the Commission or through long delay incident to the inquiry and discussion, first in the Commission and afterwards in each House, no result may be reached prior to the 4th of March. In that event the Senate will hold that its President, who may be elected for the purpose by a majority of its members, will become acting President. Thus, until another election can be held, a man not elected by a single one of the many millions of voters can retain the Executive office. Fourth—When all is done, what have we gained? We have set aside the Constitution of the United States, which requires that the votes of such Electors as the States may appoint shall be counted, and not such votes as the United States Returning Board may accept. We have broken down those simple provisions under which our fathers acted, and which they believed would not only secure an Executive independent of Congressional control, but preclude the possibility of delay and dispute as to the result of an election. This bill's possible effect is simply the Republic of Mexico reduced to a United States statute.

Henry Grady: "The End"

In the South, the work of the election commission was seen as the devil's work, a fraud, and a stain on the U.S. Constitution.

Atlanta Constitution, March 8, 1877

The farce is over—not merely the work of the electoral commission, for that was too dirty, too villainous to be called a farce—that was a tragedy with eight villains plotting to destroy the republic—but the effort to elect a president in the hundredth anniversary of American independence. That farce is over, and a majority of fully *one million* of the white voters of America has been annihilated. The conspirators will proceed to enjoy the spoils of the high office they have stolen; the receiver of the stolen office is now in Washington prepared to execute his shameful part; and there is nothing left to chronicle except to sum up the result. . . .

If the eight republican members of the electoral commission, instead of swearing to determine according to the law and the facts, had taken a horrid oath . . . to decide every point in the dispute, and the whole dispute itself, in favor of Hayes and Wheeler, regardless of the law and facts, they could not have exhibited a more shocking defiance of justice, truth and principle than they actually have presented.

QUESTIONS

1. Why was the election of 1876 such a critical one that some even believed the electoral decision might end in another civil war?
2. Why was the election commission considered by some to be unconstitutional?
3. What were the arguments in favor of the election commission?
4. Why did so few editors seem to care whether Hayes or Tilden won the election?
5. Can you predict what might have happened had the Democrats not abandoned their fight over the electoral count?

NOTES

1. William Gillette, *Retreat from Reconstruction, 1869–1879* (Baton Rouge: Louisiana State University Press, 1979), 305.

2. Charles Richard Williams, ed., *The Diary and Letters of Rutherford B. Hayes, Nineteenth President of the United States,* 3 (Columbus: Ohio State Archeological and Historical Society, 1922), 378.

3. C. Van Woodward, *Reunion and Reaction: The Compromise of 1877 and the End of Reconstruction* (New York: Oxford University Press, 1966), 17–19.

4. Ibid., 154–55.

5. Eric Foner, *Reconstruction: America's Unfinished Revolution, 1863–1877* (New York: Harper & Row, 1988), 580–81.

6. The Wormley Hotel, a favorite of Washington politicos, was owned by James Wormley, an African American entrepreneur.

CHAPTER 30

The End of Reconstruction, 1874–77

For a brief period between 1868 and 1872, Southern blacks tasted freedom. To a greater or lesser degree, they were allowed to vote, hold office, work where they wished, travel unhindered, and acquire property. Southern blacks did all of those things, despite the intense hatred of many Southern whites and open violence of such organizations as the Ku Klux Klan. However, this era of racial progress soon came to an end; an end that was driven not only by the Southern will to overcome radical rule but also by the Republicans' own self doubts about the moral origin of their own rule.

Eric Foner, in his book *Reconstruction: America's Unfinished Revolution,* lays much of the blame for the failure of Reconstruction on Republicans themselves, who began a slow dance of conciliation and compromise with Southern moderates. In part, this compromise was the result of changes in the Republican Party itself. During the period of congressional Reconstruction, much of the South's aristocracy was disenfranchised, leaving Republican leadership to come from small planters and farmers who did not share the Confederate spirit of the large plantation owners. These men, who often are referred to as the South's yeoman farmers, were primarily Unionists who welcomed congressional Reconstruction and demonstrated a willingness to work with blacks to create a biracial coalition against Democrats.

White Republicans initially supported blacks holding office, civil rights, disenfranchisement of rebels, and public school. This alliance with blacks, however, was a political necessity and did not necessarily reflect a moral philosophy of equality. Consequently, as congressional Reconstruction progressed, prejudice overcame radicalism and splits between black and white Republicans began to appear. Republicans complained that the party lost votes whenever blacks ran for office. They also lost votes because of race baiting and violence against blacks. Other issues such as white disenfranchisement, taxes, debt relief, and social equality also began to splinter the Republicans.

So serious were the splits that Northern Republicans urged their Southern counterparts to moderate their radicalism and find a middle ground where Republicans could appeal to a larger segment of white voters, even if this meant pulling away from black Republicans. For example, Republicans withdrew their support from blacks running for office and moved blacks out of leadership positions within the party. They also withdrew support from legislation supporting civil rights and integrated schools. These conciliatory tactics allowed Republicans to hold on for a year or two, but when Congress restored political rights in 1872 to disenfranchised Confederates, Republicans found themselves once again the minority party.

Other factors that contributed to the downfall of Republicans and, thus, Reconstruction, included corruption, economic problems, and the will of Northern Republicans to let the South return to "the natural order of things." Corruption was rampant in both parties and in every region of the country. But in the South, corruption took on a peculiar repugnance that raised it to a level that most people in the North and South considered out of control. The major engine that drove corruption was patronage—the centuries-old practice of giving friends, qualified or not, jobs in government. Each time Republicans passed a bill to engineer change in the South, they created another bureaucracy. Most of the patronage positions in the South went to carpetbaggers, who became an easy target for newspapers and magazines that portrayed these Northern adventurers as vile and disgusting men who ravaged the South.

By the mid-1870s, there was a growing backlash against carpetbag governments and Southern blacks. The retreat was urged on by journalists who visited the South and wrote about corruption and black ineptness. One such journalist was James Pike of the *New York Tribune,* who toured the South in 1874 and 1875 and later published his findings in *The Prostrate State.* Pike's book, which became the definitive work on the South and thus popular among Democrats and Republicans, painted a racist picture of the conduct of black legislators and carpetbaggers:

> In the place of this old aristocratic society stands the rude form of the most ignorant democracy that mankind ever saw, invested with the functions of government. It is the dregs of the population habilitated in the robes of their intelligent predecessors, and asserting over them the rule of ignorance and corruption. . . . It is barbarism overwhelming civilization by physical force. It is the slave rioting in the halls of his master, and putting that master under his feet.[1]

As Pike and others demonstrated that blacks were not ready for political equality, Republicans began to regret their part in making blacks "the party pet and the national pest."[2] President Grant's attempts to enforce voting rights and to put down the Ku Klux Klan were met with mixed feelings, as many considered it dangerous precedent to keep sending federal troops into states to prop up corrupt Republican governments, not against rebels, but against Democrats.

Added to corruption and ineptness was the economic hard times that began with the Panic of 1873. The Southern Republican legislatures were placing heavy taxes on white landowners to support public schools, railroads, and other public improvements. But, as land prices slid, landowners could no longer pay the states' exorbitant taxes, so they stopped paying taxes in many areas. In the North, voters were tired of spending millions of dollars to keep troops in the South to prop up Republican governments. They expressed their opinion at the polls in 1874 by replacing Republicans in Congress with Democrats.

The U.S. Supreme Court also dealt a major blow to Reconstruction policy in 1873 with the *Slaughterhouse Cases*,[3] when it ruled that under the Fourteenth Amendment states alone had the authority to determine the extent of their own citizens' rights. In other words, if states wanted to prohibit blacks from holding office or women from becoming doctors, that was well within their authority. The Court put the Republican Congress on notice that much of what it was trying to do to protect blacks in the South would not hold up to judicial scrutiny. Over the next 10 years, the Court would continue to emasculate the Fourteenth and Fifteenth Amendments and void most of the Enforcement and Ku Klux Klan Acts passed during Grant's administration.

By 1876, all but Florida, South Carolina, and Louisiana had been redeemed by Democrats. In April 1877, Hayes ordered the withdrawal of the last federal troops from the South. For stalwart Republicans, their worst fears were coming true. As each Southern state returned to Democratic control, all the gains that had been made on behalf of blacks were quickly abolished. It was not long before the South once again belonged to the "White Man." The *St. Louis Globe Democrat* wrote after the inauguration of President Hayes, "The untiring hatred of the Southerners has worn out our endurance, and that though we staked everything for freedom . . . we have not enough of principle about us to uphold the freedom, so dearly bought, against the persistent and effective opposition of the unrepentant and unchanged rebels."[4]

In the first section, readings point to Republican corruption and black ineptness as reasons for the North to abandon Reconstruction and leave the South to work out its own problems. The first entry, by E.L. Godkin, places the South's problems squarely on the head of black Republicans, who, having been led down the path of corruption by carpetbaggers, are incapable of ruling. The second reading, by Parke Godwin, rejoices that Georgia's carpetbag governor has been defeated and the new Democratic governor now will restore the state economically. The third selection, by Henry Grady, is a celebration of the removal of federal troops from the South. The fourth editorial in the section, by Godkin, predicts that with the last Southern state in the hands of Democrats, the division between the North and South will disappear along with all political interest in blacks.

The second section includes editorials that blame the South's problems and the end of Reconstruction on Southern whites. The first selection, by George Jones, argues that the South's economic problems rest with Southern whites who resisted all efforts by Northern entrepreneurs to restore the South after the war. The South does not seek economic renewal but seeks the total freedom to continue its violence against blacks and Republicans. The second reading, by George W. Curtis, believes that the hostilities between the North and South will end, but only if the South treats blacks fairly and with justice. The third selection, by Jones, warns that Hayes should not remove troops from the South until it is known how the new Democratic governments in the South will behave toward Republicans and blacks. The final selection, by Murat Halstead, predicts that the end of Reconstruction will bring about a realignment of parties.

SUPPORT FOR ABANDONING RECONSTRUCTION

E.L. Godkin: "Reconstruction Reassessed"

Four and a half years of Reconstruction had demonstrated to E.L. Godkin that blacks were incapable of self-government. The problem with the editor's premise is that with the exception of South Carolina, the "full and exclusive control" of state governments was in the hands of whites, not blacks.

The Nation, December 7, 1871

It is comparatively easy to reform the tariff or the civil service, or reduce the taxes, or return to specie payments, or civilize the Indians, or protect the immigrants, or get the overdue instalment [*sic*] from Venezuela, or bring Mexico to reason on that matter of "the free zone"; but it is almost as hard to give order, peace, and security to the southern half of American society as to medicine to a mind diseased, or pluck the rooted sorrow from the brain. We do not need to tell any of our readers what the state of things in that region is. It is not simply that men suddenly raised from a condition of bestial servitude, inheriting the weakness of barbarism, aggravated by the weaknesses of slavery, have been admitted to participation in the rights and responsibilities of free society; it is that they have been put in full and exclusive control of that most delicate and complicated piece of mechanism known as the government of a civilized State, with its debts, its credit, its system of taxes, its system of jurisprudence, its history, its traditions, its thousand knotty social and political problems. We say "exclusive control," because we do not call the division of power which the negroes have made with the Northern carpet-baggers a real division. . . .

In the idea that we were befriending the negroes, we gave them possession of the government, and deprived them of the aid of all the local capacity and experience in the management of it, thus offering the States as a prey to Northern adventures, and thus inflicting on the freedmen the very worst calamity which could befall a race newly emerged from barbarism—that is, familiarity, in the very first moments of enfranchisement, with the processes of a corrupt administration, carried on by gangs of depraved vagabonds, in which the public money was stolen, the public faith made an article of traffic, the legislature openly corrupted. . . . We do not hesitate to say that a better mode of debauching the freedmen, and making them permanently unfit for civil government, could hardly have been hit on had the North had such an object deliberately in view. . . .

Parke Godwin: "The New Government of Georgia"

Georgia governor Rufus Bullock was indeed one of the worst carpetbag governors in the South in terms of corruption; however, he also did much to help blacks in Georgia enjoy, albeit briefly, their political freedom.

New York Evening Post, January 17, 1872

Georgia has had its full share of robbery and corruption under the rule of the mercenary "carpet-baggers" who fastened themselves upon the state when it was reconstructed. It has been more fortunate, however, than most of the southern states in getting rid of the political vultures. Governor Bullock's ring, while it was venal and unsparing in its corrupt practices, had not the audacity of Tammany. Its leader took to his heels, and left his companions to save what they could from the wreck of the great speculation. By the moderation of those who succeeded him the state has just been saved from the lawlessness and violence which have disgraced Southern Carolina and Louisiana. . . .

The new Governor of Georgia is said to be an able and honest man, and it is to be hoped that the democrats will profit by the mistakes and crimes of their Republican predecessors to improve the government of the state. It is certain that while Bullock was Governor the administration was inefficient and extravagant. The extent of its corruption cannot be known until a correct statement of the financial condition of the state can be made. The Bullock ring, like the Scott ring in South Carolina and the Tweed ring in this city, made robbery possible by refusing to render any account of their, deeds, and the debt of Georgia is really unknown. But there is no doubt that every obligation will be honestly discharged, for the men who rule Georgia now know that repudiation will cost the state many years of stagnation in business.

Henry Grady: "New South"

This editorial not only celebrates the departure of the last federal soldiers from the South but also looks forward to the day when a prosperous South will rise from the ashes of Reconstruction. Henry Grady, who had used the term "New South" as early as 1874, would become well-known for his editorials and speeches that promoted a racist view of the New South as a prosperous land under the control of whites.

Atlanta Constitution, April 22, 1877

"The old flag" will not—if the president does not change his mind—float over a single province after high-noon of day after to-morrow. This glorious fact springs from many strange circumstances. It comes from the hands of a republican president, who was chosen by a series of returning boards. It stultifies the entire reconstruction "work" of his party. It is a blow aimed at all the means by which the administration reached power, both general and local. It snuffs out the man who led in Louisiana the republican electoral ticket several hundred votes and whose efforts were an essential part of that stupendous plot which defeated the popular will. But what of all this—Louisiana will soon be a sovereign state, and the whole south will not contain a carpetbag government.

Why our opponents are really willing to admit that the war is over and that constitutional methods should prevail, matters little to us. We can accept the fact, without inquiring why it comes so suddenly and strangely. If this great good comes from a presidential desire to quiet the presidential title by popular and just acts, let us not complain. If the presidential brain harbors the insane idea that by adopting democratic measures it can divide the democratic party in the south, unsectionalize the republican party and save it from death, we need not hasten to undeceive it. If Mr. Hayes thinks the people of the south can so easily forget the story of military interference of the past eight years as to prefer the party that is alone responsible for it, we need not rise up to tell him he is a fool. Nor is it incumbent upon us to protest if he is simply trying to save the army by confining its use within constitutional limits. Whatever the motive, the result is in every way desirable, and we need not go back of official acts. . . .

The south, the whole south, has now its grand opportunity. Freed from organized bands of robbers and bayonet rule, with a territory unsurpassed for natural fertility, with a climate that is simply superb, with inexhaustible mineral resources, with, in short, all of nature's best gifts, she is now ready to take up the real work of reconstruction and to carry it forward with that quiet determination which is born of hope and contented enterprise. The road is long and weary, but industry, energy and economy will put us over it. Let the battle begin without delay. Let our material interests have precedence henceforth, for the new life is to be practical and plodding until financially we reach solid ground. We need not trouble ourselves greatly about federal politics. There is scarcely any one so short-sighted that he cannot see that the democratic party is the party of the future—that it is to control this country for a generation to come—that it will be overwhelmingly successful in the next general elections. It is the only party in the country that is not sectional, and we have only to hold firmly to it while we battle for bread, to witness a victory that will be at least a partial compensation for the bitter trials of the past.

E.L. Godkin: "The Political South Hereafter"

E.L. Godkin is willing to go so far as to remove "the South" from Americans' vocabulary to create the rhetoric of a truly united nation. He also is willing to forget Southern blacks and relegate them to the margins while more important issues are attended to.

The Nation, April 5, 1877

The dissolution of the last sham government at the South—an event which we have a right to believe cannot now be long delayed—will place the Southern States, as regards the rest of the nation, in a position which they have not before occupied for almost a generation. Heretofore, in the discussion of nearly all national questions, the most embarrassing and vexatious element at any time to be considered, and frequently an overwhelmingly important one, was "the South." This term designated a number of contiguous States bound together by mutual interest in the maintenance of a social system which was understood to be inimical to the feelings, at least, if not to the welfare, of the inhabitants of all other States; and "the South" was always, therefore, a more definite term than "the West" or "the North." Slavery dominated every other interest, and held the Southern States together in political unity....

We believe the proposition to be almost self-evident, indeed, that hereafter there is to be no South; none, that is, in a distinctively political sense. The negro will disappear from the field of national politics. Henceforth the nation, as a nation, will have nothing more to do with him. He will undoubtedly play a part, perhaps an important one, in the development of the national civilization. The philanthropist will have still a great deal to do both with him and for him, and the sociological student will find him, curiously placed as he is in contact and competition with other races, an unfailing source of interest; but as a "ward" of the nation he can no longer be singled out for especial guardianship or peculiar treatment in preference to Irish laborers or Swedish immigrants. There is something distasteful, undeniably, in the idea of one who has played so important a part in our past political history making his final exit in the company of the Carpet-baggers; but for this unfortunate coincidence the negro is not to be blamed....

The future of the freedman will be bound up undoubtedly with that of the white man, and does not now require separate consideration. Great numbers of negroes will certainly remain upon the cotton-fields, rice-swamps, and cane and tobacco plantations, and, being employed as field-hands, their political opinions for a long time to come will inevitably reflect those of their employers. Others will learn to work in factories or become mechanics and small farmers, and, generally, all over the South for a long time, negroes will fill the places now filled at the North by Irish, German, and Chinese laborers. The political influence of the freedman, considered as distinct from that of the white man, will be almost imperceptible. His ultimate influence upon our civilization, as determined by the relative fecundity of the two races, and their action and reaction upon one another as the negro becomes better educated and more independent, is a subject which can be discussed more profitably a generation hence....

For the first time in our history we are entitled to assert that there is no danger of national dissolution. Heretofore our chief attention has been given to the saving of national life, and only incidentally have we been able to consider character or to decide upon the best methods of perfecting it. We can now devote ourselves to legitimate politics—that is, to studies of governmental science—with a fair prospect of being able to throw some light upon many of the unsolved problems of modern life.

CONCERNS ABOUT ABANDONING
RECONSTRUCTION

George Jones: "The South and the Democracy"

This editorial is skeptical that the Democratic Party can bring prosperity to the South, and it argues that Republicans are not to blame for that section's impoverishment.

New York Times, July 18, 1876

The Southern white population is represented as a unit in support of the Democracy. On the success of that party it stakes its fortunes. It sent its delegates to St. Louis with a general understanding that they should . . . accept any platform and to sustain any nomination that might seem to promise Democratic victory. The plea offered in justification of this conduct . . . is that the material exigencies of the South override all other consideration, and that upon the triumph of the Democratic Party the revival of Southern industries and the re-establishment of Southern prosperity altogether depend.

The poverty of the South does not admit of dispute. In many districts it is even more impoverished, more disheartened and distressed, than at the close of the war. In districts where some improvement has been effected, the condition of the whites is still extremely unfortunate. Land is unsalable. Labor is disorganized. The capital that is needed cannot be had. The influx of Northern and European enterprise and means, which was relied upon to feed the recuperative process, has not been forthcoming. With all its advantages of soil and climate, of timber and water-power, of mineral wealth and manufacturing facilities, the South still languishes, with no immediate prospect of relief. Judging by the prevailing tone of Southern complaints, it might be inferred that all this is the direct product of Northern malignity. The Republican policy, we are told, is responsible for the whole of it. As a matter of fact, nothing could be more untenable. When the war ended . . . energetic Northern men, with adequate capital, went into Virginia, the Carolinas, Tennessee, Alabama, and Mississippi, with no purpose but that of making for themselves homes and helping to build up a prosperous South. These were individual movements, but there would have been no limit to them had those who made the start reported satisfactory results. . . . What happened? The welcome extended to Northern people was conditioned upon the suppression of their convictions respecting the rights and future of the colored portion of the population, and the policy to be pursued by the Federal and local Governments. They were all right as long as they were buying land and contenting themselves with laying the foundations of their new homes. They were all wrong the moment they asserted the rights of citizenship and presented themselves as the advocates and supporters of the Republican Party. From that moment everything was done that could be done to render their position unendurable. They were proscribed socially. . . . If they persisted in their Republicanism, and made common cause with the freedmen, they were soon made conscious of insecurity as regards both person and property. The consequences any one might have foreseen. The flow of settlers and capital Southward suddenly ceased. No man in his senses would go into a community which thus made war upon his manhood. Some that were already there took upon their shoulders a species of martyrdom, and remained to fight it out. . . .

Now, in what way can Democratic success help the South? What possible stimulus can it give to material improvement?—to the introduction of capital and population?—to credit or enterprise, or the pacification and contentment which it requires more than either? Will victory make it less arrogant toward Republican newcomers, less hostile toward the enfranchisement, equality, and education of the Negroes? To better its condition its partisanship must be moderated, not intensified, as it surely would be under the influence of triumph. . . .

The explanation of its zeal in behalf of the Democracy must . . . be sought in another direction. What that direction is we are, unfortunately, not permitted to doubt. . . . It is not liberty that the Southern whites seek at the hands of the Democracy, as their brutal license proves. It is not the removal of inequalities, for all their outages are designed to break down the equality which the constitutional amendments have assured. What they want, what the Democracy, if successful, would readily concede, is the absolute impunity in the perpetration of outrageous wrong, which is unattainable as long as Federal authority is not on their side. Let them have a Democratic President at their back, and the coercion and cruelty, the persecution and the murders, which are now attended with a certain degree of risk, would be simple and safe enough. The letter of the constitutional amendments might remain—their spirit would be reduced to a nullity. The work of the war might not be avowedly undone, but it would be practically re-opened, and its slumbering issues would reappear, to irritate and unsettle the country, under circumstances most disastrous to its interests.

George W. Curtis: "The North and the South"

George W. Curtis, one of Reconstruction's strongest supporters, is willing to lay bitterness aside and let the South back into the fold of the nation—as long as it gives assurances that it will protect its black citizens.

Harper's Weekly, March 17, 1877

For the first time since the end of the war there seems to be an opportunity for a really better understanding between the intelligence of the Northern and Southern parts of the country. It is needless to point out how desirable such a result is, and it is useless to speculate in any recriminative spirit upon the causes that have delayed it. . . . Phrases play an important part in politics. But they are not strong enough to heal the wounds of a difference so radical and bitter as that which has long divided the characteristic spirit and ability of the old Free and the old Slave States. The actual causes of that bitter difference, however, have disappeared, and there will gradually be seen to be no reason that the representative Northern and representative Southern intelligence and interest should not be politically united. We say gradually, because the sense of injury and wrong will long rankle in the Southern popular heart. The only visible and tangible object upon which it can spend itself will be the Republican party. That will be held responsible for all that has befallen, and it will be long distrusted and opposed. The only way to meet this feeling will be to show that "the North" needs only to be assured of the security of equal rights in the "the South," and has no desire whatever to subject it to a condition which it would itself find to be intolerable.

It is this feeling which has often divided the councils of the Republican party. Its part has insisted upon a generous and patriotic Southern policy. This last spirit was represented in the candidacy of Mr. Hayes, and the policy of his administration, unless his sincerest supporters were deceived, will be in harmony with it.

George Jones: No Title

No sooner had President Hayes taken the oath of office than he announced his plan to withdraw the last troops from the South. Although this action was expected, many Republicans—even moderates—hoped that the withdrawal would be done more gradually and after more consideration.

New York Times, March 17, 1877

If the first step in the Southern policy of President Hayes be, as stated in our Washington dispatches, the immediate withdrawal of United States troops from South Carolina and Louisiana, he is on the point of making a serious blunder. No one will dispute that the withdrawal of the troops is a necessary part of any plan that may be devised for the restoration of order and stable government in these States, but such an act should follow, not precede, the making of some plan of conference and settlement. It is hardly possible that any adjustment of the claims of the rival contestants for State offices should already have been effected, either at Columbia or New-Orleans, and failing that, it is not difficult to foresee the kind of settlement which will follow the abandonment of the Chamberlain and Packard Governments to the tender mercies of their opponents. The troops cannot be withdrawn at the present juncture without the implied admission that they were sent, in the first instance, for a totally indefensible purpose, and retained without any obvious necessity. Such an opinion is certainly not that of the vast majority of the Republican Party, and it will be nothing short of a national misfortune should the President fail to carry that majority along with him. He has so great a work to do, and he has so nobly begun it, that we trust there are limitations and conditions attached to the reported stroke of policy which will render it less likely than it seems to elicit the disapproval of the intelligent and law-abiding majority of the Northern people.

Murat Halstead: No Title

Murat Halstead, a leader of the Liberal Republicans and a strong supporter and personal emissary of President Hayes, predicts that the Republican and Democratic parties will be very different in the future. The Republicans were compromising with Southern conservatives, and the old radicals were fast disappearing from the political scene.

Cincinnati Commercial, April 12, 1877

The change of policy at Washington has had the curious effect of bringing into sympathetic if not harmonious relations, extreme Democrats and Radical Republicans; and if the policy is steadily pursued by President Hayes, we may witness the novel spectacle of a political union between such old abolitionists as William Lloyd Garrison and Wendell Phillips, and such extreme Republicans as Blaine and Butler, and the irreconcilable Democrats. . . . Who could have guessed that the time would come when . . . the election of Hayes should be largely due to the conservatism of Southern members of the house? The drift of things is to the formation of a party of conservative ideas under the new administration, and the implacables of both old parties coalescing to defeat it. Evidently the time is not only ripe for a change of policy, but for a change of parties, with such combinations as will bring together those who were enemies, and arraying in opposition those who were friends. The new policy will not be confined in its effects to the adjustment of the Southern troubles and revolutions in the system of civil service, but it will cut through political organizations themselves, and have the logical result of a readjustment of party lines. Some Democrats will find themselves fair Republicans without consciousness almost of the change in their relative positions, while many Republicans will pass over to the other side by mere force of sympathy in a common crusade against the new order of things.

QUESTIONS

1. What were some of the major factors leading to the end of Reconstruction?
2. Why were Republicans abandoning the South?
3. Why were Republican state governments in the South called sham governments?
4. What role did corruption play in the downfall of Republicans?
5. Why did *The Nation* believe that the political influence of blacks would become "almost imperceptible"?

NOTES

1. James Pike, *The Prostrate State: South Carolina under Negro Government* (New York: Appleton, 1873). Reprinted in Walter L. Fleming, *Documentary History of Reconstruction* (Cleveland: Arthur H. Clark, 1907), 51–52.

2. Ibid., 258.

3. *Slaughterhouse Cases,* 83 U.S. 36.

4. *St. Louis Globe Democrat,* 31 March 1877, 4.

Selected Bibliography

Abbott, Martin. *The Freedmen's Bureau in South Carolina, 1865–1872*. Chapel Hill: University of North Carolina Press, 1967.

Abbott, Richard H. *The Republican Party and the South, 1855–77.* Chapel Hill: University of North Carolina Press, 1986.

African-American History. http://afroamhistory.about.com/cs/reconstruction/.

The African-American Mosaic: A Library of Congress Resource Guide for the Study of Black History and Culture. http://lcweb.loc.gov/exhibits/african/afam001.html.

Bailey, John W. *Pacifying the Plains: General Alfred Terry and the Decline of the Sioux, 1866–1890*. Westport, Conn.: Greenwood Press, 1979.

Bailey, Minnie Thomas. *Reconstruction in Indian Territory: A Story of Avarice, Discrimination, and Opportunism*. Cleveland: Arthur H. Clark, 1925.

Bain, David H. *Empire Express: Building the First Transcontinental Railroad.* New York: Penguin Books, 1999.

Barry, Kathleen. *Susan B. Anthony: A Biography of a Singular Feminist*. New York: New York University Press, 1988.

Beeton, Beverly. *Women Vote in the West: The Woman Suffrage Movement, 1869–1896*. New York: Garland, 1986.

Benedict, Michael Les. *The Impeachment and Trial of Andrew Johnson.* New York: Norton, 1999.

Bernstein, David E. *Only One Place of Redress: African Americans, Labor Regulations, and the Courts from Reconstruction to the New Deal*. Durham, N.C.: Duke University Press, 2001.

Bond, James E. *No Easy Walk to Freedom: Reconstruction and the Ratification of the Fourteenth Amendment*. Westport, Conn.: Praeger, 1997.

Brown, Dee. *Bury My Heart at Wounded Knee*. New York: Henry Holt, 2000.

Buhle, Mari Jo, and Paul Buhle, eds. *The Concise History of Woman Suffrage: Selections from the Classic Work of Stanton, Anthony, Gage, and Harper.* Urbana: University of Illinois Press, 1978.

Callow, Alexander B., Jr., *The Tweed Ring.* New York: Oxford University Press, 1966.

Chalmers, David Mark. *Hooded Americanism: The First Century of the Ku Klux Klan, 1865–1965.* Garden City, N.Y.: Doubleday, 1965.

Cimbala, Paul A. *Under the Guardianship of the Nation: The Freedmen's Bureau and the Reconstruction of Georgia, 1865–1870.* Athens: University of Georgia Press, 1997.

Cimbala, Paul A., and Randall M. Miller, eds. *The Freedmen's Bureau and Reconstruction: Reconsiderations.* New York: Fordham University Press, 1999.

Cox, LaWanda. *Freedom, Racism, and Reconstruction.* Athens: University of Georgia Press, 1997.

Crawford, Jay B. *The Crédit Mobilier of America: Its Origin and History, Its Work of Constructing the Union Pacific Railroad and the Relation of Members of Congress.* New York: AMS Press, 1980 (1880, year of original publication).

Cruden, Robert. *The Negro in Reconstruction.* New York: Prentice Hall, 1969.

Current, Richard. *Those Terrible Carpetbaggers: A Reinterpretation.* New York: Oxford University Press, 1988.

Currie-McDaniel, Ruth. *Carpetbagger of Conscience: A Biography of John Emory Bryant.* Athens: University of Georgia Press, 1987.

Danziger, Edmund Jefferson. *Indians and Bureaucrats: Administering the Reservation Policy during the Civil War.* Urbana: University of Illinois Press, 1974.

Dorris, Jonathan Truman. *Pardon and Amnesty under Lincoln and Johnson: The Restoration of the Confederates to Their Rights and Privileges, 1861–1898.* Chapel Hill: University of North Carolina Press, 1953.

DuBois, Ellen Carol. *Feminism and Suffrage: The Emergence of an Independent Women's Movement in America, 1848–1869.* Ithaca, N.Y.: Cornell University Press, 1978.

Feldmeth, Greg D. "U.S. History Resources: Reconstruction 1865–1877," http://home.earthlink.net/~gfeldmeth/lec.recon.html.

Fitzgerald, Michael. *The Union League Movement in the Deep South.* Baton Rouge: Louisiana State University Press, 1989.

Foner, Eric. *Freedom's Lawmakers: A Directory of Black Officeholders during Reconstruction.* New York: Oxford University Press, 1993.

———. *Reconstruction: America's Unfinished Revolution, 1863–1877.* New York: Harper & Row, 1988.

Freedmen's Bureau Online. http://www.freedmensbureau.com/.

Genovese, Eugene D. *A Consuming Fire: The Fall of the Confederacy in the Mind of the White Christian South.* Athens: University of Georgia Press, 1998.

Gillette, William. *Retreat from Reconstruction, 1869–1879.* Baton Rouge: Louisiana State University Press, 1979.

———. *The Right to Vote: The Passage of the Fifteenth Amendment.* Baltimore: Johns Hopkins University Press, 1965.

Goldman, Robert M. *Reconstruction and Black Suffrage: Losing the Vote in Reese and Cruikshank.* Lawrence: University of Kansas Press, 2001.

Gordon, Ann D., ed. *Against an Aristocracy of Sex, 1866–1873.* Vol. 2 of *The Selected Papers of Elizabeth Cady Stanton and Susan B. Anthony.* New Brunswick, N.J.: Rutgers University Press, 2000.

Gordon, Sarah B. *The Mormon Question: Polygamy and Constitutional Conflict in Nineteenth Century America.* Chapel Hill: University of North Carolina Press, 2002.

Gustafson, Melanie Susan. *Women and the Republican Party, 1854–1924.* Urbana: University of Illinois Press, 2000.

Harlow, Jennifer N. "The Compromise of 1876" (United States of America Chronology). http://campus.northpark.edu/history/WebChron/USA/1877Comp.html.

Harper, Ida Husted. *The Life and Work of Susan B. Anthony: Including Public Addresses, Her Own Letters and Many from Her Contemporaries during Fifty Years.* 3 vols. Indianapolis and Kansas City: Bowen-Merrill, 1898–1908.

HarpWeek. http://education.harpweek.com.

Harris, William C. *The Day of the Carpetbagger: Republican Reconstruction in Mississippi.* Baton Rouge: Louisiana State University Press, 1979.

Hershkowitz, Leo. *Tweed's New York: Another Look.* Garden City, N.Y.: Anchor Press/Doubleday, 1977.

Holbo, Paul Sothe. *Tarnished Expansion: The Alaska Scandal, the Press, and Congress, 1867–1871.* Knoxville: University of Tennessee Press, 1983.

Hollandsworth, James G., Jr. *An Absolute Massacre: The New Orleans Race Riot of July 30, 1866.* Baton Rouge: Louisiana State University Press, 2001.

Hoogenboom, Ari. *Rutherford B. Hayes: Warrior & President.* Lawrence: University Press of Kansas, 1995.

Hyman, Harold Melvin. *New Frontiers of the American Reconstruction.* Urbana: University of Illinois Press, 1966.

Jackson, Curtis Emanuel. *A History of the Bureau of Indian Affairs and Its Activities among Indians.* San Francisco: R & E Research Associates, 1977.

Jensen, Ronald J. *The Alaska Purchase and Russian-American Relations.* Seattle: University of Washington Press, 1975.

Kantrowitz, Stephen David. *Ben Tillman and the Reconstruction of White Supremacy.* Chapel Hill: University of North Carolina Press, 2000.

Kennedy, Stetson. *After Appomattox: How the South Won the War.* Gainesville: University Press of Florida, 1995.

Kolchin, Peter. *First Freedom: The Responses of Alabama's Blacks to Emancipation and Reconstruction.* Westport, Conn.: Greenwood, 1972.

Kousser, J. Morgan, and James M. McPherson, eds. *Region, Race, and Reconstruction.* New York: Oxford University Press, 1982.

Litwack, Leon. *Been in the Storm So Long: The Aftermath of Slavery.* New York: Vintage Books, 1979.

Lomask, Milton. *Andrew Johnson: President on Trial.* New York: Farrar, Straus, 1960.

Ludlow, Daniel H., ed. *Encyclopedia of Mormonism.* New York: Macmillan, 1992.

Lumsden, Linda J. *Rampant Women: Suffragists and the Right of Assembly.* Knoxville: University of Tennessee Press, 1997.

Mandelbaum, Seymour J. *Boss Tweed's New York.* New York: John Wiley, 1965.

Many Bloodied Plains: Western Military History. http://www.library.csi.cuny.edu /westweb/.

McBain, Howard L. *Prohibition, Legal and Illegal.* Freeport, N.Y.: Books for Libraries, 1982.

Mercer, Lloyd J. *Railroads and the Land Grant Policy: A Study in Government Intervention.* New York: Academic Press, 1982.

Nolen, Claude H. *African American Southerners in Slavery, Civil War, and Reconstruction.* Jefferson, N.C.: McFarland, 2001.

Perman, Michael. *The Road to Redemption: Southern Politics, 1869–1879.* Chapel Hill: University of North Carolina Press, 1984.

Pitman, Robert C. *Alcohol and the State: A Discussion of the Problem of Law as Applied to the Liquor Traffic.* New York: National Temperance Society, 1880.

Quill, J. Michael. *Prelude to the Radicals: The North and Reconstruction during 1865.* Washington, D.C.: University Press of America, 1980.

Roark, James L. *Masters without Slaves.* New York: Norton, 1979.

Shofner, Jerrell H. *Nor Is It over Yet: Florida in the Era of Reconstruction, 1863–1877.* Gainesville: University Presses of Florida, 1974.

Simkins, Francis Butler. *South Carolina during Reconstruction.* Gloucester, Mass.: P. Smith, 1966.

Stampp, Kenneth. *The Era of Reconstruction, 1865–1877.* New York: Knopf, 1965.

Summers, Mark Wahlgren. *The Press Gang: Newspapers and Politics, 1865–1878.* Chapel Hill: University of North Carolina Press, 1994.

Swinney, Everette. *Suppressing the Ku Klux Klan: The Enforcement of the Reconstruction Amendments, 1870–1877.* New York: Garland, 1987.

Trefousse, Hans Louis. *Impeachment of a President: Andrew Johnson, the Blacks, and Reconstruction.* Knoxville: University of Tennessee Press, 1975.

Trelease, Allen W. *White Terror: The Ku Klux Klan Conspiracy and Southern Reconstruction.* New York: Harper & Row, 1971.

Tunnell, Ted. *Crucible of Reconstruction: War, Radicalism, and Race in Louisiana, 1862–1877.* Baton Rouge: Louisiana State University Press, 1984.

Tyrrell, Ian R. *Sobering Up, from Temperance to Prohibition in Antebellum America, 1800–1860.* Westport, Conn.: Greenwood Press, 1979.

Valley of the Shadow. http://jefferson.village.virginia.edu/vshadow/.

Vandel, Gilles. *The New Orleans Riot of 1866: Anatomy of a Tragedy.* Lafayette: Center for Louisiana Studies, 1983.

Walker, Ronald, et al. *Mormon History.* Champaign: University of Illinois Press, 2001.

Wang, Xi. *The Trial of Democracy, Black Suffrage and Northern Republicans, 1860–1910.* Athens: University of Georgia Press, 1997.

Williams, Alfred Brockenbrough. *Hampton and His Red Shirts: South Carolina's Deliverance in 1876.* Freeport, N.Y.: Books for Libraries, 1970.

Williams, Lou Falkner. *The Great South Carolina Ku Klux Klan Trials, 1871–1872.* Athens: University of Georgia Press, 1996.

Woodward, C. Vann. *Reunion and Reaction: The Compromise of 1877 and the End of Reconstruction.* New York: Oxford University Press, 1991.

Zuczek, Richard. *State of Rebellion: Reconstruction in South Carolina.* Columbia: University of South Carolina Press, 1996.

Index

Abolitionist movement, 281; black suffrage and, 111, 118–19; *Boston Liberator* and, 33–34; as training ground for women's political participation, 221; woman suffrage and, 221, 222

Abolitionists, 211; carpetbaggers compared to, 216–17; Douglass, 110, 111, 114, 155, 156–57; Griffing, 32–34; Higginson, 155, 160–62; Phillips (Wendell), 227, 404; Sojourner Truth, 223

Account of the Proceedings of the Trial of Susan B. Anthony, An, 351

Act to Provide for the More Efficient Government of the Rebel States (1867), 151

Adams, Charles Frances, Jr., 332, 334, 335

Adams, Doc, 372

African Americans. *See* Blacks

Agricultural system of South, rebuilding, 43; need to keep freedmen on plantations, 43, 44

Ah Yuc, 314

Alabama legislature, Forsyth's plea against Fourteenth Amendment to, 133–34

Alaska purchase (1867), 183–91: administration of Alaska, 185; cost of, 185, 190–91; gold discoveries and, 185–86; opposition to, 186, 188–91; reports on natural resources gained, 190–91; support for, 186–88

Albany (N.Y.) Argus, Cassidy's defense of Tweed ring in, 329–30

Alcohol, sale of. *See* Sunday Liquor Laws (1866–73)

American Equal Rights Association, 224

American Journalism (Mott), xii

American Missionary Association, 31

American Woman Suffrage Association, 222

Ames, Oakes, 332, 333, 334, 337, 339, 340, 341

Amnesty Proclamation, 15, 55

Anthony, Susan B., 224, 231, 345–56: arrest of, 347; rejection of cause of, 349–53; support for cause of, 349, 353–56; trial of, 348; woman suffrage and, 222, 223, 345–56

Anti-Coolie Labor Association, 306

Anti-immigrant movement, Sabbatarian movement as, 268–69

Apache Indians, 237

Appomattox, Lee's warning at, 1

Apprenticeships, freedmen's children in, 44

Arp, Bill (Charles H. Smith), 32; opposition to Freedmen's Bureau, 38–39

Athens (Ga.) Southern Banner: Atkinson's opposition to Georgia's new Reconstruction constitution in, 167; Sledge's doubts about Ironclad Test Oath in, 64–65

Athens (Ga.) Watchman, 125; Christy's opposition to Fourteenth Amendment in, 132–33

Atkinson, S.A., opposition to congressional Reconstruction, 155, 166–67

Atlanta Constitution, xv, 171; moderate tone of, 378; opposition to black suffrage under Reconstruction Acts, 171, 176–77

Atlanta Constitution, Grady's opinions in: abandoning Reconstruction, support for, 398–99; compromises of 1876 election, opposition to, 390–91; on Hamburg massacre, 378

Atlanta Constitution, Styles' opinions in: Alaska purchase, opposition to, 190; Fourteenth Amendment, opposition to, 134; refusal to acknowledge Klan violence, 261–62; view of carpetbaggers, 213–15

Atlanta New Era, xv, 119; Bard on manipulation of black suffrage, 119, 120; on congressional Reconstruction policy, 152–53

Atlanta University, 31

Atlantic Monthly, support for congressional Reconstruction in: from Douglass, 156–57; from Higginson, 160–62

Augusta (Ga.) Constitutionalist, "correction" of criticism of Butler for Hamburg massacre in, 379–80

Augusta Loyal Georgian, xv, 16, 211; Bryant's opposition to black codes in, 50–51

Baird, Absalom, 138, 139, 140

Baltimore American and Commercial Advertiser, Garrison's celebration of Fifteenth Amendment in, 299–300

Banks, Nathaniel, 185

Bard, Samuel, xv, 112, 119–20

Baton Rouge (La.) Gazette, support for Chinese labor in, 308–9

Bayard, James, 56

Beach, Moses, antisuffrage view of, 112, 117–18

Bennett, James Gordon, xi, 17, 23–24

Bering, Vitus Jonassen, 183

Bigamy, law against, 281. *See also* Mormons and polygamy (1870–77)

Bingham, 341

Black codes, 43–54, 57, 86, 90; attitudes in the North about black suffrage and, 111; congressional legislation in 1866 in reaction to, 97–98; enforced by militia units of former Confederate soldiers, 371; lingering effect after repeal, 98–99; opposition to, 45, 46–51; prohibitions covered by, 44; support for, 45–46, 51–54

Black Hills, Indian wars over, 247–48

Black militia, 371; black troops as irritation to southerners, 76; Hamburg (S.C.) massacre of, 372–80

Black newspapers, xv; *Mobile (Ala.) Nationalist,* 34–35, 54, 115, 129, 170; reports on Klan violence in, 254

Blacks: abandonment of Reconstruction blamed on ineptness of, 394, 395–400; backlash in mid-1870s against Southern, 394–95; belief in inferiority of, 53–54, 176–77; delegates to constitutional conventions, 153, 209; *Dred Scott* decision and, 21, 123; elected to public office, 154; election of 1868 and, 291; election of 1870 and, 292; failure of Johnson's states' rights policy and, 85; freedom from 1861–1872, 393; Johnson's meeting with leaders of, 86, 110, 114–15; in New Orleans riot of 1866, 139; postponement of justice to, 19, 20–21; preference for Chinese labor over, 308–9; relegation to margins at end of Reconstruction, 400; southern opinion of character of, 52–53; violence against, 49, 85, 86, 97, 111, 151, 251–66, 291, 292, 371–80; White on role of, in Reconstruction, 9. *See also* Freedmen's Bureau (1861–72); Ku Klux Klan (1867–72)

Black suffrage (before the vote, 1865–66), 20, 24, 26, 28, 89, 103, 109–21: concerns about, 112, 117–20; freedmen's conventions and, 110–11; importance of, recognition by supporters and opponents of, 109; Johnson's idea of limited, 109–10; in North, 24, 110; support for, 111–17

Black suffrage under Reconstruction Acts, 151–53, 169–81: blacks' need for education in use of political power, 169; disenfranchisement in South before election of 1876, 382; election of 1867 and, 153, 251; Fifteenth Amendment and, 154, 171, 291–304, 357, 363, 395; Ku Klux Klan and, 253; in North, 171, 180–81; opposition to, 171–77, 223–24; support for, 171, 177–81; voter turnout, 153, 253; woman suffrage and, 222, 223–24, 227–30

Blaine, James, 333, 334, 340, 341, 343, 404

Blue laws, 267. *See also* Sunday Liquor Laws (1866–73)

Bonds, union Pacific, 333

Book of Mormon, 279, 280

Bossier (La.) Banner, scare tactics used to oppose Fourteenth Amendment in, 135

Boston, Sunday closing law in, 268

Boston Daily Advertiser, opposition to impeachment in, 203

Boston Liberator, Griffing's appeal for freedmen in, 33–34

Boston Woman's Journal, support for Anthony's cause in, 355–56

Boston women's convention (1868), 229

Boughton, Seth, 17, 24–26, 46; conservative viewpoint in 1866, 71, 76–77; support of black codes, 46, 52–53

Boutwell, George Sewall, 296, 340, 341

Bowles, Samuel, xi, 3, 10–11, 37–38: Chinese immigration and labor, opposition to, 308; Freedmen's Bureau, support for, 32; impeachment, support for, 196, 199–200; John-

son's Civil Rights Act veto, criticism of, 99, 100–101; for moderate Indian policy, 238, 244; Sunday liquor laws, support for, 269, 271–72; woman suffrage, support for, 223, 229–30

Boycott of all elections and referenda, Forsyth's advocacy of, 164–65

Bradwell v. Illinois, 347–48, 350

Bribery in Crédit Mobilier scandal, 333–34. *See also* Corruption, political

Britain: English concerns over Alaska purchase, 186–87; entry into Crimean War, 184

Brooks, James, 333, 334, 337, 339

Brown, Benjamin Gratz, 345

Brown, George T., 194

Bruce, Frederick, 186–87, 188

Bryant, John Emory, 45, 211, 217; opposition to black codes, 45, 50–51

Bryant, William Cullen, xi, 3, 7–8, 140, 326; on New Orleans riot, 140, 147–48

Buffalo (N.Y.) Express, Twain's satire on Klan lynchings in, 258

Bullock, Rufus, 397, 398

Bureau of Refugees, Freedmen, and Abandoned Lands. *See* Freedmen's Bureau (1865–72)

Butler, Benjamin, 357–59

Butler, Matthew C., 368, 372–73, 375, 376, 378, 379–80, 404

California: Chinese immigrants in, 306–7; gold strikes (1848), 235, 305, 331

Canada: gold discovered in Yukon Territory of, 185–86; white-Indian relations in, 248–49

Canby, Gen., 243

Carpetbagger myth, creation of (1867–69), xii, 153, 207–20, 255, 394, 397; backlash against, 394–95; caricature vs. actual characteristics, 207–8; delegates to constitutional conventions, 209; Klan violence blamed on, 261–62; northern viewpoint, 211, 216–20; political participation, 209; power and corruption,

209–10; southern viewpoint, 210, 211–16

Cassidy, William, in defense of Tweed ring 321, 329–30

Catherine the Great, 183

Central Pacific Railroad Company, 306, 310, 311, 312, 331; Crédit Mobilier scandal and, 334

Chamberlain, Daniel, 372, 373, 376, 377

Chambersburg (Pa.) Valley Spirit, 4

Charleston (S.C.) Courier, 47

Charleston (S.C.) News and Courier, on use of white rifle clubs to quell black violence, 377

Charlottesville (Va.) Chronicle, cooperationist stance in, 162–63

Chase, Salmon, 202

Cheyenne Indians, 237

Chicago: fire of 1871, 269; Sunday closing laws in, 268–69

Chicago Times, xi; "grandmother's" opposition to woman suffrage in, 227; on ratification of Fifteenth Amendment, 292

Chicago Times, Storey's opinions in: advocacy for patience with Mormons, 283–84; Fifteenth Amendment, opposition to, 300–301, 302–3; moderate Indian policy, support for, 245–46; Sunday liquor laws, support for equal enforcement of, 272–73

Chicago Tribune, x, xii; opposition to Alaska purchase in, 190–91; Temperance Bureau letter to, 275–76

Chicago Tribune, White's opinions in: advocacy of patience with Mormons, 285–86; black codes, opposition to, 49–50; on carpetbaggers, 215–17; compromises of 1876 election, support for, 385–86; seating of southern delegates, opposition to, 61–62; Sunday liquor laws, support for, 273–74; unconditional support of Union, call for, 8–9

Child, Lydia Maria, 222

Children of freedmen, black codes covering, 44

China, commercial relations with, 313

Chinatown (San Francisco), 307

Chinese Exclusion Law (1882), 307–8

Chinese immigration and labor (1867–72), 305–16: California gold strikes and, 305; labor competition, fear of, 311–12; laws restricting, 307–8; opposition to, 308, 313–16; support for, 308–13; views of Chinese characteristics, 309–11, 315; violence against immigrants, 305

Chirikov, Aleksey Ilich, 183

Christy, John H.: Murray's response to, 129; opposition to Fourteenth Amendment, 132–33

Churches, political rallies in, 170

Church of Jesus Christ of Latter-day Saints. *See* Mormons and polygamy (1870–77)

Cincinnati Commercial, Halstead's opinions in, xi, xii; Chinese immigration, support for, 312–13; Hayes' election in 1876, support for, 387–88; prediction of political parties of the future, 404–5

Cincinnati Commercial, on Crédit Mobilier scandal, 336–37

Cincinnati Enquirer, xi

Cincinnati Gazette, 1

Cities, impact of Sunday liquor laws in, 268. *See also specific cities*

Citizenship: for blacks, 51, 98, 123; separation of national and state, 359

Civil Rights Act of 1866, 45, 97–107, 123, 156, 169, 307, 357; basic rights of citizens in, 97–98; as conservative measure, 97; Johnson's veto of, 69, 98; opposition to, 99, 103–6; support for, 99–103

Civil Rights Act of 1875, 357–69: dilemma of, 364–65; opposition to, 360, 361–65; passage of, 359; support for, 360, 366–69

Civil Rights Cases, 359–60

Civil War: expectations of South after, 1–2; terms of peace, 1

Cole, Miriam M., 223; support for woman suffrage, 223, 231–33

Colfax, Schuyler, 57, 59, 333, 334, 340, 341, 366

Colleges (normal schools), freedmen's, 31

Commercial newspapers in North, opposition to black suffrage of, 177

Common schools, 360, 361, 368

Communalism, 112

Compromise of 1877, 383

Confiscation of rebel lands, Johnson's disallowance of, 193

Congress: Alaska Purchase and, 185; Boughton on South's representation in, 25–26; carpetbaggers holding seats in, 209; Crédit Mobilier scandal and, 333–34; election of 1866, 70, 73–75; investigation of New Orleans riot/massacre, 140; Joint Committee of Reconstruction (Joint Committee of Fifteen), 57, 69, 79–80, 123, 140, 151; override of Johnson's Civil Rights Act veto, 98; restoration in hands of, 26–27; seating of southern delegates to, 55–68; Select Committee on Freedmen's Affairs, 85–86

Congressional delegation from the South, seating (1865), 55–68: opposition to, 58, 59–63; support for, 58, 63–67

Congressional Reconstruction (1867), 151–68: carpetbaggers' appearance early in, 208–9; as moderate, 151–52; opposition to, 155, 162–67; support for, 155, 156–62

Connolly, Richard B., 319, 321, 324, 325, 327

Conservatism: Curtis' definition of, 72; support for, in 1866, 76–82

Conservative reaction to New Orleans riot, 140, 141–45

Constitutional Amendment. *See* Fourteenth Amendment (1866)

Constitutional conventions (1865), 16, 125, 208–9: black delegates to, 153, 209; black voter turnout in elections for, 153, 170; carpetbagger delegates to, 209; election of delegates to, 151–53, 169, 251

"Coolie" system of contract labor, 306, 314. *See also* Chinese immigration

and labor (1867–72); criticism of, 308; support for, 308–9

Cooperationists (moderate Southerners), 153, 162–63, 172

Copperhead Democrats, xi, 79, 161

Corruption, political, 394–95: Tweed, William Marcy "Boss," and his New York ring; abandonment of Reconstruction and, 395–400; carpetbag, 209–10. *See also* Crédit Mobilier scandal (1872–73)

Cragin Bill, 287

Crédit Mobilier scandal (1872–73), 331–44: critics of, 334, 335–39; scheme involved in, 332–33; skeptics on, 334–35, 339–43

Crime, drunkenness as cause of, 275

Crimean War, 184, 188

Crook, General, 242

Cullom Bill (1869), 281, 282

Curtis, George W., 3, 11–13, 320, 345; abandonment of Reconstruction, opposition to, 396; black suffrage, support for, 111, 112–13; Civil Rights Act of 1866, support for, 99, 101–2; Civil Rights Act of 1875, support for, 360, 366–68; Crédit Mobilier charges, skepticism of, 335, 342–43; Fifteenth Amendment, support for, 293, 295–96; Fourteenth Amendment, support for, 125, 126–27; Freedmen's Bureau Act of 1866, support for, 87, 89–90; impeachment, support for, 196, 197–98; Johnson's Reconstruction plan, criticism of, 17; Klan connected to Democratic Party by, 254, 259–60; for moderate Indian policy, 239, 248–49; on New Orleans riot, 140, 145–46; northern view of Hamburg (S.C.) massacre, 375–76; radical viewpoint during 1866, 70, 71–72; South Carolina Convention, criticism of, 21–22; Tweed ring, opposition to, 321, 325–26; woman suffrage, support for, 223, 230–31

Custer, George, 238, 239, 243, 247, 248, 249

Dana, Charles, opposition to black suffrage under Reconstruction Acts,
  171–72
Davis, David, 383
Davis, Jefferson, 1, 13
Dawes, Henry Laurens, 340, 341
Delane, John, 9
Democratic newspapers, xi, xii–xv: defense of Tweed ring by, 328–30;
  northern, on Hamburg (S.C.) massacre, 378–79; opposition to Freedmen's Bureau Act of 1866, 92–95;
  refusal to acknowledge Klan violence, 255, 260–65; scare tactics
  often used by, 112, 118–19; supporting black codes, 45–46. See also
  Montgomery (Ala.) Daily Advertiser,
  New York News; New York World
Democratic Party, 17, 27, 80; ability to
  bring prosperity to South, Jones'
  skepticism about, 401–2; ascendancy in mid-1870s, 381; Civil
  Rights Act of 1875 and, 365; concerns about black suffrage, 110;
  control of entire South by 1877, 155;
  Copperhead Democrats, xi, 79, 161;
  Curtis' connection of Klan to, 254,
  259–60; Halstead's predictions
  about, 404–5; Ku Klux Klan and,
  251, 253; liquor regulation and, 269,
  276; Marble's opposition to Tweed
  ring within, 322–24; New York Times
  concerning political corruption,
  321–22; Styles' defense of, 262; as
  "working man's party," xi. See also
  Tweed, William Marcy "Boss," and
  his New York ring
Dickinson, Anna, 111
Discrimination, Civil Rights Act of
  1875 protection from, 366–67
Disenfranchisement of former white
  officeholders in South, Fourteenth
  Amendment and, 124, 125
District of Columbia, suffrage vote in,
  169
"Doc Adams" Company of black militia, 372–73
Doremus, T., opposition to Sunday
  liquor laws of, 276–77
Dostie, Paul Anthony, 138, 139, 140

Douglass, Frederick, 110, 111, 114;
  support for congressional Recon-
  struction, 155, 156–57
Dred Scott v. Sanford, 21, 123
Dual legal system, 43. See also Black
  codes
Dunning, William, xii–xiii
Durant, Thomas J., 141, 332–33: on
  New Orleans riot, 141, 148–49

East, Chinese immigrants in the, 306
Economy: boom in the West, 331; election of 1876 and, 385–86; Panic of
  1873, 293, 395
Editors and editorial pages, politics of, x
Education: of freedmen, 31, 36–37,
  178–79; Freedmen's Bureau and,
  31; as prerequisite for suffrage,
  112–13, 295; public, 31, 367–68
Election(s): black militia used during,
  371; of 1866, 70, 73–75, 125; of
  1867, black voter turnout for, 170,
  251; of 1868, 170, 251–53, 291; of
  1870, 292; of 1872, 223, 334,
  346–47; of 1874, 381, 395; of 1876
  (see Presidential election of 1876,
  compromised); Enforcement Act of
  1870 and, 292–93; mock, black participation in, 111
Electoral commission of 1876, 383; opposition to, 384, 389–91; supporters
  of, 384, 385–89
Electoral vote in 1876 election, dispute
  over, 382–83
Elliot, W.M., 255; refusal to acknowledge Klan violence, 255, 260–61,
  264–65; Southern view of carpetbaggers, 210, 212–13
Emancipation Proclamation, 16
Enforcement Acts: of April 20, 1871
  (Ku Klux Klan Force Act), 253, 254,
  260, 395; of May 31, 1870, 292–93,
  347, 395; Second Enforcement Act
  of July 14, 1870, 293
Enfranchisement of freedmen. See
  Black suffrage entries
England, concerns over Alaska purchase, 186–87
Equal civil rights, radical viewpoint on,
  71–72

Equal representation, radical view-
point on, 71
Equal rights for blacks, 89; Civil Rights
Act of 1866 and, 97–107; Civil
Rights Act of 1875 and, 357–69; de-
mands for social rights, 154–55;
Johnson's opposition to, 98; social
rights, 357–69
Equal rights for women, 221. *See also*
Woman suffrage
Equal Rights Leagues, 111
Eutaw, Alabama, Klan violence during
elections in, 253
Excluded classes, in Amnesty Procla-
mation, 15
Ex-Confederate soldiers, violence
against Union sympathizers by,
18–19
Ex parte Milligan, 87
Extermination of Indians, advocates of,
238, 240–42, 243, 244

Factionalism within Republican Party,
154
Federal civil servants, Ironclad Test
Oath required of, 55–57
Federal government, expanding role
into affairs of states of, 29
Fessenden, Robert, 201, 202
Fetterman, William J., 237
Fetterman Massacre, 237
Fifteenth Amendment, 154, 171,
291–304, 357, 363, 395; beginning
of end of Reconstruction, 291; en-
forcement of, concern over, 297–98;
opposition to, 294, 300–303; pur-
pose of, 292; ratification, 292; sup-
port for, 293, 294–300; Supreme
Court's emasculation of, 293; view-
points during congressional hear-
ings on, 291; weakness of, 300,
302–3; woman suffrage movement
and, 222
Fisk University, 31
Flemming, Julius J., 45; opposition to
black codes, 45, 47
Florida, black codes in, 44
Foner, Eric, 393
Force Bill, 368
Forney, John W., 3, 5–7, 185

Forrest, Nathan Bedford, 251, 253
Forsyth, John, 87, 126, 140, 155; "black
republican party" in Washington,
bombast against, 99, 104–5; black
suffrage under Reconstruction Acts,
opposition to, 173; congressional
Reconstruction, opposition to, 155,
164–65; Fourteenth Amendment,
opposition to, 126, 133–34; Freedmen's Bureau Act of 1866, opposition to, 87, 93–94; harangue of
North after elections of 1866, 82; on
New Orleans riot, 140, 143
Fort Wayne (Ind.) Weekly Sentinel, support for strong military handling of
Indians in, 243
Foster, Charles, 387
Fourierism, 118, 119
Fourteenth Amendment (1866), 54,
117, 123–36, 169, 298, 307, 357,
395; as central issue in campaign of
1866, 125; citizenship and civil
rights constitutionally guaranteed
under, 123–24; as compromise, 124,
125, 126; four resolutions of, 124;
Harding's advice to South on ratification of, 62–63; Nordhoff's recommendation to adopt, 73; opposition
to Civil Rights Act of 1875 based on,
362–63; proposal of, 69–70; ratification of, 125, 153; ratification of, opposition to, 125–26, 130–35;
ratification of, support for, 125,
126–30; Supreme Court's emasculation of, 348, 349, 359, 395; woman
suffrage movement and, 222,
349–56
Fourteenth Resolution of the Republican platform (1872), 231–33
Fowler, Senator, 201
Franchise. *See Black suffrage entries;*
Woman suffrage
Fraud: Crédit Mobilier scandal and,
331–44; Tweed ring and, 319–21
Freedmen: contracts between white
landowners and, 30–31, 35; land
rented to, 30
Freedmen's aid societies, 31
Freedmen's Bureau (1865–72), 29–41,
170, 255; agents of, 30, 208; discon-

tinuation of, 37–38; duties of, 29, 30–31; education system created by, 31; financial support for, 30, 193; as first federal social welfare bureaucracy, 29; labor contracts overseen by, 30–31; opinions favoring work of, 32–38; opinions opposing work of, 38–40; responsibilities of, 85, 88; Steedman and Fullerton's report on, 32, 35, 39–40

Freedmen's Bureau Act (1866), 31, 32, 85–95, 156; black civil rights under, 86; Johnson's veto of, 31, 39, 69, 86, 88–95; opposition to, 87, 92–95; passage of, 87; support for, 87, 88–92

Freedmen's conventions, statewide, 110–11

Freedmen's schools, 31, 36–37, 208; political rallies in, 170

Freedom, franchise as ultimate sign of, 113–14

Freedom of speech, New Orleans riot as abridgement of, 141, 149

Freeman's Champion, 51–52

Fugitive Slave law, comparison of Civil Rights Act to, 99–100, 106

Fullerton, Joseph, 32, 35, 39

Fur trading in Alaska, 183–84

Galveston Weekly News, 51

Garfield, James, 333, 340, 341, 383, 384

Garrison, William Lloyd, 18, 404; congratulatory letter on Fifteenth Amendment, 293, 299–300; as foremost abolitionist, 299

Garvey, Andrew J., 320, 326, 329

Georgia: black codes in, 50–51, 52–53; Bryant portrayed as carpetbagger in, 211–12; carpetbaggers in, 397–98; Klan impact on black voter turnout in, 253; new Reconstruction constitution for, Atkinson's opposition to, 166–67; opposition to Fourteenth Amendment in, 134

Georgia Equal Rights Association, 211

German community in Chicago, protest against Sunday liquor laws by, 268–69, 272–74

Gerrymandering, 292

Gibson, A.M., 333

Glass, R.H., 155; opposition to congressional Reconstruction, 155, 163–64

Godbeites, 289

Godkin, E.L., x, 32, 35–36, 87, 90, 140, 155, 360; abandonment of Reconstruction, support for, 395–96; Alaska Purchase, opposition to, 186, 188–89; Civil Rights Act of 1875, opposition to, 360, 362–63; Civil Rights Act of 1875, support for, 368–69; congressional Reconstruction, support for, 155, 159–60; on Crédit Mobilier scandal, 334, 337–38, 339–40; Fifteenth Amendment support of, 293, 296–98; Freedmen's Bureau Act of 1866, support for, 87, 90–92; impeachment, support for, 201; on message of election of 1866, 70, 74–75; on New Orleans riot, 140, 148; northern view of Hamburg (S.C.) massacre, 373–75; rejection of Anthony's cause, 349–50; on seating of southern delegates, 58, 60–61; for strong military stand against Indians, 238, 239–40

Godwin, Parke, 211, 349; abandonment of Reconstruction, support for, 396–97; Anthony's cause, support for, 349, 354; northern view of carpetbaggers, 211, 218–19; as skeptical of Crédit Mobilier charges, 335, 340–42

Gold: Alaska Purchase and, 185–86; in California, 235, 305, 331; in South Dakota, 237–38, 247

Grady, Henry, 384, 396; abandonment of Reconstruction, support for, 396; compromises of 1876 election, opposition to, 384, 390–91; on Hamburg (S.C.) massacre, 378

Grant, Ulysses S., ix, 1, 76, 139, 194, 202, 335; attempts to enforce voting rights, 395; Civil Rights Act of 1875, signing of, 359; election in the November 1868, 160, 253, 291; Fifteenth Amendment and, 292;

Hamburg (S.C.) massacre and, 373; Indian policy and, 237, 248; Klan violence and, 253, 254; Mormons and, 284–85, 287; southern view of carpetbaggers and, 215–16

Great Nordic Expedition (1741), 183

Greeley, Horace, x, xii, 3, 5, 144, 196, 231, 335, 342; advocating harsher approach to Mormons, 282, 286–87; Alaska purchase, opposition to, 189–90; black codes, opposition to, 45, 46–47; black suffrage, support for, 111, 113–14, 171, 177–78; Civil Rights Act of 1866, support for, 99, 102–3; congressional Reconstruction, support for, 155, 158–59; Fifteenth Amendment, support for, 293, 294–95; Freedmen's Bureau Act of 1866, support for, 87, 88–89; impeachment, opposition to, 196; inconsistency and excessive conciliation of, 158; on New Orleans riot, 140, 146–47; northern view of carpetbaggers, 211, 216–18; "reconstructed" states, criticism of, 17, 19–21; for strong military handling of Indians, 241, 241–42; Sunday liquor laws, support for, 269, 270–71; as temperance advocate, 269, 270; on woman suffrage, 222

Griffin, Albert, 254; warning about Klan violence, 254, 257

Griffing, Josephine E., 32–34

Griffin (Ga.) American Union, Murray's support of Fourteenth Amendment in, 125, 129–30

Griggs, Robert G., 320

Grimes, Senator, 201

Habeas corpus, Johnson's restoration of writ of, 90

Hahn, Michael, 139

Hall, A. Oakley, 319, 327; in defense of Tweed ring, 321, 328

Halstead, Murat, xi, 384, 396; abandonment of Reconstruction, opposition to, 396; Chinese immigration and labor, support for, 308; compromises of 1876 election, support for, 384, 387–88

Hamburg, South Carolina, massacre (1876), 371–80: cause of, 372–73; election of 1876 and, 373–77, 381–82; northern view of, 373–77; southern view of, 377–80

Hampton, Wade, 20, 65

Hancock, General, 163

Harding, William W., 125, 171, 282; advocating patience with Mormons, 282, 284–85; Alaska Purchase, support for, 186–87; black suffrage under Reconstruction Acts, support for, 171, 178–79; Fourteenth Amendment, support for, 125, 127–28; Klan activities, opposition to, 254–55, 260; passion for reading and education, 178; on seating of southern delegates, 58, 62–63; for strict enforcement of antipolygamy laws, 282, 288–89; woman suffrage, opposition to, 223, 225

Harlan, James, 240

Harper Bros., 320

Harper's Monthly review of book by Mormon wife, 289–90

Harper's Weekly, 254; reports on Klan violence in, 254; on Tweed ring, 319, 320

Harper's Weekly, Curtis' opinions in: abandoning Reconstruction, skepticism about, 403; accusing Klan of being arm of Democratic Party, 259–60; call for strong Reconstruction policy, 12–13; Civil Rights Act of 1866, support for, 101–2; Civil Rights Act of 1875, support for, 366–67; complaint about emasculated Civil Rights Act of 1875, 367–68; Crédit Mobilier scandal, skepticism about, 342–43; denunciation of Johnson over New Orleans riot, 145–46; Fifteenth Amendment, support for, 295–96; Fourteenth Amendment, support for, 126–27; Freedmen's Bureau Act of 1866, support for, 89–90; on Hamburg (S.C.) massacre, 375–76; impeachment, support for, 198; Indian policy, criticism of harsh, 248–49; South Carolina Convention, criticism of, 21–22; summary of radical viewpoint in 1866, 71–72; on Tweed ring and general corruption, 325–26; woman suffrage, support for, 230–31

Harrison, William H., x

Hastings, Warren, 197

Hayes, Rutherford B., ix, 374, 376, 381, 385, 399, 403; compromised election of 1876, 381–91; on disenfranchisement of blacks in South, 382; Jones' portrait of, in *New York Times*, 386–87; Klan violence and, 254; withdrawal of last federal troops from the South, 395, 403–4

Head tax, 44

Henderson, John Brooks, 201, 244

Hennessey, R. J., 320

Herron, Andrew S., 146

Higginson, Thomas Wentworth, 155; support for congressional Reconstruction, 155, 160–62

Hillsdale (Mich.) Standard: criticism of northern states for lack of black suffrage, 180–81; opposition to seating of southern delegates in, 59–60

Holden, William, xv

Horton, Jotham, 139

Hotels in Boston, Sunday closing laws and, 268

House of Representatives: Alaska Purchase and, 185; election of 1874 and changed profile of, 381; impeachment process in, 195; investigation of Crédit Mobilier scandal, 334, 337–39

Houston, Texas, call for black codes in, 51–52

Houzeau, Jean-Charles, 45, 47–48

Howard, Oliver Otis, 30, 31, 32–33, 40, 85, 87

Howard University, 31

Howe, Julia Ward, 222, 231

Huckleberry Finn (Twain), 258

Hudson's Bay Company, 184

Hunt, Ward, 348, 350

Immigrants: befriended by Tweed ring, 319; Sunday closing law discriminating against, 268–69. *See also* Chinese immigration and labor (1867–72)

Immigration laws, 307

Impartial intelligence suffrage, 116–17. *See also Black suffrage entries*

Impeachment of President Johnson (1868), 137, 185, 193–206: cause of, 193–94; eleven articles of, 195; failure of, 195; opposition to, 196, 203–5; process, 195; support for, 196–202

Indian Bureau, 237, 238, 241

Indian policy in the West (1867–76), 235–50, 293; gold rush and, 235; moderate policy, support for, 238–39, 244–49; peace policy of Grant, 237; "removal and concentration" policy (reservations), 235–36, 237, 238, 240, 244; strong military stand, support for, 238, 239–43; treaties, 235–36, 237, 247, 248–49

Indian Wars, 236

Invisible Empire of the South. *See* Ku Klux Klan (1867–72)

Ironclad Test Oath, 16, 55–57, 58, 59, 63; Sledge's doubts about, 64–65; southern defiance of, 57

Jacksonville (Ala.) Republican, xiv

Jacksonville Florida Times, xiv

Jennings, Louis J., 171; advocating patience with Mormons, 282–83; black suffrage under Reconstruction Acts, support for, 171, 179–80; Fifteenth Amendment, support for, 293, 298–99; review of Adam's article in *North American Review*, 334, 335–36, 338–39; Tweed ring, opposition to, 321–22, 324–25

Jim Crow laws, 360

Johnson, Andrew, ix, 69, 85; Alaska Purchase and, 185; assumption of office, 85; conservative support in 1866 for, 71; Fourteenth Amendment, denunciation of, 124; Freedmen's Bureau, attacks on, 31–32; Greeley's warning to, 88–89; hope placed in, 3, 4–5; impeachment of, 137, 185, 193–206; inconsistency of, 89–90; inspectors sent to the

South by, 87; intemperate and unpresidential speeches during 1866,
77–78; Ironclad Test Oath and, 56,
57; land redistribution and, 30; on
limited black suffrage, 109–10; loyalty pledges of southern states to,
15; meeting with black leaders in
1866, 86, 110, 114–15; New Orleans riot of 1866 and, 138, 139–40,
142, 145–48; pardons to the Southern leadership, 69; Phillips' call to
unite conservatives, 78–80; power
under second Freedmen's Bureau
Act, 87; presidential Reconstruction
plan (1865–66), 15–28, 55–57, 69,
70, 85, 109; as provisional governor
of Tennessee, 2, 69; as racist, 98;
Radical Congress vs. (1866),
69–83; Reconstruction frustrated
by, 193; restoration of southern
states, 60, 61; seating of southern
congressional delegates and, 26–27,
58, 61; South's disappointment in,
76–77; speculation about postwar
policy of, 2; Tenure of Office Act,
challenge to, 193–94; veto of Civil
Rights Act of 1866, 69, 98; veto of
congressional Reconstruction act,
151; veto of Freedmen's Bureau Act
of 1866 and responses to, 31, 39,
69, 86, 88–95
Joint Committee of Congress on Chinese Immigration, report of, 311–12
Joint Committee of Reconstruction
(Joint Committee of Fifteen), 57, 69,
79–80, 123, 140, 151
Jones, George, 211, 239, 349, 360;
abandonment of Reconstruction,
opposition to, 396; Civil Rights Act
of 1875, opposition to, 360, 364–65;
compromises of 1876 election, support for, 384, 386–87; end of Reconstruction blamed on Southern
whites, 396; for moderate policy toward Indians, 239, 246–48; northern view of carpetbaggers, 211,
219–20; rejection of Anthony's
cause, 349, 350–51
Journalists: reports of conditions in
South from, 151; on southern cor-

ruption and black ineptness,
394–95. *See also specific journalists*
Judiciary Committee, impeachment
process and, 195

"Karinus," support for black suffrage
under Reconstruction Acts, 171,
180–81
Keating, John Mcleod, 238; for moderate policy toward Indians, 238, 245;
opposition to Fifteenth Amendment,
294, 301
Kemble, Fanny, 222
Knights of the Golden Circle, 256
Knights of the White Camellia, 170,
253
Kodiak Island, 183
Ku Klux Klan (1867–72), 31, 170,
251–66, 291, 375, 376, 393, 395;
campaign of terror during election
of 1868 and, 251–53; Democratic
Party and, 251, 253; founding of,
251; laws to control, 253–54; mission of, 251; opposition to activities
of, 254, 255–60; refusal to acknowledge violence of, 255, 260–65
Ku Klux Klan Force Act of 1871, 253,
254, 260, 395

Labor, Chinese. *See* Chinese immigra-
tion and labor (1867–72)
Labor contracts: between black labor-
ers and white landowners, 30–31,
35, 43; "Coolie" system of contract
labor, 306, 308–9, 314
Labor system, punitive, 70
Land redistribution policy, 30
Laurensville, South Carolina, Klan
killings in (1870), 253
Lee, Robert E., 1, 6, 29, 123
Liberal Republican Party, xii, 345, 404
Licentiousness of the press, Curtis on,
342
Lincoln, Abraham, ix, 1, 80, 109, 331;
assassination, attitudes on Reconstruction after, 8; inaugural address
(March 4, 1865), 1; wartime Reconstruction plan, 137
Liquor laws. *See* Sunday Liquor Laws
(1866–73)

Liquor license (excise) fee, New York, 268

Liquor regulation, split along party lines over issue of, 269

Little Bighorn, Battle of the (1876), 234–38: as turning point for public opinion on Indian policy, 242–43

Litwack, Leon, 111

London Times, 3, 155, 196; on impeachment, 196, 204–5; predictions about Reconstruction in, 9–10; on Sunday liquor laws, 270, 277–78; sympathy with the South in, 165–66

Los Angeles, anti-Chinese riot in (1871), 306

Louisiana: black codes in, 47–48; Constitutional Convention of 1864, 137–38; efforts to reconvene convention in 1866, 138; Klan killings by Election Day 1868 in, 252; massacre of 60 blacks in (1873), 293; New Orleans riot of 1866, 70, 137–50

Louisiana Bill, 140

Louisville Courier-Journal, xii

Lowell, James Russell, 317

Loyalty oath, 15; property rights restored to Confederates taking, 55

Lynchburg (Va.) Republican, Glass' opposition to congressional Reconstruction policies in, 163–64

Lynching, Twain's satirical protest against Klan, 258

McComb, 340, 341

McDowell, General Irvin, 163

Macon (Ga.) American Union, xv

Macon (Ga.) Daily Telegraph, Sneed's opposition to Civil Rights Act of 1866 in, 106

McPherson, Edward, 57, 64

Manifest Destiny, acquisition of Alaska and, 187–88

Marble, Manton, xi, 17, 26–28, 87, 125, 171; agreement to lead fight to clean up Democratic Party, 322–24; black suffrage under Reconstruction Acts, opposition to, 171, 174–76; Civil Rights Act of 1866, opposition to, 99, 105–6; defense of Johnson in

1866, 71, 77–78; Fourteenth Amendment, opposition to, 125–26, 130–31; Freedmen's Bureau, opposition to, 32, 40; Freedmen's Bureau Act of 1866, opposition to, 87, 94–95; impeachment, opposition to, 196, 203–4; woman suffrage, opposition to, 223–24

Martial law, rebel states subject to, 86; *ex parte Milligan* and end to, 87

Mason, Samuel W., 58; Fourteenth Amendment, opposition to, 131–32; on New Orleans riot, 140, 142–43; outrage over requirements for seating southern delegation, 66–67

Mason (mayor of Chicago), 274

Massacre in New Orleans (1866), 70, 137–50

Massacres, Indian Wars and, 236

Matthews, Stanley, 387

McLean, John, xi

McPherson, Edward, xiv

Meade, George, 134, 163, 170, 260, 261

Medill, Joseph, 269

Memphis, Tennessee, riots in (1866), 70, 140

Memphis (Tenn.) Appeal, Keating's opinions in: brutality of Indian policy, criticism of, 245; Fifteenth Amendment, opposition to, 301

Memphis (Tenn.) Daily Appeal, xv, 263–64

Meriwether, McKie, 373

Michigan, "Karinus'" on lack of black suffrage, 180–81

Military commanders, 125, 163; Boughton's complaint about despotism of, 77; Godkin's praise for, 159, 160

Military courts in South, 87

Military districts, division of southern states into, 125, 151

Military Reconstruction Act, 164

Militia, black, 371

Militia units, state, 371

Milledgeville (Ga.) Federal Union, Boughton's opinions in, xv; disappointment in Johnson, 76–77; pledge of cooperation in return for moderate policy, 25–26; support for black codes, 52–53

Ministers, voter registration by black itinerant organizers, 170

Miscegenation, 44–45, 98, 118

Missionaries in freedmen's schools, southern white hatred of, 36–37

Mississippi: adoption of new state constitution in, 17; black code passed in, 43; Johnson's limited black suffrage advice to, 109–10; white supremacists' counterrevolution in, 170

Mississippi Convention, Johnson's address to, 26

Mississippi Valley Immigration Labor Company, 305–6

Missouri, Mormon community in, 279

Mobile (Ala.) Advertiser and Register, Forsyth's opinions in, xiv, xv; bombast against "black republican party," 99, 105–6; congressional Reconstruction policies, opposition to, 164–65; on constitutional conventions, 153; Fourteenth Amendment, opposition to, 133–34; Freedmen's Bureau Act of 1866, opposition to, 93–94; harangue of North after elections of 1866, 82; reaction to New Orleans riot, 143; threats to intimidate black voters, 173–74

Mobile (Ala.) Nationalist, xv, 54, 129, 170; report of Johnson's meeting with black delegation in, 115; reports on Klan violence in, 254, 257; support for Freedmen's Bureau in, 34–35

Mobile (Ala.) Tribune, opposition to Chinese immigration and labor in, 315

Mock elections, black participation in, 111

Moderate Republican newspapers, xi

Moderates, Universal Suffrage and Universal Amnesty proposal of, 115–16

Monroe, Mayor (New Orleans), 146

Montgomery (Ala.) Daily Advertiser, 26; Screws' on constitutional convention in, 165; Screws' warning to

blacks to stay away from politics, 172–73; support for seating southern delegation in, 66

Montgomery (Ala.) State Journal, xv

Mormons and polygamy (1870–77), 279–90: advocacy for patience with, 282–86; advocacy of harsh policy toward, 282, 286–90; disturbing practices of, 280; founding of Mormon church, 279; legislation against polygamy, 281–82; violence against, 279–80

Morrill Anti-Bigamy Law (1862), 281

Mott, Frank Luther, xii

Mott, Lucretia, 221, 222

Murray, Alexander G., 125; support of Fourteenth Amendment, 125, 129–30

Nashville (Tenn.) Daily Union, 53

Nast, Thomas, cartoons of, 320; of "Boss" Tweed, 319; of carpetbagger, 208; of Klan, 252, 254; of white supremacist violence against blacks, 358

Nation, The, Godkin's opinions in, x, xii; abandoning Reconstruction, support for, 396–97, 399–400; Alaska purchase, opposition to, 189; Civil Rights Act of 1875, opposition to, 362–63; congressional Reconstruction policies, support for, 160; on Crédit Mobilier scandal, 337–38, 340; criticism of Johnson over New Orleans riot, 148; Fifteenth Amendment, support for, 296–98; Freedmen's Bureau, recognition of good work of, 35–36; Freedmen's Bureau Act of 1866, support for, 91–92; on Hamburg (S.C.) massacre, 373–75; impeachment, support for, 201; rejection of Anthony's cause, 349–50

National Anti-Slavery Standard: Garrison's criticism of Johnson's moderate policy in, 18; Stanton's support for woman suffrage in, 228–29

Nationalization of Reconstruction, 298–99

National Union Party, 70, 139–40: Philips' call to Johnson to form, 78–80

National Woman Suffrage Association, 222, 230, 231

Nauvoo, Illinois, Mormon community in, 279

"Negro Question," Reconstruction debate and, 16–17, 117, 292, 297, 303

Negro suffrage question. *See Black suffrage entries*

Nevada, White's suggestion of uniting Utah and, 286

New Orleans, segregated public transportation in, 45

New Orleans riot/massacre (1866), 70, 137–50: conservative responses to, 140, 141–45; events of, 138–40; radical responses to, 140–41, 145–49

New Orleans Tribune, xv, 18–19, 49, 254; Houzeau's opposition to black codes in, 47–48; reports on Klan violence in, 254; violence against Union sympathizers described in, 18

New South, Grady's racist view of, 398–99

Newspapers during Reconstruction, ix–xv; as political entities, x. *See also specific newspapers*

New York: State Assembly, 319; Sunday closing law in, 268, 276–77; Sunday law (1695) in, 267; Tweed and his political ring in, 317–30

New York Board of Alderman, 317

New York City, as statutory city, 319

New York County Board of Supervisors, 317–19

New York Court House, graft involved in building of, 326–27

New York Daily News: Greeley's response to, on Sunday liquor laws, 270; Wood's opposition to Sunday liquor laws in, 276

New York Evening Post, xi; support for Civil Rights Act of 1866, 99–100; on Tweed ring, 326–29

New York Evening Post, Bryant's opinions in: criticism of Johnson over New Orleans riot, 147–48; editorial of hope, 7–8

New York Evening Post, Godwin's opinions in: abandoning Reconstruction,

support for, 397–98; Anthony's cause, support for, 354; initial skepticism about Crédit Mobilier scandal, 341–42; view of carpetbaggers, 218–19

New York Evening Post, Nordhoff's opinions in: Civil Rights Act of 1866, support of, 99–100; Fourteenth Amendment, support of, 128–29; letter to *New York Times* describing NYC courthouse, 326–27; on message of election of 1866, 70, 73

New York Herald, xi, 92; Bennett's support of Johnson's moderate policy in, 23; call for Johnson to unite conservatives, 71, 78–80; on exclusion of southern congressional delegates, 58; Freedmen's Bureau Act of 1866, opposition to, 92–93; Phillips' scare tactics concerning black suffrage in, 118–19; seating of southern delegation, support for, 63–64; "squibs" describing evils resulting from civil rights for blacks, 99, 103–4; strong military approach toward Indians in, support for, 240–41; Tweed ring and, 319

New York Journal of Commerce, opposition to black suffrage under Reconstruction Acts, 177

New York Leader, Hall's defense of Tweed in, 328

New York News, Wood's support for Johnson's moderate policy in, 22–23

New York Sun, 17; Beach on state's right to decide on black suffrage, 117–18; on Crédit Mobilier scandal, 333–34; Greeley's response to, over black suffrage, 177–78

New York Times, xi, 70, 319; challenge to *New York World* and Democrats to clean up party, 321; on Chinese immigration and labor, 311; criticism of Congress in 1866, 71; on fraud of Tweed ring, 319–20; on Hamburg (S.C.) massacre, 376–77; southern view of carpetbaggers in, 210, 211–12; Stanton's support for Anthony's cause in, 353; withdrawal of support from Johnson in 1866, 70, 75–76; on woman suffrage, Curtis' response to, 230–31

New York Times, Jennings' opinions in: advocacy for patience with Mormons, 282–83; black suffrage under Reconstruction Acts, support for, 179–80; on Crédit Mobilier scandal, 334, 335–36, 338–39; Fifteenth Amendment, support for, 298–99; on Tweed's graft, 324–25

New York Times, Jones' opinions in: Civil Rights Act of 1875, opposition to, 364–65; compromises of 1876 election, support for, 386–87; parody of Indian policy, 247–48; rejection of Anthony's cause, 350–51; skepticism about abandoning Reconstruction, 401–2; skepticism about withdrawal of federal troops from the South, 403–4; view of carpetbaggers, 219–20

New York Times, Raymond's opinions in: Alaska Purchase, support for, 187–88; on benefits of impeachment, 198–99; congressional Reconstruction policies, support of, 158; criticism of radical Congress in 1866, 80–82; Freedmen's Bureau, opposition to, 39–40; on "impartial intelligence suffrage," 116–17; on New Orleans riot, 144–45

New York Tribune, x, xii, 17, 319; Doremus' opposition to Sunday liquor laws in, 277; Durant on freedom of speech, 149; letter about teachers' experience in freedmen's schools, 36–37; Pike's racist picture of black legislators and carpetbaggers in, 394; portrayal of Tweed ring, 319; Reid's opposition to compromises of 1876 election in, 389–90; Young's description of Klan activities in, 255–56; Young's support for impeachment in, 196–97

New York Tribune, Greeley's opinions in: advocacy of harsh policy toward Mormons, 286–87; Alaska purchase, opposition to, 189–90; black codes,

opposition to, 46–47; black suffrage under Reconstruction Acts, support for, 178; call for reasonable peace, 5; on carpetbaggers, 216–18; Civil Rights Act of 1866, support for, 102–3; congressional Reconstruction policies, support for, 159; criticism of Johnson over New Orleans riot, 146–47; criticism of "reconstructed" states, 19–21; Fifteenth Amendment, support for, 294–95; Freedmen's Bureau Act of 1866, support for, 88–89; strong military handling of Indians, support for, 241–42; Sunday liquor laws, support for, 270–71

New York World, xi, 319, 379; on Hamburg (S.C.) massacre, 379; portrayal of Tweed ring, 319

New York World, Marble's opinions in: black suffrage and office holding, opposition to, 175–76, 224; Civil rights Act of 1866, opposition to, 105–6; defense of Johnson's intemperate speeches in 1866, 77; Fourteenth Amendment, opposition to, 130–31; Freedmen's Bureau, opposition to, 40, 94–95; impeachment, opposition to, 203–4; Johnson's moderate policy, support for, 27–28; pledge to clean up Democratic Party, 321, 323–24; woman suffrage, opposition to, 224

Nez Perce, 237

"Nigger," Twain's use of term, 258

Nineteenth Amendment, 345, 349; ratification of, 223

Nordhoff, Charles, 73, 125; on message of election of 1866, 70, 73; opposition to Tweed ring, 321, 326–27; support of Fourteenth Amendment, 125, 128–29

North, the: black suffrage in, 24, 110, 171, 180–81; carpetbagger myth in, 211, 216–20; newspapers in, x–xii; southern harangue of, after elections of 1866, 82

North American Review, 319, 332; Adams' description of Crédit Mobilier in, 332, 334, 335–36

North Carolina, Johnson's Reconstruction plan for, 15, 17
Northwest Company, 184
Norton, Frank H., support for Chinese immigration and labor, 308, 309–11

O'Brien, James, 319
Oklahoma territory, resettlement of Indians in, 235

Pacific Railroad. *See* Union Pacific Railroad
Pacific Railway Act, 333
Panic of 1873, 293, 395
Paramilitary groups, white, 371–72
Patronage, xii–xiii, xiv; corruption driven by, 394; federal, carpetbaggers and, 215–16; Freedmen's Bureau seen as patronage scam, 94–95; Tweed ring and, 317
Perry, Provisional Governor, 21
Philadelphia Exposition, Chinese products in, 313
Philadelphia Inquirer, Harding's opinions in, x; Alaska Purchase, support for, 186–87; black suffrage under Reconstruction Acts, support for, 178–79; Fourteenth Amendment, support for, 128; Ku Klux Klan Force Act, praise for, 260; on Mormons, 284–85, 288–89; seating of southern delegates, opposition to, 62–63; woman suffrage, opposition to, 225
Philadelphia Press, Forney's hope for Unionism in South in, 6–7
Phil Kearney, massacre at Fort, 237, 243
Phillips, W.B.: antisuffrage view and scare tactics of, 112, 118–19; call to Johnson to unite conservatives, 78–80; Civil Rights Act of 1866, opposition to, 99, 103–4; Freedmen's Bureau Act of 1866, opposition to, 87, 92–93; seating of southern delegates, support for, 58, 63–64
Phillips, Wendell, 404; Stanton's prowoman suffrage response to, 227–29

Pike, Albert, 255; refusal to acknowledge Klan violence, 255, 263–64
Pike, James, 394
Plains Indians, 235, 241
Planter class, resumption of leadership in South, 193
Platte River Bridge, battle at, 240
Plessy v. Ferguson, 360
Poland Committee, 334, 339, 340, 343
Police in New Orleans riot of 1866, 138–39, 140
Political leadership in South, election of, 16–17. *See also* Constitutional conventions (1865)
Political ring. *See* Tweed, William Marcy "Boss," and his New York ring
Politics, women's participation in, 221. *See also* Woman suffrage
Poll tax, 293
Polygamy, Mormons and, 279–90
Pope, John, xiv
Poverty of the South, 401–2
Presidential election: of 1868, 170, 251–53, 291; of 1872, 223, 334, 346–47
Presidential election of 1876, compromised, 381–91: electoral vote, 382–83; Hamburg (S.C.) massacre and, 373–77, 381–82; negotiations for compromise, 383–84; opposition to compromises of, 384, 389–91; popular vote, 382; support for compromises of, 384, 385–89
Presidential Reconstruction plan (1865–66), 15–28, 55–57, 69, 70, 85, 109; critics of Johnson's policy of moderation, 17, 18–22; initial favorable responses to, 15; supporters of Johnson's policy of moderation, 17, 22–28
Printing contracts, newspaper, xiv
Private rights against state interference, 124
Protestants, Sunday liquor laws and, 268
Provisional governments, 371
Public accommodations and facilities, black access to, 359–60
Public education: Civil Rights Act of 1875 and, 367–68; in the South,

Freedmen's Bureau and, 31. *See also* Schools

Public transportation, segregation of, 44–45

Puritans, Sunday liquor laws and, 267

Quaker Indian agents, 237

Queue Ordinance (San Francisco), 307

Quotas, immigrant, 308

Race riots. *See* Riots

Racial amalgamation, 44–45

Racism, 109; of editorials in Southern newspapers, 106; of Johnson, 98; segregation through Jim Crow laws, 360; woman suffrage movement and, 222

Racist language, 171

Radical Congress, 69–83: conservative opposition to, 71, 76–82; support of radical viewpoint, 70, 71–76

Radicalism, Curtis' definition of, 71–72

Radical Republicans: black suffrage as part of plan of, 109; Hamburg massacre blamed on abuses of, 378–79; Harding on, 62–63; Johnson supporters' criticism of, 23, 24, 25, 27–28; New Orleans riot of 1866 and, 137, 140–43, 145–49; newspapers of, x–xi; Phillips' respect for, 79; presidential Reconstruction plan, reaction to, 15–16; Raymond's criticism of, 80–82, 144; southern responses to demands of, 66–67

Railroad, transcontinental. *See* Transcontinental railroad

Railway consolidations, 336

Rainey, Joseph H., 154

Raleigh (N.C.) Standard, xv

Raymond, Henry J., xi, 32; Alaska Purchase, support for, 186, 187–88; black suffrage, support for, 112, 115–17; congressional Reconstruction, support for, 155, 157–58; criticism of radical Congress in 1866, 80–82; Freedmen's Bureau, opposition to, 39–40; impeachment, support of, 196, 198–99; on New Orleans riot, 140, 144–45; with-

drawal of support from Johnson in 1866, 70, 75–76

Readmission of southern states to Union, 18, 153–54: criticism of, 17, 18; ratification of Fourteenth Amendment and, 124; requirements, 16

Reconstruction: America's Unfinished Revolution (Foner), 393

Reconstruction, end of (1874–77): concerns about, 396, 401–5; corruption and black ineptness in South and, 394–95; Panic of 1873 and, 395; Republican compromise and, 393; support for, 395–400

Reconstruction Acts of 1867, 125, 140, 357; black suffrage under, 169–81. *See also* Congressional Reconstruction (1867)

Reconstruction policy: call for a speedy and generous, 3, 4–8; call for caution and a firm, 3, 8–13; congressional (*see* Congressional Reconstruction (1867)); of Johnson (*see* Presidential Reconstruction plan (1865–66))

Red Cloud, visit to Washington of Chief, 246

Red Shirts, 253

Reformers, Sunday liquor laws and, 267–70

Refugees, slaves and former slaves as, 29

Reid, S.G., support for seating of southern delegation, 65–66

Reid, Whitelaw, 1; opposition to compromises of 1876 election, 384, 389–90

Religious movements, Sunday laws revived by, 267. *See also* Mormons and polygamy (1870–77)

"Removal and concentration" policy for Indians, 235–36, 237, 238, 240

Representation of southern states, Fourteenth Amendment and, 124, 126–27

Republican clubs, 111

Republican newspapers: *See also Harper's Weekly, New Orleans*

Tribune; *New York Herald*; *New York Tribune*; initial skepticism about Crédit Mobilier scandal, 339–42; moderate, xi; radical, x–xi; in the South, xiv, xv, 129

Republican Party: Anthony and, 345–47; black suffrage, concerns about, 110; carpetbag corruption and downfall of Southern, 210; Civil Rights Act of 1875 and, 365; conciliatory tactics of, 394; congressional election of 1866, 70, 73–75; divisions in, 154, 393–94; equal rights for blacks and, 16–17; Fourteenth Resolution adopted in Philadelphia convention (1872), 231–33; Godkin's criticism of Crédit Mobilier scandal and, 337–38; Halstead's predictions about, 404–5; Hamburg (S.C.) massacre and, 382; Ironclad Test Oath, split over, 56; Johnson's veto of Civil Rights Act of 1866 and unity of, 98; Liberal Republicans, xii, 345, 404; liquor regulation and, 269, 276; Mormon polygamy associated with slavery by, 281; organizing blacks to vote for, 170; Radical Congress of 1866, 69–83; reaction against corruption in, 381; reaction to presidential Reconstruction plan, 15–16, 17; recognition of women's rights at 1872 convention, 346–47

Reservations, Indian, 235–36, 237, 238, 240, 244

Revels, Hiram, 154

Richmond, Virginia, segregated public transportation in, 45

Richmond (Ky.) Register, opposition to Civil Rights Act of 1875 in, 364

Richmond (Va.) Enquirer, Wynne on inferiority of blacks in, 54

Richmond (Va.) New Nation, xv

Richmond (Va.) Times, xii, xv; opposition to black suffrage, 110; Wynne's reaction to New Orleans riot in, 141–42

Richmond (Va.) Whig, Elliot's opinions in, xii; refusal to acknowledge Klan violence in, 261, 264–65; warning to blacks about carpetbaggers, 212–13

Ridgway, Robert, xii

Rifle clubs, southern use of white, 377

Riots: anti-Chinese, 306, 315; fears of, 143; Hamburg (S.C.) massacre (1876), 371–80; in New Orleans (1866), 70, 137–50; in South (1866), 70

Rochester (N.Y.) Democrat and Chronicle, rejection of Anthony's cause based on Fourteenth Amendment in, 352–53

Rome (Ga.) Weekly Courier, condemnation of "black" legislatures in, 154

Roosevelt, Franklin D., 308

Ross, Senator, 201

Russell, Earl, 156

Russia, sale of Alaska to U.S., 184–85

Russian American Company, 183–84

Sabbatarian movement, 267, 268–69, 271. *See also* Sunday Liquor Laws (1866–73)

St. Louis Globe Democrat, on return of Southern states to Democratic control, 395

Salt Lake City, Mormon founding of, 280

San Antonio Express, xv

Sanborn, John B., 244

San Francisco: anti-Chinese ordinances in, 307; anti-Coolie organization of, 313; Chinatown in, 307; Chinese riots during the 1870s, 315

San Francisco Chronicle, Young's opinions in: advocacy of harsh policy toward Mormons, 287–88; Chinese labor, opposition to, 315–16; on Civil Rights Act of 1875, 361, 368–69; compromises of 1876 election, support for, 388–89; Fifteenth Amendment, opposition to, 301–2; strong military handling of Indians, support for, 242

Sanitary Commission, 29

Saratoga Convention, 148

Savannah (Ga.) Daily Herald, Mason's outrage over requirements for seating southern delegation, 66–67

Savannah (Ga.) Daily News and Herald, Mason's opinions in: opposition to

Fourteenth Amendment in, 131–32; reaction to New Orleans riot in, 142–43

Savannah (Ga.) Republican, xv

Scalawags, xiii, 153, 209

Scare tactics: against black suffrage, 118–19; against Fourteenth Amendment, 134–35

Schofield, John, 160, 163, 194

Schools: common, 360, 361, 368; freedmen's, 31, 36–37, 208. *See also* Education

Screws, W.W., 17, 26, 155, 172; opposition to congressional Reconstruction, 155, 165

Scribner's Magazine, Norton's support for Chinese immigration and labor in, 309–11

Secession acts, renunciation of, 16, 21

Second Enforcement Act of July 14, 1870, 293

Segregation laws, 44–45: Jim Crow laws, 360

Selden, Henry R., 348, 349–50, 352, 354

Select Committee on Freedmen's Affairs, 85–86

Senate, U.S.: Alaska purchase treaty, approval of, 185; impeachment process in, 195; Select Committee on Woman's Suffrage, 349; Stanton's removal and, 194

Seneca Falls convention (1848), 221

Sentiments, Declaration of, 221

"Separate but equal" doctrine, 357, 359, 360

Seward, William H., 74, 184–85, 189, 190

Sheridan, Philip, 139, 146, 236, 245

Sherman, William Tecumseh, 6, 163, 245

Sherman-Shellabarger Senate Bill, 164

Sidewalk Ordinance (San Francisco), 307

Silsby, John, 111; support of black suffrage, 111–12, 114–15

"Sioux" (former Confederate officer), support for black codes of, 51–52

Sioux Indians, 237, 243; in Battle of Little Bighorn, 237–38; Fetterman Massacre by, 237; massacre at

Wounded Knee, 238; war over South Dakota, 237–38, 247–48

Slaughterhouse Cases, The, 347, 359, 395

Slavery: comparison of "Coolie" system to, 314; Thirteenth Amendment declaring end to, 16, 123, 291

Sledge, James, 64–65

Smith, Charles H. (aka "Bill Arp"), 32; opposition to Freedmen's Bureau, 38–39

Smith, James W., 320

Smith, Joseph, 279–80

Sneed, James R., opposition to Civil Rights Act of 1866, 99, 106

Social revolution, freedom of slaves as, 91

Sons of Liberty, 256

South, the: carpetbagger myth in, 210, 211–16; Chinese immigrants in, 305–6, 308–9, 313–15; conditions in, 1, 70, 97; congressional delegation from, seating (1865), 55–68; corruption in, 394–400; division into military districts, 125, 151; fear of black suffrage in, 110; Godkin's abandonment of use of term to create unity, 399, 400; newspapers in, xii–xv; politics in, as matter of life and death, 210; poverty of, 401–2; readmission of states to Union, 16, 17, 18, 124, 153–54; "reconstructed" states, criticism of, 19–21; representation in House, Fourteenth Amendment and, 124, 126–27; republican state governments, 154; schools in, 31; speculation about future of, 3

South Carolina: black codes in, 44, 45, 49–50; Hamburg massacre (1876), 371–80; Klan killings in, 252–53; Ku Klux Klan Force Act and, 254, 260; white supremacists' counter-revolution in, 170

South Carolina Convention, Curtis' criticism of, 21–22

Southern delegation, seating of, 55–68: opposition to, 58, 59–63; support for, 58, 63–67

Springfield (Mass.) Republican, 101; Twain's humorous opposition to woman suffrage in, 225–26

Springfield (Mass.) Republican, Bowles' opinions in, xi, xii; Chinese immigration and labor, opposition to, 314; Civil Rights Act of 1866, support for, 101; on discontinuation of Freedmen's Bureau, 37–38; impeachment, support for, 199–200; moderate Indian policy, support for, 244; on restoration of Union, 10; Sunday liquor laws, support for, 271–72; woman suffrage, support for, 229–30

Stanton, Edwin, 77, 138; refusal to resign, 193–94

Stanton, Elizabeth Cady, 221, 222, 224, 225, 227, 345, 346, 347; support for Anthony, 349, 353; support for woman suffrage, 223, 227–29

State interference, private rights against, 124

State law, jurisdiction over civil rights of state citizens, 347–48, 359, 395

States' rights, 16, 21, 22, 102; Freedmen's Bureau seen as usurpation of, 29; Johnson's policy of, 85, 98

Staunton (Va.) Vindicator, Bill Arp's opposition to Freedmen's Bureau in, 38–39

Steedman, John, 32, 35, 39

Stenhouse, Fanny, 289

Stenhouse, T.B.H., 289

Steockl, Edouard de, 184–85

Stephens, Alexander H., 57, 123

Stevens, Thaddeus, 1–2, 3, 79, 126, 142, 185

Stewart, William Morris, 116

Stone, Lucy, 222, 231, 232

Storey, Wilbur F., xi; advocating patience with Mormons, 282, 283–84; Fifteenth Amendment, opposition to, 294, 300–301, 302–3; for moderate policy toward Indians, 238–39, 245–46; Sunday liquor laws, support for, 269–70, 272–73

"Straight-Out" Democratic faction, 373

Styles, Carey, 171, 255; Alaska purchase, opposition to, 190; black suffrage under Reconstruction Acts, opposition to, 171, 176–77; Fourteenth Amendment, opposition to,

134; refusal to acknowledge Klan violence, 255, 261–62; Southern carpetbagger myth and, 210, 213–15

Suffrage. *See Black suffrage entries;* Woman suffrage

Sumner, Charles, 1, 3, 118, 126, 357, 361, 366, 367

Sunday closing laws. *See* Sunday Liquor Laws (1866–73)

Sunday laws, colonial, 267

Sunday Liquor Laws (1866–73), 267–78: as anti-immigrant, 268–69; as major issue in cities, 268; opposition to, 270, 276–78; origins of, 267–68; support for, 269–75

Sweeny, Peter, 319, 321

Sweetwater Saber Club, 372, 373

Tammany Hall. *See* Tweed, William Marcy "Boss," and his New York ring

Taxes, 154

Taylor, Nat, 245

Teachers: at freedmen's schools, 31, 36–37, 208; as organizers for voter registration, 170

Temperance Bureau, 274–75

Temperance movement, 267, 269, 345

Temperance Union, 270, 274–75

Tennessee: black codes in, 46–47; handgun sales in, laws on, 45; Johnson as provisional governor of, 2, 69; Ku Klux Klan founded in, 251; ratification of Fourteenth Amendment, 124

Tenure of Office Act (1867), 193–94, 198, 203–4

Terrorist tactics of white supremacists, 170. *See also* Ku Klux Klan (1867–72)

Texas, segregation laws in, 44

Texas and Pacific Railroad, 384

Theocratic state, Mormons as, 280

Thirteenth Amendment, 16, 123, 291

Thirty-ninth Congress, seating of southern delegates to, 55–68: opposition to, 58, 59–63; support for, 58, 63–67

Thomas, Geo. H., 190

Thompson, Holland, 170

Tilden, Samuel J., 376, 381, 384, 385; election of 1876 and, 382, 383; Hamburg (S.C.) massacre and, 381; Jones' portrait of, in *New York Times*, 386–87

Tillman, Benjamin ("Pitchfork Ben"), 372, 373

Tilton, Theodore, 345

Trade: acquisition of Alaska and, 187–88; with Chinese, 313

Transcontinental railroad, 331; Chinese laborers working on, 306; civilizing effect on Mormons expected from, 283, 285–86; Crédit Mobilier scandal, 331–44; survey of a possible, 331

Transcontinental Railway Bill (1862), 331

Treason, Governor Johnson on, 69

Treasury Department, Alaska administered by, 185

Treaties with Indians, 235–36, 237, 247, 248–49

Trumbull, Lyman, 86, 97, 98, 201

Truth, Sojourner, 223

Tuscaloosa (Ala.) Times, celebration of conservative white rule, 155

Twain, Mark, 223, 254; decrying Klan lynchings, 254, 258; opposition to woman suffrage, 223, 225–26

Tweed, William Marcy "Boss," and his New York ring, 317–30: control of newspapers, 319; defenders of, 321, 328–30; fraud, evidence of, 319–21; opposition to, 321–27; political career of Tweed, 317–19; trial and conviction of, 320

Tyranny, franchise as only weapon against, 113–14

Union League, xv, 34, 111, 170, 251, 253, 255, 261

Union Pacific Railroad: bankruptcy, 334; civilizing effect in West expected of, 283, 285; construction of, 332, 333; Crédit Mobilier scandal and, 331–44; debt accrued, 333; organization of, 331, 332

U.S. Supreme Court, 254; Chief Justice of, impeachment process and, 195;

Civil Rights Cases, 359–60; *Dred Scott v. Sanford*, 21, 123; emasculation of Fourteenth Amendment, 348, 349, 359, 395; on enforcement of voting rights, 293; *ex parte Milligan*, 87; *Plessy v. Ferguson*, 360; *Slaughterhouse Cases*, 347, 359, 395; on states' legal jurisdiction over civil rights of citizens, 347–48; Tenure of Office Act overturned by, 195; *United States v. Cruikshank*, 293; *United States v. Reese*, 293

United States v. Cruikshank, 293

United States v. Reese, 293

Universal Suffrage and Universal Amnesty proposal, 115–16

Universities, freedmen's, 31

Utah: Mormon settlement in, 279–82; White's suggestion to unite Nevada and, 286; woman suffrage law in, 223

Van Winkle, Senator, 201

Violence: against blacks, 49, 85, 86, 97, 111, 151, 251–66, 291, 292, 371–80; black voter turnout and, 170; against Chinese immigrants, 305, 306, 315; Civil Rights Act of 1875 and, 357; against freedmen's schools, 31; Hamburg (S.C.) massacre, 371–80; Ku Klux Klan and (1867–72), 251–66; massacres of Indian Wars, 236; against Mormons, 279–80; New Orleans riot of 1866, 137–50; against Union sympathizers by ex-Confederate soldiers, 18; of white supremacists' counterrevolution, 170–71

Virginia, 1623 blue law enacted in, 267

Voorhies, Albert, 138

Voter registration: Anthony and, 347; black, 170, 251

Voting rights. *See Black suffrage entries*; Woman suffrage

War Department, Alaska administered by, 185

Ward politics, 317

War of races, fear of, 115, 119, 141, 143, 173, 262, 295

Washington, D.C: Griffing's appeal on behalf of freedmen of, 32–34; integration and enfranchisement of blacks in, 361

Washington Chronicle, 185

Watterson, Henry, xii

Wealth, need for black acquisition of, 296, 297–98

Wells, James Madison, 138, 146

West, the: Mormons and polygamy (1870–77); Transcontinental railroad; economic boom in the, 331. *See also* Indian policy in the West (1867–76)

White, Horace, x, 3, 8–9, 45, 210, 270, 282; advocating patience with Mormons, 282, 285–86; black codes, opposition to, 45, 48–50; compromises of 1876 election, support for, 384, 385–86; seating of southern delegates, opposition to, 58, 61–62; Southern view of carpetbaggers, 210, 215–16; Sunday liquor laws, support for, 270, 273–74

White Brotherhood, 253

White League, 252, 253

White Liners, 253, 358

White supremacist groups, 291, 358; Hamburg (S.C.) massacre and, 372–73; paramilitary groups, 371–72; terrorist tactics of, 170. *See also* Ku Klux Klan (1867–72)

Whitney, Asa, 331

Wilson, Henry, 333, 340, 341, 346

Windom, William, 244, 247

Woman's Journal, Cole's criticism of Republican's Fourteenth Resolution in, 231–33

Woman suffrage, 221–33, 345–56: abolitionist movement and, 221–22;

Anthony and, 222, 223, 345–56; black suffrage and, 222, 223–24, 227–30; Nineteenth Amendment and, 223, 345, 349; opposition to, 223–27, 349–53; support for, 223, 227–33, 349, 353–56

Women, Mormon, 282, 289–90

Women's National Loyal League meeting (1863), 221–22

Women's rights, 345. *See also* Anthony, Susan B.; Woman suffrage

Wood, Ben, 17, 22–23: opposition to Sunday liquor laws, 270, 276

Woodhull, Victoria C., 350

Woodruff, Wilford, 281–82

Woodruff Manifesto, 281–82

Wormley Hotel meeting (1877), 384

Wounded Knee, massacre at (1890), 238

Wynne, Charles H., 54; on New Orleans riot, 140, 141–42

Wyoming: admission to Union, 222–23; woman suffrage law in, 222–23

Young, Brigham, 280, 281, 283, 284–85, 287–88, 289

Young, Charles de, 282, 384; advocating harsher approach to Mormons, 282, 287–88; on Civil Rights Act of 1875, 360, 361, 368–69; compromises of 1876 election, support for, 384, 388–89; Fifteenth Amendment, opposition to, 294, 301–2; for strong military stand against Indians, 238, 242

Young, John Russell: description of Klan activities, 254, 255–56; on responsibility for Johnson's actions after impeachment trial, 202; support of impeachment, 196–97

About the Author

DONNA L. DICKERSON is Dean of the College of Arts and Sciences and Professor of Communication at the University of Texas, Tyler.